EDUCATION IN CRISIS:

A Sociological Analysis of Schools and Universities in Transition

EDUCATION IN CRISIS:

A Sociological Analysis of
Schools and Universities in Transition

RONALD G. CORWIN
Professor of Sociology
The Ohio State University

John Wiley & Sons, Inc.   New York · London · Sydney · Toronto

Library of Congress Cataloging in Publication Data

Corwin, Ronald G.
    Education in crisis.

    1. Educational sociology—United States.
2. Education—United States—1945-
I. Title.

LC205.C57 1974   370.19′3′0973   73-12844
ISBN 0-471-17522-6
ISBN 0-471-17521-8 (pbk.)

Printed in the United States of America

10 9 8 7 6 5 4 3 2 1

To the Memory of My Father,
LEONARD J. CORWIN, 1899-1971

PREFACE

This book is designed for a wide audience of scholars, educators, students, parents, politicians, and taxpayers, all of whom recently have been confronted in one way or another with the dilemmas surrounding the rapidly changing role of formal education in modern societies. In this technological age, when education has assumed special significance because of the central role it plays in the economy of modern societies, it is clear that educational institutions have entered a new era of importance. Perhaps most of us are only vaguely aware of the full range of consequences that this elevation of education is having for each individual. But most of us at least have fragmentary acquaintance with some of the issues involved in the transformation. Indeed, we cannot escape many of the problems that each day impinge on us in specific ways.

Scholars like Galbreath see universities beginning to eclipse commercial institutions as the dominant institution, because in a technological society the major resource is trained manpower, not merely financial capital. *Individual citizens* benefit from their own education: in 1966 the average college graduate could expect to earn $167,000 more than the high school graduate over the course of his lifetime, and the high school graduate could out-earn the high school dropout by $57,000. The amount of formal education a person completes also influences his life in other ways, such as whom he will marry, what kind of job he attains, and what will be his children's educational chances. The *taxpayer* is also painfully aware of the burden of financing public education. The cost of public education more than doubled during the 1960s and per capita costs for education at all levels more than tripled. During that decade the proportion of the gross national product allocated to education nearly doubled (from 4 to 8 percent). The cost of education now consumes 4 percent of all personal income. This $36 billion enterprise ranks second only to national defense in overall tax expenditures, and it is by far the most important local tax expense, consuming the large share of local tax expenditures. This cost has been a source of public resistance to the expansion of education even as it becomes a more significant element in American life.

Educational institutions, then, directly impinge on nearly everyone and all sectors of the society. Nearly a third of the nation is formally connected with educational organizations in one capacity or another—the 59 million students in colleges and schools, 3 million teachers, and the several thousands of school board members and school administrators; in sheer numbers, teachers and students have increased 30 percent in the last decade and have doubled since 1947. In addition, of course, there are the parents and the alumni. Many of these people have grown out of touch with the changes that have taken place since their own school days but nevertheless use their experience with the schools as a basis for judging the needs and goals of contemporary education.

For most *young people,* in particular, educational institutions loom large in importance. School is not only the first bureaucratic situation they encounter, but it is the one that has the most prolonged and sustained impact on their lives. Forced to attend schools by law and the economic realities, young people spend more years of their lives in educational institutions, and more days each year, than ever before. The proportion of young children between three and five years old attending "preschools" increased from 25 to 40 percent in the seven-year period from 1964 to 1971, and even more dramatic increases have taken place among older age groups. Whereas in 1910 the average adult had completed only an elementary school education, by 1970 over 6 out of every 10 adults aged 25 to 29 had graduated from high school. Over the past 20 years alone, the dropout rate from high school has declined by 25 percent; 72 out of every 100 persons who were in the fifth grade in 1959 have graduated from high school, and nearly half of those have gone on to college. If present trends continue, it is possible that by 1980 more than 60 percent of all adults in the United States will be high school graduates, more than four times the proportion found in 1910 and nearly half again the proportion in 1960. By that time, too, nearly three out of four high-school graduates will be in some kind of higher institution of education.

As if to punctuate the importance of education in American life, there are visible signs all around us that serve as constant daily reminders in the form of growth in size, number, and scale of schools and colleges. Schools are becoming larger and more "bureaucratic." The average school today is twice as large as it was only 10 years ago.

A transformation of this scale cannot take place without upsetting the rest of social life. The dramas that have surrounded these changes also have made the public painfully aware that educational institutions are at the heart of not only the economy but many of society's most critical social problems. Community struggles for control over the school, student unrest, teacher militancy, racism, and tensions among the social classes in schools and colleges are constant reminders of much broader social issues: the growing centralization of government control, bureaucratization of American life, the growing influence of the youth culture, the changing role of trained public employees, and national cleavages among ethnic and class groups in a society that attempts to democratize socially stratified communities. The problems now wracking the fabric of education are the shock waves from the repeated failures of educational organizations to adapt to these broader social changes. In some cases, schools and universities have been ahead of their time, in the vanguard of change, but they have confronted a reluctant public dragging its feet. In other cases, perhaps more typically, they have changed too slowly and are reeling under attacks from various groups because they lag behind the times.

But it remains to be seen precisely how the problems are interlaced with broader social changes and how they might be resolved. I will attempt here to unravel some of these connections and to consider alternative solutions. We shall not find all of the answers, but we can at least raise the questions that must be raised, and inventory what is known about the key issues. Where there are gaps—and there are huge ones— I will speculate about some of the implications. Hopefully, the reader will at least come away with a more comprehensive perspective.

In selecting the problems to be considered in this book, I have assumed that education is being transformed and so must be understood in terms of the *social processes* that shape institutions. Two processes are primary: *social change* and *conflict*. The reason for emphasizing institutional change is that the United States, like other Western nations, is undergoing rapid cultural, social, and structural transformations as a result of technological developments, a worldwide revolution in communications, demographic transitions, urbanization, bureaucratization, and the like. Since educational organizations are loosely integrated into the larger society—they are supported from an economic base and politically controlled—they must continually adapt to new demands made upon them as the society changes.

But in order to accurately diagnose the problems and predict the future of education, we cannot assume that educational organizations will, in fact, respond directly to social pressures in a straightforward way. Education is still less important than political and economic institutions, and schools and colleges are partially insulated from the changes taking place in other areas of society by law, custom, organizational rules, professional organizations, and independent funding and control boards.

Their autonomy sometimes enables them to resist the dominant trends and, in part, to dictate their own future. In addition, some groups inside and outside of educational institutions wield more power over education than others. The future, then, will be the product of conflict between educators and citizens, between the social strata, between those who benefit from the status quo and those who would benefit from a new social order, and between various organizational principles that underly the social institutions. While these conflicts are sometimes resolved through normal political processes, they also can take the form of direct confrontations between vested interest groups outside of normal political channels. Because the outcomes of these struggles—the compromises and the victories—set the direction and pace of change, conflict situations provide a strategic window through which to view the future.

The interplay of these two dimensions—the new demands from a changing society and the conflicts within and among educational organizations and the political and economic groups in control—means that education cannot be fully understood in terms of either what educators or what the various concerned citizens' groups would desire. It cannot be understood solely on the basis of its history or its present situation. An institution that is so dynamic and constantly in the process of transformation and compromise can be understood only by looking simultaneously to the future, emergent society, and to what is happening to the autonomy of educational organizations. I now believe that this perspective can be best achieved by concentrating on critical educational problems. By analyzing problems one is forced to examine the underlying structure responsible for them, and the conflicts and compromises surrounding the problems will determine the future.

In the course of the discussions, I try to convey the inconclusiveness surrounding many basic facts and present different sides of the controversies raging over the meaning of the available evidence. In this field, as in other fields about which the public is deeply concerned, it is important to recognize that the facts often are not so clearcut nor the answers so definitive as they have sometimes been made to appear by advocates on various sides of the controversies.

The first two chapters set the stage by describing the organizational structures and processes that underlie schools and colleges. In Chapter 1, the focus is on the complex bureaucratic *structure* that underlies the elementary and secondary *schools*. Chapter 2 amplifies this description in two ways. First, the analysis is extended to include *colleges and universities*. While many of the structural characteristics of schools also apply to universities and while they share many problems in common with schools, the latter are now at a different stage of evolution. Their experience might contain clues to the future of public schools, and it has implications for

access to higher learning in the future. Second, Chapter 2 adds a dimension of *process* to the analysis to give the reader a sense of the dynamic,
evolutionary changes that are occurring within educational organizations.
Several aspects of change in universities and their implications are considered.

Chapter 3 confronts racial and class inequities in education and sets
the stage for many of the subsequent problems to be discussed. Struggle for
access to educational institutions and for educational resources is a major
undercurrent in the schools and in colleges as well. The problems of class
and race, however, cannot be understood apart from the characteristics of
schools and colleges as organizations. For example, one of the underlying
assumptions of the movement to improve equality of educational opportunity is that the quality of the schools—how they are organized, their
resources, and the type of teachers and curriculum—makes a difference for
what the student learns. Equal educational opportunity, in other words,
is assumed to have something to do with the equality of school resources.
But accumulating evidence raises some questions about that assumption.
So we must consider how important schools really are in producing inequities in educational opportunity and, therefore, the feasibility of altering
discriminatory patterns through organizational reform.

Chapters 4 and 5 deal with the power grab within educational institutions. Chapter 4 focuses on the quest of students in both universities and
high schools for more control over their destiny. Many of the issues discussed in the preceding chapters—the changing clientele of colleges,
racism, and subtle shifts in the values of youth—converge as part of this
problem. In Chapter 5, a parallel drive of the teachers for more power,
status, and authority will be considered.

The foregoing problems can be considered to be largely the result of the
unresponsiveness of educational institutions to recent social changes.
Therefore, schools and colleges have been forced to experiment with a
variety of innovations as they cope with their problems. Some of the
proposals and experiments are reviewed in Chapter 6. In many cases, the
proposed changes are aimed at the structure of educational organization
itself. When the proposals are attempted and are successful, it is expected
that they will change the course of education for many years to come. But
the success of many of the proposed changes is still highly problematic:
often, plans that sound good are never implemented because of resistance.
Very little consideration has been given to *how* to bring about change.
Therefore, I also consider alternative *strategies* for bringing about innovation in Chapter 7.

From the way this book is organized, it is evident that I assume that
elementary, secondary, and higher education can be profitably viewed
within a common framework. In order to provide parsimony and balance

to the discussion, and because there is more research evidence on certain problems at one level of education than others, I have adopted the strategy in alternative chapters of *focusing* on one level or the other, but that will not preclude giving some attention to similar problems at other levels. In this way, hopefully, the reader will come to view elementary, secondary, and higher education from a more unified point of view than is normally available. To simplify the terminology, the term "educational organizations" will be used to apply to the full range of organizations concerned with formal education, from elementary schools, preschools, and junior colleges to universities and graduate schools.

These levels of formal education often have been artificially separated by scholars, educators, and the general public because the different people responsible for managing each type of institution tend to study their problems in isolation from one another and exaggerate the unique qualities of each setting. However, I believe that it is more efficient to use a single framework that can apply to all levels than to proliferate different frameworks. When a common perspective is used, the problems encountered at one level and the experience gained there can be used at other levels. Moreover, many of the problems themselves stem from the isolation among the various levels of education, that is, the fact that each level typically has been viewed in isolation. In a highly interdependent society, the failure to recognize actual or desirable interconnections among the various levels simply serves to perpetuate our inability to grasp and cope satisfactorily with the larger, underlying causes. Hopefully, the merit of this approach will be demonstrated in this book.

RONALD G. CORWIN
Columbus, Ohio, 1973

CONTENTS

EDUCATION IN CRISIS:

A Sociological Analysis of
Schools and Universities in Transition

CHAPTER 1

BUREAUCRACY IN EDUCATION

"Good morning, Mr. Smith," an attractive girl will say pleasantly to one of her teachers in the corridor. "Linda, do you have a pass to be in your locker after the bell rings?" is his greeting in reply.[1]

Everywhere there are schools. Accordingly, most people in this and other nations have had experience with some type of school. Also, we have all had somewhat different experiences because (1) there are many variegated types of schools and (2) each person tends to interpret his experiences from the unique vantage point of his own background. In comparison to the nineteenth century, when most Americans spent a relatively few years in a single type of school called the "common school," Americans today, from childhood to young adulthood, make their way through a maze of complex educational organizations. Critical transitions must be made between elementary schools, junior highs, comprehensive and specialized high schools, technical schools, two-year junior colleges, colleges and universities, and graduate schools. The thesis of this book is that the principles underlying these different types of educational organizations filter teachers', students', parents', and other constituents' views of one another and govern relations among these different groups. But the effects of these principles are far from being uniform. They can impinge in different ways on middle-class white children and lower-class blacks, on young children and mature youths, and on persons who value formal education and those who do not.

The way schools and colleges are organized accounts for what is truly distinctive about contemporary education. The significance of the organizational dimension is clearly demonstrated in many of the problems now rocking the foundations of public education: the struggles between community groups, teacher organizations, and administrators to control the schools; the frustrating efforts to desegregate big-city school systems; the demands from citizen groups for decentralized control; and the militant insistence of teachers on enlarging their sphere of authority in quest of professional status. A plethora of proposals has been made to restructure the schools—including plans for metropolitan-school systems, educational parks, alternative schools, nongraded schools, team teaching, and new methods of grouping students. All of these proposals are essentially organizational approaches to problems, which (often unwittingly) imply various theories about how organizations function and, ultimately, how they affect their members. It is widely assumed, then, that many of the current problems in education are rooted in the way formal education in this country is organized, and that it will take sweeping structural reforms to resolve the problems.

In this chapter, we will examine how schools are organized and consider what differences that various forms of organization can make for the students and teachers involved. The following chapter will focus on university organization.

WHAT IS THE SCOPE OF THE PROBLEM?

Although *schooling* is only one means of socializing the young, it is now an almost universal form of socialization throughout most of the world. Every year even more people throughout the world spend more of their time in schools and colleges. In the United States, for example, nearly all of the age-eligible youth now attend school—an increase of 80 percent in this age group in school during the past decade. Three out of every four U.S. high school students now graduate, and more than half of them go on to college.[2] No wonder schools have captured the interest of the American public. Probably no other organization outside the family has so prolonged a hold over the lives of so many citizens of so many nations. Schools are custodial institutions, and they are socializing agencies. Because schools are caretakers of the young, they are a convenient instrument for influencing the values of each new generation, and bitter struggles to control children take place in most modern societies.

How Rapidly Have Educational Organizations Grown?

Nearly 100 years ago, educators were becoming alarmed about the growing scale of educational bureaucracies. One observer said:

". . . In our centennial year, our common schools constitute a highly complex and differentiated, a vast and powerful system. The machinery of this system is tens of thousands of schoolhouses, thousands of libraries, vast illustrative apparatus, boards of directors and boards of examiners, normal schools and institutes, reports and bureaus, commissioners and superintendents, and more than a quarter of a million of teachers."[3]

But even the most foresighted of the nineteenth century writers probably did not anticipate the swift pace with which large scale educational systems would blanket the country. Since the beginning of this century, the volume of enrollment in public elementary and secondary schools has grown almost continually, and the number of students in both levels of American schools doubled between 1945 and 1970. Consequently, the number of educational organizations has grown at a staggering rate. There are now nearly 100,000 schools in 20,000 school districts that employ over 3,000,000 teachers and administrators and enroll 58,000,000 students.

WHAT DO THESE STATISTICS MEAN?

These impersonal statistics have a very personal meaning for the individual student and the average citizen reflecting, as they do, fundamental facts that shape both the students' learning environment and the citizen's relationship with educational organizations. The average public school in 1966 was twice as large as it had been only 10 years before, because of the failure of school building programs to keep pace with dramatic increases in enrollment.[4] The size of school *systems* also increased as their number declined by one-half during the 1960s as a result of consolidation. Today, only one-fifth of the school systems enroll 85 percent of the school population. This means that one-half of the children are enrolled in a large school system (over 12,000 students) today, whereas 20 years ago only one child in three was enrolled in a school system of that size. Comparable changes have taken place in parochial schools. These trends, of course, vary by level of education: elementary schools are becoming fewer in number and larger in size, while colleges are growing in number while growth in size is leveling off. The number of secondary schools has remained relatively stable, despite dramatic increases in enrollment.

WHY ARE SOCIOLOGISTS INTERESTED IN EDUCATIONAL ORGANIZATIONS?

An institution of the scale and growth rate described above provides a natural setting for studying worldwide movements of basic significance to all citizens, such as bureaucratization of modern life, professionalization of work, and group conflict. Accordingly, sociologists have become engrossed by the issues surrounding these perplexing events. But what can sociology contribute to the study of education? Can the discipline contribute to what is already known about educational institutions and how people learn? Many people believe that sociology can make a distinctive contribution by helping to explain how educational organizations influence what and how people learn and, ultimately, what they do with their lives. On this premise, we now consider what it means when people refer to school systems as "educational bureaucracies."

WHAT IS MEANT BY "BUREAUCRACY" IN EDUCATION?

"Education in this country is bureaucratized and schools are part of a large educational bureaucracy." Most people would probably agree with that statement. But they would agree for different reasons, because the term has different meanings for various people. Technically, bureaucracy refers to a method of organizing administrative functions. For the sociologist Max Weber, a bureaucracy represented the ultimate form of rational efficiency. It is administered by experts under the rule of law. Structurally, a bureaucracy consists of specialized jurisdictions of activity governed by rules and official documents; a system of graded levels of authority; strict compliance on the part of subordinates to the commands of their official superiors; appointment to office on the basis of expertise for lifetime ten-- ure; and guarded separation of the bureaucrat's personal life and his vocation.[5] Employees are appointed, rather than elected to office, and they must qualify on the basis of their training and skills rather than their personality characteristics alone. Incentives are used to (1) secure the bureaucrat's personal, long-term attachment to the organization and (2) assure compliance with the requirements of office. The first problem is met by guarantees of job security consisting of advancement opportunities, pensions, and seniority. The second problem is handled through penalties set for deviation, principles intended to separate the bureaucrat's personal life from his work situation and in-service training. Two principles underlie these characteristics: *specialization* and *coordination*. Specialists staff each position and are assigned tasks according to designated spheres of responsibility and authority. Their work must then be coordinated through a system of centralized authority, that is, a hierarchy of offices.

What Else Is Implied by the Term "Bureaucracy"?

To some people, then, a bureaucracy is a rational, efficient organization, in which members are responsible only for the tasks that they are competent to perform and where rewards are proportionate to one's contributions. But other people see bureaucracy quite differently. To them, it is a pejorative term, conjuring up an image of an inefficient, cumbersome organization, one that (1) is unresponsive to rapid change, (2) stifles creativity, and (3) concentrates social power in the hands of a few self-appointed, often despotic, leaders.

One can find evidence to support both images. *Rationality* and *bureaucracy* appear to be inversely correlated; that is, the more "bureaucratic" an organization is in the latter sense, the less rational and effective it can be.[6]

THE ROMANTIC CRITICS' VERSION

Several popular critics and satirists recently have depicted schools as creaking bureaucracies in the most pejorative sense of the word. Administrators and teachers are portrayed as persons who take great glee in relentlessly enforcing senseless rules. In the humorous best-seller, *Up the Down Staircase*, Kaufman sympathetically portrays the anguish of teacher Sylvia Barrett as she valiantly muddles through the bureaucratic hurdles of the New York City school system in a vain effort to reach a few of her students.[7] She is overcome by inept colleagues—the "Desk Despots, Blackboard Barons, Classroom Caesars, and Lords of the Looseleaf"—and overwhelmed by seating plans, attendance sheets, requisitions, and the library blacklist. Here is a world of time clocks and mandatory meetings, purportedly called for the superficial discussions of democracy amidst a sea of tyranny. It is all run by the J.J. McHabes and Sadie Finches—the administrators and the clerks—who, at every opportunity, spew out new memos bearing old directives: "Teachers who line up in front of the time clocks waiting to punch out in the afternoon create a crowded condition in the doorway," and "No written passes are to be issued to lavatories, since they are easily duplicated by the students. Only wooden lavatory passes are to be honored."

In a more serious vein, other authors have commented upon how the efforts to change the conservative power structure of the New York City school system have been repeatedly frustrated by a small group of entrenched, second-level administrators. *110 Livingston Street* is a trenchant criticism of the inept backwardness of the New York City school administration and its paralysis in the face of serious issues confronting large city schools.[8] Despite a long list of policy statements adopted by the school board endorsing various plans to desegregate the New York City schools, these plans have been blocked, according to the author, by the following paralyzing bureaucratic pathologies.

- The defensiveness and lack of initiative on the part of a powerless school board that is crippled by vested interest groups in the system and in the community; by the lack of necessary resources and expertise to effect change while being inundated with day-to-day trivia; and by the diluting struggles with the superintendent, who has stepped into the policy-making vacuum.
- The fact that the board and the inbred professional staff are isolated from large segments of the public because of limited provision for outside review and control; because of primitive budgeting, auditing, and

evaluation procedures used in the system; and because of endless delays and buck-passing when citizens do go to the central board for information about school policies.

- The overcentralization of most decisions on curriculum, staff, and budgeting that are made by central headquarters professionals several layers removed from the schools themselves, who must rely upon standard formulas because of their limited direct knowledge of the problems.
- The diffuseness of power and responsibility throughout the system in a system that is fragmented by isolated units, insulated from clientele by routines and by self-sufficient curricula and procedures, and that is run by chauvinistic, self-centered, and expansionist groups.
- The fact that the system is further isolated from the city government and impervious to normal democratic controls because of the school district's independent political status, lack of interagency coordination in New York City, and the absence of an electorate to whom appointed members are responsible.

"In a fundamental sense," writes Philip W. Jackson, "school is school, no matter where it happens." He notes that virtually all schools share in common certain characteristics, such as (1) the fact that children are in school involuntarily, compelled by law and the parents to be there for long periods of time; (2) the economies of scale that make school a collective experience for large groups of students; and (3) the sharp demarcation of power and authority between student and teacher, a distinction constantly impressed on the student by the fact that his words and deeds are being constantly evaluated.[9]

Friedenberg's caustic description of "Milgrim High" portrays, from the pupils' point of view, their entrapment in bureaucratic machinery that is responsible for a sullen and joyless existence.[10]

"Between class periods the corridors are tumultuously crowded; during them they are empty. But at both times they are guarded by teachers and students on patrol duty. . . . Between classes, no student may walk down the corridor without a form, signed by a teacher, telling where he is coming from, where he is going, and the time, to the minute, during which the pass is valid."

Friedenberg is relatively kind compared to some of the more damning accounts from other romantic critics. In *Death at an Early Age*, author Jonathan Kozol describes how, in his opinion, the Boston schools "destroy the hearts and minds of children."[11] His account portrays a school where children are gravely mistreated by the school teachers. They are beaten physically with rattan whips, pushed about, and shaken. Emotionally they are degraded by condescending teachers and, through coercion and intimidation, they are taught to degrade themselves, to believe that whatever happens to them is somehow their own fault, and to admit to devious acts that they may or may not have committed. Intellectually these children are ignored, judged to be inferior, and berated for their efforts when they do attempt to achieve academically. The teachers are painted as being defensive racists, condescending, and stupid. The superintendent and his staff say publicly that the Boston schools are in "good" condition, that segregation is justifiable, and that protest against the school system is indeed foolish and unenlightened. Members of the school board are racists, and the principal shows disgust for black children and considers it her mission to protect them from dialect poetry.

How Accurate Are These Portrayals?

Undoubtedly, these and other pathologies do infect many schools. There is probably a great deal of truth in some of the criticisms being leveled against educational organizations today. I have made other comparable observations:

"I came away from my visits to schools—in city after city in several regions of the country, in rural and urban settings, serving black, Indian, and white children—convinced that most classrooms are the grim, joyless places described. . . . The teachers' almost universal preoccupation with cognitive achievement, discipline, and regimen created a stifling and dogmatic environment that assaults human dignity. A depressing lack of enthusiasm for learning and the dismal disrespect that prevailed between teachers and students in the public schools was repeatedly impressed upon me. Too many schools were run on blind, deadly routines, girded by little more than a preoccupation with order. With few exceptions, monotonous regimentation could be observed in schools from the rural South to cities on the Northeastern seaboard, from the Middle West to the West Coast. The shadow of an overbearing central administration seemed to hang over the typical classroom, which prompted close supervision of students (often bordering on harassment), and which generated a pervading sense of mistrust between administrators and teachers, between teachers and students. Teachers, who generally expressed a misplaced sense of loyalty to the school administration and unbending compliance to rules and procedures, too frequently were not given the freedom to make their own decisions, and their students were not trusted even to go to the bathroom without permission. The system's need for order and coordination almost invariably seemed to take precedence over the students' interests. Although administrators insisted on assuming full responsibility for the day-to-day events in every classroom, I suspected that they were familiar with no more than the surface events. To keep this precarious colossus from collapse, it was necessary to penalize anything that was as unpredictable as creativity and innovation."[12]

However, this is not the entire story. Despite these problems, I concluded that notwithstanding our criticisms, in every school system and in every university we visited there were at least a few teachers and professors who stood apart from the rest and who were sincerely dedicated to improving the state of education.

What must be recognized, in other words, is that the situation is not uniformly bleak, that it is far more complex and variable than generally conveyed in the popular literature. While perhaps some problems have arisen because schools are too bureaucratic in some respects, perhaps others have developed because they are not *sufficiently* bureaucratic in other respects. The following discussion, then, aims to round out the picture and to provide a more balanced perspective. Our purpose is not to deny that bureaucracy has created problems in education, nor to dispute the central importance of organizational principles. The purpose is to illustrate how highly variable schools actually are, and that they cannot be accurately depicted *merely as* monolithic empires run by senseless rules, inept, authoritarian administrators and calloused, blundering teachers who exploit well-meaning children.

Several objections can be raised about such stereotypes. In the first place, it should be recognized that bureaucracy, for all of its pathologies, historically served to support public education. Mass public education in this country, in fact, probably would have been impossible without a bureaucratic system. Formal rules have protected schools against the patronage of corrupt city governments, and pupils in the larger school systems have a wider range of curricular alternatives and are more likely to have expert teachers. Moreover, centralized and standardized school systems permitted the country to accommodate the waves of children who inundated the schools at the beginning of this century in the wake of victories for compulsory free education. Standardization also helps guarantee that children will not be shortchanged as they move from one school to another, or from one part of the country to another, and it also can help to promote equal educational opportunities within a system. Generally speaking, bureaucratic procedures are largely responsible for the fact that "school has kept" in the face of increasing burdens of a knowledge explosion, rapidly changing and mobile technological society, and deep-rooted cultural conflicts within the society.

Second, the fact that schools can be perceived in so many different ways by students and parents from various backgrounds invalidates any single stereotype. If the schools were generally perceived by parents in the way critics portray them, it is doubtful that, as one poll revealed, three-fourths of the public would like to have their child take up teaching in the public schools as a career; indeed, adults with children in school, and presumably most familiar with the schools, were more favorable toward a teaching career for their child than those without children in the schools.[13] Moreover, when the public complains about the schools, they seldom complain about bureaucratic control. On the contrary, they seem to want more, not fewer controls. According to the Gallup poll just referred to, the public's greatest complaint against the schools was lack of discipline, and over half of the sample wanted more regulation of student dress. Large segments of the public do not seem to agree that schools are as detrimental to their children as the critics contend they are. Perhaps many of these parents simply do not have enough information and enough insight to perceive the problems. But perhaps, too, the schools do not impinge on their children in ways the critics believe they do.

It does seem that many people have become more disillusioned with schools within the past few years. In 1960 a survey of voters in four cities indicated that the vast majority of them had favorable opinions of the schools,[14] but when repeated only four years later, the survey indicated that the proportion of parents who considered their local schools' performance as good or excellent had declined slightly while the proportion who rated their schools as only fair or poor had increased.[15]

Even here, however, it should be noted that a *majority* of the respondents still held a favorable opinion of the schools. The major problem seems to exist among residents of the inner cities, who are more critical than residents of the suburbs. A Detroit area survey (which is perhaps worse than many cities) in 1969 indicated that there was less satisfaction among adults in the inner city than in the middle-class city or suburbs with school buildings, curriculum, and teachers.[16] Also, a national survey in 1968 indicated that a total of three out of every four members of occupations whose jobs concerned providing services to ghetto dwellers gave "education" a negative rating.[17]

Third, even in the "worst" situations there is not one but many *types* of schools representing several different *patterns* of organization, not all of which are equally detrimental to students. Havighurst identified four types of elementary schools located within Chicago's city limits.[18] There were enormous differences in pupil achievement, family backgrounds of the children, and attitudes and teaching styles of the teachers depending on the type of school. The "high status schools" were attended by gifted, motivated students and had few discipline problems. The "main-line schools" were regarded as a typical school situation with a majority of academically oriented students but also with many discipline problems and with a visible minority of children who demonstrated poor reading ability and below-average achievement. In general, the majority of parents and the community gave moral support to this type of school and its teachers. The teachers' greatest problem in such schools was the pressure of time. A third type was labeled the "common-man schools." These schools were attended by students from diverse backgrounds, who generally were not academically oriented. While the parents were inclined to support the schools, in practice they showed less concern than did main-line parents. The teachers tried to follow standard curriculum guides but, finding it difficult, gradually lowered their standards. Finally, there was a fourth type of school that Havighurst referred to as the "inner-city schools." These schools came closest to fitting the negative stereotype presented by the critics. They suffered from a syndrome of problems ranging from overt hostility of students to the teachers and intellectual apathy to lack of rewards for the teachers. Teachers were expected to follow the same curriculum used in the high-status schools even though they were given no extra resources. It was in these schools that teachers complained most about the downtown bureaucracy, that students rebelled most against the school rules and standardized curriculum, and that the teachers felt compelled to be authoritarian and spent much of their time trying to maintain control of the classroom.

While the inner-city schools tended to be concentrated in particular areas of the inner city, they were not necessarily located in the inner city in the physical sense; there were actually a number of common-man schools and even some main-line schools in areas where inner-city schools predominated. Within a specific city, or even a specific part of a city, then, there are likely to be wide variations in the problems that are created by centralization, standardization, and other bureaucratic practices.

Havighurst's typology is only suggestive of the variable forms that schools can take. Very little information is available about even how to classify different types of schools, and even less is known about the effects of different types of schools. My study of 28 high schools indicated that they can be organized in three quite different ways.[19] The reader might be able to recall various schools that he is familiar with and decide which model(s) he has observed and which type he prefers.

One pattern was "bureaucratic." These schools were highly standardized, emphasized close supervision and rules, and they were large, complex, and highly specialized. In other words, they formed a rather *consistent* pattern that I called a "reinforcement" model of bureaucracy, that is, one in which bureaucratic procedures consistently reinforce one another.

Other schools conformed to different models. Some were highly bureaucratic in only certain respects while being less bureaucratic in others. For example, a school might be highly complex or specialized, or it might have a high rate of turnover, but it was not necessarily closely supervised or standardized. Many of these characteristics were negatively correlated with one another and seemed to be interchangeable. This was called a "compensatory model" because the absence of one dimension of bureaucracy was compensated by emphasizing another. For example, a school that was highly standardized might be in a position to relax close supervision over its employees, or if a school was not highly standardized, the administration might have attempted to more closely supervise its employees. But all of these forms of control were not used simultaneously. Schools with

these characteristics can function adequately even though not fully bureaucratized.

Still another pattern that was identified in some of the schools was that
many of the bureaucratic characteristics were simply not in any way
associated with one another. That is, if a school was highly standardized,
it was impossible to predict whether or not it would also be centralized.

The evidence in that study suggested that schools were likely to become consistently bureaucratic only in the most turbulent, conflict-ridden
environments. Those located in peaceful settings were less consistently
bureaucratic. In other words, bureaucratization seemed to be a response
to conflict and the disruption associated with militant professionalism,
organizational complexity, and staff turnover. It is perhaps ironic, but
conflict and tension might be the *cause* of organization as well as a source
of disorganization. If the problems of bureaucratization are especially
acute in the low-income, inner-city schools, as the critics contend, perhaps
it is because these schools have the most disruptive environments. More
stress is placed on bureaucratic control as a way of coping with the
turmoil.

A fourth reservation regarding the popular criticisms is the implication
that the problems are caused by incompetent, malicious, or calloused
"bureaucrats," that is, the teachers and administrators. Teachers are presumed to have "bureaucratic personalities," to be mindless employees who
blindly enforce the rules, remain loyal and obedient to inept administrators, are so overspecialized that they cannot see students as human beings,
and spend their time on trivia such as collecting lunch money, taking
attendance, and keeping up with the daily lesson plan.[20] As Silberman
noted, to read some of the more influential contemporary critics of education—men like Paul Goodman, Jonathan Kozol, or Edgar Friedenberg
—one might think that schools are staffed by "sadists and clods who are
drawn into teaching by the lure of upward mobility and the opportunity
to take out their anger on their students."[21]

Although many teachers might fit these stereotypes, a growing number
of teachers are becoming militant, posing formidable challenges to the
system. Many others are trained professionals who seem to be concerned
about their students' welfare. Such teachers are more than inept, obedient
bureaucrats. But even if the accusations were true, they are open to question on still other grounds: many of the fundamental problems stem from
structural weaknesses in the organization, not the tyranny and incompetence of the people in charge. Even if there were no tyrants and incompe-
tents in teaching, in other words, many of the problems would persist.

The image of the tyrannical administrators and teachers notwithstanding, the fact is that they are in relatively *weak* positions of authority. The
criticisms tend to credit individual teachers with more influence than

they actually have. An example can be found in the New York City system. Because this is a large system (over 12,000 administrators and teachers), it might easily be assumed that those in charge must be in positions of enormous influence. But, in truth, the power has been diluted by the intricate complexity of the system and by the inbred staffing patterns. The studies of Gittell and of Rogers[22] indicate that even the superintendent of schools in New York City lacks the most essential power of a strong executive—the power to appoint and to remove key assistants who, in New York, are protected by tenure guarantees; appointments to key positions from outside the system seldom occur. In addition, the fact that the budget is controlled by a handful of administrators keeps it outside the authority of the superintendent and of district principals. Because of existing financial commitments, the budget review tends to be automatic, leaving little flexibility for top administrators and professional staff. Moreover, even when strong central leadership has been exercised, it has been met with fierce resistance from equally strong and protective interest groups, such as organized local civic and ethnic groups and teacher organizations, which have fought many reform efforts. School integration has been frustrated for several years because of deadlocks among powerful forces in the system.

Because the superintendent and individual teachers lack power, and because power is not sufficiently concentrated anywhere in the system, power cannot be effectively employed to correct problems that arise. Policy making and budgets are not sufficiently centralized to permit rational planning. Perhaps teachers do develop "bureaucratic personalities," but if they do it is because they are not in a position to successfully oppose the bureaucratic pressures on them. Blaming the teachers only deflects attention from the more fundamental aspects of the organizational structure that govern their behavior. We now consider the organizational structure of schools.

WHAT CHARACTERISTICS OF EDUCATIONAL ORGANIZATIONS ARE THE MAJOR SOURCE OF PROBLEMS?

To label schools "bureaucracies" can provide only a superficial understanding of their problems at best. Educational systems must be seen as complex, multidimensional social prisms that can and do assume many different profiles. It is impossible to understand this complicated structure in detail short of analyzing each of the unique characteristics that comprise it, one by one. Therefore, we now turn our attention to these characteristics and the problems associated with them: the goal system, recruitment procedures, internal control mechanisms, specialization, external control structures, boundary maintenance and relationship with other organizations in the environment. Taken as a whole, the discussions of these components should add up to a portrait of educational organizations.[23]

What Kinds of Problems Do Educational Goals Produce?

Since goals are normally thought to give direction to an organization, one might suppose that the goals of schools would serve as guides to their behavior and thus minimize their problems. However, the situation is quite the reverse. The goal system of American schools is responsible for several of their problems.

WHAT ARE THE PRIMARY GOALS OF EDUCATION?

Any discussion of the goals of schools must begin by recognizing two facts: the American public insists upon a great deal from its schools and colleges; and there is little consensus among the many constituents of schools on what their *primary* goals should be. Many social scientists, educators, parents, and politicians assume that scholastic achievement ("cognitive" outcomes) is the primary goal of schooling. They measure the effectiveness of schools by the readily available standardized achievement measures. Other writers, noting that the correlation between academic achievement in school and subsequent occupational success is far from perfect (see Chapter 3), insist that the outcomes of schooling must be measured by later occupational success. Still other writers see, as the primary objective of schools, their ability to influence the student's conception of himself, that is, to instill self-esteem and self-confidence and help him discover his talents. Others stress the need of schools to develop "healthy" (usually meaning conservative) political attitudes, good "citizenship," or to teach people constructive uses of leisure time.

Finally, following the French sociologist Durkheim, some writers have argued that the key to schools lies in their moral dimension.[24] Moral qualities are taught not only explicitly in the formal curriculum but also implicitly in the procedures used, teachers' attitudes, and other nuances in the school. For example, by his style of teaching, a teacher can convey to children the importance of being independent, being punctual, exercising self-restraint, striving to achieve, and the value of universalistic rules that apply uniformly to everyone regardless of his family background.[25] These general norms are ingrained in the culture of the school itself and cut across all subject-matter areas. Because of their experiences in the schools, then, children learn to accept the value and inevitability of technological change and to take a pragmatic, "instrumental" orientation toward their responsibilities, doing whatever is necessary to achieve "success." It has been suggested that grades and other rewards conferred by schools and colleges are more dependent upon the child's having conformed to these norms than upon his intellectual ability and academic motivation. Although children undoubtedly can learn these norms elsewhere—for example, in their neighborhoods—as the first formal organization that children encounter on a prolonged basis, schools undoubtedly have an important influence on the moral values of youth.

WHAT ARE THE CONSEQUENCES OF SUCH A DIFFUSE GOAL SYSTEM?

When there are so many different goals, the schools cannot rely on public consensus to legitimate the goals they chose to stress. On the one hand, without a clear responsibility for a single purpose, teachers have no grounds for rejecting demands made on them to teach a still wider range of skills. This makes them vulnerable to almost every special interest group and public demand made of them. Thus, the goal system provides no answer as to whether or not the schools should be expected to teach people to drive cars, shoot military weapons, make love, or play baseball, except as the shifting pressures of the community and of the school itself may determine. On the other hand, the wide range of goals increases the chances that some of them will be fulfilled, and the very ambiguity of the situation provides teachers with many convenient reasons for rationalizing their own conduct and for their pupils' academic failure. For example, if a student does not learn to read well, his teacher might at least take comfort in the fact that the school has helped him to become a "good citizen," or that he has gained satisfaction from interscholastic athletics.

Also, since teachers can never be entirely certain about what their ultimate objective really is, each teacher must assume some responsibility for defining and clarifying the goals and setting his own priorities accordingly. The fate of the individual student is therefore subject to the inconsistent and largely arbitrary goal definitions set by particular teachers to whom the student may be assigned. This ambiguity is a potential source of conflict as each teacher is confronted with an impossible range of objectives without enough time and resources to give any of them more than superficial attention.

Finally, the fact that every school must assume responsibility for a wide range of goals means that much of what it is trying to do will be unfeasible or inappropriate for large segments of its frequently heterogeneous student body. Conversely, many of its professed goals cannot be pursued with equal effectiveness within the fixed and limited available resources. A very important consequence is that even though educational organizations are expected to serve all children regardless of their previous backgrounds, personal objectives, or personal desires to be served, in practice schools tend to concentrate on a few objectives at a time. Schools typically slight some of their official objectives (such as vocational training) in order to concentrate on others (such as college preparation).

How Do the Recruiting Procedures Used by Schools Affect Schooling?

In addition to setting goals, all organizations must recruit new members. But recruitment seems to pose special problems for educational organizations. Different procedures are used to recruit student clientele and professional personnel.

RECRUITMENT OF STUDENTS

The way students are recruited into schools in this country has been a constant source of public irritation that has compounded the goal problem in particular. Recruiting methods can be classified into four types depending on (1) whether or not the *organization* has the power to select members and (2) whether or not the *members* can select the organization they want to join. Schools are notable examples of the type of organization in which *neither* the student member or the school has the power to decide who is to attend. Control, consequently, tends to be coercive. Attendance is compulsory for children under statutory age limits. Schools are "open door" institutions, meaning that they must accept any child within the school district. Carlson refers to this as a "domesticated" type of organization, that is, it is domesticated in the sense that schools will always have clients and are guaranteed at least a minimum amount of public resources; they do not have to appeal to, nor compete for, clients and other resources.[26] Unlike "wild" organizations, which must struggle to survive, they can operate and even flourish with less than perfect efficiency or effectiveness with full assurance that they will be "fed and cared for."

What Are the Effects of Domestication? Domesticated organizations have several unique problems. In the first place, by precluding self-selection on the part of pupils, the compulsory, open-door policy tends to maximize the variability in interests and competencies of students admitted to a particular school. This heterogeneity can produce tension in the classroom and can compound the teachers' task when they are forced to deal with such a wide range of interests, motives, and problems at the same time.

Second, domesticated organizations tend to use coercive forms of control over members. Etzioni has identified three types of control structures based on (1) kinds of power used by an organization—coercive, remunerative, and normative and (2) the basis of the members' involvement in the organization—alienative, calculative, and moral.[27] Using combinations of these two dimensions, three dominant types of organizations can be identified: (1) coercive (in which coercion is the major means of control over highly alienated members); (2) utilitarian (in which remuneration is the major means of control over members who are induced by money to participate); and (3) normative (in which members are induced to participate on the basis of their belief in what the organization stands for). It can be expected that organizations in which neither the member nor the organization can control admission will tend to be coercive, whereas organizations in which both parties exercise some control will tend to be normative. Some students find utilitarian value in schooling. Nevertheless, because of the method of recruiting, many public schools are coercive organizations. When students are compelled to attend and have little choice of the particular school to which they are assigned, and then do not succeed, they will not be highly committed to the school. Some of them rebel, either directly or passively, against its authority. School officials react by applying force.

Third, because schools cannot select their student clientele, they are under constant pressure to adapt to the abilities of those students who are in attendance. The kind of student in attendance, in other words, sets limits on what an institution can and cannot achieve. At the same time, the institution is never completely free to adjust to its clients' goals. Its latitude is severely restricted by the fact that the public expects uniform accomplishments from all schools and by required and standard procedures, curricula, and materials, all of which are uniformly enforced to at least some degree in all schools regardless of differences in the makeup of their student bodies. In view of these constraints, the school must either confine itself to making minor adaptations, or it must make all adaptations at a *sub rosa* level. In either case, the makeshift, compromise practices that result will be less effective with some students in attendance than with others.

Schools have tried to cope with heterogeneous student bodies and the large number of academically mediocre, alienated students through *informal* and even *illegal procedures* for selecting the preferred student and "cooling out" the unwanted ones. The separation of desirable and undesirable students into different tracks and courses, some of which are simply custodial "dumping grounds," is a primary way of minimizing conflict within schools. Some critics also argue that the effect is to stigmatize low achievers and seal off their fate. But school administrators and teachers persist in using the practice, sometimes justifying tracking as a method of specialization. That is, teachers find it easier to cope with students when they are all at similar stages and face comparable problems. This will be discussed further later in the chapter. As another, albeit extreme example, there are recorded instances in which school officials have encouraged outstanding athletes to move into their school district. Occasionally a school succeeds in gerrymandering the district boundary lines in order to recruit students from a favored part of the city. Finally, schools may "wink" at the truancy of "trouble makers," encouraging them to drop out before the legal age.[28]

Private Schools. Private schools provide a parallel system of schooling that does permit both students and schools to exercise a voice in who will be admitted. Private schools sometimes have the effect of segregating students and teachers who come from distinct social backgrounds and separating them from persons with opposing objectives. For example, many white middle-class parents in the major cities send their children to private schools, apparently to avoid the problems associated with public schools.

RECRUITMENT OF TEACHERS

In contrast to the compulsory basis on which students are admitted, teachers are hired on a voluntary basis and can be screened by the school administration. To some extent, tensions that arise between students and teachers can be compensated for by deliberately recruiting professional staff members who are socially compatible and technically competent enough to mediate the types of conflicts already described.

However, in practice, it is not always possible for schools to obtain the type of teachers they might prefer, even though they have the *capacity* to do so. A 1969 public opinion survey revealed that approximately one-half of the American public believed that their local schools have a hard time recruiting and keeping good teachers, and nearly half of the parents with children in school said that they knew of some teachers in the system who should be fired.[29]

What Kinds of Teachers Are Recruited? The question can be answered in terms of both the technical qualifications and personal characteristics of the teachers. The public school teacher of today is probably more technically qualified, in some respects, than his predecessors. Between 1940 and 1960 the number of teachers without four years of college declined nearly 50 percent; only 13 percent of the men and 29 percent of the women who are teaching have less than four years of college and only 5 percent of all teachers are teaching on a substandard certificate. Approximately one in four teachers in the United States now has an M.A. degree, and over half of the secondary school teachers have at least five years of college.[30]

Nevertheless, there is enormous variability in the type of teacher recruited by different schools. For example, in those schools located in densely populated middle-class communities in the most technologically advanced states, one in every three teachers has an M.A. degree; but the figure is fewer than one in five in the less-densely populated lower-class communities in the modernized states.[31] There is also a marked difference between elementary and secondary schools. Only one in six elementary school teachers has the M.A. degree, but two in every five high school teachers have completed this level of education. To take schools at the extremes, then, a student is more than twice as likely to have a high school teacher with an M.A. degree if he lives in one of the most modernized states than in the more economically backward areas of the nation.

There are comparably large variations in the types of institutions attended by teachers. Roughly half of all American teachers employed in 1965 attended a normal school or teachers' college, and many others have attended institutions where no graduate work was offered. On the other hand, many others graduated from quality liberal arts colleges or large universities.

Personal Ability. Over and above these variations in formal training, there seems to be a wide range in the level of personal competence of individual teachers. These differences were reflected in the "verbal facility" scores reported in the *Equality of Educational Opportunity* survey, which were based on a test similar to the IQ.[32] Teachers in rural areas had verbal facility skills below the skills of urban teachers. There were comparable differences between black and white teachers across the nation. However, relatively high scores among college students who were preparing to teach seemed to indicate a trend toward improved teacher quality.

Social Criteria. It cannot be assumed, of course, that formal training and verbal aptitudes necessarily measure the kind of competence that teachers need to deal with the problems they confront daily. In addition to a teacher's technical and personal competence, schools, like other social organizations, use social criteria as a basis for hiring. That is, they discriminate against people having certain social characteristics and favor people with other characteristics. For example, over two thirds of the school superintendents surveyed in the state of Massachusetts a number of years ago said that the school superintendent should not be a Negro, female, socialist, or take part in local politics, but that he should be a church member and dress conservatively.[33] These criteria may be changing following civil rights legislation in recent years, however.

Of course, using these personal criteria increases the likelihood that some technically competent individuals will inadvertently be screened out. But, organizations are normally willing to sacrifice a degree of technical competence in order to secure like-minded staff members who are committed to certain implicit goals.[34] For example, suppose that many influential citizens in a given community insist that the school system should teach children to respect the traditional institutions of marriage, religion, and the like, and that they should be indoctrinated to uphold the existing political system. The school board is likely to give priority to the more politically passive and conservative teacher applicants. The colleges of education, finding that they cannot place radical activist graduates, might discourage this type of individual from entering the profession.

Several studies suggest that college students majoring in elementary education and in physical education tend to be among the most politically conservative groups of college students (whereas students in secondary education tend to reflect more closely the attitudes of their respective teaching fields).[35] One study of Michigan State freshmen indicated that education majors not only were very conservative but were also relatively "other directed" individuals. In studies of support for civil liberties at the University of California and the University of Georgia, students in the college of education placed less value on the civil liberties guaranteed by the Bill of Rights than did students in other colleges.[36] Still another survey of teachers in one city indicated that they subscribed to the individualistic, *laissez faire* philosophy that has dominated the nation throughout most of its history.[37] Compared to social workers, teachers were more inclined to hold the *individual* rather than the society or the state responsible for social problems; were less supportive of the idea that the family and the government have responsibility for helping individuals who are in trouble; and denied that the group is responsible for the welfare of its members. They were more likely to endorse system goals, the responsibility of the individual for his own welfare, the value of struggle and self-denial for self-realization, traditionalism, and individual autonomy. The study's authors felt that in contrast to social workers, the fact that most teachers were concerned with transmitting the culture from one generation to the next made them relatively unconcerned about change. However, the same study also suggested that, in recent years, teachers participating in experiments in the inner-city schools had become more humanitarian than other teachers, with a definite leaning toward the values ascribed to social workers.

Over half of the high school teachers polled by the National Education Association (NEA) describe teachers as politically "conservative."[38] In Zeigler's survey, the proportion of teachers who were conservative varied from 41 percent of the females from high-income homes to 26 percent among males from low-income homes.[39] Approximately one-third of the relatively new teachers were classified as conservative and about the same proportion as liberals, but political conservatism increased with experience in teaching, reflecting the persistence of conservative pressures on teachers during the course of their careers. Their reluctance to speak in class about controversial topics also increased with experience, especially among the liberal teachers.

What Are the Effects of Stressing Internal Control?

If an organization is not in a position to select only compatible members who will be willing to subscribe to its goals and implicit values, it will try to compensate by first trying to indoctrinate new members; schools and colleges attempt to indoctrinate their members, not only through the formal curriculum but through an informal culture—that is, the unique values, traditions, beliefs, and goals of the particular school. When these indoctrination efforts fail, they resort to the use of extrinsic *controls* and close supervision. Definite lesson plans are prepared by the teacher for each day's work, just as an industrial supervisor lays out the day's work for the men under him. Close supervision of teachers is considered to be necessary to assure adequate performance. In order to move masses of students, the "platoon system" was devised for public schools. Under this plan, the equivalent of a factory assembly line, the students are shifted from class to class at the sound of a bell. Strict military discipline is imperative to keep the system coordinated.

The problems of maintaining control are compounded by the fact that schools are "people processing" institutions whose mission is to produce changes in their clientele (i.e., the students). This task must be performed quite differently for those students who accept the school's authority and who willingly subject themselves to its influence, and for those reluctant students who are in the school's custody primarily because they are compelled by law to be there or have no alternative way to use their time. For the latter students, the school takes on an authoritarian, "manipulative" character that discourages the kind of mutual trust from developing that is so necessary to the professional-client relationship. From what has already been said about many students' lack of intrinsic commitment to the school's objectives and procedures, it is no wonder that the typical school seems to be preoccupied with order and control.[40] In utter frustration, many schools become "custodial" institutions, where belligerent students defy the teachers and teachers are rewarded for maintaining order.[41]

WHAT CONTROL MECHANISMS ARE USED BY SCHOOLS?

Centralization. Decision making tends to be *centralized* in large school systems as a way of maintaining control. In my study of 28 high schools in the Middle West, the majority of teachers reported that the following types of decisions were made by the central administration (i.e., the superintendent's office or the school board): determining if the faculty members should receive tenure, formulating instructional policy, departmental budgets, determining what courses are to be taught and what courses are to be required, hiring new teachers, and promotions.[42] The principal's office was responsible for selection of required textbooks and setting discipline policies. It is seen that the central administration controls the major decisions. The teachers' decision-making power was confined largely to decisions *within* the classroom, such as the selection of supplementary reading materials, determining what concepts and values are to be conveyed in a particular course, teaching methods, and homework assignments.

Wittes' survey of 10 senior high schools also demonstrated the tendency of schools to rely on centralized decision-making structures.[43] According to the students' perceptions, in 6 of the 10 schools principals had more influence than any other level, and in three others the school board was perceived as the most influential level. In no case were teachers or students considered to be the most influential. Wittes identified four different types of control structures in schools based upon the way power was distributed:

1. Diffuse—where the total amount of power is perceived as small, and there are only small differences in power between the various echelons.
2. Local Control—where the principal exercises more power than any other echelon in the system.
3. Centralized—where the main sources of power reside in the superintendent and school board, outside of the school building.
4. Differentiated—where the total amount of power is perceived to be high and, therefore, while there are large differences in the power of teachers and the principal, the teachers exert relatively strong influence that is shared with the principal.

Standardization. Centralization is often supplemented by a second type of control mechanism, *standardization* or, in other words, the application of uniform policies and practices throughout a system. Several practices help to insure that all schools in a system or, indeed, throughout the nation, will use comparable procedures and practices.

• Many different school systems hire teachers from only a few teacher training institutions who are likely to have been taught similar procedures and ideologies.
• Teacher training itself is very uniform from institution to institution because of accreditation, standard textbooks used by various teacher training institutions, and the like.
• Standardized tests help to assure that the same subject matter will be emphasized throughout the system.
• Textbooks are probably the most standardizing influence on teaching; one study in Texas conducted by a governor's committee on education estimated that three-fourths of the child's classroom time and 90 percent of his homework was spent using textbooks.[44]
• Curriculum guides and uniform lesson plans are used throughout the system, state, and nation as a means of assuring that students will interpret the textbooks in the same way, although these are not uniformly enforced.
• Student mobility is another critical factor that makes national cur-

riculum standards necessary as students move from one community to another.

The prominent role that *schedules* and *routines* play in the schools is apparent in a classroom observation made by Silberman.[45] A cluster of excited children were examining a turtle with enormous fascination and intensity. The teacher insisted that they put the turtle away in order to have their science lesson. The lesson was on crabs. In another instance he reports an article from the National Education Association's journal, *Today's Education,* giving an experienced teacher's advice to new teachers in inner-city schools. Describing the procedure for walking down the stairs, the teacher reports that she lines up the children and, after appointing two line leaders and explaining to the entire class the school's rules about walking and speaking softly in the halls, she has them practice walking up and down the stairs. Each time the group is allowed to move only when quiet and orderly, she reports proudly. This reads like a leaf out of Bel Kaufman's popular satire, *Up the Down Staircase.*[46]

The Reward System. The *evaluation* and *reward* systems used to hire, fire, and promote teachers reinforce standardizing procedures.[47] One of the most insightful analyses of the evaluation system was reported over 20 years ago on the basis of a study of the mobility patterns of teachers in the Chicago public schools.[48] Regardless of the school they were in or the previous achievement of their pupils, teachers were rewarded for the scholastic achievements of their pupils and for their ability to maintain quiet, well-disciplined classrooms. Teachers naturally preferred to be assigned to schools where children were intrinsically motivated and could keep up with the lesson plans. Teachers who could not obtain jobs in these more desirable schools nevertheless stressed classroom discipline and were required to follow the lesson plans designed for intrinsically motivated pupils in other parts of the city.

Personal Controls. Schools also attempt to extend their *control* over the personal lives of their members. Schools presume to punish students who chew gum, smoke, become pregnant, get married, or refuse to pray or to salute the flag. An organization that exercises such pervasive control is called a "total institution." The prison is another example of a total institution. In prisons, attendance is mandatory; service is not compensated; rigid authority hierarchies maintain control over tightly scheduled, repetitious activities; members are closely supervised; and their personal conduct is evaluated daily. There are some obvious parallels between schools and prisons. Like prisoners, students typically must obtain permission to use the library, to get a drink of water, and to use the restroom. They seldom have choice over what they will study or do in the course of a day. They must remain in the building during specific hours. Their grooming and manners and clothing are subject to close inspection and approval by the teachers in charge and, frequently, policemen are hired to patrol the hallways.

WHAT ARE THE CONSEQUENCES OF CONTROLS?

These control procedures present some problems, but they offer some advantages as well.

Problems. On one hand, centralization and standardization have probably aggravated many of the problems that plague the public schools today. Because of such practices, schools are not as flexible as they could be to accommodate their variegated clientele, and they are not as adaptable as possible to adjust to rapid social change. Gittell analyzed the decision-making process in the New York City public school system and found that standardization and overcentralization made any innovation nearly impossible to execute.[49] The strong positions of the assistant superintendents blocked initiative and, because the superintendent normally had risen within the school hierarchy, he was unlikely to take a position different from that of the general bureaucracy. Local school boards had almost no authority in determining school policy, their role being to act as buffers between the local community and the central board.

Many students attending larger, standardized schools are perhaps less broadly educated than they otherwise would be because they are not encouraged to expand their interests beyond the narrow curriculum, and because large standardized systems are necessarily geared to the "average" pupil regardless of the fact that human beings are variable. This tendency to teach to the norm is reinforced by standardized testing. Many teachers, particularly in the suburbs, gear their courses to the external tests used for college admission to assure that their students will perform well on them, and as a result, the middle-class students have a special advantage because middle-class schools pay more attention to the standardized tests.[50]

As the practice of teaching to the test suggests, students often become highly pragmatic and even cynical about their experiences in bureaucratized school systems. Rhea's study of two elite Boston high schools, where most students were planning to go to college, revealed that the students generally regarded school as an instrumental experience designed solely to prepare them for a job or college.[51] They were primarily concerned with "getting through" and "looking good." Their main concern was not with ideas but with getting adequate grades. The majority of students would knowingly and hypocritically give the teacher a wrong answer if the teacher thought it to be a right one. This tendency to "give the teacher what she wants," was described in detail by Jules Henry.[52] The typical student in Rhea's study was engaged in building a "paper shadow," adding favorable information to his dossier through evaluations of his classwork and extracurricular activities. The students' every endeavor was heavily weighted toward "preparation" rather than "experience": 91 percent agreed that "what we do in high school is essentially preparation for what will come later; the payoff will be in college or on the job."

Contrary to what one might expect, these students showed few signs of alienation. Despite the lack of immediate relevance in their studies and the relative powerlessness of the students, they did not seem to exhibit a sense of powerlessness or feeling of depersonalization. They had learned to cope with, even to manipulate, the system. However, it is possible that students in larger, less elite systems would be less successful in controlling their own fate.

Depersonalization also is likely to be more of a problem in standardized systems. In particular, in the larger institutions the intellectual excitement of the classroom is less likely to be reinforced in the peer group outside of the classroom. Newcomb has pointed out that the major difference between large and small colleges is due to the fact that the peer group is not as strong in the larger institutions.[53]

Also, the set curriculum insulates teachers from the changing values and special circumstances experienced by different types of students. Many ghetto parents, who recently have demanded more decentralized control over the schools, are reacting to the attempts to apply routine procedures and standard curricula to their children despite the persistent failure of these methods and curricula to produce students who can compete with middle-class children.

The standardized curriculum also produces corresponding tensions between teachers and school administrators. The administrators' job is to coordinate the separate parts of the system, while professional teachers are under direct daily pressures from their students and local communities to adjust to the unique qualities, problems, and special circumstances of their students.[54] The fact that teachers work alone in self-contained classrooms also tends to insulate them from the demands of the larger system. As a result, teachers are caught between pressures from the students and from the administration.

Advantages. On the other hand, standardization and centralization provide some advantages. Students suffer less from teachers' capriciousness and from variability in the quality of instruction and grading standards in standardized schools, and a standardized curriculum helps to assure that students will learn the "essentials" at each step of the way even when they move from one part of the city or nation to another. Moreover, the standardized curriculum has permitted schools to absorb masses of children and prepare them for a complex, technological society at a relatively low annual cost per student. It remains to be seen whether a more effective means of mass education can be found of comparable combined efficiency and effectiveness.

Also, the ability of the individual student to defend himself against some of the detrimental consequences of standardization is often over-looked by the critics. Students probably learn to live with depersonalized situations and to *segmentalize* their contacts with the school, looking upon it as only one small part of their lives. Many students probably depend on other relationships outside of the classroom or outside of the school itself for their personal satisfactions. They also can learn to *rationalize* their failures. For example, a national survey of attitudes toward achievement tests reported that 40 percent of American adolescents believe that intelligence tests are more important than other qualities for determining their success in school, and 30 percent of the 5000 adolescents surveyed reported that they had changed their estimate of their own intellectual ability after they were told their scores on standardized achievement tests. Yet, less than 1 in 10 students said that they had *lowered* their estimate of their ability; whereas 1 in 4 said that their self-conception had been improved as a result of learning their test scores.[55] This tendency on the part of individuals to believe ability estimates when they are favorable and rationalize away the unfavorable results can help to cushion detrimental consequences of standardized schooling.

Size as a Special Problem

Thus far, the size of schools as a factor in control has been referred to only in passing. But, in addition to being correlated with centralization and standardization, size in itself creates special difficulties in maintaining control, and it may have some detrimental results over and above the greater need for control in large organizations.

Overcrowding. We have already commented on the growth in the size of schools. The problems of control are compounded by large, ill-equipped classrooms. Most children are being educated on a mass basis, often in shifts in large, routinized classrooms. There are now over one million pupils in excess of normal building capacity of 30 pupils per classroom, and nearly half a million in "curtailed sessions" (e.g., attending only a morning or afternoon "shift"). According to a study published in the *Congressional Record*, there is a shortage of between 100,000 and 150,000 classrooms (based on an ideal median class size of 27), and more than that number are likely to be needed to accommodate anticipated growth. Although the growth rates are leveling off, so is the public's willingness to pay for new classrooms, as reflected in the increased failure rate of school bond issues in recent years. The net effect, therefore, is likely to be continued pressures towards larger schools with accelerating problems of control unless new forms of education are found.

Some Effects of Size. Although large schools are supposed to provide *more* options for individual participation, the facts of the matter reported in a series of studies can be summarized as follows. (1) Students in small schools held an average of 3.5 responsible positions per student (members of play casts, officers of organizations, participants in athletics, and so on) ; students in large schools averaged 0.5 responsible positions per student;[56] or, every other student in the large school had only one responsible activity role. (2) Students in small schools exceeded students in large schools in having satisfying experiences related to the development of competence, to being challenged, and to engaging in important activities. (3) Students in small schools received twice as many pressures to participate, or to meet the expectations of the school, as did students in large schools.

These findings are consistent with the findings obtained from the many studies of size in factories, public agencies, discussion groups, task forces, and training-encounter groups, which indicate a negative relationship between size and individual participation, involvement, and satisfaction. When the number of persons is low there are more opportunities to participate per person, and thus each experiences the attractions with greater force.

What Types of Problems Does Specialization Produce?

Educational institutions have not always been permitted to *officially* specialize in the many diverse functions that they must perform. But this fact has not prevented them from adopting covert forms of specialization. Two types of formal and informal specialization can be distinguished: (1) "functional" specialization, which is based on (a) the selection of certain types of clientele, and (b) specialized goals or functions; and (2) "structural" specialization, based upon (a) curriculum content, and (b) the way that tasks and roles are divided.

WHAT IS FUNCTIONAL SPECIALIZATION?

This type of specialization takes place both informally among the students themselves and formally by assigning students to different programs.

Informal Specialization. Students divide themselves up informally on the basis of their common values, circumstances, and objectives. These peer cultures, like schools themselves, are very diversified. A new student in a given school might become part of one of several different types of peer groups, depending upon his background and values. Clark has identified three types of subcultures that differ from one another primarily in the emphasis on the legitimate and illegitimate academic and social goals:[57]

1. The *fun* subculture stresses sociability and extracurricular activi-

ties. It is the adolescent world of clothes, movies, cars, and dates. Status in it involves "hanging out at the right places," being "cooperative" on dates and, above all, having a "good personality."

2. In most schools, the *academic* subculture is less prominent than the fun culture; the former stresses the value of brains and of being a good student.

3. The *delinquent* subculture is characterized by rebellion. Contempt, ridicule, and defiance are expressed by these students, who not only are compelled to go to school but are precluded from admittance to the labor market. They are forced to compete for success against high odds and on terms defined by the school system. Because they are handicapped by their underprivileged backgrounds, they seek success through disapproved means.

Formal Specialization. The "dumping grounds" found in most schools and in many colleges are part of a formal system of functional specialization, although it is not always officially designated as such. Custodial courses designed for the less academic, more troublesome students segregate them from academically oriented classrooms, thus permitting the school to concentrate on academic goals with the majority of the students.

Sometimes entire departments or schools specialize in different functions. One school might specialize in preparing students for college while another specializes in vocational education. In lower-class ghetto schools, academic standards may be disregarded almost entirely in the practice of promoting children from grade to grade; they eventually may graduate, even though they may not have attained even the barest minimum of reading ability (see Chapter 3). But if slum schools have sometimes neglected the academic dimension, they perform other functions that many citizens expect of them, such as keeping students off the labor market and providing "custody" for many students who have discipline and learning problems, thus making it easier for other schools (typically in middle-class neighborhoods) to achieve their academic aims.

WHAT IS STRUCTURAL SPECIALIZATION?

To this point we have been speaking only of functional specialization, that is, a division of labor based on the assignment of *students* according to basic functions and goals of the organization. The second type of specialization—structural specialization—is based on the way the *tasks* and role assignments associated with the various functions are divided up. The distinction perhaps can be clarified with an illustration. Assume there is a school that specializes exclusively in training students for the vocations. The curriculum and related tasks associated with this function can be divided in different ways. In one case, each teacher might be assigned to teach a wide range of skills to particular individuals. Instead of limiting himself to a specific course, the teacher would be responsible for many aspects of the progress of particular students he is teaching. This illustrates functional specialization. In another case, each teacher might be assigned to teach a specific set of skills to all children in the school, one teacher teaching woodwork, another drafting, and so on. This latter situation would illustrate structural specialization. In both cases the teachers are specializing with students preparing for jobs, but the responsibilities are divided differently.

Schools at different grade levels use different forms of specialization to different degrees. According to one study, at higher age-grade levels, there was more emphasis on the transmission of specialized knowledge and skills, and there was less emphasis on preparing students with a particular type of objective in mind or instilling them with a generalized set of values.[58] But in the elementary grades, each teacher worked with a special group of students on a wide range of tasks. There was also a parallel difference in the means the administration used to deal with teachers and students. In the lower grades, appeals were made to the teachers' and students' moral obligations to conform, while at the higher grades, authority was utilitarian, based on a calculating strategy of offering such tangible rewards as money or grades.

WHAT ARE THE EFFECTS OF SPECIALIZATION?

Structural Specialization. Indeed, the public secondary schools seem to be specialized along structural lines to an exceptional degree. For example, the curriculum is broken up into small bits and pieces: American history, world history, modern European history, ancient European history, black history, the history of California, and the like. Some sociologists and educators believe that schools are too specialized in this sense, that teaching is carried out too much on a piecemeal basis. One sociologist is especially concerned that the traditional teacher role has been broken up into so many specialized roles that no one teacher is any longer interested in the "whole" child.[59] The holistic approach that he advocates would require a basic reorganization of schools. In particular, it would be necessary to increase the authority and professional competence of classroom teachers and to rely more on subprofessionals and volunteers to carry out highly specialized roles so that teachers could concentrate on developing the "affective" dimensions concerned with self-respect of students and with the moral climate.

This prescription, it should be noted, would require teachers to assume more authority for the *entire existence of the youngster outside of school,* since many of the major influences over the child and many of his problems stem from sources outside of the school. This is another form of the "total institution" approach discussed above. In other words, in addition to being a means used in the custodial type of organization, total control is sometimes advocated as a positive means of compensating for a child's family handicaps. It is part of the philosophy behind the establishment of preschools and out-of-school educational activities. Some critics even propose transforming schools into residential institutions in order to separate children from the educational disadvantages imposed by their families.

Functional Specialization. There is mixed evidence about how "grouping" children on the basis of their ability or age affects them. A few studies, such as the one reported by Goldberg and associates, have found that grouping has positive effects on the children's self-image and achievement levels.[60] However, most studies indicate detrimental effects. For example, Luchins and Luchins found that children in some tracks were stigmatized.[61] Slight gains among high ability students are probably more than offset by unfavorable effects on average and below-average students. Another limited study reported negative consequences.[62] In two Midwestern schools, noncollege prep students displayed lower academic achievement, less participation in extracurricular activities, more misconduct in school, a greater tendency to drop out, and higher rates of delinquency. However, it was not proven that these differences were produced by the track system. The losses might reflect the fact that the objective of ability grouping often is to help the bright rather than the slow students.

The evidence from the *Equality of Educational Opportunity* survey and other studies to be considered later suggests that students perform better when they are mixed on the basis of social class, although ability grouping was not directly tested. Ability grouping probably does tend to segregate students according to family background, since both prior experience and cognitive skills are correlated with social, economic, and ethnic background. Thus, Douglas found that, holding initial ability level constant, students placed in a high-ability group showed a gain in test scores from age 8 to 11, while those placed in a lower ability group experienced a decline.[63] Since the assignment was strongly correlated with the social class of the students, it is possible that ability grouping had the effect of accentuating the influence of family background. There is reason to believe that students from disadvantaged family backgrounds are more affected by the kind of students they are assigned to be with than are middle-class students (see Chapter 3).

The bright children are not only more likely to be grouped with the more motivated children but they are also likely to get the more experienced and competent teachers, since teaching bright children commands higher prestige. The *Equality of Educational Opportunity* survey shows a clear relationship between the competence of teachers, as measured by their verbal ability and level of education, and the background of their students.[64] Teacher characteristics, in fact, accounted for more variation in student achievement than all other school characteristics combined, excluding student-body characteristics. Finally, it is conceivable that ability grouping would influence the teacher's expectations, and Rosenthal's study of the effects of teacher expectations reinforces the possibility that students tend to fulfill teacher expectations (although the study has severe methodological problems).[65]

It would be premature to conclude that specialization is either categorically good or bad. There are many factors that can influence the outcome: the homogeneity of the students, how many courses they can elect, whether the objective of the grouping practice is to reduce variation in students or variation in the skills that the school tries to transmit, how much students are stigmatized by the experience, and the change in the level of competition and motivation that may occur with ability grouping.[66]

Who Controls the Schools?

Educational institutions are not merely closed systems that can be explained solely in terms of internal bureaucratic processes, however. Many of their most crucial problems stem from their relationships with outside groups. The schools' goals and policies, what they teach, how it is taught, and who is hired to teach it are all dictated by outside groups that control education. The available bureaucratic models, while of some assistance for understanding educational problems, have obscured this "other directed" nature of educational organizations. Models of organizations have yet to be perfected that fully capture the significance of the political interplay between educational organizations and their external social environments.

There are at least two types of control structures that set educational policy in this country: the legal structure and informal power structures. Policy is the product of struggles within and between both types of structures.

THE LEGAL STRUCTURE

Constitutionally, each of the 50 states in the Union is responsible for public education policies within the state. In practice, state legislatures have authorized more than 100,000 local school-board members to oversee the 19,000 public school districts. State departments of education, under the direction of state school-boards, set the guidelines pertaining to matters such as finance, school districting, general curriculum requirements, and teacher certification. Although these broad guidelines leave wide latitude for school districts, as we shall see, control over the institution is not as decentralized as implied in the notion of "local control."

Local districts *can* point to the fact that they pay most of the costs of public education as a basis for their claim to the right to control the schools. The cost of public schools, by far, represents the single most important local tax expense. Local school districts now bear over half of the burden for the cost of public education, even though local property constitutes no more than eight percent of the national wealth. Three-fourths of the local tax expenditures go to support the schools. Because citizens are trying to pay for the nation's second largest public expenditure with the least profitable form of wealth in this nation, they are understandably concerned about how the money is being spent.

INFORMAL POWER STRUCTURES

Overlapping the legal authority structure are pervasive, competitive centers of informal influence. In some communities there is a dominant monopolistic group that influences all spheres of community life.[67] Such a group might include elected city government officials, but it will also include many citizens associated with corporations, in private business, or in the professions. In many other communities the power structure tends to be "nucleated," in the sense that there are many different factions vying for power. In this pluralistic type of power structure, leaders compete among themselves, and the leaders who are influential with respect to one type of issue, such as federal aid to education, are not necessarily in the same group that has most influence over another issue, such as which textbooks should be used in specific courses.

In a survey of school systems in Massachusetts, superintendents were asked to identify the groups that, in their opinion, were the main obstacles to the schools.[68] The one group mentioned most frequently (by 38 percent) was the elected and appointed community officials in the local government, who were especially concerned about keeping rising school expenditures down. This negative role often played by government officials was especially pronounced in the larger cities.

The second most frequently mentioned group doing most "to block public education" in Massachusetts communities was composed of individual business owners and executives. Over a third of the superintendents, especially those in smaller communities, named one or more local businessmen as leading opponents of public education; many others were owners or executives of large industrial firms or retail establishments in their communities. Their main objection was to growing school costs or building new schools.

The primary supporters of the schools, also identified by the superintendents, were the PTAs (mentioned by over two-thirds of them). Also, community officials and businessmen, although they were among the opponents, were frequently mentioned as supporters as well.

The reader may sympathize with many of the demands made on the schools by these groups, and he may object to others. According to the Massachusetts superintendents, the most frequent pressures (mentioned by at least a near majority of superintendents) were to:

Protest school tax increases on bond proposals.
Demand more money for the general school program.
Teach more courses and subjects.
Introduce new services (in addition to academic instruction).
Place more emphasis on the "three R's".
Place more emphasis on the athletic program.
Protest views expressed by teachers.

What is eventually taught, in other words, not only depends upon how education is legally controlled, but also upon the informal power structure and the give and take between these official and unofficial sources of power. The kind of control that will be exercised over schools hinges on the compromises between these informal community power structures and the official seat of power, the school boards.

RELATIONSHIP BETWEEN THE BOARD AND COMMUNITY

The way school boards are linked to community power structures is still the subject of debate in lieu of answers to three closely related questions: (1) whether school board members are able to act independently of administration; (2) whether boards are responsive to local constituencies; and (3) how well school boards are insulated from politics.

How Independent Are School Boards? Different writers have reached opposite conclusions about whether school boards exert independent pressure on the school administration or whether the board is typically the superintendent's puppet. Some evidence in favor of their independence comes from the survey by Gross and his colleagues, who reported considerable disagreement between school board members and superintendents on a number of issues.[69] These disagreements suggest that boards do have independent opinions. Substantially more board members than superintendents agreed that:

- Pupils in the first six grades must meet academic standards in order to be promoted (84 vs. 51 percent).
- It is desirable to give numerical grades on report cards in the first six grades (59 vs. 9 percent).

- It is desirable for schools to teach the superiority of the American way of life in all things (73 vs. 61 percent).
- It is desirable to place more emphasis on teaching subject matter than on developing individual interests of pupils (33 vs. 13 percent).
- The superintendents should keep a watchful eye on the personal life of his subordinates (66 vs. 26 percent).
- Consideration should be given to local values or feelings regarding race, religion, and national origin in filling vacant teaching positions (41 vs. 30 percent).

At the same time, substantially more superintendents than board members agreed that:

- The superintendent should defend his teachers from attacks when they present the pros and cons of various controversial social and political issues (78 vs. 90 percent).
- A definite stand should be taken against any unreasonable demands that may come from local taxpayers (81 vs. 99 percent).

This dissent helps to explain why many of the superintendents in the Massachusetts study (one in five) stated that school boards constituted a major obstacle in carrying out their jobs in a professional manner. They were more subject to pressures when the board members were politically motivated and when the board members engaged in block voting. But while school boards sometimes exerted independent pressures, most board members in the Massachusetts study agreed to defend teachers and schools from attacks by local taxpayers.

Zeigler disputes that school-board members have enough power to act as an independent source of pressure on superintendents because individual members do not have the backing of constituent groups.[70] In most cases school boards prefer to defer to the superintendent and his staff, whom they regard as experts. Instead of serving as a conduit to channel popular views to the administrators, Zeigler contends, boards define their job as selling the administration's program to segments of the community. Arguing that most school administrators are able to coopt their boards, he concludes that the chief contribution of school boards is to *legitimate* the policies established by the administration, rather than to represent the community.

Superintendents have several sources of leverage. First, board members, who are usually unfamiliar with the technical details of running a school system, must depend upon the administrators for information and for support for their own policy decisions. That is, the "technical" authority of the superintendent takes precedence over the official (rank) authority of the school board. Second, they quickly become identified with school policies and become defensive about them. Third, they can count on public ignorance of, and apathy toward, the schools. Finally, many board members do *not* represent specific constituencies who watch their voting records and can insure reelection. If they are not committed to an outside group, these board members will be freer to support the administration.[71]

Are Boards Unresponsive? The ability of boards to act independently of the school administration, then, depends upon whether they have an outside base of support to whom they are responsible and who can provide them with leverage. Are boards as unresponsive to their constituencies as the above statements suggest? Again, views on the issue differ. According to one school of thought, school boards tend to be linked to the important segments of a community, and the main cleavages and controversies within the community consequently become reflected in the board. In their study of a rural community in upstate New York, for instance, Vidich and Bensman discovered that the school board was closely allied with prevailing community elites.[72] Others have found this to be the case in communities characterized by monolithic, elite power structures.[73] McCarty and Ramsey have argued that the structure of a community influences the structure of school boards and places limits on their actions.[74] They state that a community that is dominated by a single power structure will have a "dominated" school board and a functionary superintendent; a factional community will have a factional board and a political strategist as a superintendent; a pluralistic community has a comparably pluralistic ("status congruent") board and a professional advisor as a superintendent; and an inert community has a sanctioning board and a decision-maker superintendent. Although the evidence from 51 communities is not entirely convincing, it supports the model.

Another group of investigators classified school boards into three types: consensual, pluralistic, and factional.[75] Each type reflected the level of community tension, that is, the factional board developed within communities with high levels of tension and consensual boards in peaceful communities. Furthermore, the higher the level of community tension, the greater the boards' tendency to oppose the superintendent.

But while this might suggest that boards are reflections of their communities, the authors of the study concluded that, ironically, the factional boards were even more likely than the consensual boards to defer to the superintendent, even though their acceptance of the professional role was not quite as high as was the case for the consensual board. Despite the fact that members of factional boards opposed the superintendent, they seemed to be debilitated by the rigidity of their factions and seriousness of the disputes. In other words, when it came to struggles against the professional controls that could be exercised by the superintendent, they were not able to defend their positions.

Regardless of the amount of cleavage on most boards, there are very large segments of the population, in most communities, whose interests and points of view are not represented on the board. The vast majority of board members are males from the white, upper-middle-class. Two-thirds to three-fourths of the local school board members are businessmen, professionals, and farmers. Fewer than 1 in 10 board members (and even less in the large cities) is a skilled or unskilled manual worker.[76] They are overwhelmingly Anglo-Saxon, Protestant, and middle aged (47 years old, on the average). This composition minimizes the ability of school boards to represent the values and situations of large segments of many communities.

Although it has not been conclusively proven that the unrepresentativeness of school boards biases their decisions, there is some evidence that boards have been impervious to pressures for change that would benefit minority groups. Crain found from a case study of 15 cities that the crucial variable affecting the decision to desegregate school systems was the composition of the school board, in particular the members' political liberalism and whether they were elected or appointed.[77] Civil-rights demonstrations and other direct pressures had relatively little effect on what the boards did.

Are Boards Insulated from Politics? Some critics believe that school boards are unresponsive and not able to represent their communities because they are too insulated from politics. This insulation is caused by the independent political and financial status of the school district, the self-perpetuating nature of the school boards (since in the majority of cases, present members seek out potential candidates to run for vacant offices), closed-door meetings (practiced by at least 40 percent of the boards), low attendance at open meetings, and low turnout at school-board elections. Because of its insulation from politics, the school system seems to epitomize what Weber referred to as the emergence of a specialized bureaucracy monopolizing power through its control of expertise.

Perhaps school board members are more attuned to the political arena than the critics have recognized. In theory, perhaps, school board members are supposed to be "apolitical," impartially representing all segments of their respective communities or regions but, in practice, many members do seem to represent special interest groups. In the survey of over 100 school systems in Massachusetts, 3 in every 10 superintendents estimated that some school board members had sought to be elected in order to represent a certain group in the community, and 1 in 4 said that their school boards engaged in "bloc voting," that is, voting as representatives of special-interest blocs of factions of the community.[78] One in 5 superintendents estimated that some members of their boards were primarily interested in gaining experience in politics.

Nevertheless, the fact remains that the majority of the school board members do not seem to be politically motivated. The interests of many constituent groups in a given community are not represented on the school board.

WHAT ARE THE CONSEQUENCES OF POLITICAL INSULATION?

Insofar as schools are insulated from politics, there is the question of what difference insulation makes. Again there is conflicting evidence and opinion. First, there is evidence from the Massachusetts survey that insulation protects professional standards. The higher the proportion of board members motivated by "civic duty," the less independent pressure they exerted on superintendents and the greater their adherence to professional standards; whereas the higher the proportion of board members motivated by political experience or to represent some group in the community, the less closely they adhered to professional standards. Superintendents in the Massachusetts survey charged that politically motivated boards that practiced bloc voting were the ones that exerted independent pressures. These pressures often threatened professional standards. For example, one in four superintendents said that their board members had exerted pressures on them to award school contracts on an illegal basis and to appoint and fire teachers for reasons other than their competence. Only slightly over one in four of the politically motivated board members were judged by the superintendents to have "good motivation." The less-professional boards were found in the larger, industrial cities where the superintendency was accorded relatively high prestige. Superintendents who had boards with large proportions of members who were motivated by "civic duty" felt fewer pressures of this kind from their boards.

Second, insulation has its disadvantages. Insulation tends to promote public ignorance about educational policy and, indeed, apathy toward educational policy until a crisis erupts in the community. Most citizens know very little about the educational programs in their community. Furthermore, organized interest groups in a community normally do not involve themselves in the educational decision-making process. Many groups who are accustomed to participating in partisan elections tend to ignore school elections. This means that many people, and especially low-income groups in the large cities, will be excluded because they cannot count on even what little political influence they might have in the political party system to carry over into school policies. Thus, while insulation sometimes might promote efficiency, it does *not* lead to representation of diverse values in policy making.

What Influences Do Extracommunity Forces Have on Education?

The legal system and the local community power structures are only the top of a mammoth iceberg of outside influences on the schools. Many of the most significant influences emanate from the national, and even international sources.

Is There a National System of Education?

Ideologies about local control notwithstanding, the answer to the question is a simple, yes. But the reasons behind the answer are complex. The fundamental fact is that schools are caught up in a nationwide network of organizations that has formed in response to what sociologists call a "turbulent environment," which is characteristic of changing societies.[79] Turbulent environments are characterized by (1) accelerating rates of social and demographic change and (2) growing differentiation and complexity of interconnections among the groups and organizations in the environment. Considering the first characteristic, many sources of change can be observed: population increases, changes in the age structure, fluctuations in political leadership, changing residential patterns, and disproportionately high rates of intercity mobility that reflect the fact that most cities are integrated into a national society. The second characteristic of a turbulent environment, its differentiated structure, can be observed in the diversity of groups that attempt to influence the schools, which range from the state board of education and the governor's office to teachers associations, the PTA, and a variety of community organizations.

Both change and differentiation have the same effect: to produce *interdependence* among all organizations involved in education. Change forces realignments among schools and other organizations. Old ties are disrupted and new ones must be formed. Specifically, two shifts take place in times of change. First, new clientele evolve (or more precisely, some types of students who were previously neglected take on renewed importance) ; and second, as new clients gain power and demand better service, the priorities must shift, forcing a redistribution of scarce resources. Since all individuals are affected during such periods, there tends to be a groundswell to broaden participation in the decision making; educational organizations must provide a vehicle for expanding this influence.

New organizations must be formed to satisfy these demands, and existing organizations begin to look to one another in order to establish new standards and policy guidelines and for mutual assistance as they attempt to shift their priorities and alter their practices to meet the demands. In other words, change requires cooperation among organizations in order to permit them to work out new divisions of labor, new patterns of dependency, and new standards.

Structural differentiation reflects the other side of the coin and has similar effects. In the type of national society that has evolved in this country today, the problems are universal and large-scale. Most major cities have experienced comparable problems of integration, student and community unrest, financing, professional militancy, and the like. These problems are so large that no one organization can be equipped to tackle them. Organizations must combine in order to develop the necessary expertise and to accumulate the necessary power to implement change. It takes many different organizations, each in control of resources needed by the others, and each specializing in a small aspect of the larger problem. The organizations involved then vie for the power to coordinate the overall effort and for the authority to speak on behalf of persons who are encountering the problems, whether it be for the child, for the school system, or for education.

This turbulence has two consequences. First, the activities of any one school will be of concern to other segments of the society not directly involved in it; and second, there will be a pressing need to coordinate the work of the separate educational organizations in order to provide a concerted attack on educational problems. As the network expands in size, the problems of coordinating the combined effort and regulating conflict within it are compounded. For this reason, there is a tendency (1) for decision -making to become centralized and (2) for independent coordinating organizations to evolve as the number and range of organizations connected with schools grows. It follows that the larger the network becomes, the more subjected schools will be to outside pressures to change,[80] because as schools become more integrated with other organizations that themselves are changing, they are more likely to be affected by changes in other parts of the network.

These developments explain why, as Pellegrin concluded from his survey of innovation in education, "the greatest stimuli to changes in education originate in sources external to the field. These sources are not only outside the local community, but in most instances, outside the education profession itself."[81] This does not mean that change will be forced on schools by any single organization. Instead, organizational networks promote change through the process of compromise. Each organization pushes its own values up to the limit. The existence of other organizations imposes limits on the actions of each organization in the set.

From these general observations, three conclusions can be drawn: (1) loose *networks* of schools and other organizations tend to arise in changing, differentiated environments because such environments force organizations to become more interdependent; (2) within these networks, there is a tendency for some organizations to emerge as more central than others in order to coordinate the activities of the network as a whole; and (3) the larger the network, the more outside sources of pressure that will be exerted on schools to change.

What are the Effects of this National System? This system provides for stability as well as change. Consider first how it helps to maintain stability. Some organizations are specifically designed to maintain continuity in educational practice. First, accrediting agencies not only set limits on regional and national curriculum and personnel policies but also act as a force supporting the traditional curriculum and standards. Secondly, testing agencies exert an important standardizing influence on the curriculum although, in some cases, they also exert influence for change.[82] Seven hundred schools and over one million students take College Board Exams annually. Teachers tend to concentrate on the contents of these tests. Third, higher education imposes constraints on the freedom of schools by determining what work students must have completed in high school to be eligible for admission. They also indirectly influence the curriculum through teacher preparation programs.

Fourth, state departments of education and state school boards set and maintain minimum curriculum standards. Many subjects are required by law, such as vocational education and driver training. Although this influence is highly variable from state to state, half the states require U.S. history, for example.[83] Fifth, teacher associations have been active in implementing nationwide policy requirements, especially in areas such as home economics, driver education, vocational education, and physical education.[84] Sixth, textbook publishers and, more recently, private foundations and U.S. government agencies, have attempted to influence the curriculum by making materials generally available. The fact that over half of the schools now use the new physics and chemistry programs and two-thirds use the new biology is indicative of this influence.[85] Finally, National Educational Television potentially could have a noticeable effect on the curriculum, and might become more influential in the future. The most successful program to date is "Sesame Street," produced under the auspices of the U.S. Office of Education. Perhaps some of its methods will be mimicked by schools.

In addition to acting as a stabilizing influence, however, this national system of organizations has sometimes promoted minor reforms. As an example, Clark describes how a federation of collaborating groups and organizations produced and rapidly disseminated the "new math" curriculum.[86] A committee of private citizens, financed by a quasi-governmental agency, the National Science Foundation (NSF), set out to write a course for national school use, something that no federal agency could do directly because of congressional opposition and public fear of government control. The materials were promoted through textbook publishers and other commercial channels. NSF initiated a program of seminar institutes to teach the teachers how to use the new materials. Accrediting agencies, in collaboration with universities, gave their blessings. It was not until the new program had been widely implemented that the U.S. Office of Education directly financed the program.

DOES THE NATIONAL SYSTEM MEAN MORE
FEDERAL CONTROL OVER EDUCATION?

The fact that education in this country is so strongly influenced by a loose-knit, national network of organizations does not necessarily mean that the federal government will dominate the system. A *national* system, in other words, does not necessarily imply "federal control" if, by that term, the dictation of educational policy by agencies of the federal government is meant. Indeed, the federal government has been unable to enforce legal decisions and federal guidelines concerning desegregation and the way local schools have actually misused federal monies intended to improve the education of the poor. Government agencies represent only one of the many sources of national influence. The authority of federal agencies is restricted on all sides by controversy, congressional restraints, internal bureaucratic controls, the small proportion of the costs of education provided by the federal government, and resistance from local institutions.

As Clark has noted, the shift *upward* in the formal locus of decision making in education is more than offset by an even greater thrust *outward* in the number of voluntary relationships among public agencies and private groups that converge around and control specific issues.[87] As local control has diminished, control has shifted outward, becoming diffused among many organizations existing between local communities and the federal bureaucracy. The federal government can do no more than play a mediating role because it is only one element in a larger system of checks and balances. It functions primarily as a *countervailing power* to organizations at the local and intermediate levels.

These shifts are occurring because of the incapacity of locally and professionally controlled service institutions to respond on their own initiative to emerging national problems. A national system of education can help to overcome the provincial insulation that has traditionally shielded schools from societal changes.

SOCIAL AND CULTURAL INFLUENCES

In addition to these organizational networks, community and regional value climates also help to shape educational practices and outcomes. Even in relatively "modernized" nations like the United States, there are fluctuations from region to region in the value attached to education and in the resources available for schooling, which create systematic differences in the outcomes of schooling in different parts of the country. In 1970, for example, the percentage of the eligible high school students who graduated varied from 79 percent in the Northeast to 67 percent in the Southeast.[88] Similarly, the proportion of elementary pupils one or more years behind in reading level varied from 11 to 34 percent in various parts of the country.

A pioneering study of regional variations in the United States reported by Herriott and Hodgkins demonstrated that systematic differences in schooling can be attributed to the schools' sociocultural context.[89] Using an index developed to measure the extent that each state is modernized, the authors found that the index was correlated with attributes of schools. The more modernized the social context, the more "modern" the school's organizational structures, and the more effective their results. For example, schools in the more modernized regions reported higher proportions of teachers with M.A. degrees and higher academic achievement of students.

The impact that the social context can have on schools also can be seen in some recent cross-national studies. Nations with centralized governments often try to create highly centralized school systems that can be harnessed to their own political purposes. Centralized systems can be easily monopolized by the top political leaders.[90] On the other hand, decentralized systems are more difficult to control from the top. These systems are likely to be found in culturally diversified, multilingual nations where many groups traditionally have benefited from local control. It seems to be especially difficult for modern, rapidly growing countries to maintain centralized control because they necessarily must establish regional and neighborhood schools as the system grows.

How Do Schools Cope With Outside Constraints?

While outside groups and impersonal social forces exert constant pressures on the schools, the schools are not entirely placid pawns. On the contrary, as they have become caught up in larger networks of influence, educational organizations have devoted more of their time and resources to controlling their environments and defending themselves from outside pressures. Indeed, the test of an administrator's skill today is no longer his ability to manage the *internal* operations of the school system. The real test is his ability to relate effectively to external pressure groups without becoming a puppet. Racial and class desegregation, pressure for community control in ghetto areas, decentralization of large school districts and large universities, and militant demands from teachers and students for power represent only a few of the pressures that schools have had to cope with.

How Do Schools Defend Themselves?

The school administration is an important line of defense. Administrators occupy boundary positions that link the school and the community, serving as a buffer between teachers and outside pressure groups. In collaboration with teachers, principals carry on an essentially defensive relationship vis-à-vis parents and the community, trying to prevent any event that will give these groups a permanent place of authority in the school.[91] But, at the same time, citizens expect school administrators to represent them when they clash with teachers. The more authority that an administrator has, the more subject he will be to these community pressures, precisely because it is known that he *can* control the teachers. Recognizing that administrators are under this kind of pressure, teachers exert pressures of their own on administrators to support them when parents try to interfere with their grading or discipline practices. The general principle involved can be stated as follows: the more centralized the authority structure, the more vulnerable the central administration will be to a given source of pressure. The more decentralized the organization, the more points of external contact, which open the organization to different sources of pressure.

Teacher organizations provide another boundary defense. Powerful teacher organizations have achieved tenure guarantees that prevent teachers from being fired for reasons other than obvious technical incompetence or moral impropriety; they can provide the individual teacher with enough leverage to resist the demands of an insistent parent or school board member; and they also can bring other, often more cosmopolitan influences into the school, as when a national teacher association promotes efforts to desegregate the schools where the general community is opposed to desegregation.

It should be noted, too, that individual teachers also have ways of defending themselves apart from teacher organizations; for example, through implicit threats of retaliation against the parents' child, by not choosing him for extracurricular activities, by not giving him the benefit of the doubt in grading, or by ignoring or ridiculing him in class.

The school board provides still another link in the boundary between schools and their local communities. As mentioned, the school board serves two opposite functions: (1) it provides still another channel through which outside groups can exert pressure, and (2) it acts as a front for the school administration, providing defense against community pressures. Different writers have stressed each of these different functions, drawing very different conclusions.

The parent-teacher organizations also provide boundary defenses for school systems. PTAs can provide parents with an entering wedge with which to influence the schools. However, in practice they appear to be more often co-opted by the school administration and teachers who can stack its committees. Teachers are protected by a rule in the National PTA Charter forbidding discussion of particular children or their classroom problems at PTA meetings. The way schools co-opt PTAs was illustrated in a study of a small town where the school principal gained behind-the-scenes control of the PTA and curtailed the influence of parents while increasing his own.[92] The PTA became a "front" organization and a pressure group for his proposals. By working informally through committees, his ideas were presented to the school board as being the ideas of the parent body. The principal could not be blamed either for proposals that were defeated or for those of a controversial nature, while at the same time the PTA provided a sense of legitimacy and community support for his proposals.

Dahl reported a similar situation in New Haven, Connecticut, where a principal enlisted the support of a PTA by going to an important neighborhood leader and persuading her that "the kids in the neighborhood needed help."[93] Together they induced the PTA to endorse a hot-lunch program that required PTA members to raise funds and hire kitchen help. The principal then began to work for a new school to replace the old one and, when obstacles were raised by the city administration, he called a meeting of PTA members and other neighborhood leaders and "gave them a rousing speech asking for their help." Within 24 hours they were on the phone and in other ways bringing pressure on the administration.

What Are the Effects of Boundary Maintenance?

Boundary maintenance proves to be a very delicate problem for most schools. Schools depend upon parents to support school bond issues, and to back up the teachers when they assign homework or when they discipline the children. On the other side of the coin, parents depend upon the schools for the advancement of their children.

In view of this mutual dependence, it might be expected that the closer the relationship between home and school, the more effective the schooling will be. It is revealing that Cloward and Jones found that the involvement of parents in school affairs was positively correlated with their evaluations of the importance of education and with other attitudes toward the school as an institution.[94] Parent participation and cooperation in school affairs often leads to pupil achievement, better school attendance and study habits, and fewer discipline problems.[95] Comparing the development of three randomly assigned low-achieving junior high school student groups, Brookover, et al.[96] found that groups that received only weekly counseling sessions (or that had regular contacts with specialists in particular interest areas) did not show increased achievement; whereas the group whose parents had become more intimately involved in the school through weekly meetings with school officials about their children's development did show significant progress. Finally, Rosenthal and Jacobsen reported that children who profited from positive changes in their teachers' expectations of their abilities all had parents who were involved to some degree in their child's development in the school and who were distinctly visible to the teachers.[97]

However, it is difficult, and sometimes hazardous, for schools to co-operate closely with the home. The school bureaucracy is in many respects antithetical to the family system. The family is personal and particularistic; parents want special consideration for their child. On the other hand, the bureaucracy is impersonal and universalistic; teachers must deal with each child as part of a larger group measured against universalistic standards of performance. Given these differences, the two groups must somehow be insulated from one another, even though they must cooperate in certain respects.

The resolution of this problem depends on the type of neighborhood. Schools in middle-class neighborhoods need defenses against influential, powerful families who reside there whereas in lower-class neighborhoods, where teachers complain about the indifference of parents to their children's school work, a closer relationship seems to be called for. Coordinating mechanisms must be used to maintain a balance, to regulate the tension and the distance between schools and families.[98] Litwak and Meyer have suggested that the truant officer, neighborhood center, and the PTA perform these balancing functions.

DOES BUREAUCRATIZATION ALWAYS PRODUCE PROBLEMS?

Many of the organizational characteristics that have been identified here are potential sources of problems. But does it necessarily follow that bureaucratization always produces problems? The situation is undoubtedly more complex than has been suggested here so far. Perhaps the reader can gain some sense of how complex the problem is from my study of staff conflicts in 28 public high schools.[99]

First, it was found that certain features of schools—their size, and extent of specialization, hierarchy, complexity, staff additions, and heterogeneity—did contribute to organizational *strain*, that is, problems leading to interpersonal conflicts. Each of these characteristics independently seemed to generate conflicts. And still other organizational characteristics—participation in decision making, close supervision, and cohesive peer relations—seemed to *facilitate* conflict, but only where it was already present; these characteristics did not themselves necessarily produce problems. On the other hand, teachers' experience in the organization and close supervision seemed to inhibit problems and prevent the outbreak of major conflicts. The point is, then, that while some characteristics of schools were disruptive, others provided for integration and harmony.

But beyond that, it was found that the same characteristic was sometimes a source of strain in one context, and in another context it helped
to minimize problems. For example, levels of conflict increased in both
the most professionalized and in the least-bureaucratized schools when
attempts were made to apply bureaucratic controls such as rules, standardization, and close supervision. But in the most bureaucratic schools,
and in the least professional ones, where close control was more compatible with the organization's tradition and with the employees' willingness to accept controls, these controls created few problems. A supervisory
practice that was effective in reducing major incidents in one type of
school, in other words, could aggravate problems in another. Attempts
to control conflict seemed to be more effective in the settings that (1) are
already bureaucratic, where rules are likely to be reinforced by other
measures, and (2) in the less-professional schools where resistance from
employees is less likely to be encountered.

Finally, the role played by the structural aspects of schools depended
on the type of conflict and the people involved. Minor disagreements
tended to have different causes than overt major disputes. Also, organizational size, staff additions, standardization, and complexity all seemed
to be positively associated with conflict between teachers and administrators; but none of these variables was associated with conflict among
teachers themselves. This suggests that a practice that minimizes problems
among teachers might have the unintended effect of provoking conflict
between teachers and administrators, students or parents.

The above study was confined to teachers and administrators. It is not
known whether organizational practices would have had similar consequences for the students. But it does serve to illustrate how complicated
the relationship between organizational characteristics and educational
problems can be. In view of the complexity of the situation, it is important not to draw hasty or categorical conclusions about how organizational
structure affects schooling without further research.

HOW DO ORGANIZATIONAL CHARACTERISTICS
AFFECT STUDENTS?

One question naturally arises: What difference does all of this make
for the students? I have alluded to some possible answers to this question
in passing but, in truth, there is very little information available to
answer the question. What little evidence that is available on how organizational characteristics affect the academic achievement and educational
aspirations of students will be reviewed in Chapters 2 and 3. For now,
before concluding this discussion, we will briefly consider some of the
possible implications.

Effects of a Diversified Goal Structure

A diversified goal structure permits schools to satisfy a wide range of publics and to deal simultaneously with many types of students. But, in practice, most schools attempt only to meet the wide range of assigned objectives in a minimal way. Any particular student at most, can only hope for adequate, not superior, preparation for what he may want from the school. Many students will have to be content with only nominal attention to what they may consider to be of utmost importance.

The only way that the schools can deliberately control the range of objectives imposed upon them is for each school to specialize in terms of a distinctive goal. This seldom happens, but some schools in a particular community might specialize in working with bright, motivated students who plan to attend college, others with poorly motivated students who do not care for the academic curriculum, and in still other schools teachers would specialize with work-study groups, for example. Within each of these settings each teacher would be responsible for the total development of specific students, some teachers might work on academic objectives, and others on moral and political socialization or on how children can use their leisure time. But such schools tend to become mere custodial institutions unless principals and teachers are made accountable for the amount of improvement that occurs in the students who attend their particular type of school.

Effects of Recruiting Practices

Compulsory education, coupled with an "open-door" recruiting policy, has two important consequences. First, each school is expected to deal with such a wide range of clientele that schools cannot justify attempts to specialize among themselves with different types of students such as just described. As a result, schooling tends to become highly standardized and uniform from school to school with teaching pitched at a mediocre level. Second, a large share of the teachers' time must be spent in trying to maintain control over the situation because of the widespread alienation on the part of many students whose special circumstances must be ignored.

In defense, schools turn to informal forms of specialization. But since specialization has been worked out on a covert, extralegal level, there is no guarantee that provision will be made for *all* types of students and schools. Those who do not come from high-status families tend to be ignored.

The tendency on the part of schools to recruit relatively cautious, politically conservative teachers probably has the effect of limiting the range of opinion that students are exposed to in class. However, this conservative effect on students' values should not be exaggerated. As

Zeigler points out, liberal teachers discuss politics in class more than conservatives do. Moreover, numerous studies indicate that teachers' opinions are not nearly as important to students as are the opinions of their parents and peers.[100]

Illich points out that compulsory, universal schooling was meant to detach role assignments from a person's life history; it was meant to give everyone equal chance to any position or office.[101] However, instead of equalizing chances, he charges, the school system has monopolized their very distribution. Since educational materials and professional skills have been monopolized by schools, other institutions are discouraged from assuming educational tasks. He states, "Many students, especially those who are poor, intuitively know what schools do for them. . . . The pupil is . . . 'schooled' to confuse teaching with learning, grade advancement with education, a diploma with competence, and fluency with the ability to say something new." He forecasts that the American public will come to the conclusion that no amount of dollars can remove the inherent destructiveness of schools and other welfare institutions when they are compulsory.

Effects of Standardization

Goal priorities are implicit in the standard curriculum. Many of the most pressing practical problems confronting students—such as changing moral standards or learning how to use political power—tend to be squeezed out of the curriculum by the press of mandatory activities.

The detrimental consequences of the standardized curriculum, then, probably have more to do with *what* students learn than with *how well* they learn what is taught. For example, literally thousands of studies have produced no clear evidence that people learn any less in large, standardized classrooms. But standardization does limit the freedom of students to explore their own interests and capacities by producing uniform curricula and approaches to them.

Effects of Centralization

One justification for centralizing decisions is to assure that every student in the system will have comparable facilities, teachers, and curriculum, and to guard against special privilege. The fact that schools have not succeeded in eliminating discrimination (see Chapter 3) is not necessarily an indictment against bureaucracy. On the contrary, discrimination can arise because school systems are not *sufficiently* bureaucratized.

At the same time, a centralized and standardized decision-making structure also tends to minimize the importance of the unique backgrounds and objectives of clientele in different parts of the system and leads teachers to ignore the special problems and circumstances of *atypical* students. Moreover, in such organizations, the final decisions will be made by remote people who are least familiar with the day-to-day classroom activities.

Effects of the Division of Labor

Most schools use a division of labor that limits the opportunities of many students, one that is more appropriate for preparing particular types of students to be scholars than for preparing diverse types of students for a wide range of occupational and citizenship roles. Teaching roles tend to be organized around the age level of the children in the elementary schools and around academic disciplines ("subjects") in the high schools. Neither the child's age nor the subject matter taught directly reflect the students' interests and circumstances.

Students do not necessarily divide their own interests in terms of math and English, for example. Instead they are interested in practical *problems* that typically involve many types of academic skills. Problems such as how to buy a house, where to go on a vacation, whether the national budget is too large, whether a certain movie is aesthetically good, what is the moral value of war, or how to compute an income tax or a baseball batting average cannot be confined to a specific course in the curriculum.

Effects of External Controls

Although school districts are separate from local political units such as the city and the county government, and although educators like to think of "curriculum development" as a logical, even scientific process, schools are not insulated from politics. The decisions about what to teach *are* political decisions.[102] Theoretically, there is a broad-based participation in educational decision-making. In practice many groups, especially the students themselves, are excluded in factional competition for control. The only recourse for these excluded groups is to organize their own special interest groups and exert pressures directly on school administrators or board members or, if they become sufficiently well-organized, to confront the school system directly with boycotts and other pressure tactics. Ultimately, the excluded groups will demand that the legal decision-making process be decentralized or otherwise reorganized to permit them to participate within the legitimate control structure. Thus, if the power structure is monopolistic and exclusive, instead of being nucleated and inclusive, open conflict will occur within communities.[103] As the excluded groups compete for more power over the schools, the control structure of education is being constantly reorganized.

A national network of organizations concerned with shaping educational policy has superseded the local control structures. This national system is governed by elite groups of experts who are only vaguely subject to congressional regulation or local pressure groups. Nevertheless, the fact that a *coalition* of organizations is in control does provide a crude system of checks and balances so that no one group, including federal agencies, can completely dominate them. Thus, federal control might not be as ominous as it is often supposed, and in any case it probably is no more dangerous than politically motivated local school boards, which often insist upon imposing their own brands of patriotism, religion, or opinion on the students. At least the citizen has access to Congress through normal political channels.

Effects of School System Defenses

Without the ability to fend off the attacks of private interest groups, schools would be vulnerable to every interest group that seeks to use them for its own purpose. There would be no protection against favoritism and nepotism, no effective way to defend professional principles and the universalistic standards of fair and impartial treatment. When schools have an independent life apart from narrow political pressures, they can act as an independent spokesman for all students; they can resist the pressure to cut corners and the temptation to try to do too much with too few resources; and they can act as mediators among conflicting groups who hold different conceptions of what schools ought to be doing. In short, their autonomy allows schools to take their rightful place as one of the many sovereign checks and balances that regulate education in this country.

At the same time, sometimes educational organizations perhaps have been *too* capable of defending themselves and supremely successful in shielding themselves from the major developments within the society. Despite much rhetoric about educational reform (except for a few notable successes such as New Math and the preschool), it still takes approximately half a century for major educational reforms to trickle down to the bulk of the school systems of this country.[104] This traditionalism largely stems from the schools' "splendid isolation" (to use Cremin's term) from city, state, and national governments and from normal democratic and other political processes, which is made possible by an independent tax base, a separate system of governance, and unresponsive school boards.

CONCLUSIONS

Formal education in this country is highly bureaucratized. However, the pejorative label, "bureaucracy," provides only a superficial understanding of the problems and glosses over the more fundamental principles that underlie large scale, complex educational organizations.

It was suggested that (1) the "bureaucratic personalities" of teachers should not be overrated as a source of problems in comparison to structural sources of the problems; (2) bureaucracy is sometimes a *response* to existing problems instead of being the cause of them; (3) it is possible that some problems arise because the schools are not *sufficiently* bureaucratic rather than being too bureaucratic; (4) there is not one, but a variety of patterns of organization among American schools and colleges, some being more "bureaucratic" than others and, therefore, facing somewhat different problems; and (5) while some bureaucratic characteristics produce or facilitate problems, others seem to inhibit them.

In short, schools are more than simple bureaucracies. They are complex organizations plagued with "subterranean" conflicts between groups, using informal recruiting standards, driven by a quest for prestige and influence, and constrained by the cross-pressures from local power structures and dependence on outside groups for resources. Schools tend to "drift" as they make unplanned adaptations to the demands of clients and other constituencies and as they cope with the problem of how to reconcile standardized requirements with the uniqueness of the student clientele.

Yet, there can be little doubt that the more pathological aspects of bureaucracy have contributed to a number of educational problems, and that these structural problems are important sources of the difficulties with education today. Some problems are associated with compulsory forms of education, others with standardization, centralization, specialization, the way schools are controlled, and the like. Attempts to blindly apply standardized practices to heterogeneous students and diverse student cultures, in the face of a bewildering variety of responsibilities that the public has thrust upon the schools, have forced schools to adopt informal forms of specialization, leading to perfunctory performance of some official goals. Because coordination is difficult to achieve in view of the variety of goals and clientele, school systems perhaps overemphasize standardization.

Many of the predicaments stem from the fact that legal control over education has been delegated to local communities when most of the current problems confronting education are national in scope and must be attacked at that level. Schools and colleges must be able to defend professional standards and discourage favoritism, and yet perhaps they have been able to defend their boundaries *too* effectively considering the kind of highly interdependent, dynamic society that has emerged.

However, even the most vocal critics of the bureaucratic aspects of schools do not seem to have lost faith in the schools. The criticisms, perhaps, do not reflect a "crisis of faith" in the schools so much as optimism tempered only with disappointment that they have not achieved what they are potentially capable of achieving through effective reorganization.

With these observations, this chapter has begun to set the stage for examining a few selected educational problems in greater detail. The focus here has been on elementary and secondary schools, with occasional reference to problems of higher education. To round out the picture, Chapter 2 extends this analysis of organizational characteristics to higher education. In addition to drawing on the discussions here, in Chapter 2 we shall try to provide a more dynamic sense of organizational processes and social change than was possible here, where we tried to examine the basic structural properties of educational organizations.

REFERENCES

1. Edgar Z. Friedenberg, "The Modern High School: A Profile," *Commentary*, *36*, November 1963, 373.

2. *1970 Standard Education Almanac*. Los Angeles: Academic Media, 1970.

3. "B. A. Hinsdale in Opposition to Educational Bureaucracy in Cleveland, 1877" in *School Reform: Past and Present*, Michael B. Katz, ed. Boston: Little, Brown and Company, 1971, p. 259.

4. Abbott L. Ferriss, *Indicators of Trends in American Education*. New York: Russell Sage Foundation, 1969.

5. H. H. Gerth and C. Wright Mills, trans. and eds., *From Max Weber: Essays on Sociology*. New York: Oxford University Press, 1958.

6. Stanley H. Udy, Jr., " 'Bureaucracy' and 'Rationality' in Weber's Organization Theory," *American Sociological Review, 24*, December 1959, 791–795.

7. Bel Kaufman, *Up the Down Staircase*. Englewood Cliffs, N.J.: Prentice-Hall, 1964.

8. David Rogers, *110 Livingston Street*. New York: Random House, 1968.

9. Philip W. Jackson, *Life in Classrooms*. New York: Holt, Rinehart and Winston, 1968.

10. Friedenberg, *op. cit.*, 373.

11. Jonathan Kozol, *Death at an Early Age*. Boston: Houghton-Mifflin, 1967.

12. Ronald G. Corwin, *Reform and Organizational Survival: The Teacher Corps as an Instrument of Educational Change*. New York: Wiley-Interscience, 1973, pp. 116–117.

13. George Gallup, *How the Nation Views the Public Schools*. Princeton, N.J.: Gallup International, 1969.

14. Richard F. Carter, *Voters and Their Schools*. Stanford: Stanford University, 1960.

15. Burns W. Roper, *A Ten-Year View of Public Attitudes Towards Television and Other Mass Media 1959–1968*. New York: Television Information Office, 1969.

16. *A Study of Community Attitudes Toward the Public School System*. Detroit: Market Opinion Research, 1969.

17. Peter Rossi and others, *Between White and Black: The Faces of American Institutions in the Ghetto.* Washington, D.C.: Government Printing Office, 1968.

18. Robert J. Havighurst, *The Public Schools of Chicago.* Chicago: The Board of Education, 1964, Chapter VIII.

19. Ronald G. Corwin, *Militant Professionalism: A Study of Organizational Conflict in High Schools.* New York: Appleton-Century-Crofts, 1970.

20. Robert K. Merton, "Bureaucratic Structure and Personality," in *Social Theory and Social Structure,* Robert K. Merton, ed. Glencoe, Ill.: The Free Press, 1957, pp. 195–206.

21. Charles E. Silberman, *Crisis in the Classroom.* New York: Random House, 1970.

22. Marilyn Gittell, *Participants and Participation: A Study of School Policy in New York City.* New York: F.A. Praeger, 1967; Rogers, *op. cit.*

23. For more extensive discussions of educational organizations see Ronald G. Corwin, "Models of Educational Organizations," *Review of Educational Research: 1974,* Itasca, Ill.: F. E. Peacock, (forthcoming). Also Ronald G. Corwin, "Education and the Sociology of Complex Organizations" in *On Education: Sociological Perspectives,* (D. A. Hansen and J. Gerstl, eds.), New York: Wiley, 1967, pp. 156–223.

24. Émile Durkheim, *Moral Education.* Glencoe, Ill.: The Free Press, 1961.

25. Robert Dreeben, *On What Is Learned in School.* Menlo Park, Calif.: Addison-Wesley Publishing Co., 1968.

26. Richard O. Carlson, "Environmental Constraints and Organizational Consequences: The Public School and Its Clients" in *Behavioral Science and Educational Administration Yearbook, Part II,* Daniel E. Griffiths, ed. National Society for the Study of Education, Chicago: University of Chicago Press, 1964, pp. 262–276.

27. Amitai Etzioni, *A Comparative Analysis of Complex Organizations.* Glencoe, Ill.: The Free Press, 1961; Chapters 1, 2, and 3.

28. A. B. Hollingshead, *Elmtown's Youth.* New York: John Wiley, 1949.

29. George Gallup, *op. cit.*

30. John K. Folger and Charles B. Nam, *The Education of the American Population.* Washington, D.C.: Bureau of the Census, 1967 and Abbott L. Ferriss, *Indicators of Trends in American Education.* New York: Russell Sage Foundation, 1969.

31. Robert E. Herriott and Benjamin J. Hodgkins, *The Environment of Schooling: Formal Education as an Open Social System.* Englewood Cliffs, N.J.: Prentice-Hall, 1973.

32. James S. Coleman, Ernest Q. Campbell, et al., *Equality of Educational Opportunity.* Washington, D.C.: Government Printing Office, 1966.

33. Neal Gross, Ward S. Mason, and Alexander W. McEachern, *Explorations in Role Analysis: Studies of the School Superintendency Role.* New York: Wiley, 1968.

34. Charles Perrow, *Complex Organizations: A Critical Essay*. Glenview, Ill.: Scott, Foresman and Co., 1972, pp. 6–8; Ronald G. Corwin, M. J. Taves, and J. Eugene Haas, "Social Requirements for Occupational Success: Internalized Norms and Friendship," *Social Forces, 39*, December 1960, 135–140.

35. Carl Bereiter and Mervin B. Freedman, "Fields of Study and People in Them," *The American College: A Psychological and Social Interpretation of the Higher Learning*, Nevitt Sanford, ed. New York: John Wiley, 1962, pp. 563–596.

36. Hanan C. Selvin and Warren O. Hagstrom, "Determinants of Support for Civil Liberties," *British Journal of Sociology, 11*, March 1960, 51–73. Also William J. Crotty, "Democratic Consensual Norms and the College Student," *Sociology of Education, 40*, Summer 1967, 200–218.

37. Henry Meyer, Eugene Litwak, and Donald Warren, "Occupational and Class Differences in Social Values: A Comparison of Teachers and Social Workers," *Sociology of Education, 41*, Summer 1968, 263–281.

38. National Education Association, *What Teachers Think: A Summary of Teacher Opinion Poll Findings, 1960–65*. Washington, D.C.: NEA, 1965, p. 51.

39. Harmon Zeigler, *The Political World of the High School Teacher*. Eugene: Center for the Advanced Study of Educational Administration, University of Oregon, 1966.

40. Arthur L. Stinchcombe, *Rebellion in the High School*. Chicago: Quadrangle Books, 1964.

41. Peter M. Blau, *Exchange and Power in Social Life*. New York: Wiley, 1964.

42. Corwin, 1970, *op. cit.*

43. Simon Wittes, *People and Power: A Study of Crises in Secondary Schools*. Ann Arbor: Institute for Social Research, The University of Michigan, 1970.

44. Governor's Committee on Public Education, *Public Education in Texas*. Austin: Texas Education Agency, 1969.

45. Silberman, *op. cit.*

46. Kaufman, *op. cit.*

47. Charles Bidwell, "The School as a Formal Organization" in *Handbook of Organization*, James March, ed. Chicago: Rand McNally, 1965, pp. 972–1022.

48. Howard S. Becker, "Social Class Variations in the Teacher-Pupil Relationship," *Journal of Educational Sociology, 25*, April 1952, 451–463.

49. Gittell, *op. cit.*

50. Roald F. Campbell and Robert Bunnell, *Nationalizing Influences on Secondary Education*. Chicago: Midwest Administration Center, University of Chicago, 1963.

51. Buford Rhea, "Institutional Paternalism in High School," *The Urban Review, 2*, February 1968, 13–15, 34.

52. Jules Henry, "Docility, or Giving Teacher What She Wants," *The Journal of Social Issues, 11*, Issue 2, 1955, 33–41.

53. Theodore Newcomb, Everett K. Wilson, eds. *College Peer Groups*, Chicago: Aldine Publishing Co., 1966.

54. Willard Waller, *The Sociology of Teaching*. New York: John Wiley, 1932, pp. 6–7.

55. David Goslin and David C. Glass, "The Social Effects of Standardized Testing in American Elementary and Secondary. Schools," *Sociology of Education, 40*, Spring 1967, 115–131.

56. Roger G. Barker, et al., *Big School-Small School*. Lawrence, Kans.: University of Kansas, 1962.

57. Burton R. Clark, *Educating the Expert Society*. San Francisco: Chandler Publishing Co., 1962, Chapter 7.

58. Benjamin Hodgkins and Robert Herriott, "Age-Grade Structure, Goals and Compliance in the School: An Organizational Analysis," *Sociology of Education, 43*, Winter 1970, 90–104.

59. Morris Janowitz, *Institution Building in Urban Education*. New York: Russell Sage Foundation, 1969.

60. M. L. Goldberg, A. H. Passow, and J. Justman, *The Effects of Ability Grouping*. New York: Teachers College, Columbia University, 1966; and Dominick Esposito, "Homogeneous and Heterogeneous Ability Grouping: Principal Findings and Implications for Evaluating and Designing More Effective Educational Environments," *Review of Educational Research, 43*, Spring 1973, 163–179.

61. Abraham Luchins and Edith Luchins, "Childrens' Attitudes Toward Homogeneous Grouping," *Journal of Genetic Psychology, 72*, 1948, 3–9.

62. Walter E. Schafer and Carol Olexa, *Tracking and Opportunity: The Locking-Out Process and Beyond*. San Francisco: Chandler Publishing Co., 1971.

63. J. W. B. Douglas, *The Home and the School*. London: McGibbon and Kee, 1964.

64. Coleman, et al., *op. cit.* Chapter 9.

65. Robert Rosenthal and Leonore Jacobsen, *Pygmalion in the Classroom*. New York: Holt, Rinehart and Winston, 1968. See also R. L. Thorndyke's review in *American Educational Research Journal, 5*, November 1968, 708–711.

66. Aage B. Sorensen, "Organizational Differentiation of Students and Educational Opportunity," *Sociology of Education, 43*, Fall 1970, 355–376.

67. Ralph B. Kimbrough, *Political Power and Educational Decision-Making*. Chicago: Rand McNally, 1964.

68. Neal Gross, Ward S. Mason, and Alexander W. McEachern, *op. cit.*, pp. 331–334.

69. Gross et al., *op. cit.*

70. Harmon Zeigler, *The Irony of Democracy*. Belmont, Cal.: Wadsworth Publishing Co., 1972. This volume contains numerous additional citations.

71. Norman D. Kerr, "The School Board as an Agency of Legitimation," *Sociology of Education, 38*, Fall 1964, 34–59.

72. Arthur Vidich and Joseph Bensman, *Small Town in Mass Society.* Garden City, N.Y.: Doubleday and Co., 1960.

73. Kimbrough, *op. cit.*

74. Donald J. McCarty and Charles E. Ramsey, *The School Managers: Power and Conflict in American Education.* Westport, Conn.: Greenwood Publishing, 1971.

75. Harmon Zeigler, *The Political World of the High School Teacher, op. cit.* and *The Irony of Democracy, op. cit.*

76. Roy M. Caughran, "The School Board Member Today," *American School Board Journal, 133,* November and December 1956, 39–40 and 25–27.

77. Robert Crain, *Politics of School Desegregation: Comparative Case Studies of Community Structure and Policy-Making.* Chicago: Aldine, 1968.

78. Neal Gross, *Who Runs Our Schools?* New York: Wiley, 1958.

79. Shirley Terreberry, "The Evolution of Organizational Environments," *Administrative Science Quarterly, 12,* March 1968, 590–613.

80. Terreberry, *Ibid.*: Herman Turk, "Interorganizational Networks in Urban Society: Initial Perspectives and Comparative Research," *American Sociological Review, 35,* February 1970, 1–18.

81. R. J. Pellegrin, *An Analysis of Sources and Processes in Innovation in Education.* Eugene, Ore.: Center for the Advanced Study of Educational Administration, 1966.

82. Michael W. Kirst and Decker F. Walker, "An Analysis of Curriculum Policy-Making," *Review of Educational Research, 41,* December 1971, 479–509.

83. J. B. Conant, *The Comprehensive High School: A Second Report to Interested Citizens.* New York: McGraw-Hill, 1967.

84. Kirst and Walker, *op. cit.*

85. J. Koerner, *Who Controls American Education?* Boston: Beacon Press, 1968.

86. Burton Clark, "Interorganizational Patterns in Education," *Administrative Science Quarterly, 10,* September 1965, 224–237.

87. Clark, *Ibid.*

88. Herriott and Hodgkins, 1973, *op. cit.*

89. Herriott and Hodgkins, *Ibid.*

90. Joseph Fischer, "Education and Political Modernization in Burma and Indonesia," *Comparative Education Review, 9,* October 1965, 282–287; William Dodd, "Centralization in Education in Mainland Tangeria," *Comparative Education Review, 12,* October 1968, 268–280; Francis X. Sutton, "Education and the Making of Modern Nations" in *Education and Political Development,* James S. Coleman, ed. Princeton, N.J.: Princeton University Press, 1965, pp. 51–74; and R. S. Milne, "Mechanistic and Organic Models of Public Administration in Developing Countries," *Administrative Science Quarterly, 15,* March 1970, 57–67.

91. Becker, *op. cit.*

92. Vidich and Bensman, *op. cit.*

93. Robert A. Dahl, *Who Governs? Democracy and Power in an American City.* New Haven: Yale University Press, 1961.

94. Richard A. Cloward and James A. Jones, "Social Class: Educational Attitudes and Participation" in *Education in Depressed Areas,* Harry Passow, ed. New York: Teachers College, Columbia University, 1963, pp. 190–216.

95. Herbert J. Schiff, "The Effect of Personal Contractual Relationships on Parents' Attitudes Toward and Participation in Local School Affairs," unpublished Ph.D. dissertation. Evanston, Ill.: Northwestern University, 1963.

96. Wilbur Brookover, et al., *Self-Concept of Ability and School Achievement.* East Lansing: Bureau of Educational Research Services, Michigan State University, 1965.

97. Rosenthal and Jacobsen, *op. cit.*

98. Eugene Litwak and Henry Meyer, "A Balance Theory of Coordination Between Bureaucratic Organizations and Community Primary Groups," *Administrative Science Quarterly, 2,* June 1966, 31–58.

99. Ronald G. Corwin, "Patterns of Organizational Conflict," *Administrative Science Quarterly, 14,* December 1969, 507–520.

100. Zeigler, *The Political Life of the High School Teacher, op. cit.*

101. Ivan Illich, *Deschooling Society.* New York: Harper and Row, 1971.

102. Kirst and Walker, *op. cit.*

103. James Coleman, *Community Conflict.* Glencoe, Ill.: The Free Press, 1957.

104. Paul R. Mort, "Studies in Educational Innovation from the Institute of Administrative Research: An Overview" in *Innovation in Education,* Matthew B. Miles, ed. New York: Teachers College, Columbia University, 1964, pp. 317–328.

CHAPTER 2

ROLE CONFLICT IN THE UNIVERSITY

"Universities in America are at a hinge of history: while connected with their past, they are swinging in another direction. . . . The basic reality, for the university, is the widespread recognition that new knowledge is the most important factor in economic and social growth. We are just now perceiving that the university's invisible product, knowledge, may be the most powerful single element in our culture, affecting the rise and the fall of professions and even of social classes, of regions and even of nations. . . . This reality is shaping the very nature and quality of the university."[1]

The University of Northern Iowa is situated at the intersection of State Highways 218 and 20 in the small city of Cedar Falls, Iowa. While not of national renown, as one of three state universities within the region, it has achieved a creditable reputation for academic excellence as well as for teacher training, and it boasts several professors who have achieved national recognition. It was christened Iowa State Normal School nearly a century ago (1876), for the purpose of teacher training. But the school was to change names three more times in its short history. Each change represented another step in its continuing evolution, ever expanding its scope of objectives and increasing its structural complexity. By the time it had evolved into a teachers college (Iowa State Teachers College) in 1909, it had grown from an original enrollment of 27 to approximately 1000 students. It was to keep this identity for half a century. But in 1961, with an enrollment of 4000, its mission was no longer confined to teacher training, and for a short six-year period it was called The State College of Iowa, in deference to its aspiration to become a liberal arts college. By 1967, the college had emerged as a full-scale university consisting of five colleges, and again its name changed to reflect its new status: it is now The University of Northern Iowa. During the decade of the 1960s alone, student enrollment tripled, a growth rate that matched the entire preceding 50-year period. These name changes are only the superficial aspects of fundamental identity transformations that have been occurring not only in this college but in higher education during the past century and particularly within the past two decades.

WHAT IS THE SCOPE OF THE PROBLEMS IN HIGHER EDUCATION?

The story of the University of Northern Iowa is not unique. Indeed, the history of higher education is a history of the evolution of a larger and differentiated system of organizations that have come to assume many different forms. An unprecedented number of new universities, such as The Federal City College in Washington, D.C., and Cleveland State University in Ohio, have sprung up and swelled to capacity within a period of a few short years; enrollment in the latter institution rose from a few thousand in 1965 to over 12,000 in 1972, and projections indicate that, although the rate of growth is slowing down, it could reach an enrollment of 20,000 by the end of this decade. Hundreds of new junior colleges have been founded and existing institutions have grown to gigantic proportions in order to accommodate soaring enrollments.

Kerr writes that it was clear by 1930 that universities were changing profoundly in many directions at once, becoming many things to many people.[2] Instead of the individual student, there were the needs of the society to be considered, and instead of the generalist, there was the specialist. Newman's universal liberal man was gone forever. Today, a single institution, such as the University of California, might have an operating budget of over half a billion dollars; undertake $100 million worth of construction; employ 40,000 people; carry out operations in over 100 different locations, including experimental stations at agricultural and urban extension centers and projects abroad in more than 50 different countries; offer nearly 10,000 courses and maintain some form of contact with nearly every industry in its region and nearly every level of government. Kerr notes that over 4000 babies have been born in the University of California hospital; it is the world's largest purveyor of white mice, and it has one of the world's largest primate colonies. And (almost incidentally it seems) 100,000 students are enrolled in the University. An institution that is so many things to so many people is like a collection of feudal estates partially at war with itself. Kerr says that this is not a *university*; he calls it a *multiversity*.

During the 1950s and 1960s there was a threefold increase in the students enrolled in four-year institutions and an eightfold increase in two-year college enrollments. These enrollments increased at a rate several times faster than the growth in the college-age population although the rate of growth has declined in the past few years. The proportion of eighteen-to twenty-four-year-olds in college has doubled since 1950. Over 60 percent of the high school graduates are now enrolled in institutions of higher education.[3] The costs of higher education have increased accordingly, six times over, now standing at over $12 billion.

The number of four-year colleges and universities has also understandably increased by more than 33 percent during the 1950s and 1960s; the number of such institutions in the United States now numbers 2500. Nearly 350 new two-year institutions were founded during the same period. But despite the frantic race to keep up, the growth in enrollment has continued to outstrip the society's capacity to build new institutions, leaving the already large universities to accommodate most of the growth rate. Consequently, the state universities have grown steadily larger and, indeed, they have become the dominant institutions in higher education. Although the typical (median) *college* is relatively small (1000–3000 students), the typical *student* attends a large university; only 60 of the 2500 universities and colleges (all with enrollments over 2500) account for one quarter of the 7.5 million college students and 4 out of every 10 students attends a university that has an enrollment of more than 10,000 students.[4] The range of institutions that comprise higher education has become so complex that they cannot all be considered in this chapter. Therefore, we will concentrate on the major universities that are absorbing so much of the new growth.

There are clear parallels between the bewildering problems infecting elementary and secondary schools that were examined in the preceding chapter and the crises that have hit the colleges and universities. Like the schools, universities are complex, bureaucratic organizations, and they have been saddled with a wide range of goals that cannot possibly be effectively accommodated within the existing structures. Universities have been pressured by their local constituents and, more recently, by the federal government to provide technical services to government and industry, to train workers for technical jobs, and to undertake basic and applied scientific research. Research foundations and government agencies have penetrated deep into the universities, impelling major administrative changes. Universities *increasingly* have come under scrutiny of state legislatures and government agencies, who are anxious that monies being spent on higher education are adequately accounted for and that colleges and universities are being administered in an efficient manner. Their response to these pressures has been to develop bureaucratic procedures that have aggravated other problems.

The university today seems to be going through stages parallel to those that the public schools went through in their history. Perhaps some lessons can be learned from how the schools handled their problems that can be applied to modern universities. At the same time, universities can also provide a fresh perspective on educational problems. They are coping with some of the very problems that the nation's schools have grappled with since before 1900, but they approach these problems from a different posture and at a very unique period of history. Education now plays a vital role in the economy, and universities are part of a youth-culture transition. To understand what is happening, it is first necessary to understand universities as complex organizations.

WHAT ARE THE STRUCTURAL SOURCES OF PROBLEMS?

What Are the Goals of the University?

The European university, notes Kerr, started as a unified community, made up of masters and students, who subscribed to a central animating purpose.[5] The American university, by contrast, is a blend of institutional goals. It represents a precarious balance between (1) scholarship and undergraduate teaching functions, which is characteristic of the British university, and (2) the graduate school with its emphasis on scientific research, which has been borrowed from the German model. In addition, the American public has called upon the university in this country to (3) train students for jobs and otherwise render a wide array of services for local regions and for the nation as a whole. This range of goals has transformed the large American university of today into a series of communities and activities delicately held together by a common structure, but characterized by a great diversity of purposes. Many of its problems stem from the reluctance of professors and administrators to exchange a medieval structure that was originally adapted to single-purpose colonial colleges for a structure more suitable to the wide range of responsibilities that universities have taken upon themselves.

Indeed, the modern university has so many responsibilities that although it is generally agreed that it is among the most important institutions in our society, there is very little consensus among those involved on its role and purposes. Hutchins once described the modern university as a series of separate schools and departments held together by a central heating system. Clark Kerr thinks of the modern university as a series of individual faculty entrepreneurs held together by a common grievance over parking.[6]

WHAT ARE THE GOAL CONFLICTS?

As just indicated, American universities are expected to fulfill at least three major functions: teaching, research, and service. Probably most undergraduates, their parents, many legislators, and many professors as well regard teaching, or the transmission of existent knowledge, as the university's primary responsibility. Students are the clients of the university, insofar as it is a teaching institution; many people believe that students' interests and welfare should guide all policy decisions. But there is more than one teaching clientele. Some people want universities to emphasize a general liberal education while others see its primary function as training youth for specific vocations.[7] There is a parallel split between individuals who would stress the arts and humanities as opposed to the scientific disciplines.[8] And still other critics maintain that the university should emphasize neither academic nor vocational goals but instead focus on the human values and developmental needs of students as individuals.

Research is another important function. Funding agencies and other sponsors provide the funds to conduct research and, more generally, the society as a whole has come to depend on research for economic and technological advancement and political superiority. In addition, there are still groups who rely upon professors to give them practical assistance, to help develop new technologies, and to advise on policy issues. Professors are expected to consult with and otherwise work with practitioners in order to improve the society.

Within a particular university each of these objectives demands a different commitment of time and resources from the university. Each clientele makes different demands of the university. This complex goal structure is therefore a potential source of conflict and tension. There are two ways that universities have tried to cope with this problem: (1) by informally assigning priorities to the different goals and (2) by developing distinctive images of the university as a way of specializing.

GOAL PRIORITIES

A study by Gross and Grambsch reports one of the few attempts to empirically assess the priority given to different university goals.[9] From a questionnaire listing 47 possible goals sent to administrators and faculty members at 70 institutions, the seven top goals were determined to be (in order):

1. Protect the faculty's right to academic freedom.
2. Increase or maintain the prestige of the university.
3. Maintain top quality in those programs felt to be especially important.
4. Insure the continued confidence and hence support of individuals who contribute substantially to the finances and other material resource needs of the university.
5. Keep up to date and responsive.

6. Train students in methods of scholarship and/or scientific research and/or creative endeavor.
7. Carry on pure research.

The study indicates that there is perhaps more consensus among faculty and administrators than one might expect, but it also suggests an implicit conflict between them and students. The goals reflect a preoccupation with the faculty's self-interests, that is, protection of their academic freedom, concern with their prestige, their benefactors' good will toward the university, and their research. Only one of the top seven goals is in any way concerned with students, and that is closely associated with the scholarly interests of professors and their emphasis on pure research.

Involving students in the government of the university and emphasizing undergraduate instruction at the expense of the graduate program were among the lowest-ranked goals. This fact underscores the low priority given to student concerns and undergraduate instruction.

The study also substantiated the professor's commitment to his discipline and his professional career at the expense of loyalty to his institution. Many administrators expressed dissatisfaction with the fact that the personal ambitions and careers of highly mobile faculty members take precedence over their devotion and contributions to the institution.

Finally, the study revealed a basic antithesis between private and public universities. The private university manifested what the study's authors called an "elitist" pattern—preoccupation with the student's intellect, the well-being and satisfaction of faculty interests, and the quality and prestige rating of the university. State universities, on the other hand, were more inclined to give precedence to qualities in the student other than the purely intellectual ones, such as making a discerning consumer and effective citizen of him; they also engaged more frequently in serving the immediate community by offering adult programs, assistance through extension services, and cultural programs. These differences, in part at least, are probably due to the ability of legislators and citizens to make their influence more strongly felt on the state universities.

Distinctive Images of Colleges and Universities

The complexity of the university's goal structure has given rise to many specialized images of what a college or university is supposed to be and do. These images form a stratification system. At one extreme, large, massive, state universities have not been able to either achieve distinctiveness or announce the actual priorities that they do in fact place on different activities, such as athletics and academic and vocational preparation. The complexity of universities can be better appreciated by considering the other extreme. Many private colleges have been able to develop distinctive images that project very specific academic, social, or vocational orientations. On this point, Burton Clark reported a survey of entering freshmen at four small colleges who were asked whether the college had a special distinctive quality.[10] San Francisco State College was the only one that the majority of entering students did not consider to be greatly different from other colleges. The other three (Reed, Antioch, and Swarthmore) had distinctive images. They were not simply perceived as generally good, or small, or avant garde. The students distinguished among the three colleges on the basis of their academic standards, intellectual atmosphere, liberalism, and the experimental nature of the campus.

It should be noted that Clark's study pertains to small colleges, not to large universities, which are less likely to develop distinctive images because of their complexity and diversity of goals and students. But the point is that there are different images of academic institutions that convey sharp prestige distinctions among universities and between universities and community colleges, state colleges and universities, small private colleges, and large wealthy private universities, each of which serves different clientele and provides its graduates with more or less access to the most prized social positions. As more of the college-age group attends college, simply being a college graduate in itself will become less important as a mark of distinction than the type of college that one has attended; the type of college will be the important consideration in competition for the most desirable jobs.

Clark attempted to explain how distinctive colleges gain and maintain their distinctive identities.[11] From his case studies of Antioch, Reed, and Swarthmore, he concluded that distinctiveness is based on a unique educational innovation that comes to be identified with the college. This innovation may be attempted under any of three main conditions:

1. A new organization operating in a new context without the restraints of history and tradition is free to choose new alternatives and tends to attract reform-bent administrators and professors.
2. A crisis in an established institution can create a revolutionary context in that those in charge are forced either to give up the old ways or to give up the organization.
3. A reasonably successful college may maintain its flexibility and continue to evolve new patterns.

Clark observes that in each case the charismatic leadership of a college president was an essential ingredient for reform; in normal times charismatic leaders are avoided because they are too disruptive. However, leadership was not the only factor, because the social conditions also have to be ripe for a new leadership. In addition to a reform minded administrator, the following conditions seemed to be necessary: support for the reform among key professors who have been self-selected on the basis of their commitment to the change; modifications in the curriculum to accommodate and reflect the reform; an outside social base (e.g., alumnae, foundations, or cosmopolitan students) willing to provide the necessary economic and moral support for the college during its transition and to later support it; a student subculture that supports the idea; and a quietly fanatic ideology to maintain the momentum of enthusiasm and commitment to the innovation.

How Is the University Governed?

As a counterpart of their diffuse goal system, American institutions of higher learning have evolved an incredibly complex governance structure over the past century. Many of their problems today stem from the way they are organized and internally controlled. No aspect of the modern university is more complex than the way it is controlled. Social scientists and administrators do not agree on what holds universities together or how decisions get made. The facetious remark that universities operate only because the secretaries understand how the system works and the janitors keep it going, while an obvious overstatement, does point to some of the incredibilities in the system.

Robin Pardini writes that the study of university administration has been approached from at least four divergent perspectives.

1. The *angel above* perspective reminds us that, because the faculty is only a collection of specialists, the best interests of the complex institution can be served only by the professional administrators who alone are endowed with the "big picture" and the "long run" view of the institution.

2. The *devil above* perspective has been expressed most forcefully by Veblen. Administrators are seen as bumbling efficiency experts serving the vested interests of the businessmen and politicians who control the university; their work consists of the devious pursuit of methods to stymie the creative energies of the faculty, their skill an expression of their cunning.

3. The *angel below* perspective gives us a view of an administration that is *merely* supportive of the expert faculty members and who exist only to relieve the academic community of the burdensome worries and tedious tasks.

4. The *devil below* perspective sees administrators as policemen and as bookkeepers who have to perform the unpleasant tasks of enforcing policies, accounting for expenditures of funds and monitoring the faculty to see that they do not neglect their duties.[12]

However, even this array of perspectives is far from providing a complete list of the perspectives used. All four of the above views equate university governance with the style of administration, which most sociologists would regard as a very narrow and distorted perspective of governance. Thus, we shall consider several other images that social scientists hold about how power and authority are distributed in universities and therefore how they are governed. Each model by itself provides only an incomplete picture of university governance. All of the models of governance seem to be involved in one way or another.

THE BUREAUCRATIC MODEL

The study of universities as organizations has typically relied upon the bureaucratic model. As one writer asserts, "our assumption continues to be, then, that the prevailing basic organizational pattern of universities of higher education is bureaucratic."[13] Stroup identifies several bureaucratic characteristics.

1. Competence is the criterion used for appointment.
2. Officials are appointed, not elected.
3. Salaries are fixed and paid directly by the organization rather than determined in "free-fee" style.
4. Rank is recognized and respected.
5. The career is exclusive; no other work is done.
6. The style of life is centered around the organization.
7. Security is present in a tenure system.
8. Personal and organizational property are separated.[14]

The university has formal channels of communication and a formal hierarchy of offices, that is, students, teaching assistants, professors, deans, and presidents, for example. It is governed by a complex system of rules, as any college student knows who has tried to decipher procedures for course registration. There are library regulations, budgetary guidelines, graduation requirements, registration procedures, and rules for the use of public auditoriums.

Veblen reported one of the most perceptive analyses of bureaucracy in higher education some years ago.[15] Critical of the attempts by educators to apply the efficiency principles used in large scale business organizations to higher education, he noted that it is generally easier to justify programs whose efficiency can be accounted for than those whose efficiency cannot be easily measured. The credit and grade-point systems are the counterparts of the price system used by business. Credit hours are used as measures of the efficiency of students; that is, "failure" is failure to achieve the proper point hour within the specified period of time. Similarly, "efficient" courses can be taught in three-semester credits. Universities have also copied separate departments of accounting from businesses. Special record-keeping offices constantly evaluate student and staff efficiency, attendance, grade-point ratio and student-teacher loads. Standardized tests are used for admission to the university and as a basis for evaluating its quality. This stress on efficiency can distort the relative importance of measurement to the point where professors are reluctant to teach information that cannot be easily measured; they are tempted to test points that can be easily measured, no matter how trivial.

Another cogent discussion of universities as bureaucracies was written by Charles Page. "The most apparent indication of bureaucratization in higher education," he writes, "is to be seen, of course, in bureaucracy's most fruitful field, administration. Administration cannot escape the bureaucratic process, in whatever organization; in fact, if the organization is of any scope, its administration is, of necessity, bureaucratic."[16] He identifies several outward indications of administrative bureaucracy. The first is the elaboration of hierarchical structure with each office—chairmen, deans, and vice presidents—appropriately defined and labeled. Second, he notes how the curriculum is effected through the use of master plans, "integrated" courses, and extracurricular activities geared to institutional goals.

"Standardization and interchangeability move clearly to the front stage when we observe still another type of evidence, the textbook field . . . every college teacher is familiar with the descent of the bookmen, with their flattering pleas to submit a new course to manuscript. Why? Manifestly to gain profit for the publisher, to put money in the author's pocket, to enhance his professional prestige, to diffuse wisdom throughout the world. But also . . . to encourage the erection of similar courses wherever curriculums permit and, more importantly, in the long run to substitute the foolproof textbook for the frequently unpredictable and sometimes foolish, instructor."[17]

Third, bureaucratization can be observed in the standardization of teaching personnel. Professors are required to have a Ph.D. degree as a "union card," and the graduate school stamps the professor with its distinctive prestige level and orientation to the discipline. Page concludes that "this is the situation aptly symbolized by the expression 'educational factory.' The image provoked by this usage is, perhaps, not too misleading: freshmen raw materials; 'co-curriculum' furnishing the basic material; specialized programs or 'majors' determining the model—Sedan, Couple, even the 'convertible'; 'electives' supplying those additional accessories which are highly prized. And, smoothly moving without interruption, the assembly line: administrators and instructors following their routines faithfully, turning out the finished product, on schedule."[18]

He notes that professors adapt to the bureaucracy in different ways. One type of professor is a "ritualist," or a "bureaucratic virtuoso" who has become deeply ingrained with official protocol. Another type is essentially "neurotic," generally confused by the apparent contradictions between professional norms and bureaucratic requirements. He becomes paranoid about the diabolical machinations of his colleagues whom he believes are trying to undermine him. A third type—the "robber baron"—is like the ritualist, well adapted to the system. But instead of subscribing blindly to the bureaucracy he will ignore bureaucratic propriety altogether when it serves his own interest. He uses his courage and his realistic knowledge about how the bureaucracy functions to manipulate the system and cut red tape in order to fulfill his convictions. Finally, a fourth type, the "academic rebel," rejects the traditional academic values and university goals as well as its bureaucratic structure. His subversive activities, if successful, lead to new directions in higher education, experimental colleges, and the like.

Blau reports from his study of 115 colleges and universities that bureaucratic traits of universities have detrimental effects on academic performance.[19] A big complement of administrators, extensive use of computers, and large size produce either centralization or more levels of authority, and the students' chances of completing college are not as good in these as in less bureaucratized schools. Their progress is also hampered by a bureaucratic, impersonal attention to teaching manifest in faculty overload and few personal contacts with professors.

On the other hand, Blau's main conclusions are that large academic institutions tend to be less bureaucratic than smaller ones, contrary to popular opinion. Large institutions have relatively small numbers of administrators, authority in them is more decentralized to the faculty than in small institutions, and they are more likely to open up new academic fields by establishing new departments. Several traits usually associated with bureaucracy promote decentralization of authority, not centralization as the popular stereotype maintains: layers of administrative hierarchy, size, a large clerical staff, and a high rate of succession among university and college presidents. A paternalistic administration, not an impersonal bureaucratic one, is most likely to exercise centralized control over the faculty.

Another study of 300 colleges, universities, and community colleges in the United States supports these conclusions.[20] It was found that the larger the institution's size, the greater the control at the department level. However, there was an important qualification: major decisions in larger schools were handled in a centralized way *within* departments by strong department heads.

THE COLLEGIAL MODEL

These latter observations support contentions by many other observers who doubt that universities really fit the bureaucratic model. University professors have professional authority over and above their position in the bureaucracy, and decision making seems to be more decentralized than is characteristic of a hierarchical bureaucracy. Moreover, there are controls, both within and outside universities, that restrict the power of officials at any particular level—administrative officers that control budgets, space allocation, admissions and the like; professional associations; accrediting agencies; federal agencies; civil service; coordinating boards, state budgeting and planning offices, and the executive of the state government.

On these grounds, some writers view the university as a community of scholars. The hierarchical decision making structure is played down while coordination is achieved through consensus among coequal professors, groups, and agencies. Whereas Weber's bureaucratic model assumes that there is one line of authority dominated by the administration, in this system there is no clear-cut "line" but, instead, there is a number of autonomous individuals and groups largely free from direct control from administrative superiors making their own decisions about courses, research, and consulting. Control is exercised by peers who exert informal pressures, bestow prestige, and control hiring and promotion and other policies.

Some evidence in support of this model was reported in a survey of faculty perceptions of the power of department chairmen in a four-year college.[21] Although they attributed increasing amounts of influence to successive administrative levels (from department chairmen to state boards), the professors saw themselves as exercising considerable influence in the college. Indeed, they seemed to wield even more influence than their department chairmen. There was also some evidence that strong chairmen could actually be detrimental to some university goals: where chairmen were strong, professional productivity was lower. This probably reflects the fact that productive professors have strong contacts in their disciplines and do not have to submit to authoritarian chairmen. The author concluded that colleges are unique kinds of organizations having only a limited degree of hierarchy.

THE POLITICAL MODEL

But the collegial model rests on the dubious assumption that peers will make decisions on the basis of rational professional criteria and in conformity with the standards and goals of professional ideals. There is little reason to believe that university faculty members act any more "rationally" than anyone else when it comes to running a complex organization. Many decisions are "political" in nature. Freidson's observations about the negative aspects of collegial authority are instructive.[22] He points out that the division of labor sometimes gives a profession a position of dominance distinct from any "external" authority imposed on it by a bureaucratic framework, and that professional autonomy has effects similar to the effects that have been ascribed to bureaucracy. Thus, professionals who hold a dominant status in the organization because of their collegial authority often use their superior position with respect to clients and administrators on behalf of their own self-interests.

Baldridge proposes that universities can be more accurately characterized as political systems than either bureaucracies or communities of scholars.

"When we look at the complex and dynamic processes that explode on the modern campus today, we see neither the rigid, formal aspects of bureaucracy nor the calm, consensus-directed elements of an academic collegium. On the contrary, if student riots cripple the campus, if professors form unions and strike, if administrators defend their traditional positions, and if external interest groups and irate governors invade the academic halls, all these acts must be seen as political. They emerge from the complex fragmented social structures of the university and its 'publics,' drawing on the divergent concerns and life styles of hundreds of miniature subcultures. These groups articulate their interests in many different ways, bringing pressure on the decision-making process from any number of angles and using power and force whenever it is available and necessary. Power and influence, once articulated, go through a complex process until policies are shaped, reshaped, and forged out of the competing claims of multiple groups. All this is a dynamic process, a process clearly indicating that the university is best understood as a 'politicized' institution—above all else the Political University."[23]

Also advocating that the fundamental elements in the structure of the university are primarily political as well as economic, another writer has noted that "the heart of the matter today is political." He places the faculty in the central position of political power in the university.[24] In a study of administrative leadership in universities, Lunsford cited a growing separateness of administrators from the academic community as the primary political cleavage within the university. Growth in size, increasing specialization of the administrative functions and emerging demands upon administrators as interpreters of the university role to outside observers are all responsible for the split.[25] In coping with this conflict, administrators made surface attempts to remain in communication with student and faculty constituents. They try to operate rationally and to justify their decisions upon the best interests of the institution, pretending that their authority is based on a consensus within the university or their right to make decisions. But barely beneath the surface lies the inherently political nature of administrators' decisions, which in reality are made from a substantial power base.

THE COMPLEX ORGANIZATION MODEL

While power and conflict are characteristic of many aspects of university life, I believe that it would be myopic to view universities solely as political systems. The political model obscures the important organizational characteristics and status dimensions, whose relevance has already been commented on. The conflicts are resolved through political processes but usually within boundaries set by the organizational structure, peer groups, and status systems. The political dimension is only one of several factors involved.

In other words, universities are *composites* of the bureaucratic, collegial, and political models. Any one model by itself provides a vastly over-simplified description of universities. Therefore, I will use the term "complex organization" in describing universities. This term includes elements of each of these other models, as follows. As institutions have grown in size and complexity, they have organized hierarchically; even the faculty has had to structure itself bureaucratically in order to carry on its research, teaching, and committee work. Within this bureaucratic structure, some faculty members are able to relate to one another in a collegial form; the teaching staff elects faculty delegates to represent them on university governing bodies, and they staff committees that regulate the curriculum, research policy, and the like. In practice these collegial committees supplement and sometimes come in conflict with the administrative sphere of authority. Moreover, the real faculty power is exercised by a small oligarchy of faculty members who become politically aligned with factions of faculty members and with administrators.

In short, in the modern university, there has been a merger of political, professional, and bureaucratic forms of governance. These competing models of governance clearly promote role conflicts and tensions. Faculty members, administrators, and students who subscribe to alternative models will have different, often contradictory, expectations of one another.

Some of the complexity of university organization has been captured by Clark, who views universities as a cluster of subunits that multiply with increases in size.[26] Universities are portrayed as loosely joined federations of organizations. He notes a multiplicity of ambiguous goals and a change in academic roles from generalist to intense specialization. Students and faculty subscribe to numerous value systems, many of them centered around the individual disciplines. Authority within the universities is characteristically decentralized with the professor seeking autonomy from lay and administrative control. This decentralized decision-making structure together with professional autonomy, create elements of the collegial form of control. But, at the same time, the rules and regulations and intense specialization are more characteristic of a bureaucracy. The collegial and hierarchical structures supplement one another to form a dual decision making system; some decisions are made by professional peers and others by administrators. Often a struggle for control arises between the two groups.

The outcomes of these struggles and accommodations have produced wide variability in styles of academic governance. This variation was reflected in McConnell's review of studies of faculty roles at Berkeley, Fresno State, and Minnesota.[27] Institutional growth caused all three institutions to organize bureaucratically, and elaborate systems of committees introduced the element of representative governance in replacing the informal collegial academic community. In each institution, too, an oligarchy of tenured faculty tended to conduct business for their professional colleagues; faculty with dissenting views and younger faculty were therefore discouraged from effective participation. However, the formal relationship between faculty and administration varied with the institution. At Berkeley, central administrative officers were excluded from participation on faculty committees and consequently parallel structures of faculty committees and administration committees existed. This duality in structure fostered inconsistent decision-making and conflict between faculty and administration. At Minnesota, faculty and administration participated together on joint committees, which produced a relatively high degree of trust in faculty-administrative relationships. At Fresno State, although central administrative officers were ex-officio members of faculty committees, other variables, such as political intervention, administrative style, faculty unionism and governing board actions, produced conflict.

Whether one or another form of governance dominates depends upon the particular circumstances. For example, the size of the university and the extent to which it is insulated from outside pressures seem to make major differences. Thus, one study found that the largest universities were centralized, with a "center" at the highest organizational level that (1) served to mediate external relations, and yet (2) simultaneously permitted the faculty to exercise considerable power over the institution's policy.[28] The faculty was much more autonomous in large than in small institutions, which had more hierarchical structures. The author concluded that size often forces universities to rely upon the professional expertise of professors; whereas in smaller institutions, administrators are in a better position to exercise control from the top.

Another writer speculates that the collegial model can be maintained only where the university is relatively autonomous and not subject to strong pressures from the environment.[29] Professional autonomy, it would be expected, would be low in local community colleges because many are financially dependent on a local school district, have their student clientele entirely defined by law, and are faced with pressures toward vocational training and community service instead of the more traditional academic values. Such institutions tend to be bureaucratically controlled with work being highly standardized by means of formal contracts that usually specify not only the exact number of teaching hours but even the precise courses to be taught. Office hours are specified and checked; absences require permission from department chairmen; and there is very little freedom over financial matters. The faculty has very little control over major decisions, and there are few effective decision mechanisms for faculty input. In many ways the decision process is centralized in the administration, the departmental autonomy over hiring, promotion, and tenure is very limited. Peer evaluation is not nearly as strong as in other types of schools, and these evaluations are not as much a part of the promotion and tenure scheme. In fact, promotions are usually based on standard time schedules, not on quality of performance, much as in the public schools.

At the other end of the continuum is the large private university with heavy endowments and individual research grants for financial support. The faculty determines admission criteria and is strongly committed to academic freedom. At this end of the continuum—in the Yales, Harvards, and Stanfords—the faculty has an amazing amount of autonomy. There is much less standardization of work: the teaching hours, course loads, office hours, contractual relations, and other symbols of standardization are ambiguous and vague, allowing the professor the supreme right to be left alone. Control over major decisions is decentralized, and the faculty has great input through committees, faculty senates, and autonomous departments. Hiring, promotion, and evaluation of faculty are reserved to the faculty itself. Any intrusion into these realms is strongly and usually successfully resisted. The freedom from environmental influence allows enormous freedom for the faculty in such universities.

What Problems Are Created by the University's Recruitment Procedures?

Universities use various methods and criteria to recruit and reward students and faculty members. The kinds of students and faculty members recruited create distinctive "value climates" in different universities.

How Are Students Recruited?

At least on the surface, there are marked differences between the way that most colleges and universities recruit students and the way students are recruited by the public schools (discussed in the previous chapter). Whereas schools were described as "domesticated" organizations, many colleges and universities exist in a "wild" or competitive environment.

They can screen their members (either at the time of application or by failing wholesale large numbers of students after they have been admitted) and, on the other hand, students typically can select their own college.

However, within this dominant pattern, there are several subtypes of recruiting procedures. First, the fact that some colleges, especially the most prestigious, distinctive institutions, are able to attract a large number of applicants gives them virtual veto power over which students will be admitted, while the student has little voice in the matter. Universities that are able to skim off the best students can develop a reputation for quality, not because of what they do to the students, but because of the quality of the student recruited in the first place.

A second recruiting pattern is more typical of the mediocre institutions that, because they are not so popular, cannot afford to be selective. In this case, the student exercises the final veto. Many of these institutions find it necessary to compromise their academic standards and integrity in order to compete for students and to secure funding. Many of these institutions operate within what Clark refers to as the "enrollment economy," with financing being heavily dependent upon student tuitions.[30] Clark's study of adult education was an extreme case of how a school's need for students can affect its educational programs. The adult education program was originally justified as a means of keeping adults abreast of new knowledge in this changing technological society. However, the arts, crafts, hobbies, and related subjects had more popular appeal than the academic aspects of curriculum. Clark concluded that:

"the tendency towards service clearly changes the conception of adult education held by public school officials. In a trend that has continued unabated since the 1920's, general value symbols have become less and less closely linked to a body of educational norms. Instead, specific goals and standards of adult education are 'decided' by various schools on a temporary and educationally adhoc basis. . . . We may expect that this value adaptation, where purposes reduce to service, will be pronounced when (a) organizations attached to a precarious value (b) continue to find themselves without a dependable clientele, or more broadly, with no *specific* outside social forces to sustain them. The organizational needs of survival and security are likely to propel an adaptation to a diffuse social base, and purpose will be adjusted accordingly."[31]

Still a third recruiting pattern is characteristic of some state institutions that are required by law to admit all high school graduates from the state. In this case the university has no control over admission. Such a college was also studied by Clark. The students who chose to attend substantially modified the goals of the college.[32] This was an "open door," two-year vocational school in California, required by law to accept all high school graduates from the state who applied for admission. However, most of the students who enrolled did not subscribe to the college's vocational training objectives and instead planned to attend a state university. They looked upon the junior college as a place near home where they could earn two years of college credit before transferring to a four-year college. As the professors tried to meet the students' needs, they began to apply the kind of academic standards that the students would encounter when they went on to a four-year school. The college became inadvertently transformed into an academic-oriented institution.

In short, the "open door" policy sharply limited how far the college was able to consciously determine its own objectives. It was subjected to a sociological determinism, with control being diffused to external sources. In defense, the college attempted to protect its vocational objectives by trying to "cool out" the numerous students who did not show academic promise but who thought of themselves as bona fide college students. By using vocational interest and achievement tests, by assigning students to remedial programs, and by putting students on probation for low grades, some professors and counselors tried to reorient students from the academic program into a vocational, business, or semiprofessional program. The objective was (1) to make substitute avenues appear not too different from the ones given up, (2) to encourage gradual disengagement, and (3) to provide objective evidence of poor performance and a low probability of success in the academic program.

In the future, many more colleges may be forced to admit all applicants as rising expectations and laws of the labor market make college attendance nearly compulsory for large numbers of people. These colleges will become like the high schools of today, with little opportunity to select their clientele and little control over their goals. The colleges will be forced to either modify their goals and procedures to fit the student who is not academically inclined or put up with the discipline and alienation problems that have been characteristic of many high schools. Thus, in the future, there might not be much difference between the recruiting patterns used by schools and colleges.

This development would make it easier for young men and women from low-income families to gain admission to some type of college. At the present time, as one goes down the ability scale, the probability of enrolling in and succeeding in college decreases more sharply for children from economically and socially less-favored homes than it does for children from more-favored homes. Eleven of 17 studies published in the past two decades dealing with periods of two to four years reported a positive correlation between social class indicators and college performance.[33] And a randomly selected cohort of Wisconsin high school seniors over a seven-year period showed that, with intelligence controlled, there was a small but positive relationship between socioeconomic status and plans to attend college and college attendance, for both sexes.[34] The relative effect of socioeconomic status was greater than the effect of intelligence for females, while intelligence was more important than socioeconomic status for males. These differences in opportunity should begin to level out.

However, this leveling of opportunity may not proceed very far. The discriminatory pattern is likely to persist, in a slightly different form, for at least two reasons. First, the Wisconsin study and other studies indicate that the disadvantaged position of lower socioeconomic status students persists even after they are admitted to college. In the Wisconsin sample, even among students in college, socioeconomic status continued to exert an independent influence in determining college graduation for both sexes.[35]

Second, many low-income students will not enter the high prestige, elite colleges. In other words, some colleges are likely to remain highly selective, and the stratification among institutions of higher education is likely to become even more accentuated than it is at present. Perrucci sees growing differentiation in the quality of schools and, more importantly, in the relative success of their graduates.[36] As a result, the "sorting out" process, which was traditionally carried out at the high school level, is now being performed at the college level. He concludes that while there are more working-class students in colleges and universities, "we have at the same time moved to a more rigidly class-based system of stratification *within* the framework of higher education. The stratification has manifested itself in the over-involvement of working-class college graduates in certain occupations as well as in certain types of colleges, and in the combined impact of both social origins and the nature of college attended upon post-graduate performance and success.[37]

In support of this argument, there is evidence that differences in earning power between graduates of distinctive colleges and more obscure ones are so great that they override nearly everything else. Haveman and West concluded that "at the extremes, the Ivy League graduates do best of all financially even when they make poor grades and take a general rather than a specific course, both of which are ordinarily handicaps—while the graduates of the small schools do not get up to the averages even when they make fine grades and take the type of specific courses which ordinarily produce the biggest incomes."[38] At the same time, those students with lower economic backgrounds who do succeed in being admitted to higher prestige schools earn more than their counterparts from the less prestigious schools.

How Are Faculty Recruited and Promoted?

Some studies have shown that college students who are relatively intellectual, independent in thought, less materialistic and more politically liberal are attracted into college teaching.[39] These findings are consistent with a popular stereotype of professors as autonomous, individualistic people who reject conventional values, including the value of materialistic success. However, faculty mobility studies indicate that although professors may not be oriented to "materialistic success" in conventional terms, they are highly oriented to "success" within the academic system. Success is usually defined in terms of academic prestige rather than (or in addition to) salary. Academic mobility consists of a series of moves designed to enhance one's prestige. Prestige is closely tied to research publications. Professors tend to be highly accepting of, and conforming to, this academic system.

The higher the rank of the department in the prestige system, the higher the reputation of its individual members. This reputation tends to make them more desirable to other universities, more independent of their own, and more inclined to mobility. Caplow and McGee point out that "the faculty of great departments are generally inveterate travellers, shuttling from Teheran to Texas and from one Cambridge to another on scholarly errands which—by convention—do not need to be fully explained."[40] Faculty members are hired and evaluated on the basis of their usefulness in future staff recruitment. Each faculty member has a stake in maintaining the prestige of his department by hiring only individuals whose prestige will enhance it, since the decline in departmental prestige will be experienced by each individual member as a decline in his own prestige.

Largely because of these prestige considerations, perhaps, Caplow and McGee concluded that "when we examine the specific procedures of hiring in the American university, they turn out to be almost unbelievably elaborate. The average salary of an assistant professor is approximately that of a bakery truck driver, and his occupancy of a job is likely to be less permanent. Yet it may require a large part of the time of twenty highly skilled men for a full year to hire him."[41]

The careers of most professors in major universities in the United States today, then, depend first of all upon publication of scholarly books and articles in professional journals as evidence of research activity. Second, in addition to actual productivity, the prestige of the university from which the faculty member received his degree is an important consideration in hiring. Several studies have found that even in scientific fields, the prestige of the doctorate has more influence on who is hired by leading departments than their scholarly performance.[42] Universities can increase their stature by associating themselves with other prestigious universities.

Third, in addition to research publications and prestige of the doctorate, personal characteristics are also taken into consideration. In a study over 30 years ago, Wilson noted the prominent role that "nepotism" plays in university appointments.[43] At a typical middle-rank university at that time at least four-fifths of all appointments went to friends, kinsmen, and former students. Perhaps a third of all faculty members at that time were products of "inbreeding," that is, had received their training for their highest degree at the institution where they were currently employed. Another study conducted 15 years later showed that nepotism and inbreeding are still commonly practiced.[44] While inbreeding was generally disapproved, 40 percent of the instructors and assistant professors, and 61 percent of the professors at tenured ranks had contact with their departments before their candidacy for a position. A study of over 1100 U.S. academic scientists has found that inbred scientists, even those at leading universities, were slightly less productive than scientists trained at other universities.[45] In addition, there was evidence that the inbred professors were discriminated against in the allocation of departmental rewards. The fact that inbreeding persists despite these adverse effects on the institutions and individuals involved is testimony to the important role played by personal, particularistic considerations in the careers of university professors.

From these studies it is concluded that the prestige of the candidate's doctorate and his publication record are used as evidence that he is committed to academic norms and is technically competent, but that technical competence is not enough. It is weighed against other personal considerations. Because of the university's conflicting goals, and because of the sometimes fierce interpersonal competition that sometimes develops among scholars, department members seek out colleagues who will be personally compatible with their prior goal definitions and who will not upset the prevailing status hierarchy.

Although the academic prestige system is relatively suitable for some types of colleges (e.g., elite graduate training institutions), it tends to dominate the whole range of academic institutions. In view of the pervasiveness of this singular stratification system, faculty members frequently do not articulate their own efforts with their particular college's unique image, goals, or student ability levels and objectives.

What Problems Has Specialization Produced?

Colleges and universities have evolved both informal and formal divisions of labor.

VALUE CLIMATES: INFORMAL SPECIALIZATION

The kind of faculty members and students recruited by a college helps to establish its goals and prevailing value climate. For example, in some colleges almost all of the students come from the top fifth of their high school graduating classes, score high on college entrance examinations, and are politically liberal. Frequently, but not always, such colleges have renowned professors. Other colleges attract a high proportion of relatively mediocre, marginal students who are not politically oriented. These colleges may or may not have less-renowned professors. These different value climates lead colleges to specialize in different functions and undoubtedly influence the students. For example, a student who finds that his classmates are mediocre may also find that his own aspirations become depressed by his environment.

College and university environmental scales consisting of 160 items have been developed to distinguish among several different types of college environments. The scales tap five dimensions of college life: scholarship, awareness, community, propriety, and practicality.[46] In one type of college thus identified, students say that they work hard, set high standards for their achievements, are deeply concerned about the welfare of mankind, and are broadly interested in the arts and humanities. A second type of environment is provided by highly selective public and private universities, which are characterized by relatively strong "environmental press" toward scholarship and awareness and where the students are not usually described as friendly and helpful but are more likely to be characterized as independent, critical, and nonconformists. Whereas Antioch, Swarthmore, and Oberlin Colleges represent the first type, Harvard, Yale, and Columbia represent the second. A third type is represented by many private and public general universities, such as Syracuse University and the University of Southern California. Generally, their scores on the scholarship dimension tend to be moderate at best, whereas scores on the awareness scale range from relatively low to quite high. Still other patterns have been described for colleges that emphasize science and engineering, denominational Protestant and Catholic colleges, and institutions in which the dominant program is teacher education (where the environmental press is moderately high with respect to propriety and practicality and moderately low with respect to scholarship and awareness).

Another approach to value climates is to describe different "student cultures." One type of student culture is represented in the extreme case of the medical school. According to one study, the medical-student culture serves at least two functions: (1) providing the students a means of accommodation to difficulties of the school life and (2) providing students a basis for redirecting their efforts often in defiance of faculty ideals. The authors of the study concluded that:

"When students first enter school their emphasis on medical practice—their belief that they are in school to learn to save lives—leads them to rebel against laboratory work, essentially nonmedical, and against the drudgery of studying for intensive academic examinations. Later, they must deal with the same problem of an overload of work in a clinical setting in which examinations are not so important although the possibility of being tested and found wanting is always present. The understandings and agreements that make up student culture, by solving these problems in one way or another, allow the students to fit into the system without being constantly so upset as to be unable to function. In this way, student culture is a mode of accommodation to what the students find expected of them in school.

"At the same time student culture affects the level and direction of effort students expend while in school, by giving them a rationale for restricting the theoretically infinite amount of time and effort they might devote to their school work. More importantly, it provides them with sufficient collective support to allow them to direct their effort in quite different directions than those suggested by the faculty—considered as a unit or even considered with regard for the divisions of opinion within the faculty itself. Though members of a given department may feel that their course is really designed to put across such-and-such a brand of knowledge for this-and-that purpose, the students may remain relatively immune, drawing the strength to ignore the faculty's otherwise authoritative notions from the lore that makes up student culture. Student culture is thus the cornerstone of many faculty difficulties with students, one of the facts of life to which teachers must, in their turn, make some accommodation."[47]

However, while it is generally conceded that the college student culture has an important bearing on the behavior of college students and is often a source of strain between students and professors, the notion that there is a *general* value climate that permeates a given college or university has been questioned by several writers. Typically, there are several student subcultures on a given college campus. A simple four-way typology of students' college subcultures was suggested by Clark and Trow:[48]

1. The *collegiate*, emphasizing fraternities, sororities, social life, athletics, and campus activities. Its members tend to be from middle-class families and to resist the intellectual demands of the faculty.

2. The *vocational*, emphasizing training for a specific occupational career. Students in this group are largely from working-class backgrounds. To them college represents an opportunity to acquire economic security and social status. They tend to major in engineering, business, education, or technical fields.

3. The *academic*, committed to scholarly achievement in an academic field. Students in this group are middle class in background and have relatively well-educated parents. They are concentrated in the highly selective prestige colleges and universities and plan to go on for the highest degrees in their fields of interest. They tend to identify with the faculty and their values.

4. The *nonconformist*, repudiating the values of the above three groups. The nonconformist students may be deeply concerned

with ideas and values but reject the embrace of the college and the "system." This could include subgroups of hippies, activists, and other alienated students who are united only by their disenchantment with the established order.

One study of college students showed that many lower-class students identified with the vocational group, whereas many middle-class students were found largely in the academic subculture.[49] The greatest shift during college was toward the academic subculture; the vocational group exhibited least tendencies to reject their subculture. The four types also differed in religious values, in adherence to rules and regulations, and in their career aspirations.

These simple typologies have been elaborated in recent studies using more complex statistical procedures and other instruments. As many as 9 to 12 different subcultures have been identified in some studies. Peterson developed a series of questionnaires (the "college student characteristic questionnaires") that tapped dimensions such as the students' political liberalism, their satisfaction with the faculty's competence, with the administration, with their major, and their social conscience. These questionnaires have been used to describe college climates, as well as to identify subcultures of students. In addition to these instruments, the Educational Testing Service has developed what is referred to as an "institutional functioning inventory," which is designed to provide a description of teaching practices, governance arrangements, administrative policies, types of programs, characteristic attitudes of groups of people, and other specific aspects of campus life.[50] This instrument describes colleges in terms of 11 dimensions, such as the extent that activities and opportunities for intellectual and aesthetic stimulation are available outside the classroom, the extent of academic freedom for faculty and students, human diversity on the campus, concern for undergraduate learning, and the like.

Despite the recent interest in studying college "climates," some authors have criticized the concept because it is so closely tied to the students' sentiments that it is impossible to predict *changes* in students' sentiments and values independently from the college climate. Bidwell and Vreeland, in particular, have argued that an approach to college structure should be taken that is logically independent of, and prior to, student values if one is to determine the effects that college has on students' attitudes and values.[51] They propose a typology of university departments—the principal work place of colleges—which they then use to predict departmental effects on student attitudes. Departments were classified on the basis of:

A. Their goals—(1) technical (i.e., occupational preparation and a description of structure of the discipline, (2) moral (i.e., changing the student attitudes about the field, developing a commitment to an occupation, and liberalizing and humanizing the student), and (3) mixed.

B. Degree of faculty interest in undergraduate teaching and curriculum.

C. Intimacy and frequency of student-faculty interaction.

Bidwell and Vreeland were able to classify the departments of one university on the basis of these criteria. For example, the German and physics departments were among those that were low on both the dimensions of interest in undergraduates and the interaction between the faculty and students; whereas the history and psychology departments were high on both dimensions. Engineering was a deviant case that rated high on interest on undergraduate teaching but low in interaction.

The existence of so many different subcultures, on one hand, is a source of tension and strain among groups that support different goal priorities and create different demands on professors; but on the other hand, this variety assures that most students, regardless of their personal situation, can find some social support and will not be entirely overwhelmed by the college's dominant value system.

FORMAL SPECIALIZATION

The patterns of organization described thus far have evolved informally and are not usually officially recognized. Nevertheless, they serve as a basis for concentrating on distinctive types of students and goals, that is, as a basis of functional specialization. On the other hand, structural forms of specialization are officially sanctioned. This includes task specialization and professionalization, both of which are inherent in the collegial model of universities.

Task Specialization. Institutions of higher education have not yet learned how to cope with the growth in scope and complexity that has occurred in recent years. All professors must carry out all responsibilities. They specialize only on the basis of technical *tasks*, or content, dictated by academic disciplines (e.g., history or physics); the historian might further concentrate on nineteenth-century European naval battles and the physicist on the movement of subatomic particles under cold temperature conditions. Most professors are expected to teach graduate and undergraduate courses, to carry out research and scholarly inquiries, to publish, to provide consultant, advisory or other service functions related to their specialities, to advise undergraduate and graduate students and supervise doctoral theses, and to serve on departmental graduate faculty and university committees.

A *functional* division of labor would be another alternative—that is, different members of the permanent staff assigned to teaching undergraduates, to training graduate students, to research, and to public service activities. Instead, as Gross observes, the strategy has been to gradually redefine the professor's role to include all of these tasks.[52] Whereas many other organizations have met similar situations with new divisions of labor, the university has added function after function to the same personnel. Professors have not been encouraged or permitted to specialize in accordance with the different functions that must be performed.

Faced with an impossible set of responsibilities, professors are forced to compromise. Although the main *responsibility* of the great majority of faculty members at most universities is to teach undergraduates, they are rewarded for research and publication. Moreover, although research is rewarded, the university is not organized to carry out research; personnel assignments and budgets are based on teaching loads. As a result, many senior professors find it necessary and advantageous to give a minimum of their time and effort to their teaching responsibilities so that they can concentrate (informally specialize) on their research obligations. They are forced to go outside of the university to obtain support for their research, which often tempts them to undertake inquiries that do not represent their basic interests. There seems to be, Kerr observed, "a point of no return," after which research, consulting, and graduate instruction become so absorbing that there is little time left for undergraduate instruction.[53] Federal funding has intensified the problem, according to a Brookings study by Harold Orlans, who concluded that federal research aid "has accelerated a long-standing depreciation of undergraduate education at large universities."[54] Thus, Kerr notes a "cruel paradox that a superior faculty results in an inferior concern for undergraduate teaching. . . ."[55]

Professionalism. Excessive specialization within content fields, and the tendency to specialize informally in research and graduate study, is responsible for the preoccupation on the part of many professors with professionalism. They tend to be more identified with their own colleagues than with students, and they tend to be more loyal to their professional associations and outside funding agencies than to the university administrators; powerful research administrations, institutes, and research centers have risen to compete for control of university campuses; yet, full-time researchers are second-class citizens without faculty status in universities.

The professor's outside commitments have drastically changed his life style. Some critics say that it has become a "rat race" of business and activity, managing contracts and projects, guiding teams and assistants, bossing crews of technicians, making numerous trips, sitting on committees for government agencies, and engaging in other "distractions" necessary to keep the whole frenetic business from collapsing. Many observers are convinced that professionalism has also had the effect of devaluing teaching at the undergraduate level. Because of time-consuming professional activities, professors' teaching loads and student contact hours have been reduced (though not their overall duties), and faculty members are more frequently on leave or temporarily away from campus, with more of the instruction falling to teachers who are not members of the regular faculty.

Nevertheless, these developments are an essential part of a knowledge-based society. Professionalism establishes and maintains standards for credible research and buffers the researcher from inappropriate pressures from students and other laymen who are less able to assess the pioneering directions for research in a particular field. The problem is not professionalism *per se*, but the fact that only the research functions have been fully professionalized in universities, which has squeezed out the other, equally important functions. What is needed is a professional career ladder, with the appropriate setting and reward structure, geared to undergraduate teaching. This probably cannot be achieved as long as teaching must compete with research for recognition. More will be said about the potentialities of a parallel system of graduate and undergraduate education in Chapter 6.

How Are Universities Shaped by Social Forces?

Traditionally, colleges and universities have been looked upon as autonomous institutions. Each college and university has been controlled by separate boards, subject to the pressures of different alumni groups; it has been able to set its own hiring standards, to select its own students and to establish its own curriculum. This image of the completely autonomous college has been exaggerated, however, considering the fact that academic freedom has been in constant jeopardy in every historical era, either from religious, business, or political groups seeking to control and censor professors.

Moreover, whatever autonomy institutions of higher education once had has been eroded since World War II by a series of social, political, and economic crises, including the growing dependence of the nation upon universities to solve national problems, explosive growths in enrollment, increased costs of state-supported programs, the growing complexity of the system of higher education, and the like. As a result of these changes, the location of power has gradually moved from inside to outside the original boundaries of universities. The federal and state governments have exerted greater influence over higher ducation, as witnessed in the GI Bill, scholarship programs, multibillion dollar research funding programs, and statewide master planning for higher education.

Kerr identifies two great impacts that, above all other forces, have molded the modern American university system into a distinctive organization. Both come from sources outside of the universities, both primarily from the federal government in response to national needs.[56] First was the land grant movement, reflected in the Morrill Act of 1862. Universities were to assist the rapid industrial and agricultural developments in the United States through research that would advance farming and manufacturing and through service to many segments of the society. As Kerr points out, nowhere before had universities been so closely linked with the daily life of so much of their societies.

The second great impact on universities began with federal support for scientific research during World War II. Major universities had begun to obtain the bulk of their research funds from the federal government. These research budgets constituted 20 to 50 percent of a university's total expenditures, most of them handled outside of normal channels. Kerr concludes that the emergence of these "federal grant" universities over the past 30 years has developed more by force of circumstances than by conscious design. These federal monies have had profound effects. Universities must commit some of their own funds to most projects, assign space, and provide time for research. To a large extent, outside funds determine which areas of the universities will grow fastest. Federal research money has given a great impetus to the development of science departments within universities. And the federal research effort has been concentrated in a few major universities, thus accentuating the size of already mammoth institutions.

These and other crises in higher education have made individual colleges and universities more interdependent than ever before, forcing them to cooperate more closely than in the past. They are being forged into an integrated national network. There are both informal and formal modes of cooperation.

WHAT FORMS OF INFORMAL INTERDEPENDENCE OCCUR?

Frequent reference has been made throughout this chapter to the informal institutional system of higher education. We have noted both (1) an implicit division of labor among the institutions that has evolved because various colleges perform similar functions and specialize in one or another of a wide range of goals and (2) a system of stratification among colleges and universities whereby some of these institutions have more access than others to prestige and necessary resources and can place their graduates in more desirable positions. Both dimensions are important.

The Division of Labor. There is limited but convincing evidence that the way institutions of higher education relate to one another has fundamental consequences. Comparing universities in England, France, and

Germany, Ben–David finds that the scientific productivity of these nations can be traced to the amount of competition among their universities.[57] Nations where higher education has been dominated by one or two institutions, or where the number of professorships has been restricted, have had lower productivity than nations in which universities could expand in growing academic fields and were forced to compete with one another for the most creative researchers. The competition forced individual institutions to make changes in order to attract new professors, which kept them in the forefront of new developments.

The Stratification System. It has been noted that there is a hierarchy of institutions based upon how they are linked to the political economy; some universities are in a better position than others to place their graduates in the most coveted social positions. Meyer argues that a college's ability to inculcate students with certain information and values depends on the college's position in this hierarchy and on the position that students will assume after graduation.[58] The high school, college, law school, or medical school that a person has graduated from entitles him to claim the title and the prerogatives of "college graduate," "attorney," or "physician." The fact that the individual has acquired such a status probably does more to determine how others will act toward him, and how he himself acts, than the values and technical knowledge he may have acquired from the formal curriculum. And, conversely, the college will not be able to create changes in the values and attitudes not validated and reinforced by the positions graduates enter.

There are three reasons why students learn what they are supposed to learn. First, students actively monitor the curriculum, sorting and selecting out what is actually important for the next career stage, whether it is entry into college or practicing a certain occupation,[59] and they disseminate these informal expectations to new students.[60] Second, practitioners (college professors, factory superintendents, physicians, or engineers) exert their influence on the schools and colleges to produce the desired qualities in graduates. Third, the career ladder continues to filter, shape, and refine the new graduates during the course of their careers.

The extent of a college's influence on students will depend on characteristics of the jobs its graduates take—such as the *distinctiveness* of their positions—and the degree that it *monopolizes* entry into these positions. For example, medical schools, which have sole authority to prepare medical doctors, will be more effective socialization agents than undergraduate liberal arts colleges, which do not prepare people for a specific career; a high school that can guarantee graduates entry into a few Ivy League colleges will have more influence than one whose graduates go to a wide range of colleges. It also follows that schools that prepare people for the elite social and political positions within highly stratified *societies* are likely to have more effect on their students than lower prestige schools in societies without exclusive elites.

What Forms Do Formal Networks Take?

A formal hierarchical structure of educational institutions in this country extends from primary through secondary to higher education. Attendance at one level is a prerequisite to entrance into the next level. This system permits social mobility from one level to another. Although the bond between universities and public high schools is not as strong as between high schools and elementary schools, the admission requirements of universities have a strong influence on the high school curriculum, just as (as indicated above) some high schools can virtually guarantee their graduates admission to certain colleges. But this bond is complicated by links with businesses that employ the graduates of both high schools and colleges.

Various institutions of higher education themselves are loosely knit together in formal arrangements. Statewide and regional planning has been forced upon higher education by some of the same forces already mentioned—the growth of student enrollment, the rising costs of state supported programs, duplication of programs caused by competition among institutions within each state, and the growing complexity of systems of higher education. Many states now have a single board of control responsible for coordinating higher education within the state, and the majority have or are developing master plans for higher education.[61] Also, several interstate compacts, both regional and nationwide in scope, have been established to encourage cooperation in higher education, for example, the Western Interstate Commission for Higher Education, Education Commission of the States, and exchange programs among Big Ten universities.

Little is known about the effects of these efforts to forge a more rational formal system of higher education, however. If these efforts at coordination were successful, the different institutions could form a career ladder that would allow students to be mobile, that is, to use less prestigious institutions as a stepping stone into more prestigious ones. But universities are not likely to quickly relinquish their autonomy. One study of statewide planning in four states concluded that as colleges and universities have become amalgamated into networks of interdependent institutions, an inevitable tension has arisen among the institutions because their individual interests and autonomy are compromised, and because of the ambiguity of statewide goals, competition for the scarce resources, and the difficulty of maintaining the innovativeness of the system.[62] Although the study did not support the view that coordination and planning at the state level necessarily resulted in uniformity, mediocrity, and rigidity, it did indicate that planning had brought fundamental changes primarily to the smaller, public, two-year and four-year colleges, which constitute the majority of the institutions within a statewide system. The large public universities were not responsive and continued to be strong and diversified. Changes in smaller institutions appeared to restrict their autonomy. Although there was not evidence that these smaller institutions had been debased, nevertheless some of the colleges did report instances of being dominated by the state university or being manipulated by a planning agency to suit the purposes of the whole system.

BOUNDARY MAINTENANCE

Some institutions of higher education, then, are less vulnerable to external influence than are others. Major universities, in particular, are blessed with structural defenses that protect them from outside pressures. A glimpse into the nature of these defenses was provided in a study of academic freedom reported during a period of history in this country during which universities were subject to political repression.[63] The pressures emanated from many legal and extralegal sources including the state legislature, alumni groups, private citizens, university administrators and students. One-fifth of the 2400 social science professors in the sample reported perceptible increases in pressures from alumni, trustees, the community, and legislators or local politicians over the seven years prior to the study.

Administrative support for the professors who were attacked by outside groups was related to the structure of the university. First, support for academic freedom was related to the "quality" of the college, as reflected in the ratio of library books to undergraduate students, annual budget per student, percent of Ph.D.'s on the faculty, and percent of graduates receiving scholarships and other honors. Superior colleges gave the faculty more than four times as much voice in matters of academic freedom as medium- or low-quality schools. The proportion of faculty members who reported that attacked personnel were protected by the administration increased directly with the quality of the colleges. But, significantly enough, the number of persons attacked also increased with the measure of quality, and with it the apprehensiveness of their faculties.

Secondly, the universities with more prestigious faculties received more support than those with mediocre faculties. The most liberal social science professors also tended to be the most productive and had the most prestige within their disciplines. Therefore, in order to defend the school's academic reputation, the administration was forced to defend the very persons who were most likely to embarrass the university in terms of its public relations. Once an administration decided that the university wanted to compete for academic prestige, it was forced to defend the prestigious, though outspoken liberal professors.

Third, the larger public institutions (compared to smaller ones) tended to give more support to academic freedom, perhaps because they had more sources of financial support and were less dependent upon any one pressure group, such as the state legislature or a large donor. Privately endowed colleges were less subject to pressure from politicians and trustees than were tax-supported institutions, presumably because of their independent sources of income.

Another study arrived at similar conclusions. The financial and political independence of junior colleges influenced their ability to defend academic freedom. The study was based on 74 junior colleges in 15 states. Relatively autonomous colleges, that is, colleges that had their own tax district and a board of governors, were distinguished from the less autonomous colleges that were attached to public school districts.[64] It was found that staff and faculty in the autonomous colleges were more likely than those attached to public school districts to (1) approve the discussion of controversial issues and (2) approve the expression of personal viewpoints of instructors on traditional values. Social science professors were the most approving, while administrators, librarians, and instructors in applied fields were least approving of these classroom practices.

Who Controls Higher Education?

Most of the nearly 2500 colleges and universities are publicly controlled, with the remainder being controlled by private groups. In nearly all cases this means that a board of control consisting of laymen representing various sectors of the public has been appointed to oversee the development of major policies of the college or university. However, historically, the trustee's influence has never been very substantial, particularly in comparison to the role of administrators and faculty members who have controlled most matters of significance in the educational community— although, occasionally, the trustees do make their influence felt, especially in public institutions where they have full legal authority. Unfortunately, the few available studies are essentially descriptive, concerning the typical size of governing boards, how they are selected, the source and nature of board authority and basic board functions. Less is known about the degree of influence exerted by trustees on university affairs, how the influences are exerted, and what types of activities are influenced. But it is possible to make some inferences.

In 1947 Beck surveyed over 700 trustees and found that over 70 percent of them were business leaders. Only 10 percent were connected with education in any formal capacity.[65] There were no clerical, skilled, semi-skilled or unskilled workers in the sample. Nearly half were over 60 years of age; one in five was 70 or over. They could be classified as political conservatives on the basis of their voting records and party affiliations. Much the same picture was drawn by a more recent survey.[66] In general, trustees today are still male, in their fifties (with more than a third over 60), white (fewer than 2 percent of the sample are black), well educated, and financially well off (more than half have annual incomes exceeding $30,000). They are typically in prestigious occupations—medicine, law, and education, but even more frequently in business; one-third of the total sample are executives of manufacturing, merchandising, and investment firms, and at private universities nearly half hold such positions. The majority of the trustees identified themselves as Republican (58 percent) and most often regarded themselves as politically moderate (61 percent) or conservative (21 percent). Only 15 percent regarded themselves as liberal. Nearly 40 percent of them and well over half at certain types of institutions are alumni of the institutions on whose boards they serve.

Such men can create important links between universities and powerful sectors of society; they can lend their personal prestige to the institution, help secure and manage endowments, and exert influence in the legislatures. However, as Beck observed, they clearly lack a basis for identifying with either underprivileged groups or youth. The biased representation of middle-class occupations puts them in a position to divert the resources and potentialities of higher education to the service of a special class. Nor do such men have any special competence in the affairs of higher education. As Veblen sardonically noted, "Plato's classic scheme of folly, which would have philosophers take over the management of affairs, has been turned on its head; the men of affairs have taken over the direction of the pursuit of knowledge."[67]

Trustees in the recent study generally seem to favor an "open door" philosophy of education. The vast majority say that there should be opportunities for higher education available to anyone who seeks education beyond secondary school and agree that colleges should admit socially disadvantaged students who appear to have the potential, even if the students do not meet normal entrance requirements. Nevertheless over 90 percent of them still regard attendance at *their* college to be a privilege, not a right. This is true even of trustees in public junior colleges, who also share the privilege-not-a-right sentiment. Generally, the trustees probably believe that *other* colleges should employ more flexible admission criteria allowing their own institution to maintain high standards; or if they do accept the open door policy for their own institution, they probably want to be able to protect the institution against "unacceptable" student conduct.

Generally speaking, trustees who are business executives consistently favor "running a college like a business" more than trustees from other occupations. They prefer a modified "top-down" hierarchical form of institutional government, often preferring to exclude even members of the faculty from those decisions having to do with the academic program of the institution. For example, over 50 percent of the total sample of trustees believe that faculty and students should *not* have major authority in 8 out of 16 typical campus decisions. The proportion feeling that trustees or administrators alone should have major authority in making the decision exceeds 40 percent in 12 of the 16 decisions. At the same time, the trustees themselves shy away from direct decision making, except when it comes to selection of the president and matters of finance, the physical plant, and "external affairs." In other cases they prefer that college officials make the decisions.

From their responses to several statements in the recent survey concerning academic freedom, it is clear that most trustees do not accept a liberal notion of academic freedom. For example, over two-thirds of them favor a screening process for all campus speakers. There are many instances (e.g., in the fall of 1968 at the University of California) where university trustees have attempted to interfere with university speakers. Nearly half of the trustees feel that students already punished by local authorities for involvement in matters of civil disobedience off the campus should be further disciplined by the college. Over half of the trustees at institutions located in the South agree that the content of the student newspaper should be controlled by the institution, although only about 30 percent of the trustees in New England and the Mid-Atlantic institutions hold this view. Trustees of public junior colleges, 42 percent of whom are elected by the general public, appear to be the least freedom-oriented in terms of their responses to the questionnaire items.

There are wide differences of opinion about academic freedom between trustees and persons who occupy academic positions. The trustees are generally more conservative than the faculty in terms of political party affiliation and ideology and attitudes about higher education. Trustees generally do not read the more relevant higher education books and journals.

In the final analysis, however, trustees do not "control" universities despite their legal authority. They are only one of several "governing" groups, often rubber-stamping decisions made by professors or administrators. Some of these other groups have already been identified: state planning agencies, alumni groups, donors, accrediting agencies, employers, and research funding agencies (in addition to professional associations).

What is the role of trustees, then? The overall impression conveyed by the study is that most trustees, especially the elected members of public institutions, do not see their role as defending the university from most of these other groups. Traditionally, perhaps, trustees saw their role as spokesmen for the university. But their power to represent the university has been curbed by faculty professionalization. Without a faculty constituency, they are more likely to take the role of "protector of the public interest." There is a potential basis of conflict between the typical trustee and most university professors who not only disagree politically, but also have different educational philosophies and, above all, hold competing conceptions of university governance.

Corson argues that the trustee has an important responsibility for interpreting to the faculty the evolving needs of the society.[68] But, because of the ideological differences between faculty members and trustees, Hartnett concludes that "we might expect greater conflict and disruption in the academic program, a deeper entrenchment of ideas of competing factions, and, worst of all, an aimless, confusing collegiate experience, where the students' program is a result of arbitration rather than mutual determination of goals and purposes."[69]

WHAT PROBLEMS IS SOCIAL CHANGE PRODUCING?

In view of the obvious importance of these external forces, it follows that the future of universities cannot be understood apart from the major social changes impinging on them. Therefore, we will now consider the meaning of several critical developments for universities: (1) the "knowledge explosion" and society's growing dependence on research; (2) the rise of mass higher education; and (3) the emergence of "moral orthodoxies" on campus. The way each of these changes is transforming universities will be reviewed.

What Will the "Knowledge Explosion" Do to Universities?

It is abundantly clear that research, like education, is no longer a luxury item. Funds for research and development increased 10 times between 1945 and 1955 and doubled again between 1955 and 1960. As the nation's gross national product doubled in recent years, total funds available for basic research alone increased more than six times. A nation cannot be technologically productive until its population has achieved a relatively high research capacity. There is an insatiable demand for research in all fields.

According to some estimates, education explains one-fourth to one-third of the growth in total national income and over 40 percent of the growth in per capita income in the United States over the period of 1929–1957.[70] The production, distribution, and consumption of "knowledge" in all of its forms is said to account for 29 percent of the gross national product, according to Machlup's calculations, with "knowledge production" growing at about twice the rate of the rest of the economy.[71] While the exact figures have been challenged, the principal fact is that knowledge production and transmission are major economic forces in the American economy. It is axiomatic that universities and other organizations involved in the production and the transmission of knowledge will assume a central position in the society. This position is only partly dependent on the importance of technology.[72] In addition, university professors have been thrust into important policy-related roles. As Lane points out, political leaders are looking for practical information, and because they are freer from their constituencies today, they are in a better position to use knowledge as a basis for policy decisions.[73]

What Are the Effects of this New Status? If university-based researchers are tackling larger and more complex problems, and if the implications are important enough to influence public policy, an important corollary follows: *research can no longer be conducted exclusively on a part-time basis by professors who spend large portions of their time on other activities.* The growth of policy research will change the basic structure of the universities. At least one change is already clear: the new linkages that universities have established with external groups, that is, the politicians, professional organizations, independent research groups, businessmen, community leaders, and consumers.

The university's role as a major producer of applied knowledge has been a source of several problems. First, policy research plunges universities into complex issues that cannot be resolved with existing competence and available resources. The sciences, including the social and behavioral sciences, are sometimes regarded almost as magic fetishes capable of delivering mankind from a wide range of problems. In fact, however, science has not been able to solve many of these problems. Merton has called attention to the "indeterminancy" of behavioral science findings, in particular. There is a wide disparity between the social scientist's potential authority as a consultant and the actual meager state of his knowledge.[74] As long as social scientists were considered to be impractical thinkers, they could make reckless proposals and exaggerated claims without fear of hurting anyone. But the Equal Educational Opportunity Survey, the "Pygmalion" study and the recent work of Arthur Jensen (to be discussed later) are only a few examples of how the work of competent researchers is now being used—wisely or unwisely—for policy decisions.[75] When social scientists are wrong today there is more at stake than a "null hypothesis." They can no longer pretend that their work is only part of an academic puzzle.

A second problem is the loss of insulation from popular pressures that invariably accompanies practical applications of knowledge. Academic disciplines often seem to need protection until they develop sufficient maturity to tackle the most difficult problems. Some writers believe that the physical sciences, for example, were able to develop their explanatory powers precisely because scientists initially limited thir concerns to those problems that could be solved with the existing scientific theory and technology; and conversely, they avoided problems that outside authorities may have considered to be important when there was no foreseeable scientific solution.[76]

Politicization of the university is an important consequence. In view of the potential influence of research on public policy, it can be expected that political leaders will seek to influence research in order to better rationalize and guide their actions. This means that researchers will be enlisted in partisan causes and, in view of the policy implications coupled with the indeterminancy of their findings, they will be in a particularly vulnerable position for political attack.

In view of these costs, what will be the "payoff" for the society? Will this nation make wiser policy decisions as professors become more centrally involved in policy? Not necessarily. Although social scientists, like other intellectuals, historically have been fascinated with power, there is little reason to believe that they know how to use it effectively. Although intellectuals sometimes have played an important role in certain periods of U.S. history, as in the constitutional convention for example,[77] Coser's review demonstrates that their forays into the political domain usually have ended rather disastrously.[78] Merton describes the honeymoon between intellectuals and policy makers as typically brittle and short. Lasky and de Tocqueville also called attention to the limits of rule by "experts."[79] The latter believed that the qualities that are meritorious in the writer are a vice in the statesman: "the very qualities which go to make great literature can lead to catastrophic revolutions."

Even if social scientists do have more information at their disposal than the average layman, there is no calculus by which value-ladened conclusions can be derived from factual premises. For example, there is no scientific way, short of political conflict, to prove that, because black children learn to read more readily in integrated schools, the schools should be racially integrated. It also depends on who possibly will be harmed and the value one attaches to reading.

Many of the social scientists who themselves were instrumental in overthrowing the myth of the rational economic man have substituted in its place the rational social scientist acting on his specialized knowledge. Lippmann's warning is still apropos: "It is only knowledge freely acquired that is disinterested. When, therefore, men whose profession it is to teach and to investigate become the makers of policy, become members of an administration in power, become politicians and leaders of causes, they are committed. Nothing they can say can be relied upon as disinterested. Nothing they can teach can be trusted as scientific. It is impossible to mix the pursuit of knowledge and the exercise of political power and those who have tried it turn out to be very bad politicians or they cease to be scholars."[80]

How Will Universities Cope with these Problems? In anticipating how universities will react to those problems we can draw upon a wide range of sociological theory, ranging from Durkheim to Blau, and derive another proposition: *as a result of the growth in importance and scale of knowledge, research settings will become more specialized and differentiated.*[81] Social organizations tend to evolve more and more complex structures. The greater the need for knowledge, the more specialized the research system that produces and transmits knowledge will become.

Evidence of structural differentiation in universities can be seen in new activities and settings and a proliferation of professors' roles as professors have tried to combine political action with scholarship and research. Some roles permit professors to exercise *influence.* This power is in marked contrast to the traditional basis of recognition, which is *academic scholarship.* A *dual* reward system has arisen, then, based on both influence and knowledge.[82] Since influence is awarded by laymen, it is a special threat to the internal controls normally exercised by university scientists over their own colleagues by giving and withholding recognition.[83] Trying to reconcile their newfound influence and orientation to laymen with the traditional academic system, professors have developed a variety of roles that give different priorities to influence and prestige. Some of these roles are outlined in Table 2-1. In the table, two dimensions are used (Scope of Activity and Basis of Authority) to identify six academic roles.

1. Basic research scholars concerned with broad intellectual issues and rewarded by prestige among colleagues (Cell I).
2. Applied researchers and technicians focusing on specific problems, which are often more directly comparable to the interests of laymen (Cell II).
3. The scholarly critics and commentators attempting to exert a broad social influence through persuasive rhetoric (Cell III).
4. Their counterparts functioning as expert consultants within limited areas of social policy research (Cell IV).
5. The academic politicians using the university as a basis to exercise political power (Cell V).
6. The political advocates seeking to advance specific political causes, sometimes through use of pressure, force, or other non-legitimate means (Cell VI).

Table 2-1 A typology of academic roles.

SCOPE OF ACTIVITY	BASES OF AUTHORITY		
	Knowledge	Influence	Power
Broad	I Basic research (scholar)	III Social criticism (scholarly critic)	V Organized political activity (politician)
Specific	II Applied research (technician)	IV Policy research (consultant)	VI Pressure group activity (advocate)

Individuals, of course, may attempt to combine several roles, but special settings are likely to arise appropriate to each type of role, both within universities and, on a broader basis, within the society as a whole. It will become difficult for universities to effectively accommodate the range of evolving research and scholarly roles within a single structure and setting. Some of the possibilities will be explored in Chapter 6. For now, it is sufficient to note that some types of research are likely to be separated from undergraduate teaching in order to reduce the strains from attempting to perform the knowledge production and transmission function simultaneously.[84]

What Will Mass Higher Education Do to Universities?

These events can be more fully understood within the context of still another development of revolutionary proportions: the swelling enrollments in institutions of higher education caused by the needs of technology, status competition centered in jobs, urbanization and mobility, and growing egalitarianism. The universal education movement that began in the primary schools less than 100 years ago is now reaching into colleges and universities. If "mass education" is defined as the point where one-half the age group is enrolled in an educational institution, then mass education has reached the universities. The fact that college enrollments nearly tripled in the past 30 years—and in recent years they have increased four times over—amounts to a revolution in higher education.

In addition to the sheer increase in size, there has been a change in the nature of the student body. If, on the average, undergraduates seem less frivolous and more mature than undergraduates of former days, as they do to some sociologists,[85] there is also greater variability among them in commitments and interests. Preliminary reports from the Carnegie Commission Study of Higher Education indicate that skyrocketing tuition and fee charges eventually might allow only the rich and socially mobile, subsidized poor to attend college. Enrollment increases have brought academically mediocre middle-class and lower-class youths to college. Many of these youths are there because of social pressure and not aspiration for education. Given the trend toward mass enrollments as high as 70 percent of the relevant age group in the next few years, universities simply no longer can count either on selectively recruiting the academically inclined and the socially mobile who are willing to accept the university system, or simply expel "those students who don't belong." Diversified performance standards will evolve in response to the heterogeneity. Being flooded with students who are seeking neither social mobility nor a particular kind of job training, colleges will be under pressure to provide less specialized undergraduate programs, even as research work in some ways becomes more specialized.

WHAT ARE THE IMPLICATIONS FOR THE PROFESSOR'S ROLE?

Parallel events in the history of the public schools provide some ominous clues about what mass education might do to professors. The transformation taking place in colleges today parallels what Trow calls "the first transformation" that occurred in the high schools with the advent of compulsory education laws before the turn of this century.[86] Masses of lower-class children who had little intrinsic aspiration for further education were retained in this formerly elite system. A bureaucratic structure arose to accommodate the new students, bringing about devastating changes in the teachers' and the students' roles and statuses. Under a public cry for efficiency an often ill-trained army of teachers, marginally committed to teaching, was assigned heavy work loads, charged with responsibility for motivating and disciplining their reluctant charges with differing backgrounds, abilities, and interests. John Dewey's reforms, designed to individualize instruction and to promote relevance in education, were addressed to these problems but fell on deaf ears.

There are clear parallels between the first transformation of the high school and what seems to be happening in higher education today. Like the nineteenth century public schools prior to mass enrollments, colleges before World War II were select schools for a few upwardly mobile, middle-class youths studying classical education and preparing for the professions. And also like the schools, colleges today are becoming "compulsory" for many of today's college students, who have few alternatives in the labor market and who are pressured by parents and friends to enter college. The college students echo the complaints of their high school counterparts about impersonal treatment, standardization, irrelevant courses, and poor teaching.

Changes comparable to the transformations experienced by high school teachers may be in store for the professor—a return to an earlier day perhaps, when professors were classroom teachers and disciplinarians, primarily concerned with motivating students and with guiding their intellectual and character development. The public is demanding that professors spend more time in the classroom, and in place of lecturing, they are now compelled to find new methods of teaching and materials that will motivate skeptical undergraduates.

Under these conditions, it seems clear that, just as research cannot be done on a part-time basis, teaching undergraduates no longer can be treated as a part-time job. Not withstanding the criticisms about universities overemphasizing research, in practice it may become more difficult to meet research obligations if these obligations are to be paralleled by the obligations for undergraduate teaching.[87] In short, in view of the challenge of undergraduate teaching on top of the demand for policy research and the other responsibilities, it is going to be more difficult for professors to handle teaching on a part-time basis as they have done in the past; pressure to separate teaching, research, and other roles and to provide specialized settings for each role, is likely to increase.

Parallel to this shift of roles, the sources of tension between professors and administrators appear to be becoming more pronounced.[88] Research professors, in particular, can develop an expertise that is valued by laymen and colleagues alike. This expertise provides them with a source of autonomy and influence within the university. At the same time administrators are evolving advanced subspecialties and live in a diverging social world from that of the faculty; it is impossible for most administrators to meet regularly with substantial proportions of faculty members—they face different pressures and have different responsibilities. Also, there are growing demands by government officials for accountability and closer scrutiny of universities, which require administrators to exercise more control over faculty members. Yet, the administrator cannot command authority solely on the basis of his claim to specialized competence, which is, at best, precarious in comparison to the expertise of faculty members. The tension between researchers and administration will limit the ability of administrators to stimulate closer coordination between teaching and research.

What Did Student Activism Do to Universities?

Student activists subscribe to a highly orthodox, uncompromising set of values. The content of these values will be discussed in Chapter 4. For our immediate purpose, it is sufficient to note that activist students tend to be rigid and dogmatic. This uncompromising moral orthodoxy is an important exception to the many parallels already alluded to between the nineteenth-century high school and what is happening in universities today. What is illuminating about activism—and the "hippie" movement as well—is that students are conforming to a new, evolving status and value system. This status system is not merely a negative reaction to money and prestige but, in a more positive sense, it represents fierce competition for moral superiority that is perhaps typical in polarized societies. Moral orthodoxy takes the form of a "moral one-upmanship" in which each person tries to express more self-righteous crusading indignation than his peers.

WHAT PROBLEMS DOES MORAL ORTHODOXY CREATE?

There is a touch of irony about this self-righteousness: well-meaning youths have created another breeding ground for a type of bigotry and moral tyranny more demeaning of human integrity than money or prestige ever were.

Some of the consequences can first be seen in the teaching roles. Manheim believed that the ability of the intellectual to transcend political party affiliation, in order to maintain his objectivity on the total situation, was the major contribution that the intellectual could make to the political process.[89] If one follows John Stuart Mill and John Dewey, the teacher can make a comparable contribution to education. His responsibility, they said, is to confront the student with challenging ideas that are *contrary* to his own,[90] to teach students to recognize what Weber called the "uncommon facts."[91] Indeed, the presentation of alternative viewpoints is what distinguishes "education" from "indoctrination."

Liberal behavioral scientists have found this mission of providing perspective to be agreeable in the past, when they faced a classroom of naive, middle-class youngsters largely from conservative homes. But they are likely to find it to be personally more distasteful to present "the other side" to steadfastly liberal and radical students when it is the conservative side that they have not examined. In an age when students evaluate their professors and otherwise play more influential roles in the university, behavioral scientists will be tempted to tell their students and their colleagues only what they want to hear. Flattered to find that students suddenly are listening to what they have been saying about the social system being responsible for social problems, many behavioral scientists will eagerly welcome students as political allies in a hostile society.

There is an analogous problem with respect to research. Not only will students elicit pressure for research along certain lines, but researchers who are competing for the students' approval of their self-righteousness will find it more difficult to maintain a balanced perspective towards members of the establishment and may feel personally degraded by associating socially with such individuals. The morally unorthodox are put into categories on the basis of their personal or political predispositions. Thus, Arthur Jensen has been censored as a bigot by colleagues because he arrived at the conclusion that some groups have lower intelligence than others (see Chapter 3). This kind of stigmatization can be as dehumanizing as Jensen's. When a behavioral scientist avoids those with whom he does not agree, he risks developing a fatal blind spot. Once researchers allow themselves to become known primarily as partisans in the ideological wars, the credibility of their research will be in even greater jeopardy than now. The public will understandably be reluctant to cooperate in projects that they have reason to fear could be twisted to support the researcher's own personal vendettas.

WHAT IMPACT DOES COLLEGE HAVE ON STUDENTS?

Having considered a range of factors (both within and outside) that can affect the university, we come to the question of what difference all of this makes to the college student. It is not possible here to review all strands of evidence concerning the separate influence of each factor, and in any event, the truth is that very little is known for sure about how college structures do influence learning, value change, or other dimensions of student life. But recognizing the difficulties, we will review at least a sample of the available evidence.

A number of studies have shown that students tend to change their attitudes, values, beliefs, and career plans during their undergraduate years.[92] In general, students tend to raise their educational aspirations during the undergraduate years. While it is true that some students drop out of college at least temporarily, or abandon all plans for a bachelor's degree, many more decide to go on to a master's degree or a doctorate. In the course of these changes students tend to shift their undergraduate fields of study; typically more students switch out of the natural sciences, mathematics, and engineering than transfer into these subjects while students are more likely to transfer into the fields of business, the social sciences, and the arts and humanities.

One of the most consistent patterns of change concerns the students' attitudes and beliefs. In general, the students tend to become less orthodox and more liberal toward religion, politics, and many other areas during the course of their college careers. They become less authoritarian, less dogmatic, less prejudiced and less politically conservative. At the same time, they tend to become more intellectual, independent, dominant, and impulsive. The student's interests and values tend to shift toward the dominant values of his college. In other words, he becomes progressively more conforming to the dominant value climate with respect to his career preferences, field of study, religious orientation, and political values. This means that a student with a particular political orientation is more likely to retain it if he attends an institution where most of the other students hold the same values.

However, it should be noted that many young people who do not attend college show many of the same changes, although to a lesser extent than do college students; thus it is not clear how much college experience itself contributes to some of these changes.

It would be very misleading to try to draw a general conclusion about the impact of college without considering the many different types of colleges involved. It has been generally concluded that differences in the impact of different types of colleges on their students' development are relatively small in comparison to the students' personal characteristics. Nevertheless, several different characteristics of universities have been found by Astin and others to be associated with the way the college affects students, including:

1. *Size*—institutional size seems to have a negative effect on the student's continuing in college and on his educational aspirations, but it seems to have a positive effect on his interest in obtaining a professional degree.

2. *Selectivity of the college*—peer groups in highly selective institutions tend to be competitive, independent, and permissive; whereas student groups in less selective colleges appear to be more cohesive and more involved in classroom activities. However, quality institutions do not necessarily provide better environments for learning than do lesser quality institutions. Students appear to develop their cognitive skills at the same rate no matter how selective or unselective the institution they attend; even the highly able student who attends a highly selective institution proceeds at the same pace as if he had attended a less selective one. However, students at selective institutions are more likely to persist in college and to go to graduate school, and they are less likely to enter education, business, engineering, physical science or medicine and teaching but more likely to major in the arts and humanities or social sciences. A student of a certain level of ability is likely to earn lower grades at a highly selective institution than he would had he gone to a less selective one.

3. *Curricula*—compared to students in the universities, those in liberal arts colleges are less likely to drop out and more likely to increase their interest in attending graduate school. Students in liberal arts colleges tend to be channeled into the arts and humanities and the social sciences and away from business, educa-

tion, and engineering. In contrast, universities tend to shift students away from majors or careers in the natural sciences and into careers in business, and they are more likely to drop out if they attend a university. Students in teachers' colleges tend to lack independence and are conscientious about attending classes, although their classroom participation is relatively passive and their personal interaction with instructors is limited. Students in teachers' colleges feel there is little academic competitiveness, that the student as an individual is somewhat neglected, and that the school spirit is poor. Teachers' colleges also tend to be somewhat repressive against student aggression and initiative, although they are relatively permissive toward cheating.[93]

Several other characteristics have been found to be associated with student conduct and academic performance, including the source of control, the predominant sex of students in the institution and the predominant race. However, the above findings are illustrative.

The research to date on the effects of college on students is subject to some very serious reservations. Most of these studies have presumed that there would be some kind of uniform effect throughout the college or university as a whole. Few of them have taken into account variations within a college or the variety of social structures that are typically found on a given university campus (such as illustrated in the Clark-Trow or Bidwell and Vreeland typologies described above).[94] Consequently, changes that occur in different directions among the different segments of a college population that can cancel out each other tend to be obscured.

One of the few attempts to identify how universities *differentiate* different students was reported by Selvin and Hagstrom in the course of their study on the determinants of support for civil liberties.[95] They found wide differences in the support of civil liberties among students in the different disciplines. Men in the social sciences and humanities were about twice as likely to be highly libertarian as those in engineering, education, and business administration. The physical sciences and life sciences fell between these extremes. The libertarianism of the women was less influenced by their choice of major, although they were more affected by certain nonacademic aspects of university life, notably the place where they lived. Students whose major subject was education were among the least supportive of civil liberties. The authors concluded that, although there was a strong selective process operating, what students learned in their courses partly accounts for these differences. There was some evidence of accumulated learning, although the differences were not large.

HOW DO SCHOOLS AND COLLEGES DIFFER
FROM OTHER ORGANIZATIONS?

We have been assuming that there are many similarities between schools, colleges, and other types of organizations and, therefore, that concepts conventionally used to describe organizations in other fields, such as hospitals, prisons, and factories to mention a few, can be profitably applied to educational organizations. The similarities *among* educational organizations and *between* them and other types of organizations stem from their common underlying structural characteristics, that is, how members are recruited, the degree of centralization and standardization, diversity of the goals, the division of labor and the other characteristics considered in this chapter. Therefore, *it would be far more meaningful to classify educational and other types of organizations on the basis of variations in these structural characteristics than according to the conventional labels, "hospitals," "colleges," "universities," "high schools," or "elementary schools."* For example, a large high school, a state college, and a general hospital might all have very similar authority structures, even though they might have very different types of goals. Only by concentrating on these common structural characteristics can general theories of organization be developed and utilized to help explain educational problems.

Are Education Organizations Unique in Any Respects?

But, we do not want to leave the impression that there are no unique qualities about educational organizations. They do perform some unique functions that separate them from many other organizations. Therefore, it may be instructive at this point to consider several of these unique aspects.[96]

First, education is a service that deals directly and intimately with people. Schools and colleges try to do things *to* people as well as *for* them. This can produce tension, especially when students have no choice in whether to attend school. Also educators must share their authority over the student with parents and other groups who often disagree among and between themselves about the proper course of action and the proper policies.

Second, the development of "critical attitudes" is a central part of most educational philosophies, especially in some of the more specialized types of institutions. The public *expects* some objectivity of the public school system as well. This analytical attitude, supported by ideologies of academic freedom, occasionally becomes aimed toward highly valued aspects of the society. In this way schools and colleges, sometimes inadvertently, encourage pupils to revolt against certain aspects of the established order.

Third, there is often widespread disagreement over which standards and procedures should be used to evaluate the success of educational organizations. Businesses are judged on the basis of their size and profit, hospitals on their recovery rates, and prisons and drug centers on the recidivism of their clientele. But the policy statements about "career training" or "good citizenship" issued by schools do not establish firm criteria for the measuring success of schools. It may take years in order to determine whether, and in what direction, students have changed their skills or attitudes as a result of their schooling, and even then they will have been simultaneously influenced by so many different forces that it is hazardous to attribute the change specifically to the particular curriculum, method, or type of school.

Fourth, a large share of the schools and colleges in this country are publicly controlled. Public-school administrators have almost no legal status, and their job is subject to the school board's pleasure. Their weak official position puts administrators in a vulnerable position with respect to special interest groups in the community and sometimes compels them to use subterfuge.

Fifth, the staffs of schools and universities are professionally trained at relatively high and homogeneous levels, and professors and teachers have as much education as the chief administrator of the organizations. Their level and type of training—together with legal tenure and support from professional organizations and the fact that their work situations (behind closed doors) do not easily permit close supervision—can give the teaching faculty a high degree of autonomy. In addition, professors and teachers are trying to organize in order to further improve their professional status.

Finally, the physical structure of schools and many universities makes them a somewhat special case. Unlike many organizations, such as hospitals, the school and college are parts of a system of units, physically dispersed throughout the community and state; many universities are part of a state system. The physical remoteness of the controlling boards and administrative officers compounds problems of communication and control.

Taken one by one, perhaps, many of these characteristics are shared with one or another type of organization, such as hospitals or social work agencies. But few organizations have precisely the same *combination* of characteristics. Therefore, while organizational theory can be useful for understanding educational problems, caution must be exercised in drawing direct parallels from noneducational organizations.

CONCLUSIONS

Universities have grown in size, in extent of diversification, and in number of responsibilities. This growth reflects the vital role that knowledge has come to play in the economy. Their new responsibilities have thrust universities into the midst of social issues that in turn are creating a new crisis for higher education. Professors are conducting research that has serious policy implications; they serve as consultants; and they sometimes lead social action groups and political causes. But the university is ill-adapted for many of these activities. Its commitments to *produce* knowledge and to put it to practical use compete with its traditional responsibility to *transmit* knowledge to more and more students. Professors have assumed so many responsibilities that it is doubtful that all of them can be achieved within the university.

The need of universities to establish *priorities* among their responsibilities often has not been clearly recognized and, in fact, it has been deliberately obscured by apologists attempting to demonstrate that teaching and research are complementary and compatible functions. It is true that research can contribute to the teacher's technical competence in the classroom, and conversely, teaching can help guide research and offset the excessively narrow focus that is required for much research. However, these functions can be fulfilled simultaneously only under ideal conditions not present in most universities. In practice, research must compete with teaching for time, resources, and recognition. At present, it is left to the individual professors to work out personal compromises, but in the long run, institutional solutions must be found in the form of new roles and more role differentiation within universities. These solutions will be discussed in Chapter 6.

REFERENCES

1. Clark Kerr, *The Uses of the University*. Cambridge: Harvard University Press, 1963, pp. v–vi.

2. *Ibid.*

3. *Standard Education Almanac*. Los Angeles: Academic Media, 1970.

4. *Ibid.*

5. Kerr, *op. cit.*

6. *Ibid.*, p. 20.

7. Robert M. Hutchins, *The Learning Society*. New York: Praeger, 1968.

8. C. P. Snow, *The Two Cultures and a Second Look*. New York: New American Library, 1964.

9. Edward Gross and Paul Grambsch, *University Goals and Academic Power*. Washington, D.C.: American Council on Education, 1968.

10. Burton R. Clark, "College Image and Student Selection," in *Selection and Educational Differentiation*, T. R. McConnell, ed. Berkeley: Center for the Study of Higher Education, University of California, 1960, pp. 155–168.

11. Burton R. Clark, *The Distinctive College: Antioch, Reed, and Swarthmore*. Chicago: Aldine Publishing Co., 1970.

12. Robin J. Pardini, "A Problem for Every Solution: Perspectives on the Study of University Administration," *Journal of the Society of Research Administrators, 4,* Summer 1972, 6–27.

13. G. L. Anderson, in T. Lunsford (ed.), *The Study of Academic Administration,* Boulder, Colo.: The Western Interstate Commission for Higher Education, 1963, p. 17.

14. Herbert H. Stroup, *Bureaucracy in Higher Education.* New York: The Free Press, 1966, Chapter 4.

15. Thorstein Veblen, *The Higher Learning in America: A Memorandum on the Conduct of Universities by Businessmen.* New York: Huebsch, 1918, pp. 77–78.

16. Charles Page, "Bureaucracy and Higher Education," *Journal of General Education, 5,* January 1951, 94.

17. *Ibid.,* p. 95.

18. *Ibid.,* p. 97.

19. Peter M. Blau, *The Organization of Academic Work,* New York: Wiley-Interscience, 1973.

20. J. Victor Baldridge, "College Size and Professional Freedom," *Change, 5,* May 1973, 11–12, 63.

21. Winston W. Hill and Wendell L. French, "Perceptions of the Power of Department Chairmen by Professors," *Administrative Science Quarterly, 11,* March 1967, 548–574.

22. Eliot Freidson, "Dominant Professions, Bureaucracy, and Client Services" in *Organization and Clients,* William R. Rosengren, ed. Columbus, O.: Charles E. Merrill, 1970, pp. 71–92.

23. J. Victor Baldridge, *Power and Conflict in the University,* New York: Wiley, 1971, pp. 19–20.

24. McGeorge Bundy, "Faculty Power," *The Atlantic Monthly, 222,* September 1968, 42.

25. Terry F. Lunsford, "Authority and Ideology in the Administered Community," *The American Behavioral Scientist, 11,* May–June 1968, 5–8.

26. Burton R. Clark, "Faculty Organization and Authority," in *Academic Governance: Research on Institutional Politics and Decision-Making,* J. Victor Baldridge, ed. Berkeley: McCutchan Publishing Corp., 1971, pp. 236–250.

27. T. R. McConnell, "Faculty Government" in *Power and Authority: Transformation of Campus Governance,* Harold L. Hodgkinson and L. Richard Meeth, ed. San Francisco: Jossey-Bass, 1971, pp. 100–109.

28. Walter R. Boland, "Size, Organization, and Environmental Mediation: A Study of Colleges and Universities," in *Academic Governance, op. cit.,* pp. 69–70.

29. J. Victor Baldridge, "Environmental Pressure, Professional Autonomy, and Coping Strategies in Academic Organizations," *Academic Governance, Ibid.,* pp. 508–527.

30. Burton R. Clark, *Adult Education in Transition*. Berkeley: University of California Press, 1956.

31. Burton R. Clark, "Organizational Adaptation and Precarious Values: A Case Study," *American Sociological Review, 21,* June 1956, 327–336 (quote, pp. 335–336).

32. Burton R. Clark, *The Open Door College*. New York: McGraw Hill, 1960, pp. 168–176. "The Cooling-Out Function in Higher Education," *American Journal of Sociology, 65,* May 1960, 569–576.

33. Bruce K. Eckland, "Social Class and College Graduation: Some Misconceptions Corrected," *American Journal of Sociology, 70,* July 1964, 36–50.

34. William H. Sewell and Vimal P. Shah, "Socioeconomic Status, Intelligence, and the Attainment of Higher Education," *Sociology of Education, 40,* Winter 1967, 1–23.

35. *Ibid.*

36. Robert Perrucci, "Education, Stratification and Mobility" in *On Education: Sociological Perspectives,* Donald Hansen and Joel Gerstl, eds. New York: Wiley, 1967, Chapter 4.

37. *Ibid.,* p. 115.

38. E. Havemann and Patricia West, *They Went to College*. New York: Harcourt, Brace, and Co., 1952, p. 180.

39. Ian D. Currie, Henry Finney, Travis Hirschi, and Hanan C. Selvin, "Images of the Professor and Interest in the Academic Profession," *Sociology of Education, 39,* Fall 1966, 301–323.

40. Theodore Caplow and Reece J. McGee, *The Academic Marketplace*. Garden City, N.Y.: Anchor Books, 1965, p. 107.

41. *Ibid.,* p. 114.

42. Diana Crane, "The Academic Marketplace Revisited: A Study of Faculty Mobility Using the Cartter Ratings," *American Journal of Sociology, 75,* May 1970, 954–964 and L. L. Hargens and W. O. Hagstrom, "Sponsored and Contest Mobility of American Academic Scientists," *Sociology of Education, 40,* Winter 1967, 24–38.

43. Logan Wilson, *The Academic Man*. New York: Oxford University Press, 1942 and A. B. Hollingshead, "Ingroup Membership and Academic Selection," *American Sociological Review, 3,* February 1938, 826–833.

44. Caplow and McGee, *op. cit.*

45. Lowell L. Hargens and Grant M. Farr, "An Examination of Recent Hypotheses About Institutional Inbreeding," *American Journal of Sociology, 78,* May 1973, 1381–1402.

46. C. Robert Pace, *College and University Environment Scales and Technical Manual*. Princeton, N.J.: Educational Testing Service, 1963; Frank H. Bowles, C. Robert Pace, and James C. Stone, *How to Get Into College*. New York: Dutton, 1968; and Alexander W. Astin, "Impact of College on Students," *The Encyclopedia of Education,* Vol. 2, New York: Macmillan and The Free Press, 1971, pp. 221–227.

47. Everett C. Hughes, Howard S. Becker, and Blanche Geer, "Student Culture

and Academic Effort" in *The American College*, Nevitt Sanford, ed. New York: Wiley, 1962, pp. 515–530 (quote, p. 529).

48. Burton R. Clark and Martin Trow, "The Organizational Context" in *College Peer Groups*, T. N. Newcomb and Everett K. Wilson, eds. Chicago: Aldine, 1966, pp. 17–70.

49. David Gottlieb and Benjamin Hodgkins, "College Student Subcultures: Their Structure and Characteristics in Relation to Student Attitude Change," *School Review, 71*, Fall 1963, 266–289.

50. Richard E. Peterson, *College Student Questionnaire: Technical Manual*, Princeton, N.J.: Educational Testing Service, 1965.

51. Rebecca S. Vreeland and Charles Bidwell, "Classifying University Departments: An Approach to the Analysis of Their Effects Upon Undergraduates' Values and Attitudes," *Sociology of Education, 39*, Summer 1966, 247–254.

52. Neal Gross, "Organizational Lag in American Universities," *Harvard Educational Review, 33*, Winter 1963, 58–73.

53. Kerr, *op. cit.*, p. 65.

54. Harold Orlans, *The Effects of Federal Programs on Higher Education*, Washington, D.C.: The Brookings Institution, 1962.

55. Kerr, *op. cit.*, p. 65.

56. Kerr, *op. cit.*

57. Joseph Ben-David, "Scientific Productivity and Academic Organization in Nineteenth Century Medicine," *American Sociological Review, 25*, December 1960, 828–843.

58. John A. Meyer, "The Effects of the Institutionalization of Colleges in Society" in *College and Student: A Sourcebook in the Social Psychology of Education*, Kenneth A. Feldman, ed. Elmsford, N.Y.: Pergamon Press, 1971.

59. Hughes, Becker, and Geer, *op. cit.*

60. Walter L. Wallace, *Student Culture: Social Structure and Continuity in a Liberal Arts College*, New York: Aldine, 1966.

61. Lionel J. Livesey, Jr. and Ernest G. Palola, "Statewide Planning," *The Encyclopedia of Education, 4*, New York: The Macmillan Co., 1971, pp. 397–403.

62. Ernest G. Palola, "Statewide Planning and Higher Education: Institutions at the Institutional Level," Center for Research and Development in Higher Education, Berkeley: The University of California, 1969.

63. Paul J. Lazarsfeld and Wagner Thielens, *The Academic Mind*. New York: The Free Press, 1958.

64. Herbert Maccoby, "Controversy, Neutrality, and Higher Education." *American Sociological Review, 25*, December 1960, 884–893.

65. Hubert P. Beck, *Men Who Control Our Universities*. New York: King's Crown Press, 1947.

66. Rodney T. Hartnett, *College and University Trustees: Their Backgrounds, Roles and Educational Attitudes*. Princeton, N.J.: Educational Testing Service, 1969.

67. Thorstein Veblen, *The Higher Learning, op. cit.*, pp. 77–78.

68. John J. Corson, *Governance of Colleges and Universities*. New York: Mc-Graw Hill, 1960, p. 58.

69. Hartnett, *op. cit.*, p. 53.

70. Theodore W. Schultz, "Education and Economic Growth" in *Social Forces Influences American Education, 60th Year Book of the National Society for the Study of Education*. Chicago: The University of Chicago Press, 1961, pp. 46–48 and Mary Jean Bowman, "The Human Investment Revolution in Economic Thought," *Sociology of Education, 39*, Spring 1966, 111–137.

71. Fritz Machlup, *The Production and Distribution of Knowledge in the United States*. Princeton, N.J.: Princeton University Press, 1962, pp. 374–399.

72. John Kenneth Galbraith, *The New Industrial State*. Boston: Houghton Mifflin, 1967.

73. Robert Edwards Lane, "The Decline of Politics and Ideology in a Knowledgeable Society," *American Sociological Review, 31,* October 1966, 649–662.

74. Robert K. Merton, "Science and the Social Order" in *Social Theory and Social Structure*, Robert K. Merton, ed. New York: The Free Press, 1957.

75. James Coleman, et al., *Equality of Educational Opportunity*. Washington, D.C.: U.S. Department of Health, Education, and Welfare, Government Printing Office, 1966; John C. Flanagan, *Project Talent: One Year Follow Up Studies*. Pittsburgh: University of Pittsburgh Press, 1966; Arthur R. Jensen, "How Much Can We Boost I.Q. and Scholastic Achievement?," *Harvard Educational Review, 39,* Winter 1969, 1–123 and Summer 1969, 449–483; and Robert Rosenthal and Lenore Jacobsen, *Pygmalion in the Classroom*. New York: Holt, Rinehart and Winston, 1968.

76. Don Price, *The Scientific Estate*. Cambridge, Mass.: Belknap Press of Harvard University Press, 1965 and Thomas Kuhn, *The Structure of Scientific Revolutions*. Chicago: University of Chicago Press, 1962.

77. Merle Curti, *American Paradox: Conflict of Thought and Action*. New Brunswick, N.J.: Rutgers University Press, 1956, pp. 9–18.

78. Lewis A. Coser, *Men of Ideas: A Sociologist's View*. New York: The Free Press 1965 and Merton, *op. cit.*

79. Harold J. Lasky, "The Limitations of the Experts," and Alexis de Tocqueville, "How Towards the Middle of the Eighteenth Century the Men of Letters Took the Lead in Politics and the Consequences of this New Development," both reprinted in *The Intellectuals*, George B. deHuszer, ed. Glencoe, Ill.: The Free Press, 1960.

80. Walter Lippmann, "The Deepest Issues of Our Time," *Vital Speeches*, July 1, 1936, quoted in Arthur Schlesinger, Jr., *The Politics of Hope*, Boston: Houghton Mifflin, 1963, p. 147.

81. Emile Durkheim, *The Division of Labor in Society*, Glencoe, Ill.: The Free Press, 1947 (translated) and Peter Blau, "Formal Theory of Differentiation in Organizations," *American Sociological Review, 35,* April 1970, 201–218.

82. Alvin Gouldner, "Organizational Analyses," *Sociology Today*, Robert K. Merton, ed. New York: Basic Books, 1959, pp. 400–428.

83. Norman Storer, *The Social System of Science*. New York: Holt, Rinehart and Winston, 1966 and Warren O. Hagstrom, *The Scientific Community*. New York: Basic Books, Inc., 1965.

84. It is expected that this trend will grow at an accelerating rate during the present decade, continuing to increase at a slower pace thereafter. This prediction is based on the premise that both teaching and research will continue to grow at accelerated rates during the decade, and that the universities will continue trying to accommodate both functions by adopting specialized structures to provide for the different requirements of each activity. The likely success of this strategy depends on other developments that we will now discuss.

85. Christopher Jencks and David Riesman, *The Academic Revolution*. Garden City, N.Y.: Doubleday, 1968.

86. Martin B. Trow, "The Second Transformation of American Secondary Education," *International Journal of Comparative Sociology*, 2, March 1961, 145–166. Elsewhere Trow notes a very clear parallel between what was happening to the curriculum in our colleges and universities about 1970 and the transformation of the secondary school curriculum in the first two or three decades of this century. In colleges and in universities, as in the secondary schools before them, the growth of involuntary attendance forced changes in the curriculum away from the intrinsic logic of the academic disciplines and toward the interests that students bring with them to the classroom. See Martin Trow, *The Expansion and Transformation of Higher Education*. Morristown, N.J.: The General Learning Press, 1972.

87. Research is not a principal occupation of many behavioral scientists within universities. A study reported by Hirschi and Zelen suggests that many of the students who aspire to be college teachers are inclined to hold radical activist sentiments but often do not subscribe to the traditional academic orientation nor expect to make a significant contribution to their field of knowledge. It can be expected that many of the most competent graduate students will find more challenge in the prospect of teaching undergraduates than in doing research, particularly with the encouragement of the doctor of arts and related nonresearch advanced degrees. See Travis Hirschi and Joseph Zelan, "Student Activism: Theoretical Perspectives and An Empirical Test," paper presented at the 65th Annual Meeting of the ASA, Washington, D.C., 1970.

88. Lunsford, *op. cit.*

89. Karl Mannheim, *Ideology and Utopia* (translated by Louis Wirth and Edward Shils). New York: Harcourt, Brace, and World, 1969.

90. John Stuart Mill, *On Liberty*. London-New York: Longmans Green and Co., 1921 and John Dewey, *Human Nature and Conduct*. New York: H. Holt and Co., 1922.

91. Max Weber, "Science as a Vocation," *From Max Weber*, H. Gerth and C. W. Mills, eds. England: Oxford University Press, 1958, p. 214 ff.

92. K. A. Feldman and T. N. Newcomb, *The Impact of College on Students*.

Vols. 1 and 2. San Francisco: Jossey-Bass, 1969 and Burton R. Clark, *Educating the Expert Society*. San Francisco: Chandler, 1962.

93. cf. Astin, *op. cit.* Also by the same author, *The College Environment*. Washington, D.C.: The American Council on Education, 1968; *Predicting Success in College*. New York: The Free Press, 1970.

94. Allen H. Barton, "Studying the Effects of College Education" in *The College Student and His Culture: An Analysis*, Kaoru Yamanoto, ed., pp. 326–330. Boston: Houghton-Mifflin, 1968 and James S. Coleman, *The Adolescent Society*, New York: The Free Press, 1961: Also Clark and Trow, *op. cit.* and Bidwell, *op. cit.*

95. Hanan C. Selvin and Warren O. Hagstrom, "Determinants of Support for Civil Liberties," *British Journal of Sociology*, 11, March 1960, 51–73.

96. Willard Lane, Ronald G. Corwin, and William Monahan, *Foundations of Educational Administration: A Behavioral Analysis*. New York: Macmillan Co., 1966, pp. 46–48.

CHAPTER 3

EQUALITY OF EDUCATIONAL OPPORTUNITY: Poverty and Racism in American Schools

"You walk into a narrow and old wood-smelling class-room and you see before you thirty-five curious, cautious and untrusting children, aged eight to thirteen, of whom about two-thirds are Negro. Three of the children are designated to you as special students. Thirty percent of the class is reading at the Second Grade level in a year and in a month in which they should be reading at the height of Fourth Grade performance or at the beginning of the Fifth. Seven children out of the class are up to par. Ten substitutes or teacher changes. Or twelve changes. Or eight. Or eleven. Nobody seems to know how many teachers they have had."[1]

"Why does a society as rich as ours, a society with a respect for formal education approaching awe, educate its citizens at less than their capacities?"[2]

The school in Western civilization is not an agency to which students come seeking traditional knowledge, as it is in preliterate societies.[3] As we have observed, it is instead an agency seeking out the "captive" student to indoctrinate him with newly acquired knowledge and values; the teacher's competence is measured by his ability to change the actions and beliefs of others. In highly interdependent technological societies people who are not trained cannot make an economic contribution and must be subsidized by the state. Schools and other agencies are assigned the responsibility to train and "rehabilitate" the individuals who do not "fit in." But morally this role is difficult to reconcile with respect for the individual and with democratic principles, and at the practical level, groups disagree over who has the right to change whom and whose values are to be inculcated.

These moral and practical questions have always plagued the efforts of schools and colleges to cope with children from the different social classes. Historically, teachers have considered it their mission to "assimilate" youngsters from minorities by holding them accountable for the majority's standards of behavior. This approach was justified with the "great melting pot" ideology that holds that in the United States, differences among immigrant groups usually disappear after a few generations, blending all Americans into a coherent whole based upon consensus on the dominant values. Scientist-educator James Conant, among others, credits the "comprehensive" school composed of all types of children as the agent primarily responsible for the rapid cultural assimilation that has often taken place throughout the nation's history.[4] The children who measured up to the universalistic standards were promoted through the educational system; those who could not (or would not) meet the standards were expelled or shunted aside in custodial institutions.

In their zeal to select the deserving students, teachers evaluated the child's "conduct," "deportment," "citizenship," and "character" as well as his academic achievement. Both the Protestant Ethic (with its stress on character training), which guided the early formation of schools, and the "mental health movement" (with its "whole child" philosophy), that dominated schools during part of this century, legitimated the right of schools to regulate the ethics, etiquette, personal appearance, and moral and religious values of children. Even those children who passed the scholastic tests might fall down on the latter criteria. These were quite often the children from ethnic minorities and lower-class homes.

However, although lower-class children have always posed academic and moral problems for the schools, only in recent years, with the "war on poverty" and growing racial tensions, have these problems been recognized as a critical *national* concern. Lower-class groups have never been so powerful nor so vocal. The superiority of the middle-class value system has never been so seriously challenged. The melting-pot theory has been discredited, as it has become apparent that many ethnic enclaves continue to thrive in the major cities after many generations. Whereas schools were seen primarily as a source of *upward* mobility, it has become clear that at best there is room for only one out of four lower-class children to move up in the social class systems. Thus, in effect, schools functioned as "sorting and selecting agencies," determining who would and who would not be socially mobile.[5] The authority of the schools to make that judgment, to impose the dominant values on all children, and to set achievement standards that favor middle-class children is being openly challenged.

This chapter deals with some of the issues that have arisen from these developments. Some social-class differences will be briefly described, and then we will consider the evidence pertaining to unequal opportunities in education. The way that certain organizational characteristics of schools can aggravate or perhaps help to alleviate the problems of poverty and racism in the schools will also be discussed.

WHAT DO THE CRITICS SAY ABOUT THE SCHOOLS?

Growing intolerance toward the posture that schools traditionally have taken toward lower-class children has plunged educational institutions into a bewildering swirl of ideological attacks from organized lower-class groups, social scientists, and romantic critics.

What Is the Case Against Low-Income Schools?

Kohl uses two poems written by school children to illustrate the "irrelevance" of schools for many lower-class children.[6] One is an innocent description of how "shopping with Mom" makes the child and her mother closer to one another; the other is a description of the "pitiful cry of junkies" as they pass dope on the streets while "the cops pass idly by." The first poem was accepted by the school paper. The second was rejected on the grounds that the child could not possibly know what a junkie was and that other children would not be interested in such a topic anyway; besides, it didn't rhyme properly and the meter was poor. Kohl charges, "We have only to convince ourselves that a lie will be 'better' for the children than the truth, and we will lie."

Another critic contends that the problems stem from the fact that schools are incapable of dealing with human variety. They are forced to deal with children as a homogeneous mass, handling all situations uniformly.[7] Goodman sees the whole process of conventional education as "brainwashing."[8] Silberman calls the schools "grim, joyless places." "It is not possible to spend any prolonged period visiting the public-school classrooms," he writes, "without being appalled by the mutilation of spontaneity, of joy in learning, of pleasure in creating, of sense of self. . . ." The fault, he says, is that nearly all grade schools treat children as miniature adults.[9] Still another author, Farber, in his book, *The Student as Nigger*, says, "And it's not *what* you're taught that does the harm, but *how* you're taught. Our schools teach you by pushing you around, by stealing your will and your sense of power, by making timid square apathetic slaves out of you—authority addicts."[10]

Kozol, author of *Death at an Early Age*, candidly subtitles his book, "The Destruction of the Hearts and Minds of Negro Children in the Boston Public Schools." Drawing upon his experiences as a teacher in a Boston school, he describes the authoritarianism and malicious irrationality of genteel middle-class teachers and administrators who seek to impose their misplaced values on helpless children.[11] His book opens with a passage about Stephen, an eight-year-old, who sometimes talks to himself and at other times laughs out loud in class for no apparent reason. He is a mild and unmalicious child, but he cannot do any of his homework very well. His math and reading are poor. In the third grade he was in a class that had substitute teachers much of the year. Stephen often came to school badly beaten, but he was more concerned about hiding his abased condition from his teachers than he was in escaping from it. However, nobody complained about the things that happened to Stephen. He had no mother or father; he was a ward of the state. Although Stephen did poorly in school work, he was a fine artist, according to Kozol. However, his art teacher constantly rebuked him because his paintings were not neat, orderly, and organized, but were often casual, messy, and somewhat unpredictable. Most of all, he seldom followed the instructions he had been given to produce "real drawings." After Kozol took Stephen to tea at the home of a Cambridge friend, he was forbidden by the principal to "take further risk" of driving a child home. The reading teacher told him that he must learn that he could not teach the children if he was going to be in a position of a friend, and that a parent or onlooker might wonder why a normal man should take a peculiar interest in a particular child. When Stephen swore at a substitute teacher, he was suspended, but he kept coming back to school, hoping to be admitted to class. The reading teacher "kept her fingers crossed" in hope that he would go away.

In still another descriptive critique, Kohl reported a revealing incident concerning Robert. When Robert stopped coming to his music and art lessons, Kohl inquired about him from the guidance counselor and was told that Robert was a "bad boy, not the kind we want here." Kohl writes,

"Then she drew close, pencil in hand, and said: 'You know we're very good to . . . here in school.'

"She hastily wrote 'Negroes' on her note pad, then rubbed it out as ears perked in the office and eyes rolled at her unperceived. 'But Robert is just not our type of boy; he doesn't fit in.' "[12]

One of the most careful observers, Friedenberg, chastises the schools for denying students the right to go to the bathroom without a pass and the privilege of determining how they will cut their hair or wear their clothes, and for their arrogance for presuming the right to inflict personal punishment.[13] He condemns the school for being basically contemptuous of the students, for neglecting their real characteristics as human beings, and for being indifferent to their needs and feelings as individuals. "In the blandest possible way," he writes, "they have been pushed around." He adds that they have been pitted against one another, seduced with little awards of leadership, and spanked for displaying reasonable ardor. "If this is not enough . . . young people are ruining their chances with their record in school. The record is being very carefully kept."

In city after city the critics level their sights and take aim on the schools. Hardly anyone in the nation's capital, says Susan Jacoby, reporter for *The Washington Post*, wastes time quibbling over whether the Washington public schools are really as bad as the critics say they are. "The school system has been declared a failure by white families who have fled to the suburbs in more massive numbers than in any other American city; by middle- and upper-income Negro families, who are enrolling their children in private schools at a rapidly increasing rate; and by poor Negroes, who are becoming increasingly vocal in their outrage at the deteriorating public schools they do not have the money to escape."[14] And similar complaints can be heard in less racially impacted cities like Chicago, which one writer declares is a "legacy to an Ice Age."[15] Sociologist Philip Hauser characterized the Chicago system as "a giant of inertia, inequity, injustice, intransigence, and trained incapacity."[16] Reputedly, from journalistic accounts, many principals in that system have discouraged PTA activities by banning evening meetings. At some schools it is reported that teachers have been told that they may not, even on their own time, belong to community organizations without their principal's permission. Even the telephone numbers of Chicago schools have been unlisted at times, and one West Side kindergarten teacher recalls that when she mentioned to her principal that a visiting mother had observed that there were 57 children in the class, the principal shouted, "Parents have no business in your room!" Teachers say that the premium in Chicago is placed on not presenting problems to the person above, and in many classrooms the prime objective is to maintain an atmosphere of control, not to teach. There is reportedly an unwritten rule that a teacher should flunk no more than three percent of her students. "You have to keep them moving," says a first-grade teacher at an inner-city school, "or you destroy the image."[17] The *median* reading level of the eighth-grade class in one year was at the fifth-grade level, and many students ranged as low as the second-grade level.

What Can Be Said For the Other Side?

However, some social scientists have taken exception to this dismal view. Robert Havighurst, himself an author of a controversial and critical study of the Chicago public schools, accuses the critics of making exaggerated statements, of being what he calls "nonresponsible," that is, for making statements that are probably not true, but in any case are easily misunderstood and misinterpreted.[18] Chiding *The New York Times* for a headline, "City Pupils Losing Ground in Reading and Arithmetic," he complains that *The Times* did not point out the fact that almost 300 of the 650 elementary schools had reading averages for their second grades of 3.0 or higher—three-tenths of a year above the national mean. Nor did *The Times*, he says, report that 44 elementary schools had reading scores for their fifth grades averaging 7.0 or more—1.3 of a year above the national average. As noted in Chapter 1, Havighurst's own survey of public schools of Chicago identified four types of schools in the inner cities, only one of which met the conditions usually described by the critics. Certainly, he says, not all poverty schools were of this type. Havighurst maintains that big city schools are doing a better job than ever before of educating the kind of children who come to school "ready and eager to learn." Public schools, he says, "are probably doing as well, in their sphere, as our local government, police traffic departments, welfare departments, church federations, and other civic and municipal groups." Many of the vocal critics of the big city schools, he charges, "have a naive faith in what the school can accomplish when it is not aided by the family."[19]

DO SOCIAL CLASSES EXIST IN THE UNITED STATES?

Before continuing with these indictments and the defenses, one might ask whether it any longer makes sense to talk about "poverty schools" in view of the fact that the United States has become a remarkably affluent society in recent years.

Is the Lower Class Still a Significant Part of the Economy?

The "other America," as MacDonald calls it, still does constitute a very large segment of this country.[20] While it is true that the income of the working class as a whole has been rising, many low-income people have not experienced these increases, and moreover, the income of the professional-managerial group has been rising at a much faster rate. The proportion of families and individuals with personal incomes below $3,000 has declined from 50 percent in 1929 to only 10 percent in 1972. Nevertheless, there are still more than 5 million families today (representing about 20 to 30 million individuals) with incomes below $3,000. They constitute 10 percent of all families in the U.S. but they receive only two percent of all income. The 20 percent of the families with the lowest incomes receive less than six percent of all income.

According to a 1970 study for the Committee on Economic Development:

- As measured by the official criteria of the Social Security Administration for subsistence income ($3553 for a nonfarm family of four), the absolute number of poor declined from 40 million in 1959 to 25 million in 1968. But, measured in relative terms, there has been no decline in poverty in the past 20 years. In 1947, for instance, the bottom 20 percent of the country's population received 5 percent of the total income. By 1968, this share had increased to only 5.7 percent.

- Of the 13 million poor who live in metropolitan areas, two-thirds are white and one-third is black, Puerto Rican, Chicano, Oriental or American Indian. In the central cities, though, the nonwhites account for nearly half the poor, and their proportion is growing fast. By 1985, the number of whites in central cities will have actually declined, while the "poverty-prone" nonwhites will have almost doubled, leaving them with absolute majorities in Chicago, Philadelphia, Detroit, Cleveland, St. Louis, Baltimore, Newark, Oakland, and New Orleans.

- Within ghetto areas of the major cities perhaps 60 to 70 percent of the families earn less than enough to maintain a minimum decent standard of living. These poor families account for double the number of poor families whose male heads work sporadically or are unemployed.

- Hardest hit are the 5.4 million children who account for 42.2 percent of the urban poor. Undernourishment, which exists in 63 percent of poor families, can cause brain damage. Also, growing up in chaotic families, poor children get little of the tactile or mental stimulation necessary for creating the curiosity that makes for success in the school.

- Roughly half of the poor are young. They will be flooding the labor market so fast in 1975 that the Department of Labor expects 25 percent more 16- to 19-year-olds looking for jobs than in 1965—and 50 percent more black youths. This will happen at a time when blue-collar positions for which they will be competing will be opening up at a rate of about 15 percent a year. Consequently, the jobless rate among teenagers in big-city slums is over 30 percent. In other words, there is a very real possibility that many, even most, of the children of the poor will become the fathers and mothers of the poor.

- Over half of the nonwhite children under 18 in this country live in poverty, as compared with 15 percent of the white children, making the proportion of nonwhite children in poverty four times that of white children. The white families also have been escaping from poverty at a faster rate. However, since the white population is almost eight times as large as the nonwhite population, the number of white children classified as poor is larger than the number of poor nonwhite children— about 9 million as compared with about 6 million.

Differences in Values

These variations in economic class are reflected in a variety of value themes associated with the different strata. Although it is illuminating to understand these differences, as far as they exist, it would be a mistake to exaggerate the importance of value conflict. Basically, the differences between the classes in this country, and the ensuing struggles, reflect differences in power, not values. Nevertheless, values do provide guidelines for solving life's problems. Since people in each economic stratum are confronted with different problems, they tend to adopt different value systems.

To understand these differences, it is first necessary to understand the dominant and variant values in the United States, which anthropologists have helped to describe.[21] The dominant values are, by and large, associated with the middle class, while the lower class and upper class have adopted variant value patterns. According to this system of classification, several alternative focal values found in America represent different solutions to five major types of problems that all people must resolve: (1) man's relationship to nature; (2) man's view of himself; (3) the valued personality type; (4) man's relationship to other men; and (5) man's orientation to time (see Table 3-1).

Table 3-1   Dominant and Variant Value Patterns[a]

TYPE OF PROBLEM			
Man's relationship to nature	Subjugated to nature (LC)	Part of nature (UC)	Superior to nature (MC)
Man's view of himself	Good (LC)	Perfectable (UC)	Evil (MC)
Valued personality type	Being (LC)	Being-in Becoming (UC)	Doing (MC)
Man's relationship to other men	Hierarchical (LC)	Collateral (UC)	Equalitarian (MC)
Man's orientation to time	Present (LC)	Past (UC)	Future (MC)

LC=associated with the lower-class value system.
MC=associated with the middle-class value system.
UC=associated with the upper-class value system.
[a]Adapted from Table XXIX, Florence Rockwood Kluckhohn, "Dominant and Variant Value Orientations" in Clyde Kluckhohn and Henry Murray, eds., *Personality in Nature, Society, and Culture,* New York, Alfred Knopf, 1953, p. 346. To be republished by The Greenwood Press, Westport, Conn., in early 1974.

MAN'S RELATIONSHIP TO NATURE

Man can (1) feel *subjugated* to nature, (2) consider himself to be a *part of nature,* or (3) consider himself to be *superior* to his natural environment. If people feel subjugated, they are likely to adopt a "mystical" view of the world, sometimes worshiping objects of nature (such as the sun, moon, or mountains), or alternatively simply resigning themselves to whatever comes with little hope of effecting the course of events. People who feel subjugated to nature and unable to control their own destiny often turn to "other-worldly" religions for consolation. Growing interest in the occult in this country in recent years perhaps reflects an intensification of a feeling of subjugation.

At the other extreme, some people learn a sense of mastery over nature. They adopt a mechanistic, impersonal view of the world, relying upon science or magic to control the material world. The world, to them, is not an object of worship but a challenge to conquer. Several focal values dominate such cultures. First, *materialism* is often associated with this perspective, since a person's ability to master the physical world is assumed to be reflected in the artifacts he owns and the wealth he has accumulated. "Success" and "failure" are interpreted in terms of material wealth. A second focal value associated with the mastery syndrome is a high regard for *hard work*. It is thought that a person can achieve whatever he sets out to do if he is willing to work hard enough, and conversely, one's failure is attributed to his laziness. It is dignified to work hard; idleness is "sinful." Even the person's leisure time often entails hard work, whether it be sports, hobbies or club work. Finally *youth* is glorified in such cultures, as reflected in the widespread use of cosmetics, hair dye, and other evidence of anxieties about growing old. This high regard for the young is partly in deference to the greater capacity of youth for vigorous work and partly in recognition that progress will bring changes that will outmode the older generation.

As a third alternative, some people feel "at one" with nature. They are not awed or intimidated by their environment. They might be fatalistic in that they do not attempt to control the universe, but they do not feel overwhelmed by nature nor hopeless in the face of it, and when they do look to the future through fortune tellers or astrology, they are concerned with predicting what is to be rather than trying to control the future.

MAN'S VIEW OF HIMSELF

People may think of themselves as basically (1) *evil*, (2) *good*, or (3) *neither* inherently good or bad, but *perfectable*. Christianity adopted the first alternative, allowing for perfectability only through faith and salvation. "Sin" is a key problem in societies that regard man as innately bad. They tend to be morally repressive on the assumption that man's desires must be controlled. On the other hand, in societies that assume that people are basically good, people will have little sense of conflict between their moral standards and their personal desires. Such societies, therefore, tend to be permissive and to value self-expression. Finally, some people make no judgments about the innate character of men; they do not become preoccupied with either the problem of sin or self-indulgence.

VALUED PERSONALITY TYPE

Man's view of himself also determines the dominant type of personality in the society. If people are considered to be basically good, they need no further justification other than the fact that they are alive. This kind of group tends to stress the value of existence, or just "being." If, on the other hand, people are considered to be evil, they must justify themselves on the basis of their *good works*. They must be doers. Finally, if people are not assumed to be either good or bad, but capable of perfection, their status will change with stages of the life cycle; it is assumed that one will automatically fulfill his destiny in the course of maturization, and so the individual naturally evolves into a better person over the course of his lifetime. He must not merely exist but he must *become* something better than he is through the natural process of aging.

MAN'S RELATIONSHIP TO OTHER MEN

Some people are accustomed to (1) a hierarchical or *"lineal"* relationship with others, in which there is a dominant and subordinate party to the relationship; (2) others relate to each other as *equals*, that is, an equalitarian relationship; and (3) still others relate to the *group as a whole* rather than to an individual, the group welfare being the major determinant of how an individual behaves.

In the lineal society, it is expected that people will show deference to certain social positions regardless of the personality traits of those who occupy them. *Authority*—not popularity—is admired, and the elite—not the common man—deserves the esteem of others.

Equalitarian societies, by contrast, tend to stress the importance of *popularity* and willingness to conform, and value the outgoing "personality." Popularity contests, in which the opinions of all members of a society are equally important, validate the above qualities. Openness is also valued, as evidenced, for example, in picture windows, open front yards. Finally, the "common man" is elevated to a position of superiority in such cultures.

In the collateral society, esteem is based on neither the individual's personal traits nor his authority. Instead, esteem is reserved for the individuals who are most dedicated to the group's values and its welfare. They seek neither popularity nor authority but strive for respect based on their contributions to the group.

MAN'S ORIENTATION TO TIME

Finally, some people are oriented primarily (1) to the *past* and to the history of their group; (2) others look to the *future*; and (3) still others live for the *present*. Groups that worship the past are traditional in nature. They typically have achieved a high social position and look back with pride on the customs and the triumphs that brought them to their position. Because they are at the apex of the society, they hope for a future without change, or perhaps one that offers a chance to return to the past.

By comparison, the *future-oriented* groups are optimistic about continued progress in the future based on their successes in the past. As in the case of the traditional peoples, they typically have had a history of accomplishment, but they have not yet reached the pinnacle of the society and, therefore, continue to look toward the future. Successes in the past provide grounds for hope of still further accomplishments in the future. The ability to plan ahead, to *defer* one's desire to gratify his immediate needs, and to save money in order to accumulate the resources and skills necessary to achieve in the future are all admired.

Finally, the groups that are oriented to the *present* tend to be sensate, emphasizing the desirability of satisfying personal pleasures, expressing one's "self," and experiencing intense personal feeling.

How Do the Social Classes Differ?

Social scientists disagree about whether or not there are systematic differences in the values of different classes. For purposes of the discussion here, a middle ground will be taken. I believe that while social classes do not necessarily differ systematically on all of these focal values, certain alternatives are more typically associated with one or another of the social classes. For example, the American *middle* classes tend to assume that man is master of his environment. They are a self-sufficient, "this worldly," and materialistic people who value hard work and rely on scientific technology. They have learned to defer their need for gratification and are optimistic about continued progress in the future. Even credit cards are a middle-class invention, since they require self-control and ability to budget for the future. Members of the middle class also are suspicious of each other and of their own innate desires, believing that man's morals must be policed for his own good. Each person must "prove" himself, as measured by what he accomplishes during his lifetime, particularly by the material goods he has accumulated and the social status he has achieved. Children are valued because they are needed to carry on the family name. Family planning reflects the value that middle-class parents place on being able to care for a few children well. Since their actions outside the family reflect on the family name, children are held to strict codes of propriety, although children, as all people, are believed to deserve respect and dignity. Competition is brutal, although it is often polite, implicit, and subtle rather than direct and explicit.

By contrast, the lower class in America traditionally has been more subjugated because of a lack of economic resources and low social standing.

Neither planning for the future nor materialism makes much sense for a family with a low income, living in substandard housing, and suffering malnutrition and extreme economic insecurity. While they value materialistic goods, materialistic values are less accessible.

The unpredictability of a slum existence focuses the attention of its residents on the present, immediate problems that arise. Layoffs, relocation, fluctuating land values, and invasions into the neighborhood by outsiders competing for jobs and housing, all confound the future. Their energy and resources are quickly consumed in the course of day-to-day living, and therefore, there is little incentive to defer gratification or to plan ahead for an unpredictable future.

While they are accustomed to working as a necessary condition of life, work does not have the moral mystique that it does for the middle class, nor does idleness necessarily have the same connotation of sin. Such people have little need to "justify" themselves; having survived is justification enough. They often turn to "other-worldly," fundamentalistic religions for consolation. Such religions offer in the next world what cannot be achieved in this one. Although rigid behavioral codes of conduct may be prescribed, since people are not regarded as inherently evil, lower-class peoples are not preoccupied with conventional moral standards designed to protect the individual from himself. This is not to say that lower-class people are "immoral," but that they have an alternative moral system, one that is relatively undogmatic; lower-class people are not intent on imposing their moral system on others. Indulgence of sensuous desires is considered to be a natural part of living, and the ability to experience pleasure is the essence of consciousness.

Insecure with "objective goals" (such as a stable career or high income), which they have little hope of achieving, they try to find pleasures in interpersonal relationships among their friends and peer groups. The street gang is a source of social support, not merely a "means of killing time." In contrast to the subtle competition of the middle class, the lower class emphasizes direct verbal and physical aggression. The ability to fight is admired. An extended family system also helps lower-class children compensate for unstable and often unsatisfying relationships with those within the immediate nuclear family and with the outside, impersonal, middle-class world.

Street gangs are organized in rigid hierarchies in which leaders often use their power arbitrarily. Similarly, the lower-class family is not especially "democratic." The father often is an authoritarian head in the traditional lower-class home. Such families tend to be "adult centered," rather than "child centered." Since children typically are not planned and are expensive, they are expected to adjust to adult routines. Yet, because their actions are not likely to tarnish the family name in the community, they are permitted a great deal of freedom outside of the family.

We have obviously portrayed a caricature. These are only general tendencies, which are based more on speculation than systematic evidence and, in any event, should not be generalized to individuals. Moreover, it should not be assumed that lower-class individuals do not admire the middle-class values. The point is that in their circumstances it is often not feasible to try to follow middle-class value patterns. Many of the dominant values are only remotely relevant to their personal lives. Therefore, the middle-class values are not central to their own thinking.

What Implications Do Lower-Class Values Have for Schooling?

Even this brief synopsis of value differences between the classes suggests critical points of tension that are likely to arise in the schools. Schooling assumes the ability to defer gratification. It is ultimately valuable to the extent that one can reasonably expect that his education will provide him with a better occupation or a more satisfactory life style at some future date. Grades act both as a form of praise and as promissory notes that can open or close doors to economic and social opportunity. As far as grades are the former, the child must respect the teacher's opinion. But it is often difficult to convince an alienated child that he should work hard to overcome the many obstacles in his way just to win the esteem of an impersonal and alien person in authority. As far as they are the latter, grades are remote from the immediate situation. The lower-class child, uncertain about where his food will come from next month, whether the family will be able to pay the rent, or whether there will be coal in the bin next week, is scolded at school for turning in a messy paper, or coming to school late. Sharing a three-room apartment with six siblings and a television set, he is reprimanded for failure to complete homework on time.

Still another difference stems from the priority given to friendship and personal relationships in the slum neighborhoods in contradiction to the impersonal, professional "objectivity" that they find in their teachers. When the slum child turns to his friends on the playground for his personal satisfactions, he is reprimanded for "hanging around on the corner" or for "fighting on the playground" to gain recognition among his peers. The lower-class boy who may have achieved leadership within his group is seldom admired by his teachers for his status; indeed, it may be a mark against him. At the same time teachers seldom see a need to punish the backbiting gossip characteristic of admired middle-class students.

The bureaucratic rules on which the teacher's authority rests force children into a passive role that, in the case of lower-class children, deprives them of adult status they often have already earned in their own families. At the same time, notwithstanding the bureaucratic *rules*, many lower-class parents object to what they consider to be lax *supervision* and disrespect for authority characteristic of many schools. They are especially critical of the laissez-faire, child-oriented classrooms. Perhaps one reason is that the lower-class family is based on a precarious authoritarian system. The lack of discipline in the classroom challenges the adult-centered foundation of the lower-class family.

But while we have stressed the value differences, they should not be exaggerated. The racial conflict in recent years, as well as much of the criminal activity in the ghettos, occurs because many individuals in the lower class *do* subscribe to middle-class values and resent being excluded from the material and other benefits of the middle class. A growing number of lower-class people refuse to be simply resigned to their condition and are determined to alter their position in life, but often lack either the necessary assistance or the skills to do so. Moreover, as we shall see in the next chapter, the middle-class values are going through an important transformation with the growing influence of the "counterculture."

DOES SCHOOLING MAKE A DIFFERENCE?

My purpose to this point has been to describe the social class system in order to lay a foundation for some of the tensions in the schools and help to understand the reasons for differences in educational opportunity. But before proceeding to describe the magnitude of these differences, we should first consider how much the success of lower-class children in school pays off and how much they might be handicapped by a lack of formal education.

Unfortunately, most social scientists who have researched this issue have been preoccupied with the question of social mobility and, therefore, have interpreted the issue almost exclusively in reference to whether education enhances the individual's job prestige and income. There are, of course, many other plausible effects of schooling on individuals that might be equally important, such as the influence of schooling on the student's personal values, his uses of leisure time, and the like, as discussed in Chapter 1. However, the available evidence forces us to confine the discussion to the effects that schooling has on vocational success, on which there is extensive evidence. Specifically, we shall concentrate on two implicit aspects of the general question: (1) How important is formal education for occupational success? (2) How does socioeconomic status affect access to formal education?

Does Education Determine Occupational Success?

Occupational success can be estimated from both the individual's occupational status and his level of income. Most of the evidence is based on the *amount* of schooling rather than the quality or type of school attended.

EFFECTS ON OCCUPATIONAL STATUS

There is now nearly conclusive evidence that schooling has a modest, positive effect on occupational status. Using a sample of males 20 to 64 included in the U.S. Census, Blau and Duncan reported that educational level was one of the most important determinants of occupational achievement.[22] They also demonstrated that the more educated the parent, the more educated the child and the higher his level of occupational achievement, indicating that schooling affects social status indirectly through one's family as well as directly. A study of Wisconsin high school graduates reached a similar conclusion.[23]

It should be noted that although the correlations are *relatively* high (approximately $r = .50$), educational attainment accounts for only one-fourth of the variance in occupational attainment in the above studies. In fact, Berg contends that the correlation between formal education and job success has been grossly exaggerated by educators and social scientists.[24] He reports that the relevance of formal education to the advancement of civil service employees was relatively low at all levels (tau $= .34$); and more important, the higher the grade at which the better-educated employee entered the government, the less relevant his education would be for his promotion prospects. For example, half of the men filling one technical, complicated, high-level civil service job had no formal education beyond high school. He concludes that schools are too diverse to permit inferences about how formal education will affect life chances. From the standpoint of the individual, schooling is no guarantee for occupational success. Nevertheless, it can improve his chances somewhat.

EFFECTS ON INCOME

Similarly, it is well known that persons with more schooling receive higher earnings throughout their lifetime.[25] The worker with one to three years of high school can expect to earn $37,000 more than the worker with an elementary school education, and the high school graduate can look forward to a $94,000 advantage over his elementary school counterpart. Also, within occupational groups, income rises as education advances. Two economists studying a representative sample of males suggested that the number of years an individual spent in school has a significant and strong association with his earnings, which is in addition to the apparent effect measured by achievement tests.[26] When Hanoch employed stringent statistical controls on socioeconomic background he also found a strong correspondence between schooling and earnings.[27] After Dennison and others made adjustments to compensate for original differences in ability, motivation, and social class, for example, they estimated that about 60 percent of the differences in income was the result of schooling.[28] Again, schooling is certainly not the only factor involved, but it is a persistent and important factor nonetheless.

A number of these studies also substantiated that the better schools, in particular, have fewer dropouts and higher student achievement, both of which are related to higher earnings and greater economic opportunity. Even after adjustments have been made for individual ability and other intervening influences, the influence of schooling persists.

Nevertheless, these findings, too, have been challenged.[29] After reviewing available research findings, Jencks and his associates concluded that the cognitive skills taught in schools have very little association with income. They find a high degree of economic inequality among those who score high in standardized achievement tests in the general population. They estimate that eliminating qualitative differences between elementary schools would reduce the range of scores on standardized tests in sixth grade by less than 3 percent, and desegregation and eliminating tracking would raise black elementary school students' test scores by a few points at most. According to them, the outcomes of school seem to depend almost entirely on luck and the characteristics of the entering children, especially their personalities.

THE ACHIEVEMENT OF MINORITY GROUPS

The evidence can be used to support two contradictory conclusions, depending upon how one places the emphasis. It boils down to a matter of perception—is the water glass half-empty or half-full? First, the modest correlations between schooling and both occupational achievement and income can be taken as evidence that schooling is an important factor in one's social mobility. The Jencks analysis seriously underestimates the effect of educational skills and cognitive achievement on income by failing to control for region and other sources of variation, and by emphasizing the *unexplained* part of the problem. In fact, educational level is the strongest measurable characteristic (other than age) in determining income levels. Granted that a large part of the difference in income is not explained, correlations that explain from one-fifth to one-half of the variation are not bad for the social sciences. Moreover, Jencks' analysis was limited to variations among individuals. Group inequities were virtually ignored. Yet, as will be noted later, there is evidence that schools have their chief impact upon poor children.

Second, looking at the "slippage" between formal education and subsequent achievement, it is clear that schooling is no guarantee for occupational attainment. The positive correlations are far from perfect and, as a matter of fact, *most* of the variance in occupational status cannot be explained by educational attainment, and years of schooling is only one of many variables that must be used to account for occupational income.

Why is there not a greater assurance that formal education will lead to occupational success, especially for the poor? Three possible explanations are that (1) many individuals do not have the necessary personality and social skills; (2) teachers have not been able to adequately train many children, especially children from low-income families and members of minorities, with the necessary skills while they are in school; and (3) many people are discriminated against in the labor market.

Cohen endorses the first explanation. He questions the general assumption that has prevailed in this country since the late nineteenth century, that is, that minority group members can overcome their status handicap by attending school.[30] This would be true only if adult social and economic status were determined on the basis of standards similar to those used to evaluate school performance: intelligence, order, discipline, and respect for authority. Moreover, it is not entirely clear that schooling has "worked" even for immigrants who arrived from Europe around the turn of this century. The fragmentary and sketchy body of evidence suggests that, in the first generation at least, children from many immigrant groups did not have an easy time in school. Pupils from these groups were more likely to be retarded than their native white schoolmates, more likely to make low scores on IQ tests, and they seemed much less likely to remain in high school. This was as true in the 1920s and 1930s as during the first part of this century. Cohen concludes that assimilation of immigrants into American society may have been more directly the effect of their *contact* with urban American society (and presumably their social skills) than with what the schools teach.

Welch prefers the second explanation. Noting that low returns from schooling persisted for blacks at least until the last decade, he concludes that, to a Southern rural black between 1920 and 1960, schooling was a poor investment. A nonwhite with no schooling could expect to receive 31 percent of the income of a similar white, but school attendance for nonwhites increased income at a rate of only 38 percent of the corresponding increase for whites.[31] Returns to blacks schooled in the 1920s and 1930s were so low that, relative to whites, black income fell as school completion level rose.

However, according to Welch, recent evidence shows that returns, as a fraction of earnings, for blacks schooled in the 1950s and 1960s exceed returns to whites. These estimates imply that income gains that were earlier realized by whites as average educational levels increased are now being realized by blacks.

Welch dismisses the discrimination explanation, that is, that discrimination against blacks is now occurring less frequently than before, on the grounds that explanation does not adequately account for comparable changes in the white sector. Instead, he attributes much of the shift to the improved quality of schooling for blacks in recent years. For example, in the segregated South important black-white differences in enrollment, attendance, and expenditure patterns have diminished as have black-white expenditures (and achievement test differences) in the North. If Welch is correct, it would mean that in the future formal education will become an even more important avenue of mobility for minority group members than it has been in the past. Their access or lack of access to schools and colleges will be the critical link in their ability to improve their social status.

However, there is reason to question Welch's optimistic assumptions that improved academic skill on the part of minority group members will be justly rewarded. The connection between *academic test achievement* and occupational attainment is even lower than the correlation with *years of schooling.* At best, academic achievement accounts for no more than one-fifth of the variance in occupational attainment and it accounts for no more than a third of the variance in years of schooling. Indeed, from an extensive review of the literature, one researcher concluded that when the number of school years completed is held constant, studies show little relationship between accomplishments in many areas and the individual's grades or test scores in academic skills.[32]

This leaves us with the third explanation—the possibility that job discrimination is at the bottom of the problem and the changes that have been occurring. To the extent that discrimination is involved, improvements in the academic quality of low-income schools will not in themselves necessarily lead to greater economic opportunities for children from low-income families. This interpretation rests upon a very different theoretical model than do the other two models. The second and, to some degree, the first explanations (which assume that employability is based on the quality of one's education and socialization experience) are part of a more general *functional* model.[33] The premises of this model are (1) that formal education provides the training necessary for the skilled jobs, and (2) that individuals are rewarded for their skill (or penalized for lack of skill). However, available evidence does not provide much support for this model. Regarding assumption (1), the educational level demanded by employers has gone up far faster than the technical skill requirements of jobs would require. Generally speaking, organizations do not force their employees to use their full capacity of skills because of informal controls, "red tape," empire building, and norms against "rate busting." Formal education requirements, in other words, do not merely reflect an objective assessment of economic demand. Regarding assumption (2) it has already been pointed out that better-educated workers are not necessarily more productive; in most cases, they are less productive.

The argument that employability is based on discrimination is a specific application of another model, the *conflict* model. From the standpoint of this model, education is used as a criterion for entry into a status group. Levels of education are raised in order to exclude people who have other social characteristics usually associated with a low level of education; but if some members of lower status groups achieve disproportionately high levels of education, they might be excluded on still other grounds (e.g., nationality, race, or religion). The basis of entry into an occupation and subsequent promotion, in other words, is power; education is only a strategic barrier used to control entry. Collins has made a convincing argument for this interpretation by pointing to evidence that schooling equips individuals with a status culture and acts as a sorting and selecting mechanism, and that employers are more concerned about acquiring "respectable," well-socialized employees than obtaining people of high technical competence.[34] From this perspective, the improved employment opportunities for educated blacks are probably the result of their advances in political and economic power in recent years rather than either a change in the quality of their schooling or upgrading of job skills demanded.

In the final analysis, then, it can be concluded that formal education plays a *limited,* if nonetheless important, role in social mobility. Reducing the barriers to formal education and improving the quality of education for lower-class children will certainly improve their chances. But more and better education is not the only answer and in itself will not guarantee equality of economic and social opportunity. This fact should not be forgotten; but neither should it be used as an excuse to ignore the problem of discrimination in education.

Does Socioeconomic Status Affect Access to Education?

Having considered the rather limited but important role that education plays in occupational success, we can turn to the question of how serious the barriers to formal education are for lower socioeconomic groups. One, there is an impressive body of research that says that the educational and occupational statuses of a boy's father present only minor handicaps or advantages in his educational attainment.[35] For example, in a survey of Wisconsin high school graduates, there were only low correlations between the person's socioeconomic status and either his educational attainment or his academic performance in school.[36] (The correlations were in a magnitude of $r = .26$ and $r = .34$). When these crude correlations were adjusted for other variables (such as the influence of "significant others" on the student's motivation) the relationships were even lower; although the influence of the significant others (i.e., parents, friends, and teachers) was itself correlated with socioeconomic status. Most of these studies show that mental ability has a more important influence on academic performance and years of schooling than does socioeconomic status, and that there is only a low correlation between mental ability and status. On the basis of these studies Hauser concluded that "although the persistence of racial differentials in academic achievement at given grade levels cannot be ignored, the prospective gain in social and economic achievement resulting from their elimination cannot be great."[37]

However, social background has more influence on educational attainment than is revealed in the correlations. In the first place, though the correlations are low, socioeconomic status does have a *persistent* effect, and socioeconomic status operates *indirectly* on achievement through the individual's intelligence, the influence of significant others, and his educational aspirations. Second, most of the evidence in the social mobility studies is based on large samples and linear correlations that obscure large variations among different subgroups, especially disparities between social classes that arise at critical turning points in the educational career, such as at the point of graduation and college entrance. Some writers have concluded that the influence of socioeconomic differences disappears after a high school graduate gets into college, but Eckland's study of a midwestern state university presents evidence to the contrary. Most of the social class measures (except family income) were significantly related to final graduation rates, especially among students who were only average students in high school.[38] Moreover, with the exception of Eckland's study, most of the studies do not include the school dropouts, who are the most educationally and socially disadvantaged group.

Finally, other methods of analysis reveal striking discrepancies in the educational attainment of different social classes. Among males of comparably high ability, in 1967, 95 percent of those in the upper socioeconomic strata attended college compared to only 65 percent of those from lower socioeconomic status homes. From his research on the Wisconsin high school graduates referred to above, Sewell reports that, the low linear correlations notwithstanding, when the sample was divided into four socioeconomic classes,

"A high SES student has almost a 2.5 times as much chance as a low SES student of continuing in some kind of post-high school education. He has an almost 4 to 1 advantage in access to college, a 6 to 1 advantage in college graduation, and a 9 to 1 advantage in graduate or professional education. In the middle SES categories the rates are consistently between these extremes: the lower the SES group, the more limited the opportunities at each higher level of education."[39]

Even when academic ability was controlled by dividing the sample into fourths according to the students' scores on standardized tests, higher SES students continued to have substantially greater post-high school educational attainment than lower SES students.

"For example, among students in the lowest fourth of the ability distribution, those in the highest SES category have a 2.5 times advantage over those in the lowest SES category in their chances to go on to some form of post-high school education. For students in the highest ability fourth, the chances of continuing their schooling are 1.5 times greater if they are from the highest rather than the lowest SES category. Similarly, in the lowest ability fourth the rate of college attendance is 4 times greater for the highest SES group than for the lowest SES group. Among the top quarter of students in ability, a student from the lowest SES category is only about half as likely to attend college as a student from the highest SES category. A similar pattern holds for the chances of graduating from college, where corresponding ratios range from 9 to 1 among low ability students to 2 to 1 among high ability students."[40]

In addition to these points, there are at least two other considerations that are usually ignored in these discussions: (1) differences in the quality and type of institutions attended by members of different social classes; and (2) changes that are occurring in the significant "screening out" points in the education system. Regarding the first consideration, students from the lower socioeconomic strata tend to attend community and junior colleges and low-status state schools, which provide them less prestige and fewer opportunities to obtain the most desirable jobs. The lower, discounted social value of these schools is not usually taken into account in the statistical calculations, although careful observers are aware of these subtleties. The second consideration refers to the changing value of a high school diploma and, more recently, of the college degree. It has been pointed out that in the short 10-year span between 1957 and 1967, the proportion of high ability lower-socioeconomic status males attending college increased from 39 percent to 65 percent, and among the low ability group from that class the progress was even more striking, from 6 to 48 percent who attend college.[41] However, these individuals are gaining admissions to college at precisely a time when college has become less of a mark of distinction. Admission to graduate school has become the mark of distinction. Simple correlations between socioeconomic status and *total* years of schooling therefore only minimize the relationship and obscure the important question: *Do lower class individuals have equal access to the levels of education and the types of schools that are of the greatest social value?* The answer is still *no.*

We shall now consider, in more detail, the magnitude of differences in educational achievement among the children from different social classes and some of the reasons to account for it.

DIFFERENCES IN EDUCATIONAL OPPORTUNITY: THE CURRENT STATUS

Francis Keppel wrote that the first revolution in American education dealt with *quantity,* providing everyone some sort of education; the second revolution underway today concerns *equality* of educational opportunity; and "the next turn of the wheel must be a revolution in quality."[42] There is reason to believe that schools have yet to come to grips with the second revolution. Evidence of continuing discrimination with respect to facilities and treatment comes from study after study. Earlier surveys by the Urban League in Chicago, NAACP in New York City, and Patricia Sexton in Detroit all reported school inequalities.[43] To assess the full magnitude of this problem, in 1965 Congress commissioned a massive sociological survey of over 4000 schools, which included 600,000 children in grades one, three, six, nine, and twelve.[44] The survey documented the extent of racial and ethnic segregation. It revealed that the gap was smaller than many critics had expected with respect to facilities; lower-class children are likely to attend schools that are only slightly inferior to schools attended by middle-class children. But there was clear evidence that they perform less well on academic tests. For example, the verbal achievement of lower-class white twelfth grade children was more than two years below their upper-class counterparts.[45] In the metropolitan areas of the Northeast they scored only in the mid-tenth grade achievement level, whereas the performance of the upper-class whites exceeded the twelfth grade norms. With the exception of pupils of Oriental family background, the average pupil from the minority groups studied scored distinctly lower on achievement tests at every grade level than did the average white pupils. The achievement differences between whites and blacks and Puerto Ricans were very great. Eighty-five percent of the black students scored below the white average. The minority group's scores were as much as one standard deviation below the majority of pupils in the first grade, and the deficit increased as the children progressed through school. At grade six, the average black child in the North was more than one and three-fourths years behind the average white child in reading comprehension. At grade nine, he was more than two and one-half years behind the average white. And, by grade twelve, he was nearly three years behind. The record of Puerto Rican performance was even poorer than that of blacks except in twelfth grade mathematics. Something happens, then, over the school years that widens the gap in achievement between whites and the minority groups. In no instance was the initial gap narrowed rather than widened as a result of intervening educational experiences.

The Education of Black Children

The education of black children in the United States represents an extreme case of a group whose historical, economic, and educational handicaps have been compounded by racial disadvantage.

YEARS OF SCHOOLING

The gap between black and white attainment has been rapidly narrowing. For example, in 1940 the difference in formal education between nonwhites 25 to 29 years old and whites of similar age averaged nearly four years (7 versus 10.7 years). By 1970, the difference had dropped to .4 years (12.2 versus 12.6 years of school). Arbitrary barriers to equal employment opportunities also were falling during the same period.

And yet, these apparent gains were not translated into equality of rewards. The median differences in the family income of nonwhites and whites increased from $1550 in 1949 to $3515 in 1970. There was a substantial increase in the income of both groups even after adjustment for inflation, but (although the gap is narrowing) the median nonwhite income still lags behind at about 65 percent of the median income for whites. In number of dollars the economic gap between the races increased.[46]

QUALITY OF EDUCATION

As already indicated, probably the major reason for this anomaly is that blacks encounter more discrimination on the labor market than they do in the schools. In addition, as was noted above, at least part of the answer might be in the low quality of education that blacks receive while they are in school. To the extent that quality is involved, a finding from the Equality of Educational Opportunity survey (EEOS) is important. It concluded that black and Puerto Rican students, compared to white students, in the metropolitan North, attend schools that are older, larger, and more crowded, with cafeterias and athletic fields also being in shorter supply. Their elementary school teachers also score slightly lower on a short vocabulary test.[47] For the nation as a whole, the survey showed that white children attended elementary schools with a smaller average number of pupils per room (29) than do the minorities (32-33). Nationally, at the high school level the average white had one teacher for every 22 students while the average black student had one teacher for every 26 students. There was a marked degree of overcrowding in "all-Negro" high schools, almost double that of whites. All-black schools were more than twice as likely to be ancient buildings, at least in Northern metropolitan areas. On the other hand, faculties of Northern metropolitan black schools were more stable, the staff was more likely to have chosen to teach there, and teacher absenteeism in Negro schools was lower than in white schools.

SEGREGATION PATTERNS

The educational prospects of nonwhite children probably will not improve much as long as large numbers of low-achieving children are segregated in poorly staffed schools. For one thing, children in racially isolated schools do not benefit from the protection of powerful white middle-class parents who are willing and able to constantly badger school officials to make continual improvements in the learning environment for their own children.

Because of federal intervention, *Southern* public education is not as tightly segregated as it was 20 years ago. Since the 1954 Supreme Court ruling against *de jure* segregation of public schools, there have been slow, but fundamental, alterations. A majority of biracial Southern school districts, especially in the border states, have begun at least token desegregation programs. According to a survey by the Department of Health, Education and Welfare the percentage of blacks enrolled in schools with a majority of whites more than doubled in the 11 states of the South, up from 18 percent in 1938 to 37 percent in 1972; the number of black students attending 100 percent black schools dropped from 68 percent to 11 percent, and over the same period the number of blacks enrolled in 80 to 100 percent black schools dropped from 79 percent to 39 percent.[48]

However, as *de jure* segregation of schools in the South has decreased, *de facto* segregation in the *North* has rapidly increased. The growing black ghettos in the major cities, combined with the neighborhood-school principle, has established an entrenched pattern of racially separate education. The problem is particularly serious at the locally based elementary level. Black children growing up in these areas have generally had far *less* equal-status contact with whites in their formative years than blacks in earlier generations.[49] The great majority of children in this country attend schools in which most of the students belong to the same ethnic group. More than two-thirds of all black pupils in the first grade attend schools that are between 90 and 100 percent black, and two-thirds of the twelfth-grade blacks attend schools that are over 50 percent black. Moreover, the average black child also has fewer middle-class classmates, that is, classmates enrolled in a college preparatory program and whose mothers have graduated from high school.

Despite the efforts of federal agencies and the courts, the situation has not shown much improvement. According to the Civil Rights Commission, all-black elementary school enrollment in most city school systems has risen in recent years. For example, 84 percent of the total black increase in 15 city school systems was absorbed in schools that were 90 to 100 percent black, and 97 percent in schools that were more than 57 percent black. In Cincinnati, Ohio, to take one case, the black elementary school enrollment doubled in 15 years, but the total of black children in majority-black schools almost tripled; in 1950, 7 out of every 10 black elementary school children in Cincinnati attended majority-black schools but, in 1965, nearly 9 out of 10 did. In Oakland, California, almost half of the black elementary school children were in 90 to 100 percent black schools in 1965, but only five years earlier less than 10 percent were.

Teaching faculties are equally segregated by race. According to the Equality of Educational Opportunity survey, black teachers rarely teach white children, but over 60 percent of the black children are taught by black teachers. This practice of assigning teachers to schools on the basis of race casts serious doubt on the validity of administrators' claims that segregated schooling patterns are entirely a result of housing patterns and beyond the school's control. The segregation of teachers is largely the product of informal and official administrative policies.

What are the Barriers to Integration? Pettigrew has identified three major barriers to desegregated education in the South.[50] Many of the same factors are also present in the North.

1. Social structure—Rural, traditional, and impoverished areas with high concentrations of Negro population resist racial change most intensely. This is a function of these areas' implanted anti-Negro traditions, of less Negro insistence, of less-structural differentiation between "public" and "private" sectors, and of greater emphasis upon ascriptive, diffuse, particularistic, and affective orientations.
2. White resistance—Apart from violence and economic intimidations, whites resist with restrictive state legislation and active *de facto* segregation through residential separation.
3. Negro insistence—The historical failure of blacks to insist on racial change also has slowed desegregation; such failure is a function of the avoidance-learning cycle of fear and withdrawal, the entrenched role of "Negro," and vested interests in maintaining Negro communities created by segregation.

Despite these barriers, however, Pettigrew sees definite indications that Southern education has entered upon a new era of more rapid desegregation. To begin with, the hard-core "black belt" areas caused by the migration of Negroes to the urban areas of the South and North are shrinking. Moreover, some of the basic values are being changed with industrial development and higher levels of education. Also, desegregation itself brings its own acceptance among many white Southerners. Where school desegregation has already taken place, the proportion of white adults favoring desegregation has increased substantially. In other words, public opinion tends to accommodate itself to new arrangements after the fact. Forced desegregation may create a temporary "backlash" but, over the long run, it can be expected to gain acceptance.

Efforts to desegregate the big city schools in the North confront even more stubborn structural barriers in the form of residential segregation patterns that are reflected in school districting policies. School districts and municipal boundaries are the major obstacles to integration in the metropolitan North. Patterns of residential segregation, which have their counterpart in socially segregated schools, produce relatively homogeneous schools. Almost the entire increase in the total black population since 1950 has been in the central cities, while most of the increase in the white population has been in the suburbs. With the exodus of whites to the suburbs, the proportion of nonwhites in the schools in many cities has increased dramatically. For example, in one 10-year period in Los Angeles, the proportion of nonwhite children in the schools increased 167 percent. Over 90 percent of Washington, D.C. enrollment and over half of New York City enrollment is nonwhite. The consequences of these patterns can be seen in Baltimore. Even though over a 10-year period twice as many white children were attending schools that also enrolled at least a few blacks, the proportion of blacks attending entirely segregated schools actually increased in the same period.

Nevertheless, there are some encouraging signs for the future. While there has been some resistance to desegregation efforts in specific places, whites have become more favorable toward desegregation over the past 30 years. Public opinion polls between 1942 and 1963 indicate that acceptance of school desegregation by Southern white parents increased from 2 to 30 percent and from 40 to 75 percent among Northern white parents. According to more recent polls, this trend is continuing. While parents in both the North and South resist plans that would put blacks in the majority, there is little evidence that a white backlash has developed in response to either court-ordered school desegregation or to the urban riots of the late 1960s.[51] The trend toward growing acceptance of integration in housing and schools continued during the period of widespread, severe urban disturbances after 1963. At most, riots and related events appeared to temporarily slow down the rate of increased acceptance of desegregation, not halt or reverse the long-range trend toward acceptance of desegregation.

HOW CAN THE DIFFERENCES IN EDUCATIONAL ACHIEVEMENT BE EXPLAINED?

It seems indisputable, then, that lower-class children do not do well on academic achievement tests, and they are often segregated in poorly equipped schools. But it remains to be seen whether these differences in achievement are caused by poor facilities, incompetent teachers, segregation, and other characteristics of the schools. Other explanations have been offered. Therefore, it will be instructive to consider various explanations that have been advanced to account for the relatively poorer educational achievement of lower-class children.

Do Some Groups Have Inherently Inferior Intellects?

For example, could not the differences in achievement be accounted for by differences in the *innate intellectual abilities* of social class and racial groups? Some social scientists believe that certain ethnic and racial groups have genetically inferior minds. The achievement test scores of blacks, they maintain, might accurately reflect the biological inferiority of black children. They contend that this also could explain why compensatory education programs have not been very successful. If this is so, it follows that schools and teachers should not be blamed.

Recently this question of the relative role of heredity and environment in the determination of human intelligence was reopened by a respected psychologist, Arthur Jensen. His article, devoted to a lengthy exposition of how the relative role of heredity and environment can be determined, concluded that heredity has a far greater role to play than environment in explaining differences between the IQ of blacks and whites.[52] Jensen based his argument on the concept of "heritability" of IQ. The fact that heritability estimates for the white population (the only group we have estimates for) are quite high (.80) means that the IQ of children can be predicted from their parents' IQs with a high degree of reliability, suggesting that IQ is inherited.

However, the fact that test achievement is systematically related to entire ethnic, racial, and class groups indicates that more is involved than variations in the biological ability and motivation of *individuals*. To prove the biological argument, it would be necessary to demonstrate that learning capacity is genetically fixed for large *groups*. This assumption, however, is hard to reconcile with the known variation within groups, and with the established fact that the intelligence of racial groups often improves within a few years after the group has migrated to a favorable intellectual environment. Moreover, even apparent biological differences are conditioned by diet. Thus, the average height of Japanese males has increased several inches over the past generation because of an increase in protein in the Japanese diet.

Studies of identical twins in similar and different social environments suggest that, at best, no more than 40 to 60 percent of the variance in educational achievement can be accounted for by IQ. Jencks estimates that about 45 percent of the variance in Stanford-Binet IQ scores in the population are related to genetic variation, about 35 percent to environmental variation, and about 20 percent to genetic-environmental covariance. This last factor represents the fact that bright children are typically raised in superior environments and thus environmental and hereditary factors cannot be unraveled in these cases.

A group of concerned psychologists ("Psychologists for Social Action") reacted to Jensen's article with a prepared statement that began:

"The suggestion that there is a scientific basis for drawing conclusions about race differences in intelligence is based on the following premises:

"1. That intelligence tests provide a reliable measure of a scientifically understood entity called 'intelligence.'

"2. That there has ever been a single black child in this country who has not suffered from some form of racial oppression.

"3. That there is a body of accurate information based on the administration of intelligence tests to black and white children under comparable circumstances.

"4. That intelligence is inherited as a fixed trait.

"5. That the science of genetics provides a basis for the definition of intelligence in terms of innate and acquired components.

"6. That hunger and malnutrition, prenatally and during early childhood, do not seriously impair and debilitate intellectual performance.

"All of the above premises are either obviously false or seriously questioned by many competent scientists working on these problems."[53]

Apparently most teachers do not accept Jensen's conclusions either, although many of them do. When teachers in one Midwestern city were asked to rank various reasons to account for the poor educational performance of their students, one out of three teachers in the inner-city schools rated "limited capacity of the students to learn" either first or second in priority of the possible reasons.[54] That may be an alarming number, but at least the majority of teachers in low-income schools see it another way. The limited-ability explanation was more likely to be used by teachers in middle-class schools, over half of whom had doubted the ability of their children. In other words, teachers used ability differences to explain individual variations in achievement within the middle class, but the majority of teachers did not explain the lower performance of entire classes in these terms.

Is Poor Motivation the Answer?

If innate ability is not the answer, can the class- and race-linked achievement differences be explained by variations among the groups' *motivation* to learn? Many teachers and other observers believe that lower-class children are often "lazy" and unconcerned about getting an education. In the previously cited study of teachers in Columbus, Ohio, teachers in lower socioeconomic schools rated their students' academic motivation lower than the teachers in middle-class schools rated the motivation of their students. They typically attributed the source of this problem to the child's family background and neighborhood.

It is often said that academic achievement is not encouraged by the lower-class children's parents and friends, that their families do not provide sustained encouragement and assistance with school work that would prod them to work, that lower-class parents do not have the necessary financial and intellectual resources to support teachers, and that they do not reward and punish their children as consistently as middle-class parents do for their child's school performance. Thus, children simply do not expect to do well in school or to go on to college. The Equality of Educational Opportunity survey (EEOS) provided some support for this thesis. Family background was more closely correlated with academic achievement level than any other type of variable considered, except the child's own sense of control over his destiny. Family background accounted for over one-third of the achievement of sixth-grade black pupils in the North.

But while teachers probably cannot rely on lower-class parents to reinforce what they do in school as much as they can rely on middle-class parents, this does not mean that lower-class parents think education is unimportant. On the contrary, several public opinion surveys during the past few years have shown that the vast majority of lower-class parents want their children to do well in school and often want them to go on to college.[55] Perhaps the main difference is that educators have not devised procedures to capitalize on these parents' interests as effectively as they have learned to use the support of middle-class parents.

To the extent that poor motivation is involved, it can be interpreted in another way. It can be argued that if children are going to be compelled to attend school, the schools have an obligation to appeal to *their* interests, to demonstrate the relevance of schooling to them. Instead of signifying the children's laziness, masses of unmotivated children serve as an indictment against the schools. The solution might be to elevate the problem of motivation to *central* priority in teaching and reward teachers for motivating pupils instead of for efficiently covering a given body of subject matter and maintaining order in the school.

Does the Fault Lie With the Teachers?

The first two explanations of poor school performance on the part of lower-class children emphasize the inadequacies of the *child*. This reflects the assumption behind much of the earlier research, which was conducted in small town schools attended by children from all social strata. The school was taken as a given, fixed element in the situation; its appropriateness was not questioned. The question then centered on why certain individuals were unable to adjust to it.

However, in recent years, two important shifts in perspective have taken place. First, attention has shifted from the inadequacies of the learner to the shortcomings of the *teachers*. As Herriott and St. John have observed, instead of asking why the academic achievement of lower-class pupils is so low, it is more instructive to ask why teachers are not more successful with these pupils.[56] Second, the preoccupation with the social class background of the individual child is being supplemented with information about the social-class composition of the *schools*.

The tendency to blame the teacher is reflected in the writing of most of the romantic critics who, as already indicated, have variously charged that too many teachers hold inhumane and disrespectful attitudes toward their pupils, and worse, that teachers often inadvertently or deliberately discriminate against or otherwise mistreat the children. Friedenberg is especially vocal on this point. He bluntly attributes the dreadful conditions of schools directly to the personal characteristics of the teachers. The urban slum schools, he contends, are run by awful people—the tyrants, the silly, the malicious and experienced teachers, and the trivial and vulnerable beginners. He states, "We are dealing here with people who have a lot of faith in punishment, manipulation, and taking orders from above." They are people, he concludes, who are "not going to be improved by instruction or therapy; they do not have good intentions; and so long as they dominate the schools, the schools are not going to be improved from within."[57]

Several different hypotheses have been advanced to account for the presumed detrimental effects of teachers, all of which stem from the middle-class status of the teachers: the "Culture-Gap Hypothesis," "Horizontal Mobility Hypothesis," and the "Self-fulfilling Prophecy Hypothesis."[58]

The *culture-gap hypothesis* holds that because teachers have middle-class origins, and because teaching is a middle-class occupation, teachers subscribe to values that differ radically from their slum-school pupils. Moreover, their middle-class professional status acts as a barrier to understanding lower-class children. Thus teachers are biased against lower-class children.

The *horizontal mobility hypothesis* asserts that teachers do not like to teach in low-income schools and, as a reward for their loyalty, inner-city teachers are promoted to middle-class schools. The lower-class schools soon end up with the less-experienced teachers who do not want to be there. A chief advocate of this hypothesis found that relatively defenseless new teachers in Chicago were assigned against their wishes to inner-city schools and eventually sought to be transferred away as soon as they had developed sufficient seniority in the system.[59]

The *self-fulfilling prophecy*, as expressed by Clark and, more recently, in a controversial study by Rosenthal and Jacobsen, maintains that children tend to achieve at the level *expected* of them by their teachers.[60] If teachers have low esteem and little hope for their pupils, the argument goes, they will teach in a perfunctory way and convey their attitudes in a variety of ways; the children will sense this and gauge their own expectations and performance accordingly.

What Is the Evidence that Teachers Are Biased?

Several studies report some evidence to support the charge that teachers are biased against lower-class children. There is evidence, dating back to Becker's study mentioned above, that the lower the socioeconomic status of the school, the greater the proportion of teachers who would want to move into a school in a better neighborhood. The Herriott and St. John study found that the lower socioeconomic status schools had less experienced teachers who also had been in the present school for shorter periods of time. Similar findings were reported in a study of the Los Angeles schools conducted shortly after the 1965 Watts riots.[61] Also, according to the Equality of Educational Opportunity survey, in comparison to teachers in Negro schools, higher proportions of teachers in all white schools would rather stay in their school. In still another instance, one in five Columbus, Ohio teachers teaching in lower-class schools wanted to move to a better neighborhood; eight percent of the teachers in middle-class schools said that they wanted to move. Nearly half of the requests for transfer in Columbus came from first- and second-year teachers, most of whom specifically requested middle-class schools. The majority of those who listed "discontent" as their reason for transfer were beginning teachers in inner-city schools.

Reservations. And yet, the charge that teachers are biased against lower-class children because of their own middle-class backgrounds must be qualified on the basis of several reservations. First, it should be noted that people in teaching come from a wide range of backgrounds. National Education Association figures indicate that one-quarter of the teachers come from farm families, and another quarter from skilled or semi-skilled homes. Seven percent have fathers in clerical sales work. Only 15 percent come from professional or semiprofessional homes and a third from families with a managerial or self-employed father. Although beginning teachers are more likely to come from white collar than from blue collar or farm families, in comparison to medical, law and dental students, they are less likely to have white collar origins.[62] Thus, while teachers *tend* to come from the middle ranges of the population, all strata are represented among teachers.

A second and related point is that there seems to be a natural selection process through which middle-class teachers tend to end up in middle-class schools and lower-class teachers in lower-class schools. The previously cited study of 500 school principals found that the lower the school's socioeconomic status, the higher the proportion of teachers whose fathers were in blue-collar occupations.[63] A tendency toward self-selection was also apparent in the Columbus, Ohio survey.[64] Inner-city teachers seemed to be more, not less, sympathetic toward the values and the problems faced by children in inner-city schools. Several examples can be cited. More teachers in inner-city schools would permit male students to wear long hair; opposed segregated staffing policies; opposed the "neighborhood school" concept if it created racial imbalance; supported busing; supported compensatory education and the policy of assigning the best and most experienced teachers to the more difficult schools; identified closely with lower-class children; and communicated more frequently with parents. In other words, self-selection seems to minimize status barriers, and a policy that indiscriminately assigned teachers from the outer-city to inner-city schools could aggravate the culture gap, notwithstanding apparent advantages such a policy might provide toward a more equitable distribution of qualified teachers, fairer promotion policies, and racial integration.

Third, sociologist Emile Durkheim believed that occupations themselves determine how people in a modern society will behave. The teaching culture probably exerts its own pressures on teachers. Insofar as travel, education, morality, and public service are encouraged among teachers, teaching probably does have a unique influence on teachers' values. On the other side of the coin, teachers are not well integrated into many communities; in many respects they are sociological "strangers" who remain outside the basic class structure of the community. Often excluded from political and community leadership positions, teachers are not necessarily the most representative members of the upper middle-class community or its value system.

Fourth, although traditionally perhaps teaching has been dominated by the Protestant Ethic that has played so vital a part in molding the values of the middle-class business community in this country, there is evidence that the teaching culture has been changing in recent years in response to the growing public concern about the problems of poverty. One study comparing the humanitarianism of teachers and social workers found that the former were more inclined to hold the *individual* rather than the society or state responsible for social problems, that they were less supportive of the idea that the family and government have a responsibility for helping individuals who were in trouble, and that they were more supportive of traditional, conservative school practices.[65] Moreover, teachers seemed to be socialized into this value system. For example, when the 16 schools in the study were grouped on the basis of the average length of experience of the teachers in the schools, it seemed that the members who were in the minority in the building had adopted the values of the majority, and that the longer they had taught in their present schools, the more their educational philosophy had changed.

But the same study revealed evidence that the teaching culture may be changing. Teachers in the inner-city had become more humanitarian over the course of the study. Initially, the teachers who were participating in experimental projects in the inner-city schools held more humanitarian values than teachers in the schools without such projects. But two years later, these differences had disappeared. Teachers in all schools had become more humanitarian. Inner-city schools have been the focus of many major government projects that have given teachers in these schools more recognition than they had in the past. Moreover, it is possible that a different type of reform-minded teacher is now coming into the profession. In any event, it is misleading to categorize teachers simply as "middle-class people," without recognizing the strong independent pressures operating on them through their own distinctive occupational cultures.

Finally, it should be recognized that teaching is only one of a large number of professions faced with disaffection from, and ineffectiveness with, lower-class clientele. Similar evidence is available about physicians, psychiatrists, lawyers, social workers, and nurses.[66] If the problem were due exclusively to the type of people in these professions, it would mean not only that more than a million individuals in this country are uniformly inept and prejudiced but that there are a similar number of these bad people in other professions. Before accepting such an indictment, it would be wise to explore other interpretations.

Does the Organizational Structure Make a Difference?

We have seen, then, that social scientists originally explained poor educational performance as being the result of the learner's inadequacies—his ability, motivation, and family background. These factors are still considered to be of great importance—especially the child's family and neighborhood situation. But today social scientists also have begun to pay more attention to the ingredients of learning that schools directly control. This includes, as we have just seen, the personal characteristics of teachers—their competence, social class background, and occupational values. In addition, it includes the *structural* and other organizational features of the educational system, such as facilities, professional norms, official policies, and the value climate established by the type of student body. We shall now consider these factors.

This brings us to a critical question, the answer to which will have a direct bearing on the lives of students, teachers, administrators, and social scientists alike. Stated cryptically the question is: *Do schools make a difference?* The term "schools" is used in a generic sense to include many different characteristics of educational organizations of all types—elementary and high schools, junior colleges, vocational schools, and colleges and universities. The question is meant to suggest that the way schooling is *organized* might affect the immediate and long-run learning outcomes. Note that the question posed in this way differs from merely asking whether "schooling" (or *amount* of education) makes a difference, which is what most of the data already reviewed actually pertains to. Educators have always assumed that the quality of education is associated with the size of classes, availability of special courses, laboratory facilities, the quality of the teacher, the curriculum, grading policies, and the like. But is there any evidence to support these assumptions?

The EEOS provides some illuminating evidence. The influence of school characteristics on students' verbal achievement was compared to other factors. Specifically, the study assessed the independent effects of each of three types of characteristics:[67] (1) attitudes of the individual pupils, such as interest in learning, self-concept, and their sense of ability to control their environment; (2) the pupils' family background characteristics, such as parents' educational level, interest, size of family, and family resources; and (3) school factors, that is, teachers' characteristics, various types of facilities, and composition of the student body. It was concluded that in comparison to the first two elements, which exerted strong effects on achievement, school factors had relatively little effect. To be more precise, the influence of the variables examined ranked as follows:

1. *Pupils' sense of control over their destiny.* It was concluded that out of all the variables measured in the survey, including all measures of family background and all school variables, these attitudes showed the strongest relation to achievement at all three grade levels (sixth, ninth, and twelfth).

2. *Home background.* Family background and attitudes accounted for over one-third of the differences among sixth-grade Northern whites, over one-fourth among sixth-grade Northern Negroes, and 40 percent among sixth-grade Puerto Ricans.

3. *Proportion of schoolmates from middle-class homes.* "Attributes of other students," the authors concluded, "account for far more variation in the achievement of minority group children than do any attributes of school facilities and slightly more than do attributes of staff." Individual achievement seemed to be facilitated when a student attended school with peers who were socioeconomically advantaged and whose parents were more interested in school success.

4. *Teachers' competence.* Teacher characteristics were more influ-

ential in explaining variations in verbal achievement than facilities and curriculum. Teachers made only about a 2 percent contribution to the differences in the achievement of sixth-grade Northern whites and Negroes, but they contributed more for Puerto Ricans (8.1 percent). Among the teacher characteristics that showed the most marked effects were educational attainment of the teacher's mother (and her socioeconomic status), years of teaching experience, localism of the teacher, educational attainment of the teachers themselves, vocabulary test scores, teachers' preference for teaching middle-class and white-collar students, and proportion of teachers who were white.

5. *School facilities.* This included per pupil expenditures on staff, volumes per student in library, science laboratory facilities, extracurricular activities, size, school location, and several indicators of quality of curriculum. Facilities and curricular measures for twelfth-grade Northern Negroes accounted for only 3.1 percent of the achievement scores. Class size and pupil-teacher ratio showed no consistent relationship with achievement.

WHAT ARE THE IMPLICATIONS OF THE EEOS FINDINGS?

In short, the study suggests that schools have relatively little effect on academic achievement. The authors themselves concluded that the quality of the school does not make a crucial difference in what pupils learn; schools, therefore, are unable to offset the child's handicap if he comes from an educationally disadvantaged family. They arrived at this conclusion for at least three reasons: (1) because minority children have serious educational deficiencies at the start of their school careers (i.e., in first grade), (2) because more variation in student achievement is found within the same school than between schools, and (3) because of the small apparent influence of either school facilities or teacher competence. Hauser is even more insistent that the effects of schools are small. He maintains that being "in" school is far more important than the school one attends, and asserts that it is misleading to be preoccupied with school quality.[68]

A similar conclusion has been stated even more emphatically by Jencks and his associates.[69] After reviewing available research findings, they have concluded that making schools more equal by improving their quality will not have much effect on equalizing educational opportunity, and that in any event, equalizing educational opportunity will not do very much to reduce poverty. As noted above these conclusions are based on evidence (1) that the quality of schools does not affect cognitive learning and (2) that academic achievement itself is not highly correlated with income. Consequently, they conclude that although school reform might be important for improving the lives of children, reform should not be expected to improve the child's life chances. They speculate about the reasons that school quality has so little effect on test scores: the greater influence of home, peers, and TV; inability of administrators to control the way students and teachers actually treat one another; and the overwhelming influences in later life that counteract whatever temporary influence that schooling might have.

Such conclusions have been used politically to support quite opposite interpretations. Racists welcomed the conclusions that the sources of inequality reside in the home, and that the school has little responsibility for them. Teachers and administrators could take comfort in the finding that the teachers and the school can do little to change students' performance and, therefore, cannot be blamed for low achievement. Advocates of school integration found ample support for their position from a subsequent analysis showing that children do better in schools that are mixed by race and social class than in segregated schools. At the same time, separatists could now argue that inferior facilities in black schools do not necessarily mean that they will get an inferior education. The conclusion that educational achievement was unrelated to the expenditure of money or to the nature of physical facilities was welcomed by many politicians and taxpayers who want to believe that all that is needed are new methods of teaching, and not more money. And finally, the conclusion that achievement is related to the child's "sense of control over his environment" was welcomed by all who want to believe that attitudes alone are responsible for learning—liberals and conservatives alike. The conservatives call it the "lack of get up and go," the liberals call it the lack of self-confidence, but in either case, the implication is the same: the problem is all in the minds of the children and can be successfully resolved by changing the individual children; there is no need to change the educational system, the power structure, or the available jobs and housing opportunities.

How Accurate Are These Conclusions?

These conclusions, if valid, could be of revolutionary significance. That students learn more in "good" schools than in "poor" ones has long been accepted as self-evident. However, the authors who dispute this conclusion have had to rely on inadequate, even inappropriate, measures of school quality. As already noted, most of the studies have concentrated on *amount* of education (schooling) rather than the *quality or type* of schools. Moreover, the available data on quality pertain to "resources," which is only one aspect of quality. Therefore, inferences about whether *schools* make a difference are dubious at best. There are several specific reasons for questioning the conclusion that schools do not make a difference:

- Three of the five major factors in the EEOS were actually organizational characteristics that could be controlled by administrators: the type of students enrolled, the type of teachers recruited, and the facilities and programs available. While perhaps none of these features by itself was as important as the child's home background and his self-conception, taken together they can have an important influence on learning outcomes.

- In the EEOS, during the time when the influence of the child's family background diminished (between the sixth and twelfth grades) there was a growing likelihood that he would be influenced more and more by what took place in the school. In another study, as children grew older, variations in characteristics of the student's peer group played an increasingly larger role in the shaping of values and aspirations; while simultaneously the importance of family characteristics declined.[70]

- A series of other studies has consistently identified school characteristics that are associated with academic achievement, for example: peer group composition, characteristics of teachers (education, race, experience, verbal ability, and attitudes toward integration), salary of teachers, composition of the curriculum (including mathematics offering), cost per pupil, number of specialists on the staff, urbanism, and geographic location.[71] Also, some studies have indicated that the type of *college* attended explains a small but significant proportion of variance in whether a student will graduate from college beyond his intelligence, rank in school, socioeconomic background, and level of occupational aspiration. Moreover, different types of colleges have different effects for students of different socioeconomic intelligence levels.[72]

- Similarly, many previous studies by economists have found that schools do appear to affect earnings far more than Jencks and his associates allow. Part of the difference might stem from their failure to control for critical variables, such as regional variations in incomes and price levels (which affect real income).[73]

- Many of the conclusions are based on the rather subjective issue of what magnitudes of difference are important. Findings presented by Jencks, for example, indicate that an extra year of elementary or secondary schooling appears to boost future income by about 4 percent, an extra year of graduate school by about 4 percent. According to these data a comparison of high school graduates and college graduates, who were otherwise identical, would show the college graduates earning about 30 percent more than their less-educated peers.[74] This is not an inconsequential difference for the individuals involved.

- Similarly, even though the quality of the school explained only 10 to 20 percent of the students' achievement scores in the EEOS, this figure means that improving schools could spell the difference between failure and success for a large number of borderline students.

- School characteristics in the EEOS had a far more important influence on lower-class than on middle-class students; the former is precisely the group whose futures rely so heavily on what the schools do because they have so little support in the home. In the South, for example, compared to the white pupils, 40 percent more of the achievement of Negro pupils was associated with the composition of the schools they attended. Therefore, it is for the most disadvantaged children that improvements in school quality will make the most difference in achievement.

- The EEOS reports high correlations between the characteristics of schools and the socioeconomic backgrounds of the children who attend them. Most writers have arbitrarily attributed all of this overlapping correlation to the socioeconomic characteristics of the children (or to other factors such as their intelligence, which are indirectly related to their social status). This approach already presumes that schools are not the overriding factor, and that socioeconomic status should take precedence in the explanation. As a result, school characteristics have not really been given a fair test.

- Linear correlational analysis used in most of the studies is an inappropriate technique for identifying the influence of organizational structure, since the extremes are obscured and washed out by small variations within the middle range. The crucial test is the differences between so-called innovative schools and typical schools.[75]

- The indicators of school organization that have been examined have been selected on a common sense or pragmatic basis rather than on the basis of theory about organizations (see Chapter 1). Consequently, there is little correspondence between the indicators of organizational structure used in most of the research and the concepts that guide the theoretical literature. For example, Coleman concluded that per-pupil expenditures, books in the library, and a host of other facilities show virtually no relation to achievement if other aspects of the school are held constant.[76] Coleman is referring to school facilities, not organizational structure, that is, the kind of characteristics that were discussed in Chapter 1. Nevertheless, the final implication is that schools do not make a difference. Moreover, as Levin has pointed out, even the measures of facilities are not adequate. The "host" of other facility measures used in the regression analysis of verbal achievement turns out to have been rather limited.[77] At grades one, three, and six, the *only* facility measure used was volumes-per-student in the school library. At grades nine and twelve, the library variable was supplemented by one representing the presence of science laboratory facilities, but it is not clear why science laboratories should have any effect on verbal performance and, in any case, it seems unlikely that the effects of the entire physical plant, instructional aids, and other facilities on educational achievement can properly be assessed by considering only library books and science laboratories. In view of these criticisms, it is remarkable that even small relationships can be demonstrated.

In short, the evidence about whether the characteristics of schools influence a child's academic performance is far from being conclusive, one way or the other but, on balance, there is reason to believe that, in some circumstances at least, school characteristics can make an important difference for some children. It will be instructive, then, to consider which characteristics are likely to make this difference.

WHICH ORGANIZATIONAL CHARACTERISTICS MAKE A DIFFERENCE?

Several school characteristics appear to have a particularly crucial bearing on not only how well children perform in school but also on their later career chances and life styles.

Membership Composition: SES

COLLEGE PLANS

First, as indicated above, there is now persuasive evidence that the *composition of the student body* affects college plans and academic achievement. Since the type of student admitted to a school depends on the recruiting policies, student body composition can be considered as an organizational characteristic.

Wilson's research suggested that the educational aspirations of lower-class children increased when they attended schools with predominantly middle-class peers. Thirteen high schools in the San Francisco area were classified into three groups on the basis of the proportion of the student body who planned to go to college. Whereas only one-third of the sons of manual workers who were attending schools in predominantly working-class areas (where few of the children intended to go to college) themselves anticipated going to college, 59 percent of these same types of working-class students had plans for college when they attended middle-class schools with predominantly college-oriented student bodies.[78] Wilson later showed that after controlling for the child's first-grade IQ, the social-class composition of the primary school had a significant effect on sixth-grade reading level and the reasoning scores.[79] In other words, students seem to be influenced by one another at least as much and probably more than they are influenced by their IQ or home background.

ACADEMIC ACHIEVEMENT

In addition to the effects of student body composition on college plans, other investigators have found that the composition of schools affects students' academic achievement. The EEOS confirmed that the composition of the student body can independently affect the students' academic achievement. The authors of the survey concluded that attributes of other students accounted for more variation in the achievement of minority group children than did any attributes of school facilities and slightly more than attributes of the staff; in general, as the educational aspiration and backgrounds of fellow students increased, the achievement of minority group children increased. The performance of minority children of comparable social class background was better in schools that had a higher proportion of middle-class children. The school climate seemed to have a more striking effect on lower-class than on middle-class children.

The authors explained that the Northern metropolitan Negro or Puerto Rican student brings to school a burden of background disadvantages. When his burden is joined with those of his peers, he

"attends a school where his fellow students generally come from economically poorer, less stable homes, which are more poorly equipped to give stimulation to the educational pursuits of the children. The families are larger and, less frequently, have both real parents living at home; the parents' level of education is lower, and the homes more frequently lack modern conveniences and reading materials such as daily newspapers, encyclopedias, and home libraries. Of all the characteristics of schools that distinguish the education being provided the average white and Negro students, it is the environment provided by the fellow students where the differences are most dramatic."[80]

Wilson had found that the *aspirations* of middle-class children declined when they attended lower-class schools. However, the academic *achievement* of middle-class children in the EEOS did not seem to decline when they attended predominantly lower-class schools. The authors concluded that if a child comes from a middle-class home that is strongly supportive of education, he can hold his own when mixing with less-able students. But in the absence of strong support for academic achievement in the home, lower-class children seemed to be much more dependent upon the caliber of their schoolmates.

The effects of attending different types of schools are graphically portrayed in Figure 3-1, which reports the achievement scores of twelfth-grade black and white students in the metropolitan Northeast. The scores have been translated into grade-level norms. In the figure the individuals are matched by race, social class, and by the social class composition of their respective schools. The figure shows that the social class composition of the student body (the first line) makes a substantial difference for indi-

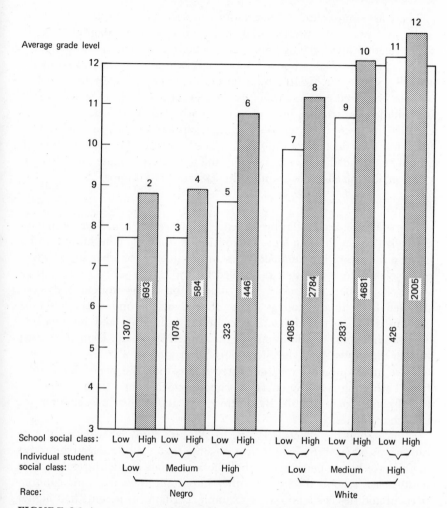

FIGURE 3-1 Average grade-level performance of Negro and white twelfth-grade students by social-class level of the school and the social-class origin of the student; metropolitan Northeast. *Note*: the numbers in the bars represent the number of cases. *Source*: USCCR analysis of *OE Survey* data. See App. C 1. From Figure 3, *Racial Isolation in the Public Schools*, U.S. Civil Rights Commission, Government Printing Office, p. 85.

viduals of the same race and from comparable social-class backgrounds. For example, among lower-class blacks, students who attended lower-class schools tested at or below the eighth-grade level, while students who attended middle-class schools scored at nearly the ninth-grade level. Upper-class blacks attending middle-class schools were two years ahead of their counterparts in lower-class schools.

There are comparable differences for white students as well. Lower-class white students in the twelfth grade tested at only the tenth-grade level if they attended lower-class schools, and at the eleventh-grade level if they were in middle-class schools. Upper-class whites, on the other hand, achieved above the twelfth-grade level when they were in middle-class schools. Upper-class blacks tested at the eleventh-grade level when attending middle-class schools, but below the ninth-grade level when they were enrolled in lower-class schools. Thus, regardless of race, a child's performance was affected not only by his class background but by the type of school he attended. This suggests that the normative climate of the school can override the effects of an individual's social class origins.

RESERVATIONS

But while the accumulating evidence is impressive, it has not been conclusively proven that student composition is itself the determining influence on the aspirations and achievement of students. Another study, based on an elaborate design that controlled for the child's sex, IQ, and family social class, found that social class composition of the student body contributed little to the college plans of students beyond what could be accounted for by the characteristics of the individual and his family.[81] Still another study of adolescents in the United States and Denmark raised further questions about the effects of the peer group.[82] Parents were found to have more influence on their career plans than did peers. In samples from both countries, the effect of school socioeconomic status on educational plans was negligible. By contrast, parental influence was important in both countries.

Even though the effects persisted in Wilson's study when parents' education was taken into account, it is possible that a subtle selective process might have been operating, so that the lower-class child who enrolled in middle-class schools differed in other important ways from his counterparts in middle-class schools; for example, perhaps his parents had higher aspirations for him. In view of the small number of black children in middle-class schools, they were clearly a select group.

Beyond that, it should be noted that a method of grouping that is beneficial for some children might be detrimental to others under some conditions. The *middle-class* child's aspirations in Wilson's study seemed to *decline* when he enrolled in a predominantly lower-class school. Whereas 93 percent of the children from professional homes enrolled in middle-class schools wanted to attend college, that proportion dropped to only 64 percent for comparable students attending lower-class schools.[83] And another investigator reports an even more curious twist. The schools that were composed of students of *higher* than average ability had a *negative* effect on the college plans of students from the lower class.[84] The author conjectured that, even though high-ability schools provide incentive for many students, sometimes they also set unrealistically high competitive standards for others. As a result, many students in highly competitive academic settings are likely to learn to view themselves negatively in comparison to their most brilliant peers. But nevertheless, it should be noted that when this negative effect is added to the positive influence that these schools can have on some students, the effect of student body composition is rather impressive.

The studies to date have not given adequate consideration to the type of friendship patterns that develop in homogeneous and mixed schools. That is, perhaps lower-class students will not be affected by the school's composition *unless* they are able to form close friendships with middle-class students. For example, Wallace found that as college freshmen became socialized into the college peer group, their own levels of aspirations for grades while in college and their plans for graduate school became changed.[85] This change of aspiration among freshmen was related to the extent of their contacts with upper classmen. The effect of these friendships with upper classmen was greatest where the student's greatest achievement and job aspirations had been relatively low. Most of the studies of student composition are based on schoolwide or classroom composition, not on actual friendship groupings.

Something else that needs to be taken into account is the opportunity of lower-class students to gain recognition from their peers. Two sociologists have reported that over a 40-year period, students who had high status among their peers raised their aspirations while the aspirations of the nonleaders dropped, regardless of fathers' education.[86] By the senior year, the students' status in their peer group accounted for larger differences in their aspiration levels than did their family status, especially for boys. The authors concluded that the student's desire for future success may rest almost as much on his personal achievements and on status among his peers as on the family he comes from.

Finally, as we have already stressed, the *criterion* used to assess the effects of student composition and other organizational variables needs to be questioned. The way students perform on cognitive achievement tests represents a very limited objective of schools, albeit one that is generally considered to be important. The preoccupation with aspiration measures reflects a narrow status bias on the part of many middle-class sociologists, who seem to presume that social mobility within the economic system is the only important outcome that reasonably could be expected of educational organizations. While many people accept the mobility ideology, an increasing number of young people seem to have rejected it. The question is: *What do schools do to and for them?* Too little attention has been given to the broader, often unintended consequences of schooling on students' future life styles—that is, their political participation, initiative and compliance predispositions, and their use of leisure time.

Membership Composition: Racial Segregation

ACADEMIC ACHIEVEMENT

Racial segregation is a separate dimension of student body composition that deserves independent consideration. Whether or not attending a racially integrated school affects a child's educational achievement is still being debated. In the EEOS, differences were found between educational performance in racially mixed and in segregated schools. But the authors attributed these differences to the *social class* differences between whites and Negroes, rather than to racial differences *per se*. It seemed to the study's authors that there were few benefits from racial integration beyond those that could be attributed to social class differences. Wilson reached a similar conclusion.

However, this conclusion was contested by a group commissioned by the U.S. Civil Rights Commission to reanalyze the EEOS data. It was found that when twelfth-grade black students from the same social class attending schools of comparable social-class composition were compared, the more white classmates a black student had, the higher his test scores. (See Figure 3-2). For example, lower-class twelfth-grade black children attending segregated lower-class schools achieved at only the seventh grade level, but if at least half of their classmates were white they achieved well beyond the eighth grade level. The results were similar for lower-class black students attending middle-class schools and for middle-class blacks in both lower-class and middle-class schools. Even when disadvantaged black children were in class with similarly disadvantaged whites, their average performance improved by more than a full grade level. When they were in class with the most advantaged whites, their performance improved by more than two grades.

Further reanalysis of the data supported the commission's conclusions and showed that *school* desegregation was associated with higher achievement of black pupils only if they were in predominantly white classrooms, but *classroom* desegregation was favorable regardless of school percent white. Other findings of the survey indicated that:

- There was a consistent trend toward higher academic performance of Negro students the longer they were in schools with whites.
- Negroes who attended desegregated schools were more likely to have fathers in white collar occupations than Negroes who attended racially isolated schools.
- Negroes who attended desegregated schools were more likely than those

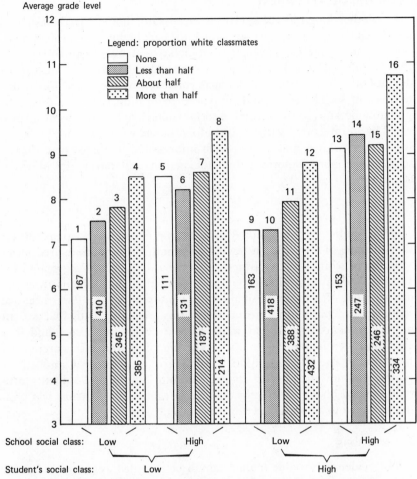

FIGURE 3-2 Average grade-level performance of twelfth-grade Negro students by individual social-class origin, social-class level of school, and proportion of white classmates last year; metropolitan Northeast. *Note*: the numbers in the bars represent the number of cases. *Source*: USCCR analysis of *OE Survey* data. Taken from *Isolation in the Public Schools*, U.S. Civil Rights Commission, Government Printing Office, Figure 5, p. 90.

who attended racially isolated schools to reside presently in interracial neighborhoods.
- The relationship between achievement and racial composition remained strong regardless of home cultural background of the parents, their education, and material possessions.
- The effects of desegregation were reduced or eliminated if *classrooms* in an otherwise integrated school remained segregated.

OCCUPATIONAL ATTAINMENT

In another longitudinal study, an investigator found that blacks who had attended integrated schools not only had higher test achievement, but were more likely to graduate from high school and attend college and to have better jobs and higher incomes throughout at least the next three decades of their life.[87] The differences could not be accounted for by differences in social background or type of education. These effects were probably because of the favorable social conditions for achievement provided by an integrated setting—including contact with white adults, learning to trust whites, and access to job information. Perhaps these characteristics are more important than the personal characteristics of white classmates.

ATTITUDES

Other studies have attempted to assess the effects of desegregation on the attitudes of the children toward one another. Singer compared racial attitudes of white students from a school that had been desegregated for 13 years and an all-white school, and found that the students from the desegregated school showed significantly more positive and fewer negative stereotypes of blacks and greater desire for associating with blacks than did the students from the all-white school.[88] Whitmore also found that eighth- and tenth-grade white students became significantly less prejudiced five months after desegregation as compared to before.[89] Campbell reported a significant positive change in white high school students' attitudes toward blacks six months after desegregation; this change was positively related to amount of classroom contact.[90]

RESERVATIONS

The evidence available to date cannot be regarded as conclusive. From her review of available research, St. John concluded that before and after studies of desegregation of school systems suggest that following desegregation black students generally perform no worse and in most instances better. But it is still possible that students who participate in desegregation projects are typically a select group to start with.[91] Also, the available data sometimes have been misconstrued, and many side effects have not yet been taken fully into account. For example, one table in the Civil Rights Commission reanalysis showed that white students in predominantly Negro classes scored well below those in all-white classes after controlling for parental education and social composition of the school. This again raises the possibility that integration can have detrimental effects for certain individuals under some conditions. One cannot ignore the *tension* that often develops in integrated situations. Several studies report that, as a result of school desegregation, many black youngsters experience extreme stress, fear, rejection, hostility, and physical and emotional brutality from their white classmates.[92] The Equality of Educational Opportunity survey showed that in schools where few white teachers reported the existence of racial tension, students were more likely to want to go to college, to believe in the virtues of hard work, and to score higher on verbal achievement tests than students in schools where at least half the teachers reported racial tension.

The Official Structure

Up to this point, we have considered only one type of organizational variable—student composition. Much of the recent research has concen-centrated on this interpersonal dimension. By comparison, relatively little attention has been given to impersonal organizational characteristics, such as the official *standards* of education and other organizational variables that were discussed in the first chapter.

To illustrate, an index of school characteristics was associated with academic achievement in the EEOS, notwithstanding the authors' pessimistic conclusions. An index of "school quality" was also devised from the EEOS by the U.S. Civil Rights Commission Team, which consisted of measures of the availability of scientific laboratories, comprehensiveness of the curriculum, and extracurricular activities. As Table 3-2 indicates,

Table 3-2 School Quality, Student Performance, and the Social Class Composition of Schools[a]

Individual's Parents' Education (Social Class of Students)	School Average: Parents' Education (Social Class Level of School)	School Quality Index	Achieve-ment Level
Less than high school (low)	Less than high school graduate (low)	Low	7.4
		Medium	7.8
		High	8.2
	High school graduate or more (medium to high)	Low	8.5
		Medium	8.6
		High	9.2

[a]Average verbal achievement test scores, 12th grade, by school quality index, parents' education, and school average of parents' education, expressed in grade level equivalents; metropolitan Northeast. (From *Racial Isolation in the Public Schools*.)

for children from lower-class families (measured by parents' education), the higher the quality of the school, the higher the level of the students' achievement. This is true for all lower-class children, whether they are attending lower-class schools or middle-class schools. When Column 1 is read down, there are variations in student achievement that relate to quality of educational facilities and programs. If an index as flimsy as this can begin to detect structural influences, it would seem to be fruitful to launch more sophisticated studies.

Levin suggests that, instead of the variables used in the Coleman study, it would have been far more meaningful to study a wide variety of instructional aids, particularly such representatives of the "new technology" as educational TV and computer-aided instruction. But even those variables do not begin to tap the variables that both sociological theory and the experience of many students, teachers, and administrators demonstrate are the vital ones. None of the studies to date have attempted to assess the effects of even the most fundamental properties of organizations (some of which were discussed in Chapter 1). However, it is possible to at least illustrate the potential importance of organizational properties by considering how variations in a selected number of variables could influence learning outcomes.

THE INTERNAL CONTROL STRUCTURE

This includes, for example, the degree of centralization and decentralization, as well as the flexibility with which schools can adapt to clients and to variable local circumstances. A survey of another type of service organization—a social work agency—is suggestive in this regard. Some departments were found in which workers had become very bureaucratic because they had to work under procedure-oriented supervisors; the workers in these departments were less oriented to case-work service than when they worked for less procedure-oriented supervisors.[93] The insecure newcomers, not thoroughly familiar with procedures, were especially rigid in their adherence to official procedures. But they became more flexible as they gained greater experience, especially when they had strong peer-group support.

There is some reason to believe that low-income schools have relatively rigid control structures. For example, corporal punishment seems to be used more frequently in lower-class than middle-class schools. It may be partially because maintaining order is officially rewarded, because lower-class children pose more disciplinary problems than middle-class children and because physical coercion is more acceptable to lower-class parents and children.[94]

The administrators of lower-class schools also seem to exercise authoritarian control over the teachers. The most widely criticized schools, the ones in the lower-class neighborhoods, are the very ones that teachers often say are not innovative and that provide them with less opportunity to work on the solutions to the problems. Herriott and St. John, for example, found that in the lower socioeconomic schools fewer teachers were satisfied with the method of making decisions on the curriculum and disciplinary matters and still fewer judged their colleagues to be unwilling to try out new ideas.[95] Similarly, in Columbus, Ohio, 40 percent of all teachers in the lower-class schools said they were only minimally involved in making school policy (in comparison to one-quarter of the teachers in middle-class schools who made this assessment).[96] Compared to middle-class schools, nearly twice as many teachers in poverty schools rated their principal's willingness to support innovation and change to be either poor or below average. There were also indications that teachers in ghetto schools were less likely than those in middle-class schools to take initiative. Asked whether teachers in their schools were likely to "stick out their necks" and take a definite position about an interpretation of school rules when a controversy arose, 39 percent of the teachers in the schools in the middle-class areas said that the teachers in their schools stick out their necks, but only one-fourth of those in ghetto schools made this assessment of their colleagues.

The unanswered question is how these types of controls affect the students. One of the few efforts to assess the direct impact of bureaucratic controls on students concentrated on the level of educational aspiration among Canadian high school students.[97] Using measures of several dimensions of bureaucracy (including amount of control) that were based on respondents' judgments, the authors concluded, after controlling for other variables, that their measures of bureaucratization had a small relationship to educational aspiration, although the relationship was not large.

THE REWARD SYSTEM

The fact that teachers are rewarded for the academic achievements and conduct of their pupils produces a distinct pattern of mobility among teachers wanting assignments to the schools with ambitious, bright and well-behaved students.[98] Similarly, school administrators, like supervisors of other large-scale organizations, evaluate their employees on the basis of the number of clients processed, as well as their adherence to procedure. This reinforces the desire of staff members to work with the achievement-oriented clients who will be "receptive" to treatment and willing to conform to bureaucratic procedure.[99]

Within the classroom, some writers have argued that the degree of competition among children for grades, and the degree that children from different social classes find grades a meaningful reward, is another aspect of the reward system that can affect their motivation to learn.

GROUPING PRACTICES

A single-item indicator of grouping that was included in the Coleman Report is too simple to tap the complexity of this dimension. One study comparing student achievement in Denmark and the United States indicated that the access of students to high-quality academic programs had a strong independent effect on academic achievement. The way students are grouped determines this access. In the United States, among students

of comparable IQ and social class background, those who were participating in a college preparatory program scored higher on achievement
tests than those who did not.[100] In the Canadian study cited above the
type of program to which students were assigned had more effect on the
educational aspiration than any other variable (including the student's
age, sex, and socioeconomic status). The different programs and procedures
for assigning students to them certainly represent important dimensions
of organization.

EDUCATIONAL STANDARDS

The importance of the school's official posture toward learning was
underscored in a survey of a sample of Canadian high school girls, which
concluded that the peer group influence on students' attitudes and values
was less important than the educational standards endorsed by the school
and the community. Differences in emphasis on maintaining standards
were found between schools located in large and small communities.[101]

CLASSROOM STRUCTURE

From cross-cultural studies of the education process, Bronfenbrenner
notes that classmates put more pressure on one another to work on their
studies where the classroom is organized around small cooperative groups
of students than where individual students are pitted against each other.[102]
Coleman reached similar conclusions about U.S. schools, and suggested
that schools ought to be deliberately restructured to establish small cooperative *groups* competing with each other toward a clearly defined
goal.[103]

Another dimension of the classroom structure is the way teachers themselves relate to one another. Does the child learn better in a self-contained
classroom setting, or in a team-teaching situation? Preliminary research
at Stanford University suggests that team teaching and other forms of
differentiated staffing are in some ways more effective than the self-
contained classroom. (See Chapter 6.)

Professional Norms

Some social scientists are becoming convinced that there is something
about professional work that interferes with service to lower-class clients.
This seems to be true not only in teaching but of other professions as well.
Speaking of social work, Cloward and Epstein speculate that the aspirations of this occupation for status predispose social workers to disaffiliate
themselves from the stigma of working with exclusively lower-class
clientele.[104] They point out that the intensive casework techniques that
social workers use are based on the assumptions that problems can be
resolved by talking about them and through self-understanding. These

assumptions are foreign to lower-class clients who want to see changes in their environment and who need concrete, impersonal services, such as care for children, housing, and unemployment and old age assistance.

At best, professional norms have a mixed effect. Merit examinations and "objective" tests can help to minimize the amount of discrimination and caprice that teachers can inflict on children. However, objective standards sometimes have the effect of reinforcing discrimination because lower-class children with poor intellectual background tend to perform more poorly than the middle-class children on "objective" examinations.

Persons who criticize professionalism and persons who defend it often fail to acknowledge the two sides of this dilemma. In their zeal to maintain standards, professionals are often oblivious to the unintended ways that their actions reinforce the social class system, since lower status individuals are less likely to meet rigid standards. But, in their attempts to introduce flexibility into the professional standards and to discount the importance of cognitive achievement, the humanists may be doing a disservice to precisely the group of youngsters who most need to improve their academic skills in order to compete in a larger society.

Quality of Schools and Teachers

Meyer constructed an index of the quality of the schools attended by 35,000 students based on classroom size, accreditation, specialists, and the students' familiarity with scholarship programs. He concluded that, with school social composition controlled, school quality had no effect on the students' college plans.[105] However, the differences in achievement of students in the Equality of Educational Opportunity survey were consistently related to the quality of the teachers. An index of teacher quality was constructed consisting of measures of educational level, type of college major, desire to continue teaching in the current school, and years of teaching experience. Table 3-3 shows that these differences in qualifications of teachers have a systematic relationship to student performance.

Table 3-3 Teacher Quality, Student Performance, and the Social Class Composition of Schools[a]

Individual's Parents' Education (Social Class of Students)	School Average: Parents' Education (Social Class Level of School)	Teacher Average Index	Grade Level Performance
Less than high school graduate (low)	(A) Less than high school graduate (low)	(1) Low	7.7
		(2) High	8.1
	(B) High school graduate or more (medium to high)	(1) Low	8.6
		(2) High	8.9

[a]Average grade-level performance of low-social-class 12th grade Negroes, social-class level of the school and teacher quality; metropolitan Northeast. (From *Racial Isolation in the Public Schools.*)

Consider, for example, the first row (A) that depicts disadvantaged black students attending schools with a majority of disadvantaged students. When such students have less qualified teachers (row 1), they do less well than when their teachers are more qualified (row 2). The same relationship holds when disadvantaged black students are in schools with a majority of disadvantaged students (B). At each school social-class level, students with more qualified teachers perform at higher levels than those with less qualified teachers.

Several other studies conducted in this and other nations also confirm a small but persistent relationship between teacher experience or level of formal training and student achievement. A national survey taken in a sample of 171 primary schools in England indicated that the quality of teachers—as measured by their degree of responsibility in the school, experience, in-service training, and an outside evaluation—was more closely related to student achievement than any other variable assessed.[106] The "International Study of Achievement in Mathematics" also established a slight relationship between pupil performance and amount of teacher training.[107]

The Informal Peer Culture and Extracurricular Activities

Another dimension of schools that seems to have an important effect on students is the peer group culture. College student subcultures were considered in Chapter 2. Here we can note the evidence on one aspect of the student subculture (i.e., sports) that Coleman himself emphasized in another study. Coleman found in his study that, holding IQ constant, academic achievement was lower in schools dominated by a sports culture than in schools where academic norms were more highly valued. But, speaking more generally, Coleman concluded that:

". . . the variation among schools in the status of scholastic achievement is not nearly so striking as the fact that in all of them, academic achievement did not 'count' for as much as did other activities in the school. Many other attributes were more important. In every school the boys named as best athletes and those named as most popular with girls were far more often mentioned as members of the leading crowd, and as someone to 'be like' than were the boys named best students.

"The relative unimportance of academic achievement . . . suggests that the adolescent subcultures in these schools exert a rather strong deterrent to academic achievement."[108]

For the lower-class youth, such an environment simply becomes an added barrier to his own mobility. If he decides to pursue intellectual objectives, he does so at the expense of lowered status within the school status system. As a double burden, he would probably also lose status among his lower-class peers outside the school.

A subsequent study by other investigators did indicate that students who participated in extracurricular school activities, especially in athletics, had developed *higher* educational aspirations than students who did not.[109] This does not necessarily mean that these students go on to fulfill their aspirations, however. Spady's evidence indicates that, even though high school athletes tend to aspire for college, their aspirations are frequently not fulfilled.[110]

Formal Curriculum versus Informal Social Organization

Cross-national studies recently have uncovered a relationship between years of schooling and the extent that an individual holds "modern" values, that is, is open to new experiences, is independent from parental authority, and takes an active part in civic affairs. The writers agree that schooling (in addition to occupational experience) is a powerful factor in the shaping of modern values. But they disagree on precisely what it is about schooling that has this effect. Inkeles argues that values are not shaped by the formal curriculum but, instead, by the social organization of the school—its informal, implicit, and often unconscious program for dealing with children.[111] Other investigators, while confirming that modern value orientations (of Africans in this case) were closely associated with years of schooling, disagree with the stress that Inkeles places on the organizational dimension. They conclude instead that these values could be attributed to the school curriculum, not the social organization aspects of the schools.[112]

There are often subtle but important differences even within the formal curriculum among different schools, and indeed even within the same type of course. For example, a content analysis of textbooks in civic education programs in three schools revealed different views of the political process were conveyed in schools of different socioeconomic composition.[113] The material presented in the working-class school did not "encourage a belief in the citizen's ability to influence government action through political participation." The material in middle-class schools, on the other hand, stressed political participation as a means of influencing political processes and political decision making.

CONCLUSIONS

Sociologists can be divided into two groups: the *reductionists*, who see social problems as the result of the social backgrounds and related personal characteristics of the individuals involved; and the *structuralists*, who believe that the way people act depends not only on their native intelligence, personal backgrounds, and attitudes but also on the pressures in their current situations. The widely publicized research on social class has made the public acutely aware of the importance of the home and other influences *outside* the schools. But in addition, other types of influences deserve more attention, including both the positive and the detrimental effects of the organizational structure, professional norms, official policies and rules, and the informal culture. As thousands of lower-class children rebel, or leave school in despair, and find themselves judged as academic failures, the reductionists find the schools flawless and faultless. Perhaps the structuralists have been too quick to blame the schools for the failures, and perhaps neither group has given schools enough credit for the successes (e.g., the growing sophistication of students). Credit is given instead to the mass media or other institutions. One need not subscribe to the cheerless indictments of the romantic critics to suspect that schools have some responsibility for both some recent improvements in education and the widely publicized failures.

But, it should be noted, even if further research does verify that the basic source of inequality lies in the home and in the cultural influences immediately surrounding the home, that fact in itself also has some profound implications for school organization. For it would signal an urgent need to *design* new structures that are capable of freeing the school and the child from the detrimental aspects of the child's home and neighborhood. Such structures would either (1) provide better insulation or (2) establish more effective linkages with lower-class homes. Proposals to start schooling at an earlier age and to create boarding schools that require students to live away from home move schooling in the first direction. Attempts to increase community control and parent participation move it into the second direction.

In either event, if sounder theory and ultimately sounder school policy are to be developed it is now imperative to distinguish the *institutional* forms of discrimination that are anchored in organizational structure and official and professional norms from (1) personal values of teachers (i.e., favoritism shown toward the middle-class students in extracurricular activities and in grading); (2) the policies adopted by administrators and school boards (i.e., inequitable distribution of facilities) ; (3) pressures imposed by the peer group and by family background; and (4) the biological sources of intellectual inferiority. Then the personal values and skills of the people involved—the middle-class composition of the student body, the middle-class values of the teachers and the school boards—will be seen in proper perspective as only one of several forces that contribute to differences in levels of achievement. Once the magnitude of the institutional barriers has been fully grasped, it will become clear, if it is not already clear, that teaching teachers to be "nicer" and to have tolerant attitudes, though helpful, will not be a solution. If some problems stem from the organizational structure, then the solutions must involve nothing short of reorganization of the present school system. It is an optimistic sign that most of the organizational characteristics identified in this chapter can be manipulated as a way of improving the schools and, perhaps ultimately, of improving the society itself.

In closing this chapter, I once again remind the reader that social mobility and academic achievement, on which we have been forced to concentrate by the available evidence, are only two of the many possible ways that school characteristics might affect students. Considering the fact that academic achievement explains less than a third of the variance in *either* occupational status or number of years of schooling, it is perhaps not the most important effect. Much more important, perhaps, is how much children learn to conform, to submit to social control, to learn to cope with the bureaucracy, and to exercise influence, for example.

Moreover, we should not forget that schools perform larger social functions that are easily obscured when the focus is on the individual learner. In particular, schools play a *linkage* role that mediates the larger societal events with the personal experiences of students. For example, schools are a means through which governments are able to monopolize and control the socialization process. Also, schools constitute one of the arenas where normative conflicts in the society are resolved, and they act as mediators between rapid social change and the social structure. Too little is known about what role school structures might play in fragmenting or unifying a society.[114] Do comprehensive schools help to homogenize the society? Does the existence of specialized schools based on meritocracy promote cleavages among groups? And what roles do schools play in promoting or blocking social change?

This larger perspective on schools was illustrated in the author's study of the Teacher Corps. Schools in less-modernized areas of the United States (e.g., the rural South) were less able to resist the attempts of an outside group to promote educational innovation than were schools in modernized areas.[115] One reason was that schools in the latter areas had several structural defenses not available to schools in less-modern regions, such as centralized administration, strong teacher organizations, and specialized competence of teachers. Teachers in the former regions relied for their defense on traditional, conservative value patterns, referred to by Parsons as "fundamentalism." While fundamentalistic values helped to protect these schools from rapid change, they did not seem to be as effective against change-oriented outsiders in their midst as were the structural defenses available to schools in other parts of the country. More research of this kind needs to be undertaken in order to fully appreciate the importance of organizational characteristics.

While the focus in this chapter has been on social mobility and academic achievement, then, there are many other consequences that different forms of organization might have. Sociologists still have not identified or examined all of the outcomes that school characteristics *do* effect. Certainly, it would be premature and irresponsible to conclude that the organizational characteristics of schools do not make a difference. ·

REFERENCES

1. Jonathan Kozol, *Death at an Early Age*. Boston: Houghton Mifflin, 1967, p. 187.

2. Raymond W. Mack, *Transforming America: Patterns of Social Change*. New York: Random House, 1972, p. 71.

3. Margaret Mead, "Our Educational Emphasis in Primitive Perspective," *American Journal of Sociology, 48*, May 1943, 633–639.

4. James B. Conant, *Education and Liberty*. Cambridge, Mass.: Harvard University Press, 1953.

5. W. Lloyd Warner, Robert J. Havighurst, and Martin B. Loeb, *Who Shall Be Educated?* New York: Harper and Row, 1944.

6. Herbert Kohl, *Thirty-Six Children*. New York: The New American Library, 1967.

7. Jules Henry, *Culture Against Man*. New York: Random House, 1964.

8. Paul Goodman, *Compulsory Mis-education*. New York: Vintage Paperback, 1964 and Paul Goodman, *Growing Up Absurd*. New York: Random House, 1960.

9. Charles Silberman, *Crisis in the Classroom*. New York: Random House, 1970, p. 10.

10. Jerry Farber, *The Student as Nigger*. New York: Pocketbooks, 1970, p. 17.

11. Jonathan Kozol, *op. cit.*

12. Herbert Kohl, *op. cit.*, p. 201.

13. E. Z. Friedenberg, *Coming of Age in America*. New York: Random House, 1965 and E. Z. Friedenberg, *The Vanishing Adolescent*. Boston: Beacon Press, 1959.

14. Susan L. Jacoby, "Big City Schools IV—Washington's National Monument to Failure," *Saturday Review, 50*, November 18, 1967, 71–73, 89–90.

15. Charles and Bonnie Remsberg, "Chicago: Legacy to an Ice Age," *Saturday Review, 50*, May 20, 1967, 73–75, 91–92.

16. Philip Hauser, *Integration in the Chicago Public Schools*. Chicago Advisory Panel on Integration, 1964.

17. Charles and Bonnie Remsberg, *op. cit.*, p. 91.

18. Robert J. Havighurst and A. Farber, "Professor Scores 'Unresponsible' Critics of Big City Schools," *The New York Times*, January 28, 1968, p. 56.

19. *Ibid.*, p. 56.

20. Dwight MacDonald, "The Other America," *The New Yorker, 38*, January 19, 1963, 82–132; Herman P. Miller, *Rich Man, Poor Man*. New York:

Thomas Y. Crowell, 1971; and Anthony Downs, *Who Are the Urban Poor?* New York: Committee for Economic Development, 1970.

21. Cora Dubois, "The Dominant Value Profile of American Culture," *American Anthropologist, 57,* December 1955, 1232–1239: Also, Florence Kluckhohn, "Dominant and Variant Value Orientations" in *Personality in Nature, Society, and Culture,* Clyde Kluckhohn, et al., eds. New York: Knopf, 1953, pp. 342–360. To be republished by The Greenwood Press, Westport, Conn., 1974.

22. Peter M. Blau and Otis Dudley Duncan, *The American Occupational Structure.* New York: Wiley, 1967.

23. William H. Sewell, Archibald O. Haller, and Alejandro Portes, "The Educational and Early Occupational Attainment Process," *American Sociological Review, 34,* February 1969, 82–92.

24. Ivar Berg, *Education and Jobs: The Great Training Robbery.* Boston: Beacon Press, 1971.

25. Henry M. Levin, et al., "School Achievement and Post-School Success: A Review," *Review of Educational Research, 41,* February 1971, 2–16 and H. P. Miller, "Annual and Lifetime Income Relation to Education," *American Economic Review, 50,* December 1960, 962–986.

26. I. W. Hanson, B. Weisbrod, and W. J. Scanlon, *Determinants of Earnings: Does Schooling Really Count?* Madison, Wis.: University of Wisconsin, Economics Department, April 1968 (mimeo).

27. G. Hanoch, "An Economic Analysis of Earnings and Schooling," *Journal of Human Resources, 2,* Summer 1967, 310–329.

28. E. Dennison, *The Sources of Economic Growth in the United States and the Alternatives Before Us.* New York: Committee for Economic Development, 1962. See also Barry R. Chiswick and Jacob Mincer, "Time Series Changes in Personal Income Inequality in the United States from 1939, with Projections to 1985," *Journal of Political Economy, 80,* May/June 1972, S34–S71. Also James S. Coleman, Peter Rossi, and Zabora Blum, "Longitudinal Effects of Education on the Incomes and Occupational Prestige of Blacks and Whites," *Social Science Research,* September 1972.

29. Christopher Jencks, et al. *Inequality: A Reassessment of the Effect of Family and Schooling in America.* New York: Basic Books, 1972. See also Mary Jo Bane and Christopher Jencks, "The Schools and Equal Opportunity," *Saturday Review of Education, 55,* October 1972, 37–42. For critiques of these authors' works, see James S. Coleman's and Thomas Pettigrew's discussions in "Review Symposium," *American Journal of Sociology, 78,* May 1973, 1523–1527.

30. David K. Cohen, "Immigrants and the Schools," *Review of Educational Research, 40,* February 1970, 13–27.

31. F. Welch, "Black-White Differences in Returns to Schooling." New York: National Bureau of Economic Research, 1972 (mimeo).

32. James M. Richards, "Assessing Student Performance in College," ERIC Clearing House on Higher Education, Report 2, May 1970.

33. Randall Collins, "Functional and Conflict Theories of Educational Stratification," *American Sociological Review*, 36, December 1971, 1002–1019; John K. Folger, and Charles B. Nam, "Trends in Education in Relation to the Occupational Structures," *Sociology of Education*, 38, Fall 1964, 19–33; and Naville Pierre, "Technical Elites and Social Elites," *Sociology of Education*, 37, Fall 1963, 27–29.

34. Collins, *op. cit.*

35. Blau and Duncan, *op. cit.*

36. Sewell, Haller, and Portes, *op. cit.*

37. Robert M. Hauser, "Schools and the Stratification Process," *American Journal of Sociology*, 74, May 1969, 587–611 (p. 588).

38. Bruce K. Eckland, "Social Class and College Graduation: Some Misconceptions Corrected," *American Journal of Sociology*, LXX, July 1964, 36–50.

39. William Sewell, "Inequality of Opportunity for Higher Education," *American Sociological Review*, 36, October 1971, 793–809.

40. *Ibid.*, p. 795. Also Cornelius J. Lammers, "Student Unionism in the Netherlands: An Application of a Social Class Model," *American Sociological Review*, 36, April 1971, 250–263.

41. K. Patricia Cross, *New Students and New Needs in Higher Education*. Berkeley: Center for the Study of Higher Education, 1972.

42. Francis Keppel, *The Necessary Revolution in American Education*. New York: Harper and Row, 1966, p. 1.

43. Chicago Urban League, *An Equal Chance for Education* and Patricia Cayo Sexton, *Education and Income*. New York: Viking, 1961.

44. James Coleman, et al., *Equality of Educational Opportunity*. Washington, D.C.: U. S. Government Printing Office, 1966.

45. U.S. Civil Rights Commission, *Racial Isolation in the Public Schools: A Report of the U.S. Commission on Civil Rights*. Washington, D.C.: U.S. Government Printing Office, 1967.

46. *Ibid.*; *Information Please Almanac, Atlas and Yearbook 1971* (25th Edition), Dan Golenpaul, ed. New York: Dan Golenpaul Associates, 1971; and U. S. Bureau of the Census, *Historical Statistics of the United States: Colonial Times to 1957*. Washington, D.C.: 1960.

47. Coleman, et al., *op. cit.*

48. James Cass, "How Much Progress is Enough," *Saturday Review*, July 17, 1971, 41 and "HEW Survey Reports Desegregation Gains," *Columbus Dispatch*, April 13, 1973, 43B.

49. Thomas F. Pettigrew, "Complexity and Change in American Racial Patterns: A Social Psychological View," *Daedalus*, 94, Fall 1965, 974–1008.

50. Thomas F. Pettigrew, "Continuing Barriers to Desegregated Education in the South," *Sociology of Education*, 38, Winter 1965, 99–111.

51. See Andrew Greeley and Paul Sheatsley, "Attitudes Toward Racial Integration," *Scientific American*, 225, December 1971, 13–19; Melvin J. Knapp and Jon P. Alston, "White Parental Acceptance of Varying Degrees of

School Desegregation: 1965 and 1970," *Public Opinion Quarterly, 36,* Winter 1972–73, 585–591; and Gwen Bellesfield, "White Attitudes Toward Racial Integration and the Urban Riots of the 1960's," *Public Opinion Quarterly, 36,* Winter 1972–73, 579–584.

52. Arthur Jensen, "How Much Can We Boost I.Q. and Scholastic Achievement?" *Harvard Educational Review, 39,* Summer 1969, 1–123.

53. Psychologists for Social Action. Mimeo., December 1969.

54. Ronald G. Corwin and Marilyn Schmit, "Teachers in Inner City Schools: A Survey of a Large-City School System," *Education and Urban Society, 2,* February 1970, 131–155.

55. Frank Riessman, *The Culturally Deprived Child.* New York: Harper and Row, 1962.

56. Robert Herriott and Nancy St. John, *Social Class and the Urban School.* New York: Wiley, 1966.

57. Edgar Z. Friedenberg, "Requiem for the Urban School," *Saturday Review, 50,* November 18, 1967, 77–79, 92–94 (quote, p. 94).

58. Corwin and Schmit, *op. cit.* and Herriott and St. John, *op. cit.*

59. Howard S. Becker, "Social Class Variations in the Teacher-Pupil Relationship," *Journal of Educational Sociology, 25,* April 1952, 451–465.

60. R. Rosenthal and L. Jacobsen, *Pygmalion in the Classroom.* New York: Holt, Rinehart and Winston, Inc., 1968; and K. Clark, *Dark Ghetto.* New York: Harper and Row, 1965.

61. Kenneth Martyn, "Report on Education to the Commission on the Los Angeles Riots," Los Angeles: California State College, November 1965 (mimeo).

62. National Education Association, *What Teachers Think: A Summary of Teacher Opinion Poll Findings, 1960–1965.* Washington, D.C.: Research Division, 1965, p. 19; Ward S. Mason, *The Beginning Teacher.* Washington, D.C.: U.S. Government Printing Office, 1961.

63. Robert Herriott and Nancy St. John, *op. cit.*

64. Corwin and Schmit, *op. cit.*

65. Henry J. Meyer, J. Eugene Litwak, and Donald Warren, "Occupational Class Differences in Social Values: A Comparison of Teachers and Social Workers," *Sociology of Education, 41,* Summer 1968, 263–281.

66. Richard A. Cloward and Irving Epstein, "Private Social Welfare's Disengagement from the Poor: The Case of the Family Adjustment Agencies." Proceedings of Annual Social Work Day Institute, School of Social Welfare, University of New York at Buffalo, May 1965 and reprinted in M. Zald, ed., *Social Welfare Institutions.* New York: Wiley, 1965: Also August B. Hollingshead, *Social Class and Mental Illness.* New York: Wiley, 1958 and Ozzie G. Simmons, "Implications of Social Class for Public Health," *Human Organization, 16,* Fall 1957, 7–10.

67. Coleman, et al., *op. cit.*

68. Hauser, *op. cit.*

69. Jencks and others, *op. cit.*

70. E. L. McDill and J. S. Coleman, "Family and Peer Influences on College Plans of High School Students," *Sociology of Education, 38,* Winter 1965, 112–126.

71. See Henry S. Dyer, "School Factors," *Harvard Educational Review, 38,* Winter 1969, 38–56.

72. Eldon L. Wegner and William Sewell, "Selection and Context as Factors Affecting the Probability of Graduation from College," *American Journal of Sociology, 7,* January 1970, 665–679.

73. Henry M. Levin, "Schooling and Inequality: The Social Science Objectivity Gap," *Saturday Review—Education, 55,* December 1972, 49–51.

74. *Ibid.*

75. Critics have attacked the methodological design and execution of this study on numerous other grounds, including (1) low response rate for schools (only 59 percent) and high nonresponse on individual questionnaire items (e.g., 41 percent of the sixth graders); (2) inadequate control for background variables, that is, parents' educational attainment is an insufficient indicator of socioeconomic level; (3) the fact that curriculum should have been controlled because tests of achievement used in the study are more closely related to college preparatory curricula while minority group children are more likely to be enrolled in general or vocational curricula; (4) failure to take student migration into account, that is, the characteristics of the school in which the student is currently enrolled may not be typical of the quality of all schools to which he has been exposed during his educational experience; (5) inadequacy of the multiple regression analysis used to assess the influence of different characteristics on verbal achievement because explanatory variables were highly correlated with each other; for example, the fact that lower-class schools are located in lower-class neighborhoods makes it difficult to find and compare schools in the slums and suburbs that have comparably good and poor staffs and facilities and student bodies. Concerning this last point, the decision to enter family background characteristics into the equation before entering school factors has the consequence of underestimating the effect of school characteristics. One task force commissioned to study the statistical evidence in the report concluded that "the things used to control were so highly correlated with things being adjusted that school effects were largely removed." See also Frederick Mosteller and Daniel P. Moynihan, editors, *On Equality of Educational Opportunity.* New York: Random House (paper), 1972.

76. James Coleman, et al., *Equality of Educational Opportunity, op. cit.* Also "The Concept of Equality of Educational Opportunity," in *Equal Educational Opportunity,* by the Editorial Board of *Harvard Educational Review.* Cambridge, Mass.: Harvard University Press, 1969, pp. 9–24.

77. Henry M. Levin, "What Difference Do Schools Make?" *Saturday Review, 51,* January 1968, 57 ff.

78. Alan B. Wilson, "Residential Segregation of Social Classes and Aspirations of High School Boys," *American Sociological Review, 24,* December 1959, 836–845.

79. Alan B. Wilson, *Consequences of Segregation: Academic Achievement in a Northern Community.* Santa Barbara: Glendassary Press, 1970. Also Edward McDill, "Educational Climates of High Schools: Their Effects and Sources," *American Journal of Sociology, 74,* May 1969, 567–586.

80. James S. Coleman, et al., *Equality of Educational Opportunity, op. cit.,* p. 205.

81. William Sewell and Michael Armer, "Neighborhood Context and College Plans," *American Sociological Review, 31,* April 1966, 159–168.

82. Denise Kandel and Gerald S. Lesser, "Schools, Family, and Peer Influences on Educational Plans of Adolescents in the United States and Denmark," *Sociology of Education, 43,* Summer 1970, 270–288.

83. A. Wilson, *op. cit.,* 1958.

84. John W. Meyer, "High School Effects on College Intentions," *American Journal of Sociology, 75,* July 1970, 59–70.

85. Walter L. Wallace, "The Institutional and Life Cycle Socialization of College Freshmen," *American Journal of Sociology, 70,* November 1964, 303–318 and Walter L. Wallace, "Peer Influences and Undergraduates' Aspirations for Graduate Study," *Sociology of Education, 38,* Fall 1965, 275–393.

86. James S. Coleman, "Academic Achievement and the Structure of Competition," *Harvard Educational Review, 29,* Fall 1959, 330–351 and J. S. Coleman and Edward McDill, "Educational Climates of High Schools: Their Effects and Sources," *American Journal of Sociology, 74,* May 1969, 567–586.

87. Robert L. Crain, "School Integration and Occupational Achievement of Negroes," *American Journal of Sociology, 75,* January 1970, 593–606.

88. D. Singer, "The Impact of Interracial Classroom Exposure on the Social Attitudes of Fifth Grade Children." Unpublished study, The University of Michigan, 1964.

89. P. S. Witmore, Jr., "A Study of School Desegregation, Attitude Change, and Scale Validation," *Dissertation Abstracts, 17,* 1957, 891–892.

90. E. O. Campbell, "Some Social Psychological Correlates of Direction in Attitude Change," *Social Forces, 36,* 1958, 335–340.

91. Nancy H. St. John, "Desegregation and Minority Group Performance," *Review of Educational Research, 40,* February 1970, 111–133.

92. M. A. Chesler and P. Segal, "Characteristics of Negro Students Attending Previously All-White Schools in the Deep South," Unpublished manuscript, The University of Michigan, 1968 and M. A. Chesler, S. Wittes, and N. Radin, "When Northern Schools Desegregate," *American Education, 4,* 1968, 12–15.

93. Peter Blau, *Dynamics of Bureaucracy.* Chicago: University of Chicago Press, 1955.

94. Walter Philips, "The Influence of Social Class on Education: Some Institutional Imperatives," *Berkeley Journal of Sociology, 5,* Fall 1959, 63 ff.

95. R. Herriott and N. St. John, *op. cit.*

96. R. Corwin and M. Schmit, *op. cit.*

97. Barry Anderson and Ronald M. Tissler, "Social Class, School Bureaucratization and Educational Aspirations," paper read at the American Educational Research Association annual meeting, April 5, 1972.

98. Howard S. Becker, "The Teacher in the Authority System of the Public Schools," *Journal of Educational Sociology, 27,* November 1953, 128–144. Also Benjamin Hodgkins and Robert Herriott, "Age-Grade Structure, Goals, and Compliance in the School: An Organizational Analysis," *Sociology of Education, 43,* Winter 1970, 90–104.

99. Gideon Sjoberg, Richard A. Brymer, and Buford Farris, "Bureaucracy and the Lower Class," *Sociology and Social Research, 50,* April 1966, 325–337.

100. Denise Kandel and Gerald Lesser, *op. cit.*

101. Meyer, *op. cit.*

102. Urie Bronfenbrenner, *Two Worlds of Childhood.* New York: Russell Sage Foundation, 1970.

103. J. S. Coleman, "Academic Achievement and the Structure of Competition," *op. cit.*

104. Richard A. Cloward and Irving Epstein, *op. cit.*

105. John W. Meyer, *op. cit.*

106. Central Advisory Council for Education. *Children and Their Primary Schools: A Report of the Central Advisory Council for Education, Vols. I and II.* London: Her Majesty's Stationery Office, 1967.

107. Torsten Husen, *International Study of Achievement in Mathematics.* New York: Wiley, 1967.

108. James Coleman, *The Adolescent Society.* Glencoe, Ill.: The Free Press, 1961, p. 265.

109. Richard A. Rehberg and Richard E. Schaeffer, "Participation in Inter-Scholastic Athletics and College Expectations," *American Journal of Sociology, 73,* May 1968, 732–740.

110. William J. Spady, "Lament for the Lettermen," *American Journal of Sociology, 75,* January 1970, 680–702.

111. Alex Inkeles, "Making Men Modern," *American Journal of Sociology, 74,* September 1969, 208–225.

112. Michael Armer and Robert Youtz, "Formal Education and Individual Modernity in an African Society," *American Journal of Sociology, 76,* January 1971, 604–626.

113. Edgar Litt, "Civic Education, Community Norms and Political Indoctrination," *American Sociological Review, 28,* February 1963, 69–75.

114. Robert J. Havighurst, editor, *Comparative Perspectives on Education.* Boston: Little, Brown and Co., 1968.

115. Ronald G. Corwin, *Reform and Organizational Survival: The Teacher Corps as an Instrument of Educational Change.* New York: Wiley-Interscience, 1973, Chapter 8.

CHAPTER 4
STUDENT ACTIVISM

"For reasons not definitely known, a spirit of discontent which had been growing culminated in open revolt. The students barricaded, fortified, and stocked Old North, and elected two counsels who 'held sway over an elaborately organized state.' A citizens guard was mobilized in town to defend the college. Students were expelled. At a judicial assembly, 'when this business was about to begin, one of the leaders of the association rose and gave a signal to the rest, and they rushed out of the hall with shouting and yelling.' "[1]

The previous chapters identified several important trends that have been transforming the educational system—the emergence of a complex, sprawling bureaucratic system; inequities in educational opportunities; unresponsiveness of the system to the changes imposed by growth, new clientele, the demands of knowledge production and teaching; and the emergence of new youth cultures. These conditions lie at the heart of both student and teacher rebellions that have received so much publicity in recent years. This chapter is concerned with the dramatic emergence of an unprecedented level of student activism and romantic protest against science and norms of academe in this country during the 1960s. Developments within the past few years and the course that activism is likely to take in the future are considered in Chapter 6.

At least since 1964, when a series of student demonstrations erupted at University of California's Berkeley campus, journalists, social scientists, students, and politicians have been trying to explain the ominous sporadic outbreaks of student activism on college campuses, and often in public high schools.[2] Traditionally the church, the state, the military, and business groups attempted to use universities for their purposes. Today, the demands are also being made by organized, polarized groups within the university. Its structure provides no ready protection from this immediate source.

Berkeley was a turning point. "No other student uprising in the United States," writes Feuer, "has impressed the public's imagination as much as that which took place at the University of California in the fall of 1964."[3] On Tuesday, September 29, 1964, in defiance of university rules, four student organizations set up tables to solicit funds and volunteers for civil rights sit-ins. A university investigation soon prompted a sit-in, and several students were suspended. This was followed by a clash with the police. Further massive tactics of civil disobedience followed the arrest of student leaders, whereupon the police, acting under orders of the governor of the state, arrested over 800 students and nonstudents who were "sitting in" in the administration building.

The U.S. President's Commission on Campus Unrest referred to this scenario as "The Berkeley experiment." It involved several elements: protest initiated by a small group of student radicals; a combination of off-campus and on-campus issues; use of disruption tactics that denied others their fundamental liberties; police intervention; strong reaction to police intervention that created widespread sympathy on campus for the protesters; a fragile alliance between radical student leaders who wanted political action and liberal student leaders who wanted university reform; and lack of concrete change from the effort.[4]

Four years later, on April 23, 1968, 300 students occupied Hamilton Hall at Columbia University. The student leader, Mark Rudd, announced that they would stay there until the university agreed to discontinue construction of a gymnasium in the surrounding black community that was being built amidst the complaints of several community residents. He also demanded that the university disengage from involvement with a military research organization, the Institute of Defense Analysis. Meanwhile, a split developed between the black-power students and the white leftists. The blacks were less interested in university reform than in retaliating against what they considered to be white racist encroachment on the Negro community.

The President's Commission on Campus Unrest identified several ways in which the Berkeley invention was modified at Columbia and after: destruction of property, papers and records; counterviolence against protesters by law enforcement officers, including several student killings; university unpreparedness; threats against university officials; acts of terrorism; university disciplinary action; public backlash against campus unrest; and repressive legislation and delay or cutbacks in appropriations.[5]

However, while the confrontations were growing intense, the Commission also referred to the "paradox of tactics." Instead of following the extremists, the most moderate students often reasserted their commitment to nonviolence and their determination to work within the system. The more violent the extremists became, the more determined many moderates became to effect change through nonviolent means. They would help to control crowds and to plan peaceful demonstrations, thus vindicating the good intentions and self-discipline of most protesters. Their effect was to cool off the movement even as it gained momentum so that overall, violence remained isolated. In part, the moderates were effective because they outnumbered the extremists. In part, it was because they succeeded in setting up programs of action designed to provide politically viable alternatives to violent action. Princeton University, for example, rescheduled its fall classes in 1970 to allow students to work in political campaigns for the two weeks before election day and peaceful antiwar demonstrations were organized.

During the four years intervening between Berkeley and Columbia, student rebellions rapidly spread. The intensity of campus conflict and violence increased, and official response hardened, as evidenced in the increasing use of National Guard troops on many campuses during 1969 and 1970. Since this climactic period, the intensity has abated with only isolated outbreaks.

The observer is struck by two anomalies in the reports. First, the discontent often appears to be aimed at precisely the most liberal, and by usual standards, the most successful universities, and it is typically spearheaded by the most liberal, academically successful students. Secondly, there appear to be marked contrasts between the politically active students of the 1960s and students of the 1950s and 1970s. During the 1950s, professors were chiding students for being apathetic and unconcerned about anything except finding a good job, a good marriage, and establishing a home and family. A similar passiveness seems to have emerged in the 1970s. What causes these metamorphoses in American students, that is, how can the pattern of activism in this country be explained? According to some popular analyses, the sources of dissent can be traced to the loss of certain traditional American virtues, and especially the breakdown of the American family, "softness" of American living, and an overindulgence on the part of university authorities. How do these views compare with the social scientist's analysis? Let us first consider the dimensions of this very complex problem and then review alternative explanations.

WHAT IS THE NATURE OF STUDENT ACTIVISM?

Is Student Unrest a Recent Development?

First, let us put the problem in perspective. Is student activism a strictly contemporary problem? So it might seem. Less than a decade before Berkeley, the Jacob Report, based on a survey of college student opinion, described that generation of students as "gloriously contented" in their present activity and in their outlook for the future. They were self-centered, aspiring, materialistic—not militant.[6] Sociologists were predicting the "end of ideology," the permanent demise of romantic idealism that spurs social movements.

But, in retrospect, the "silent generations" might be historical interludes, quirks in the chain of history. Student unrest extends back through the history of this nation and, indeed, outward throughout the world. The quotation that opens this chapter describes a student rebellion at Princeton University, not in 1970 but in 1807! The issue might have been the marking system, as it was in Williams in 1868, or it might have been directed against *in loco parentis,* as it was in countless other instances during the nineteenth and twentieth centuries. There were student uprisings about these and other issues during almost every generation at Harvard College. The "nonconformist" subculture has always been a part of the American college scene.

Some of these revolts created history. Certain colleges in the United States were almost destroyed by student power. Almost all of the attempted assassinations of Austrian officials between 1910 and 1914, reports Feuer, were by members of the student movement.[7] Social revolutions in Russia, China, and Burma sprang from student movements, in some cases toppling entire governments.

Was Student Activism of the 1960s Unique?

The National Task Force on Violent Aspects of Protest and Confrontation (The Skolnick Report) identified several unique, unprecedented qualities about student activism in the United States during the 1960s:[8] there were more students involved over a wider distribution of places throughout the country; protests were more militant and sustained; they had spread into the high schools and junior highs; students had learned to use some sophisticated strategies of confrontation, to provoke police, and to stage events through the mass media in such a way as to mobilize the sympathy of neutral students and to radicalize "middle-of-the-roaders" who are forced by such incidents to take sides; and they had the support of a new youth culture and were better organized. On this last point, the President's Commission on Student Unrest observed:

"Student unrest was increasingly reinforced by a youthful 'counterculture' that expressed itself in new kinds of art and music, in the use of drugs, and in unorthodox dress and personal relations. Students were receptive to this culture's accent on authenticity and alienation. Many university communities began to attract nonstudents who also participated in the new youth culture. These 'street people' in turn played a prominent part in some student demonstrations, violence, and riots, and complicated responses to campus unrest."[9]

As one of the leaders of the "Vietnam summer" told Keniston, ". . . now the kids that are coming up have a very different experience. . . . More kids are coming into college really so disgusted by American life, so alienated as high school kids that they just stay very close together."[10]

The key difference, however, is that students had become more hostile to established authority institutions, not only within the university but within the society as well.[11] Student unrest in previous eras was provoked by specific grievances about their colleges or professors—food, favoritism, grading practices, the curriculum, and the autocratic use of power by educators. Only seldom in this country have students developed a sustained national movement bound together by a political ideology. Historically, most of the activists have been loyal to the nation, have accepted the society and its premises, and have subscribed to most of the academic system itself. They usually have sought the redress of specific grievances and to arrive at a more equitable administration of basic principles.

Today by contrast, as the Skolnick Report concluded, almost uniformly participants in the mass protests see their grievances rooted *outside* the university, and in particular, in the existing arrangements of power and authority in contemporary society. The President's Commission on Campus Unrest noted that the zealous defiance of authority that characterized the traditional school riot has been merged with youthful idealism, including social objectives of highest importance.

The initial thrust in the 1960s was toward reforming the society rather than the university as such; the university was perceived as a neutral ground from which to launch constructive attacks on the society. But as the movement grew and more ferment took place on the campus, the connection between the university and the larger society became clearer to student leaders. The university came to be perceived as a microcosm of the larger society. Students learned that by attacking the university they could attack the larger institutions on which the university was built— centralization of authority, the status inconsistencies of youth, and the dominant role of the military in the society, all of which were reflected within the structure of the university. Thus, university reform became a direct step toward more basic social reform.

This new dimension is closely linked to the fact that student activism in the 1960s was heavily influenced by the growth of militancy and of political and cultural self-consciousness among blacks and other minority group students, including Puerto Ricans in the East and Chicanos in the West and Southwest.

Perhaps, as Feuer observes, the closest parallel to the 1960s arose during the 1930s at the peak of the Great Depression as students became disillusioned with Wilsonian liberalism and came to fear the rise of Nazism in Europe. Both the activism of the 1930s and the 1960s had strong pacifistic overtones, but in the 1930s the activists identified with the labor movement (rather than the black power and Civil Rights movements). The coalition with labor, paradoxically, turned out to have a stabilizing and conservative influence. Behind the labor movement in this country has always been a materialistic drive on the part of workers for a bigger stake in the existing social order. Unlike the black power and student movements of the 1960s, there was no underlying disillusionment with the values of the society itself. The workers' complaint was that they were not getting an equitable share. By contrast, student movements in recent years have attacked the basic assumptions of the society itself.

How Widespread Is Student Activism?

Is student activism an isolated phenomenon, the part-time concern of a relatively few, odd young people? Or has it become an inherent ingredient of educational institutions as they are structured today? The question can be answered, in part, by examining the prevalence of incidents and the numbers of students involved in recent years.

PREVALENCE

How many institutions have been involved? While there are fluctuations in the overall trends, it is safe to say that a large number of universities and high schools were the target of demonstrations during the past decade. Two surveys indicate that, during the short span between 1965 and 1968:

- The number of campuses experiencing organized protests regarding the Vietnam war almost doubled.
- Activism toward a larger student role in campus governance increased substantially.
- Civil rights activism among white college students declined significantly, while race related incidents on campus increased.
- The number of colleges with student left groups doubled.[12]

Thirty percent of the 1230 universities and colleges surveyed by Hodgkinson reported increases in student protests and demonstrations during the 1960s.[13] A national student association survey reported that during the first six months of 1968, 222 demonstrations had occurred at 101 colleges and universities, involving nearly 40,000 students.[14] According to Peterson's data, in 1965, there were "student left" organizations on only 25 percent of American campuses but, by 1968, that number had nearly doubled (to 46 percent).

One of the remarkable features of student activism during the 1960s was its spread into the high schools. A Columbia University study reported that 348 American high schools in 38 states experienced some form of disruption during the winter of 1968-1969, and another 239 schools suffered "serious episodes."[15] By May of 1969 more than 20,000 protests had been counted. A U.S. congressional subcommittee reported in 1970 that 18 percent of nearly 30,000 high schools surveyed had experienced "serious protests."[16]

In a 1969 survey, 60 percent of high school principals reported some form of protest in their schools and many others expected it in the future.[17] A special survey of disruptions in high schools in 19 cities, conducted by Syracuse University in the spring of 1970, reported that one-third had experienced student boycotts, walkouts, or strikes; one-fourth had experienced picketing or parading; and one-fifth reported rioting.[18] (One in five also reported *teacher* boycotts, walkouts, or strikes.) When various kinds of unorganized protests were included—such as property damage, arson, student-teacher physical confrontations, and abnormal unruliness—a total of 85 percent of the schools had experienced some type of disorder, and many had experienced several forms of these problems.

There is evidence of an increased incidence of certain types of problems in high schools in recent years, notably, physical violence against teachers and truancy. For example, armed police patrol the halls of half of the schools in the city of Chicago. Only six percent of the principals in the 1965 Equality of Educational Opportunity survey reported physical violence against teachers, and even in racially mixed lower-class inner-city schools of the big cities violence occurred in less than one in every three schools. But, by 1970, 39 percent of the principals included in a survey of disruption in urban secondary schools reported physical confrontations with teachers.[19] The incidence was uniform across communities but increased directly with proportion of minority students enrolled. Truancy rates also appear to have increased between 1965 and 1970. Only 12 percent of the school principals surveyed in 1965 reported average attendance figures below 90 percent, and even in the big cities, only one-fourth of the schools failed to achieve this standard. But in 1970, one in three principals, including 41 percent in the big cities, reported low attendance rates. In both surveys, schools with high absenteeism had high proportions of students from racial and ethnic minorities; only one-fourth of predominantly black and one-half to two-thirds of racially mixed large schools in the big cities reported average daily attendance over 90 percent in 1970.

The incidence of disruption in colleges and high schools should not be exaggerated of course. Feuer points out that the United States has never had a massive student movement of the national proportions of those of Russia and Japan.[20] The 20,000 students who participated in the peace march on the Capital in the late 1960s represented only a small fraction of the 2,000,000 students in colleges at that time. Even the widely publicized American student government in the 1930s was relatively small in number; for example, there were perhaps no more than 20,000 members of the American Student Union in 1939.

Moreover, the statistics obscure important differences in the *types* of institutions involved. The new left organizations that spearhead the student movements are associated mainly with the larger, more prestigious universities. Numerically, there are fewer of these colleges than of the more conservative, church-affiliated, Southern, and nonmetropolitan, vocationally oriented colleges. A 1965 survey of deans of students in 849 institutions, for example, reported a total absence of radicals in three-fourths of these institutions.[21]

It would be misleading, then, to assume that the typical *college* is subject to disruption. But, since more students attend the large universities where these episodes take place, it is fair to conclude that the typical *student* is likely to be attending a disruption-prone college.

FORMS OF STUDENT PARTICIPATION

Apart from the number and diversity of institutions involved, how widespread has the discontent been among the students on any particular campus? Is this a case of radicalism for the few, or is there a broad base of support? Here again, different conclusions can be drawn, depending upon the criteria used.

Generally speaking, only a relatively small number of students are actively involved at any one time. For example, Lipset estimated no more than 25,000 members and supporters of the new left out of 6,000,000 students. During 1968 less than 3 percent of American college students were involved in demonstrations.[22] The college deans surveyed by Peterson estimated that probably less than 2 percent of the national student population were active in any one issue with perhaps another 10 to 12 percent strongly sympathetic and capable of being mobilized for specific issues.

But student organizations are no different from other voluntary associations in that typically a few leaders carry the burden of most of the work. Therefore, one must assess to what extent student leaders reflect a broader concern, how much *moral* support there is for political demonstrations on campus. Moral support for political activism seems to have increased during the 1950s and 1960s. In one study, surveys of men undergraduates in 1952 were replicated at Dartmouth in 1968 and at the University of Michigan in 1969 in an attempt to measure value changes. It was found that commitments to political participation had become stronger and privatism had become weaker than in 1952. "Other directedness" and embeddedness in groups diminished, and the students' criticism of social institutions intensified. There was decreased commitment to traditional beliefs and forms of religion. (The effect of changed selection of students on the survey responses accounted for less than half of the changes since

1952.)[23] According to a 1969 *Fortune* magazine survey, roughly two-fifths of the student population expressed some support for "activism."[24] Although only 11 percent of American students in a Harris poll identified themselves as "radical or far left" in 1970, three-fourths of them believed that "basic changes in the system" will be necessary to improve the quality of life in America, and 44 percent thought that social progress was more likely to come about through "radical pressure from outside the system" than from the actions of major established institutions. Eighty percent of the respondents were attending schools that had experienced protests or demonstrations in May 1970, and three-fourths of the students at these schools favored the goals of the protesters; most (58 percent) of them had participated in protests.[25] Over half of the college students polled by *Newsweek* magazine in 1965 said that they had contributed money for a cause or signed a petition; 29 percent had participated in a demonstration; and one in five had boycotted a restaurant or store, joined a picket line, or defied school authority.[26] Although fewer than 1 in 10 said that they had violated a law or had gone to jail for a cause, over one-fourth of them said that they would be willing to violate a law, and 43 percent would go to jail if necessary. Over half would be willing to defy school authority.

Probably the majority of high school students also want more power, but a large number seem to be willing to work within legitimate political channels. According to a national Harris poll in 1969, 58 percent of high school students wanted more opportunity to participate in setting up school rules and deciding the curriculum.[27]

The *means* available to students for expressing their dissatisfaction makes a big difference in the way they answer these questions. Generally the less violent the means of protest, the more students who will become involved. The majority of students polled by Harris in 1969 did not accept violence as an effective means of change,[28] but many students who would not sanction direct confrontations sympathized with the causes and would participate through legitimate channels. In the 1964 Berkeley episode, only one-third of the students approved the *tactics* used in the demonstration, but two-thirds of them supported the *goals* announced by the student leaders. Sommers developed the following classification system from his survey of the Berkeley students after the 1964 demonstrations:

1. The militants—those who supported both the goals and the tactics of the Berkeley revolt (approximately one-third of the student body).

2. The moderates—those who supported the goals but not the tactics (approximately 30 percent of the student body).

3. The conservatives—those who opposed both the goals and the

tactics of the demonstration (approximately 22 percent of the student body).

4. Others—those who could not be classified (approximately 20 percent of the student body).[29]

Smith and his colleagues developed a more extensive typology of what they refer to as "student involvement":[30]

The *uninvolved students*—which includes (1) the inactives, who report no participation in political or social organizations; and (2) the conventionalists, who are members of fraternities and sororities, who are below average on the number of protests and social service activities they have engaged in, but who are not members of right-wing organizations.

The *activists*—which includes the (1) constructivists, i.e., students who are involved in one or more social service activities and one or fewer protest activities, (2) the social service workers, who work as volunteers in the hospital, volunteer tutors, and social agency volunteers, and (3) the social protesters, who have engaged in picketing, demonstrations, peace marches, work for civil rights, and sit-ins.

The *dissenters*—which includes students who have been involved in two or more protest activities *and* have not been engaged in service activities.

The *broad-spectrum* activists—which includes students who have engaged in one or more service activities and two or more protest activities.

But even these classification schemes do not do justice to the full complexity and shifting nature of student participation. A survey of Harvard students three weeks after the seizure of University Hall and the "police bust" in the spring of 1969 revealed that although most students initially did not think the sit-in was justified, a substantial number had changed their opinions during the course of events, moving toward support of the militants.[31] There was a striking tendency for attitudes toward the strike to become consistent with the students' general political perspectives. Thus, the farther to the left the student placed himself, the higher the probability that he would become more sympathetic toward the militants; while a student on the right, by contrast, would express more approval of the university's decision to call in the police. Over one-third of the leftist students had changed their opinions about whether the students' takeover of the building was justified, but less than two percent of the students on the far right changed their opinions.

Two ingredients in the situation helped to explain the shift. One was the prevailing climate of opinion. According to the study's author, Harvard students not only had leftist tendencies, but their beliefs were so tightly organized that events within the university and outside of it were easily connected. This kind of connection, he contends, can be made only by the best-informed, best-educated people (which he believes may help to explain why prestigious colleges and universities are so often involved in protests). The second factor was the issues chosen by the militants. The question of ROTC and accusations of university "imperialism" both linked the university with the outside world, and calling in the police confirmed this linkage.

In the final analysis the numbers of students involved may be a less important factor than this discussion may have implied. As Feuer points out, numbers have never been necessary to produce a student movement capable of changing the history of the world. Moscow University, the center of unrest in the early nineteenth century, had fewer than 1000 students. Social movements are spearheaded by a few leaders. The student activists have many of the characteristics of such leaders, and they are based in the most influential institutions. The fact that only a minority of students on any one campus might become actively involved is less important for assessing the long-range impact of activism on education than the fact that those who are involved are potentially a very influential group.

What Types of Issues Are Involved?

The Scranton Commission on Student Unrest concluded that three great issues were involved in the rising tide of student protest during the 1960s: (1) the position of racial minorities and of black people in particular; (2) the war in Southeast Asia; and (3) denial of personal freedoms within the university.[32] College deans surveyed by the Educational Testing Service similarly indicated that the largest numbers of students were stirred by (1) off-campus issues, such as the war in Vietnam, civil rights, and the draft; and (2) administrative regulations over their personal conduct—dormitory rules, food service, dress codes, and drinking regulations.[33] Protests regarding Vietnam or dormitory regulations occurred on one in three campuses in 1967–1968. But the latter survey also revealed marked variation in the issues involved among different types of institutions. Whereas two-thirds of the private universities reported protests about the Vietnam War, this type of protest was found in only one in five teachers' colleges.

As already suggested, historically, there appears to have been an evolutionary trend in the type of issues that provoke students. Initially students were concerned with educational problems on the local campus. They then turned their attention to political problems at the national level. Finally, they settled their focus on social issues representing a merger of these two levels. The support and momentum for student power seems to have increased at each new stage. The major student organization in Japan—the Zengakuren—evolved through such stages.[34] During the early period this federation of college student governments, which began with the labor movement after World War I, focused primarily on local issues that arose on individual campuses, such as the purge of the militaristic professors, which took place after the war, and complaints about fee raises. As the national government began to change its policies toward education, the issues became national, including threats to academic freedom. Students united and organized nationwide strikes. Then, in the third stage, the issues shifted entirely to the political, such as nuclear testing treaties and Japanese militarism. During this stage the student organizations established cooperation with nonstudent political organizations. This shifting nature of the issues and character of student movements makes it difficult to interpret the statistics collected in any one stage.

In contrast to the external targets of the college protests, activism in the high school has not yet evolved into or involved a comparably high level of social consciousness. Where they occur, disruptions in urban high schools still seem to be directed primarily toward internal problems, especially disciplinary rules, dress codes, school services, and facilities and curriculum policy. Vandalism is also a prevalent problem in high schools. According to data from the Equality of Educational Opportunity survey in 1965, about three-fourths of the high schools sampled in the study reported some property damage.[35] The incidence of vandalism varied from 95 percent in racially mixed schools in the inner ring of big cities to 11 percent in the rural areas. However, social issues may soon assume a more prominent role in high school activism. There have been strong undertones of civil rights issues in many of the incidents. In large schools (over 1000 students) racial issues are factors in more than half of the protests reported. According to Bailey's high school disruption poll, student boycotts, walkouts, or strikes occurred twice as frequently in racially mixed or black schools as in predominantly white schools (46 percent versus 22 percent).[36] There was a similar pattern for picketing; principals of three-fourths of the large, big-city schools with predominantly nonwhite enrollments reported that they had been picketed by students. (Less than one-third of the schools in the Equality of Educational Opportunity survey in 1965 reported having problems of tension between racial or ethnic groups.) The incidence was slightly higher (41 percent) for the largest schools, and it was much higher for racially mixed schools; thus, 61 percent of the racially mixed schools in the inner cities reported racial tension, compared to less than one-third that number in predominantly white or black schools located in similar areas. There also was a corresponding rise in the incidence of racial issues in the universities in the late 1960s.

HOW CAN STUDENT ACTIVISM BE EXPLAINED?

Having described the parameters of the problem, we are now ready to consider its "causes." Since education never has been a completely autonomous institution, various theories of educational change, including theories of student unrest, have sought to relate activism to family, business, political, and even forms of secular-religious institutions. Several types of explanations have been frequently offered, a few of which will be briefly reviewed in the following discussion. We shall identify four types of conditions that must exist simultaneously for activist movements to emerge: (1) *predisposing conditions* that incline certain types of individuals to become activists; (2) *conducive or facilitating* conditions that establish a value climate favorable to activism; (3) *structural supports* that sustain activism; and (4) *triggering mechanisms* that provoke it in particular instances where these other conditions are present.[37]

Is Activism Caused by a Certain Type of Person?

Many people believe that activism is caused by a few people with peculiar personal backgrounds and personalities who are perennial "trouble makers." As far as the problem can be explained in this way, activism could be minimized by screening out certain types of students and faculty, that is, the intellectual, humanistic individuals from liberal middle-class homes, those majoring in the humanities and social sciences, those from out of state, and those who are not preparing for a specific vocation. There is perhaps some truth in this assumption since, as reported in Chapter 2, many studies of higher education have shown that the social climate of colleges depends more upon the kind of students who are attracted than upon the special characteristics of the individual institutions; the "post-modern" youths who most aggressively reject the middle-class ethos attend the disruption-prone colleges. However, in the course of the discussion we shall note some serious reservations, too.

Who Becomes Involved in Student Causes?

Keniston notes that the "stereotypical dissenter" is popularly portrayed as both a bohemian and political activist. Bearded, wearing Levis, long-haired, dirty, and unkempt, he is seen to be profoundly disaffected from his society and is often influenced by Marxist, Communist, or similar radical ideas as well as being an experimenter in sex and drugs, and generally unconventional in his daily behavior.[38]

However, this "deviant" image is not supported by the evidence. Studies consistently reveal at least five major findings about the characteristics of student activists.

1. The relationship between social class and political orientation is not entirely uniform from nation to nation, but in general, activists both in this and other nations come from *high-status, middle-class families*. For example, Feuer notes that in Yugoslavia, stu-

dents from middle-class homes comprised only 13 percent of the population, but contributed almost half of the student activists. Flack's study of a sit-in at the University of Chicago revealed that students from upper-class status backgrounds were predominantly involved. The sit-in participants reported higher family incomes, higher levels of education for their parents, and overwhelmingly perceived themselves to be "upper middle class."[39] But important exceptions have been reported in Japan, the Netherlands, and elsewhere.[40] In highly stratified countries, the few working-class students in universities are probably not typical of their class and, in some nations, the liberals are more generally found in lower than in middle-class stations of life.

A particular segment of the middle class in this country seems to be disproportionately involved. Flacks has observed that the fathers of activists are typically employed in the less commercial, creative occupations—such as the arts and communication media, public service, education, and the professions. These positions are economically secure but sufficiently removed from traditional middle-class commercial interests to encourage the families to question the status quo and to search for alternatives.

2. Most have *politically liberal* (but not necessarily radical) *fathers*. They are often of Jewish, liberal Protestant, or unreligious origins. Approximately half of the student activists in the 1964 Berkeley demonstrations, for example, came from liberal, democratic homes.[41] Braungart's study (based on a sample of 1200 college students representing extremes of the ideological spectrum from 10 universities and from two national conventions) showed that the political activity of members of the leftist college groups was closely and positively correlated with parents' political identification (and family religious status).[42] Family politics, in other words, was by far the strongest predictor of student political identification and more important than social class *per se*.

3. Most of the activists choose to *major in the social sciences and the humanities*. Nearly half of the rank-and-file activists in one survey who had participated in social protest demonstrations or marches or civil disobedience were majoring in the social sciences or humanities.[43] Only 12 percent were in preprofessional programs. Separate surveys of students at the Universities of California and Georgia both revealed systematic differences in support for civil liberties among students majoring in different disciplines.[44] When University of California students' support for civil liberties was compared with a national cross-section of the population, community leaders and social science teachers, the

students (not just the activists) were much more libertarian than are other members of the society. Students in the social sciences and humanities were especially liberal, and their libertarianism increased steadily from year to year with the initial differences of opinion diminishing. Students at the University of Georgia were less supportive of civil liberties but, nevertheless, the majority (52 percent) were classified as libertarian (compared to 80 percent of the University of California students). Since these studies were conducted in a period of relatively little student activism, they cannot be directly generalized to this problem. However, they are at least suggestive of a general pattern of variation. There is more recent evidence from 19 countries showing that, on the whole, students in the social sciences, law, and the humanities are more likely to be politicized and left than their colleagues in the natural and applied sciences.[45]

4. Most of the activists are intellectually oriented. The California study confirmed that twice as many students with high grade-point averages were highly libertarian as those with low grade points; although grade point made less difference during the first two years of college than during the third and fourth years.[46] A study at another university indicated that almost twice the number of arts and humanities majors as majors in business, commerce, and other vocationally orie ted disciplines believed that it is as important to obtain knowledge as to obtain a degree.[47] This intellectual dimension, together with the high academic standing of the activist, suggests that intellectual ferment may lead to dissent, and dissent to organized forms of protest.

5. Most subscribe to *highly humanistic philosophies*. Lewis reported that students in the arts and humanities, behavioral sciences (disciplines that produce activists), and education more frequently embraced humanitarian values than those in business, commerce, and engineering. Ironically, as mentioned in Chapter 2, the students' sensitivity to their fellow man sometimes produces an almost fanatically rigid brand of idealism. By comparison to the class struggles in the labor movement, which centered around the distribution of income, student activism tends to be compulsively ethical and dedicated to absolute moral standards. Thus, while student movements are comprised predominantly of middle-class students, they self-consciously reject narrow economic, class interests. "For, of all social movements," writes Feuer, "those composed of students have been characterized by the highest degree of selflessness, generosity, compassion, and readiness for self-sacrifice."[48] Accordingly, student movements

have sometimes been the bearers of the society's noblest ideals. The Cox Commission report on university disturbances concluded, "The ability, social conscience, political sensitivity, and honest realism of today's students are a prime cause of student disturbances."[49] One student observed during their investigation, "Today's students take seriously the ideals taught in schools and churches, and often at home, and then they see a system that denies its ideals in its actual life."[50]

In conclusion, it is clear that, aside from the *numbers* of students involved in activistic causes, the activists come from the sectors of society and of the university that produce the leaders in other spheres of life. Activists are academically successful students from secure middle-class homes, attending the large, prestigious academic institutions—which makes activism significant beyond the sheer number of places and people involved.

RESERVATIONS

However, while certain types of individuals might be predisposed toward activism, this in itself does not explain why demonstrations and acts of violence, for example, occur in some places and not others. In addition to the people involved, the *situation* must be ripe for change; that is, the value climate must be conducive to activism, and there must be structural support for it. The crucial role of these contextual factors has been demonstrated in a number of studies. For example, the simple relationship between a student's socioeconomic class and his political activism largely disappears *within* colleges of similar quality levels, suggesting that the apparently higher rate of activism among students from high-status families might result from the fact that they are concentrated in the higher-quality schools.[51] The *concentration* itself probably fosters the emergence of a student activist subculture and, moreover, the educational policies of these schools and the nature of their faculties might tend to provoke and encourage the students.

Academic performance in the study just cited was unrelated to student activism at the *lower*-quality schools; even the better students in these schools were not very active. But at the better institutions, where the rates of activism were high, the better students were very active in comparison to the other students. Finally, although generally students in the social sciences and humanities were more activist than those in more technically oriented fields, this too was influenced by the quality of the institution. The propensity of the former types of students to be active materialized in only certain kinds of institutions.

A comparable study of Argentine university students focused on voting behavior instead of protests, but it leads to similar conclusions.[52] Students who were located in departments in favor of the students having a voice in university government were far more likely to have voted leftist than students in other departments, regardless of their family background or their personal attitudes toward student government.

Finally, there is evidence that the actions taken by university professors during the Columbia University disturbance in the spring of 1968 were more strongly influenced by the attitudes of their colleagues and the students in their departments than by their own personal preferences.[53] Very few of the faculty members who supported the demonstration held regular classes if their friends also supported it, but over twice as many faculty held regular classes if their friends opposed the demonstration. In other words, if colleagues supported the strike, it was difficult for professors to hold regular classes, whatever their personal beliefs. Social support was so important that when it was lacking less than half of the faculty members acted in accord with their own predispositions.

In view of the influence a social setting can have on people, it seems naive to hold a few individuals responsible for a national and worldwide problem on the basis of their personal inclinations. We shall have to look for more sophisticated explanations. Many writers subscribe to a notion that activism is the response of immature adolescents to authoritarian controls exercised over them in certain types of situations.

Are the Student Activists Immature Adolescents?

According to this popular view, student activism is associated with adolescence; it is one way that immature, mischievous adolescents "let off steam." Universities, seen as parent substitutes, become logical targets for an increasing number of students who face an extended period of adolescence and are testing the limits of their freedom. Adolescents are "marginal men and women," dependent on adults, plagued by the status inconsistencies that come with the confusing transition between childhood and adulthood.

On the one hand, students have a high level of incentive. They are sheltered most of their lives within idealistic academic institutions where they are taught to adhere to the culture's basic values in absolute terms. Their moral principles have not yet been tested by personal experience and the necessity of compromise. Aristotle's observation that young people "do things excessively and vehemently," and "have exalted notions because they have not yet been humbled by life or learnt its necessary limitations" is probably still true. They have few social roots and little investment in the society. They typically do not hold full-time jobs, own real estate, or have the responsibility of raising families, all of which are decisively conservative forces.

On the other hand, the risks are not high. They are protected by the academic freedom afforded by the university and an *in loco parentis* tradition (which curiously shelters them from civil law enforcement agencies and from courts that have been somewhat tolerant of them on occasion because of their youth, idealism, and presumed naivete); and they are assured of a secure future by virtue of their middle-class backgrounds, an affluent economy, and their own academic standing. And although risks are involved, today's youth have not had many occasions to encounter first hand the terrors of power. They fail to understand that people with power might exercise that power—might occasionally discriminate against, intimidate, jail, and even shoot student revolutionaries.

RESERVATIONS

There are elements of truth in this picture, but it is nevertheless a distorted, exaggerated account. It would be a gross error to view the period between ages 17 and 24 merely as an extension of adolescence as though young activists were simply going through the "rites of passage" into adulthood or only "proving themselves" for adulthood. As already suggested, it is precisely the status of adulthood and the moral order underlying it, they seem to be rejecting. To the many members of the younger generation who have lost faith in the ability of adults to solve the world's problems, the older generation represents a blatant dogmatism and self-righteousness that have produced two world wars, a depression, a political inquisition, a rising crime rate, dehumanization of the city, and perennial war.

Such fundamental rebellion is not characteristic of *adolescence*, but instead it mirrors a new stage that seems to have emerged between adolescence and adulthood, which sociologists call the period of "youth."[54] Whereas adolescence is a period during which the child reluctantly adjusts to adulthood status, and he may even be reluctant to give up his dependence on adults, the youth subculture frees the individual from excessive dependency on his parents, enabling him to assume an independent and mature posture. Youths of today are not immature; on the contrary, they are mature enough to realize that their parents are not necessarily appropriate role models for their own adult lives. Caught in the gap between adolescence and adulthood, the youth culture has fashioned its own roles, values, and ways of behaving—not simply a combination of the values of adulthood and childhood, but a new, independent style of life. In short, the youth culture is not merely a negative rejection of adulthood, since it provides a more positive chance to develop a sense of identity that can bridge the discontinuity between the generations.

The fact is that universities have no trouble accommodating themselves to the purely adolescent forms of mischievousness. They learned to live with and tolerate the panty raids of the 1950s, football demonstrations, May Day bed races, and "sex" on the campus riverbanks and in the dormitories. Regardless of how costly or embarrassing these activities might be, universities tolerate them precisely because they do not represent a serious threat to the authority system. It is the *maturity,* not the immaturity, of student activism that has sometimes frightened university officials and the general public. In the early part of the movement, perhaps one reason why universities were so ineffective in coping with demonstrations is that they did insist on treating demonstrations as another phase of adolescence.

Is Student Activism Another Aspect of the Generation Conflict?

The immaturity theme is a superficial aspect of the more fundamental "conflict of generations" explanation that has been advanced by many social scientists. A propensity for unrest is regarded as an inherent aspect of childhood socialization within the authoritarian educational system. The value system and authority structures are seen as the sources that generate and sustain activism. During the last century, the Russian writer Turgenev wrote a compelling account of how values sustain the conflict between fathers and sons.[55] It is believed that as most young people stay in school longer, the conflict between generations will be more frequently played out in universities, administrators replacing parents as targets of hostility. This would help to explain the frequency with which issues arise over administrative regulations over student conduct.

This explanation takes two different tacks. Some theorists stress the psychological dimensions of the explanation while others concentrate on the cultural dimensions.

PSYCHOLOGICAL INTERPRETATIONS

From his monumental study of student movements throughout history, Feuer concludes that they are founded on a *generational consciousness,* in the same sense in which workers' movements are founded on class consciousness.[56] But unlike the workers, who have been separated by wide economic differences from nation to nation (the assembly line workers in the United States, for example, have little in common with coolies in Malaya), the world's intellectuals share a common culture and a common sense of being suppressed by the generation in power. Drawing upon a Freudian analysis, he concludes that student movements occur whenever the elder generation, through some historical failure, has become "deauthorized" in the eyes of the young. They arise, in other words, wherever social and historical circumstances combine to cause a crisis that undermines their confidence in the adult generation.[57]

The key assumptions are evident in his interpretation of the motives of

Jewish student activists. Why, he asks, are Jewish students frequently at the forefront of student protest? His answer calls upon two psychological forces. On the one hand, the Jewish youth, he says, are ashamed of their often illiterate immigrant parents who have been persecuted throughout history and emasculated by Nazi terror. The young Jew's protest against American institutions symbolically severs his identification with his parents. On the other hand, the Jews cannot escape their sense of destiny as a people chosen for genocide and pogroms, which would help to explain the self-destructiveness of many demonstrations.

Reservations. Perhaps there are some elements of symbolic struggle for many young people attempting to make up for their sense of guilt and the sins of their "shameful" parents, but (in addition to its anti-Semitic bias) this interpretation is entirely speculative and so slippery that it defies empirical test. Moreover, these somewhat strained attempts to convert objective problems into a symbolic war between children and their parents have the effect of reducing critical issues to mere gestures and figments of the psyche, thus obscuring the fundamental *institutional* sources of the problems. A serious explanation of the causes of student activism must go beyond the inner conflicts of those who protest and take into consideration the crises of institutions in this country and throughout the world.

CULTURAL CONFLICTS

Many of these crises stem from value conflicts embedded in the larger cultural system, which is a different side of the generational conflict theme. Many demonstrable differences in cultural values do separate the generations. Many youths today subscribe to a parallel culture that has emerged alongside the old middle-class value system (described in Chapter 3) that dominates the thinking of the older generation. Slater writes:

"The old culture, when forced to choose, tends to give preference to property rights over personal rights, technological requirements over human needs, competition over cooperation, violence over sexuality, concentration over distribution, the producer over the consumer, means over ends, secrecy over openness, social forms over personal expression, striving over gratification, Oedipal love over communal love, and so on. The new counterculture tends to reverse all of these priorities."[58]

The core of the old culture, says Slater, is scarcity. The assumption that there is not enough to go around justifies fierce competition and discrimination against the underdog and even war itself. "Success" is measured by the resources that one has managed to accumulate, possessions taking precedence even over human life. Structured inequality is a natural consequence. The ability to defer gratification is also highly valued because scarcity encourages people to postpone their desires for immediate gratification so that they can plan for an uncertain future. This future orientation is so central to coping with the problems that arise from scarcity that the individual learns to exercise restraint not only in the economic sector but in his personal appearance, dress, manners, and leisure pursuits.

By contrast, the new culture, which emerged in a period of affluence, is based on the assumption that important human needs can be easily satisfied with the plentiful resources available. Equality and peace are now logical alternatives. Restraint gives way to the creative impulse and sensual stimulation—psychedelic cultures, amplified sound, erotic literature, bright clothing, erratic extreme fashions, and sexual freedom.

A related theme that separates the generations is what sociologists refer to as the consistent pressure toward "universalism," that is, an increasing extension of principles of equality, equal opportunity and fair protection of law to all groups within the society, and the world. As they have come to believe in these doctrines, youths have become increasingly skeptical about the fundamental premises of an industrial, technological society and more critical of middle-class America.

The four dominant value patterns that Flacks identified among the activists in his sample also suggest that a new value system is emerging:

> *Romanticism:* aesthetic and emotional sensitivity to beauty and art, quest for self-expression.
> *Intellectualism:* a concern with ideas and desire to realize intellectual capacities with broad intellectual concerns and reaction against doctrinaire ideology.
> *Humanitarianism:* a concern for the plight of others in society and a desire to help others, value on compassion and sympathy and a desire to alleviate suffering, egalitarianism, and emphasis on community.
> *Rejection of moralism and self-control:* antipathy toward the importance of strictly controlling personal impulses, adherence to conventional authority and morality including moralism about sex, drugs, and alcohol and rejection of arbitrary rules, centralized authority and "careerism."[59]

While these themes have been expressed by writers and social critics throughout American history, today the number of intellectual critics is growing, their power has increased. Moreover, the activist subculture shares some values in common with the parallel "hippie movement." A religious quality permeates both youth cultures. The hippies and the radical students are in a sense the new generation's pioneers, oriented to the present and experimenting with new forms of life and uses of time better geared to a leisure society. Their intense devotion to their own brand of moral dogma feeds their ambivalent sense of shame and idealism, inflaming their rebellion. The difference between these groups is that "hippies" rebel passively by "dropping out," while activists retaliate directly against authority.

What Are the Structural Sources of the Generation Gap?

The roots of the generation gap, then, extend deep into the social structure.

DEMOGRAPHIC STRUCTURE

A "polarized" demographic structure—where a relatively large older group possessing disproportionate economic and political power and social status that is matched against a high proportion of young people— is one source of tension. Many nations of the world have such a population structure. According to U.N. estimates, by 1980 one in every three persons in the world will be in the 12–25 age bracket.[60] Youth will begin to predominate in world affairs. In this country, in 1960, the center of population gravity was in the 35–40 age group—older than it had ever been before. Then, suddenly within five years, the center shifted all the way down to age 17—younger than it had been in our history since the early 19th century—with nearly half of the population under 25. At the same time, more people are living to an older age, and control remains in the hands of older people. As pointed out in the first chapters, members of university boards of control are typically in their fifties and have high annual incomes.

SOCIAL STRATIFICATION

Correspondingly large differences between the economic and educational statuses of the elites and the rank-and-file citizens also reinforce the generation gap. Whereas the average adult over 40 has approximately only eight years of formal education, most youths have over 11 years of schooling and one-half of the high school graduates are entering college. In some underdeveloped countries where this educational gap is even greater, the intellectual elite constitute the sole competitors to the military elite for political power.

SOCIAL CHANGE

Perhaps the hypothesis most repeatedly advanced is that youth protest is set in motion by rapid rates of social change that create sharp discrepancies between the formative experiences of parental generations and those of the younger generation.[61] Americans equate scientific and technological innovation with progress and are willing to pay the price even when it requires the destruction of traditional institutions.[62] Industrial progress has left in its wake the dire signs of pollution, and technological advances in military weapons even threaten to destroy the world. As a result of technological change, notes Keniston, adults and their children stand at different intersections in the crossroads of time, moving in different directions.

The number of years it takes to produce a major difference between generations collapses as the pace of change accelerates. Thus, as Keniston points out, differences in the America of 1950 and of 1960 were greater than the differences between 1900 and 1910. Social changes that once would have taken a century now occur in less than a generation. Many young people today have traveled as much as, or more than their parents and teachers, they have access to mature reading materials, and are confronted with complex social problems through television and movies. Many college students are married, employed, and generally older today than they were several generations ago. The effect is to decisively "de-authorize" the existing power structure in the eyes of the younger generation.[63] Adult experience, and hence the wisdom and values that guide adults, becomes outmoded. Youths confront new situations and must adopt new moral guidelines. It is no coincidence that the authors of the report on violence in America concluded that if any generalization can be made, it would be that student movements arise in periods of transition.[64]

The facts of rapid social change cannot be easily reconciled with the future orientation that drove the present adult generation. The younger generation has learned that if the future is more important, it has also become more remote, uncertain, and unpredictable. The drive to "get ahead" and plan for the future no longer make sense to them. For the youth, then, the immediately knowable present assumes a new significance.

Cultural change also takes its toll on the adults, who begin to question their own values. Keniston finds that one of the activists' major complaints against adults is the adults' hypocrisy—that is, their failure to live up to their own *espoused* values.[65] This hypocrisy, he believes, stems from the fact that many middle-class parents moved during their own lifetimes from a Victorian ethos in which they themselves were brought up, to a less moralistic, more humanitarian, "expressive" value system in their own adulthoods. Reared in homes where obedience to authority, hard work, deferred gratification and self-restraint were emphasized, many of today's adults have witnessed the "emancipation of women" movement in the 1920s, went to college in the 1930s where they were influenced by progressive, liberal, and psychoanalytic ideas, and during the 1940s and 1950s were strongly influenced by "permissive" views of child rearing that clashed with the techniques by which they themselves were raised. Their traditional values no longer fit these events. Though perhaps the gap between parental preaching and practice "objectively" is no greater than that which confronted many other generations of young people, today's youth sense an unusual amount of *ambivalence* on the part of their parents over the very values that parents successfully inculcated into their children. Thus, the young radicals typically come from families where parents disapprove of discrimination against blacks in principle but are uneasy about their own children's interracial friendships.

Reservations. A number of studies have found that while American youths, particularly those from higher status groups, are highly peer oriented, the values promoted by their peers are not necessarily divergent from those of their own families.[66] Since radical protesters come from predominantly liberal homes, there is little basis for the claim that they reject their parents' values. In any event, Kandel and Lesser found that the aspirations of youths in the United States and Denmark are more influenced in some matters by their parents than by their peers.[67] In 1966 only 1 in 7 college students with Republican parents had turned out to be Democratic, and 1 in 11 from Democratic homes had converted to Republican.[68] Moreover, the great majority of the radicals in Keniston's study said they were applauded by their parents who approved and accepted their activities; and while some parents were ambivalent about the extent of their sons' or daughters' commitment to the new left movement, their reservations were often based on practical considerations. If sons share the ideals of their fathers, they cannot be said to be in "revolt" over anything but the *means* to be used.

If there is a generation conflict, then, it is far more complicated than children acting out their hostilities toward their *own* parents. Another possibility is that activists are rebelling against the "older generation" in a more general sense, if not their own families. Even so, there seems to be more involved than a conflict of values. The "hippies" who have dropped out of society seem to subscribe to the *same* ideals as the activists. Although social change and value differences can fuel activism, then, something else must account for why certain epochs of rapid change lead to student activism while others have not, and why, within *the same society*, some individuals respond by becoming politically and socially active while most of their peers do not. Therefore, we shall turn to consider the cultural contradictions that impinge on youth in different ways, that is, the conditions that link the value climate to the individuals involved.

What Types of Status Inconsistencies Do Youths Encounter?

Variations in rates of change across a society produce *inconsistencies* for some individuals that are not experienced by others. Activism is the response of individuals who experience one of three types of inconsistencies: (1) *status inconsistencies*—a young person is defined as a child in some respects and an adult in others, as when 18-year-olds fulfill adult military responsibilities and can vote but cannot join a labor union, marry without parents' consent, or purchase liquor; (2) *discontinuities* between different stages in the life cycle, that is, status expectations and values inculcated in one stage of life are not rewarded later, which occurred in France where student unionism was initiated by students who had fought in the underground resistance movement against Nazism and refused to revert to the subordinate status of minors when they returned to college; and (c) *disparities* among institutional sectors, e.g., as discussed in Chapter 3, values endorsed in the home might be contradicted in the school or college.

Several versions of these inconsistency themes and some of their sources will now be considered.

CHILD-REARING "PERMISSIVENESS" AND STATUS INCONSISTENCY

As they have lost some of their authority, middle-class adults have become more permissive toward their children. Youths often respond by turning to their own peer group for authority, for example, "everyone is doing it." Authoritarian relationships have been replaced by negotiation. Parents and children bargain about what is proper in areas of personal grooming, sexual conduct, smoking, drinking, curfew hours, vacation plans, and the family car. In this "child-oriented" society, middle-class parents select their residence and even build their careers around the kind of playmates and schools available to their children. The child also learns that adults easily can be made to feel guilty about not having sufficiently provided a proper social atmosphere for their children; shaming adults for their failure to provide the right kind of society has been a widely used strategy within the student movement.

Young people who have this kind of "influence" within the family, it can be argued, will expect no less within high schools and colleges. Thus, the *in loco parentis* philosophy that permeates educational institutions produces a sense of status deprivation. It is probably no accident that the parents of activists in Flack's study were "more permissive" than parents of nonactivists in their child-rearing practices.[69] Many youths resent the "status offenses," tabooed for them but considered proper for adults. They see taboos against swearing, drinking, smoking, fornication, addressing adults by their first names, criticism of teachers, administrators and police as forms of discrimination designed to keep them in their "place." The incidents that activists select to protest often highlight these inconsistencies.

Reservations. The intriguing notion that "overpermissiveness" is responsible for activism might be referred to as the "Dr. Spock theory" of revolt, after the author of a popular medical book on child rearing who has been widely blamed for encouraging middle-class mothers to raise a generation of overindulged, disrespectful children. But, Dr. Spock was only a spokesman for a new philosophy of child rearing that had spread through the society, and if he had not rationalized what the mothers did, middle-class mothers would have found other ways to rationalize it. Permissive child-rearing, in other words, was a response to social change, not its cause.

It should be remembered, too, that permissiveness is a middle-class development that cannot plausibly explain the activism among lower-class youth, many from black families that have a more traditional, authoritarian structure. From the perspective of many lower-class parents, the *schools* are too permissive. The lower-class student's situation is more comparable to that of university students in many underdeveloped nations, where a curiously contradictory explanation is used to account for student unrest. Whereas U.S. youths are presumed to be rebelling against the authoritarianism of universities because they are accustomed to more freedom at home, in underdeveloped countries the university student comes from a traditional, authoritarian home and presumably engages in protest as a way of exercising his new found freedom in the open climate of the university away from parents' watchful eyes. If there is any way to reconcile these contradictory explanations, it is perhaps that the *inconsistency* between home and university is more important than whether one institution or the other is the more authoritarian.

DISCONTINUITY BETWEEN TRAINING AND OCCUPATIONAL OPPORTUNITY

This is a two-pronged explanation. First, as mentioned in Chapter 2, many college students are essentially compelled to attend college because there are few post-high school alternatives. Employers give preference to college-trained applicants even though a college education might not be necessary to perform the job. Moreover, many jobs do require better trained personnel today. In either case, the result is the same: it takes more formal education today than a decade ago to obtain a job of the equivalent prestige and income. Thus, students who a decade ago would not have considered college feel compelled to attend. On the other hand, for many high school and college graduates, their years in school will not necessarily lead to desirable jobs. This frustrating lack of "pay off" can be a source of young people's aggression. Indeed, political revolutions are said to take place in nations where the educated elite is underemployed or unemployed and denied access to political positions.[70]

The magnitude of the problem in this country perhaps does not approach the situation in Japan, where in some years more than one-half of the 120,000 college graduates were unable to find jobs commensurate with their skills, leading to both high suicide rates and strident militancy among students. Nevertheless, some theorists maintain that the college graduate in capitalist societies has essentially become a low-paid member of a growing, alienated, and powerless new class of professional employees. The growing enrollments in the United States are certainly a threat to the prestige and economic value of the diploma and degree, which were being held out to youths as an almost sacred prize during the 1960s in the wake of Russia's space triumph in 1958. After facing several years of anxiety in hope of entering college, many students probably experience disillusionment not only with the college itself but with the increasing amount of competition for the skilled jobs. The problem is highlighted in aerospace engineering where many young men during the 1950s, wanting to enter the challenging space program, limited their social life, postponed marriage and studied demanding subjects, only to find that in 1970 there were no jobs available. A comparable situation has developed in teaching during the 1970s. The youth of today perhaps has some reason to rebel against meritocracy and the competition and pressures on him to succeed in the wake of growing competition.

This hypothesis could help to account for the fact that the brightest and academically successful social science and humanities students tend to be centrally involved in the student movement. Activists typically major in subjects that are least likely to directly lead to productive occupations (i.e., the social sciences and humanities). Their very success in college, in comparison to their uncertain career prospects, creates a sense of relative deprivation not experienced by either less successful students in these disciplines or by the successful students in the vocational fields. Conversely, students in vocationally oriented colleges such as business administration seldom demonstrate. This explanation might also help to explain why law students have been actively involved in leading student movements primarily in those countries with an oversupply of lawyers. It also could help explain why black ghetto youth become involved in high-school disruptions; the employment rate for graduates from black ghetto schools is nearly as high as for those who dropped out of school (69 percent versus 49 percent). If the hypothesis is correct, students in engineering, education, and other overcrowded fields are likely to produce more activists in the future.

Stinchcombe advanced a similar explanation of rebellion in high schools.[71] Whenever the goals of success are strongly *internalized* but *inaccessible*, he argued, and when adults cannot promise that one's present performance in school will promise a satisfactory future, adolescents rebel against authority. Although all youths are expected to conform to the same standards of behavior, they have different chances for later success. In other words, he sees the future, not the past family history, as the real source of adolescent rebellion. The most rebellious students in

Stinchcombe's sample expected to enter lower-status jobs after graduation. Since there was no statistical relationship between a student's social class and his rebelliousness in the high school, it is doubtful that lower academic performance *per se* produced rebellion. It seemed to be produced by the disparity between high commitment to success and the prospect of failure.

Reservations. This economic interpretation is based on the assumption that, when all is said and done, student activists are merely out to promote their own self interests, just as the union members of the 1930s were out to increase their stake in the economy. The source of activism, then is seen to be *status threat,* not *idealism.* Notwithstanding the students' moral objections to the Vietnam war, what really bothered them, says Bereday, was the threat of the draft.[72]

Recent events provide some support for this conjecture, as we shall see in Chapter 6. Undoubtedly, narrow self-interests are involved for a large segment of upwardly mobile rank-and-file members. However, this interpretation does not explain the idealism bordering on ideological self-destructiveness that drives the activist *leaders* and that permeates an entire counterculture. Keniston denies that the young radicals are dissatisfied with the opportunity to satisfy their *own* aspirations; they seem to be relatively unconcerned with enhancing their own economic status.[73] This martyrlike posture of many activists has puzzled even casual observers of student demonstrations. What explains the students' apparent willingness to risk censor and even jail? Why are they also so disdainful of material success, careerism, and the drive to "get ahead"?

It is not merely, as Aristotle said, that "the young love victory and honor more than money, which they have not yet learned what it means to be without" because, for most of these students, there is little prospect that they will *ever* learn what it means to be without. Indeed, the affluent economy provides a cushion, which minimizes the risk of permanent failure and frees young radicals to identify with *others* who are oppressed. The radicals' basic goal is not only to achieve new freedoms, opportunities, or benefits for themselves but, instead, to extend to everyone the freedoms, opportunities, and benefits that they themselves have experienced. Their very financial security and lack of corresponding responsibility adds an emotional quality to their activism. Students constitute a new leisure class, unpreoccupied with narrow career interests, who can afford the time and incentive to read and talk about broader social concerns.[74] They may be seeking self-respect, influence, or martyrdom, but there is little reason to believe that economic threat is their only concern.

All of this casts serious doubt on any interpretation that presumes that *scarcity* of employment is the only source of dissatisfaction. As Slater has observed, youths who are part of the new culture refuse to celebrate their economic affluence and are not anxious about their social position.[75] Affluence can make possible the rejection of the very foundation that produced affluence.

During periods of prosperity and affluence, when many individuals experience improved conditions, even dramatic economic gains cannot satisfy high expectations fanned by past gains. Thus, paradoxically, discontent grows faster during precisely the periods when a group is experiencing improvement in their condition. Sociologists call this phenomenon *the revolution of rising expectations*. One way that governments promote this is to promise too much.

CONTRADICTIONS IN INSTITUTIONAL PRACTICES

Finally, many contradictions can be found in the priority given to ideals in different areas of life. For example, a church that preaches that the poor need and deserve help and that war is evil might invest in profitable slum housing property and weapons industries. The sources of some of these contradictions during the 1960s were identified in the Skolnick Report.

- Failure of the national administration to fulfill promises to stamp out poverty and urban decline.
- Failure of the political system to deal effectively with problems of race despite the administration's rhetoric that fed rising expectations.
- Escalation of an expensive undeclared war in Vietnam that drained resources from the war on poverty and that relied on the arbitrary conscription of youth who could not accept the immorality of the war.
- The brutality exercised against civil-rights workers and Negroes by Southern police officials and white racists.
- Brutal encounters with the police on campus.
- Reduction in student draft deferments, an action that was perceived by many young people as a retaliation against student activists.
- Cooperation of academic institutions with the war effort and with the military agencies generally.
- The success of the students at Berkeley and elsewhere in publicizing the student's condition and demonstrating that massive protest could be successful.[76]

Similar conditions were cited by Bailey as causes of disruptions in high schools: violence in America, and squalor, spontaneity and impulsiveness of slum life styles, black rage, and white and black racism.[77]

The federal government's "war on poverty" and its support for the civil rights movement during the 1960s might have fueled activism by promising improvements that could not be delivered. Idealistic and politically naive young people, in particular, were victimized by the rhetoric of the 1960s. The effect was to accelerate the revolution of rising expectations referred to above. Thus, racial discrimination became a symbol of widespread violation of American ideals. Black students were involved in more than half of the total 292 protests during the first half of 1969, according to a study by Urban Research Corporation.[78] Between 1964 and 1968, the number of American Negroes attending college increased at twice the rate of the total college enrollment (85 versus 46 percent), much of this increase at institutions that traditionally enrolled a predominance of white students. Many of these students encountered barriers to full assimilation into the traditionally white subculture on many campuses. One study found that black students are only minimally involved in campus life.[79] The extracurricular programs in most colleges were shaped by and for what has long been the dominant student culture. The student life of blacks is limited by taboos against interracial dating, and they are discriminated against by fraternities, sororities, and other social clubs. Moreover, since a university degree has become more economically relevant for upwardly mobile blacks, traditional and inflexible university standards have also stood in their way. Therefore, gaining "black recognition" on what had been traditionally white campuses became a leading protest issue.

While the university remained relatively immune from the civil rights movement during the early 1960s by virtue of the absolutism of scientific standards and its remoteness, in recent years, the black militants have realized that the university is more vulnerable to attack from the inside by some students. Regarding admissions and hiring practices as symbolic of the myth of white western cultural superiority, many young blacks worked for more voice over how university resources are distributed and over the curriculum.

Reservations. These cultural contradictions and status inconsistencies are undoubtedly important, but they still deal with only one side of the equation, that is, why some types of individuals might be predisposed toward activism. The other side of the equation must explain why these predispositions do not always materialize. For the answer, we shall examine the types of structural supports in the society that feed militant actions.

How Does the Political System Support Activism?

The political system can play an important role in activism. Student movements can arise only where students are strategically situated in positions that give them access to power. Universities today sometimes provide that access because they have been politicized—not by student activism but, as discussed in Chapter 2, by the fact that they have entered the service of the commercial, technical world by producing technicians and through scientific research. Student political activity is only a logical outcome of the university's attempt to be more useful and influential. "Social relevance," in other words, is a two-way street. A university cannot be involved in vocational training and applied science and still remain insulated in other respects. It will therefore be fruitful to consider in more detail how universities are linked to politics. We shall see that political activism is a product of a convergence of (1) a loose affiliation between the university and the political system, (2) a relatively mature student body from influential families, and (3) a changing, nucleated political structure.

TYPE OF AFFILIATION

Relationships between universities and political systems can take one of three forms: (1) remote, (2) close-knit, or (3) loosely linked. When universities are remote from political parties, they are insulated from the social forces that produce activism and relatively peaceful. At the other extreme, in nations where universities are closely linked to political parties, student activists can expect to be rewarded at a later time with political careers; student protest is constrained by the fact that activism becomes a direct stepping stone into politics and government jobs. The effect of the second option can be seen in Japan since the Meiji restoration. The *state* universities have been close to the government and have supplied civil servants and political leaders.[80] Consequently, opposition to the government in Japan usually has not come from the students in state universities; instead, it has come from the less well-connected *private* universities, which are less-directly linked to civil service careers.

Finally, there is sometimes a very *loose* but firm linkage between universities and the political system. Student movements seem most likely to arise under this condition. Because they are linked to the polity, universities will be stimulated by political turmoil, and yet their independence prevents them from being *co-opted* by the political and civil service systems. In these situations, activism tends to focus on only those issues that are directly linked to the political system, such as the war in Vietnam and civil rights. But, lacking a sustaining outside political base, activism arises rapidly and dies out just as quickly.

Weinberg and Walker have embellished this typology by distinguishing between two types of linkages between universities and the government: (1) whether or not the government controls the university and its financing; and (2) whether or not students are recruited into political careers through party sponsorship.[81] Where both of these links are present (as in Latin American nations) student politics tends to take the form of factional competition among political party branches. Where both are absent, university student government prevails. Where recruitment is low and government control is strong, national student unions predominate, and where the reverse conditions pertain, as in the United States, political party branches and clubs prevail. In the latter situations, activists tend to be without specific political career goals but seek to create novel, *ad hoc* organizations to carry out their activities. The fact that such organizations lack structural links to the university student government and to national political parties weakens their impact and encourages tendencies toward extremism. Indeed, as Lipset has argued, the basic leftward thrust of American society, with its liberal ideology, makes it difficult for liberal students to innovate unless they do go to radical extremes.[82] When this happens they find themselves so far to the left that they have very little popular support, which minimizes their impact. In Latin America and, to some extent in the French case, the tighter structural linkages between the university and national politics provide a stronger base for the organizational protest, increasing the likelihood of either the movement's partial success or its incorporation into existing political organizations.

Weinberg and Walker see activism in this country as a *substitute* for more legitimate political activity. If they are correct, presumably, activism would decline if activists were to become more closely linked to the major political parties. But it seems equally plausible that a close association with the political system would only tend to *stimulate* other forms of political activity, including protest demonstrations. Support for this latter alternative was found in a limited study using a sample of UCLA students.[83] The majority of demonstrators, instead of being unattached to the larger political system, had worked in political precincts for national parties. This suggests that integration into the political system did not curb other forms of political activity; on the contrary, politically oriented students seemed to be using alternative forms of activity to achieve their purposes. Co-opting students into the political system, then, will not necessarily curb activism and could serve as a stimulus to it.

THE STATUS OF STUDENTS

Student movements seem most likely to evolve where students occupy an elite, responsible status in the society, one that can provide an independent source of power to them. In many of the underdeveloped countries, where two-thirds of the population is under 30, students are mature adults, not immature adolescents. For one thing, the elite students are already identified with the existing system; however, they are in a powerful position if they do choose to revolt. Their affinity with political elites gives them leverage that lower-class students cannot hope to have.

Many black student leaders who have entered white institutions in recent years are a type of elite with roots in the black community and often steeped with ideals of black militancy. An Educational Testing Service survey revealed that black students entering integrated institutions have higher aptitude scores, are more independent, liberal, concerned with social justice, and aspire to more years of formal education than their counterparts who enter traditionally Negro colleges.[84] Many of these differences are correlated with their scholastic aptitude scores. They provide the militant black community with a political wedge into universities that heretofore did not exist.

NATURE OF THE POLITICAL SYSTEM

Regardless of how much leverage the students might have or how closely linked the university is with the political structure, student activism might not materialize unless two other characteristics are present in the political system. First, apparently the political structure must be in the process of *rapid change*. When students are affiliated with elite political groups during normal periods they tend to become co-opted. But once the structure begins to change, and the elites lose control, they can no longer guarantee employment and other opportunities to loyal students. Disillusioned student elites have been especially active in nations that have been undergoing rapid political change and revolution.

Second, it appears that the political structure must be *divided*. The greater the political cleavage in society, the more critical that the role played by a small, organized group of students can be in the shifting political balance. For this reason, student movements have been very influential in countries split by several political parties. It is probably no accident that the student movement in the United States rode the momentum of the liberal and the conservative third-party movements in the United States. The Eugene McCarthy campaign for President in 1968 represented a "third party" around which students could rally.

THE ROLE OF OUTSIDERS

Many protests also seem to involve an unorganized contingent of people who are only loosely affiliated with either universities or politics. Over half of the incidents connected with demonstrations were caused by "outsiders" not immediately connected with the demonstration, according to the Skolnick Report, and over half of the high school principals in Bailey's study also reported the presence of unruly, unauthorized, nonschool persons in their schools during 1970.[85]

There is little evidence that these people are backed by political groups. One study found that the typical "nonstudent" turned out in greater frequency than members of the student body for civil rights functions and protests against the war in Vietnam. He was a young person alienated from society and estranged from his family but not political in the conventional sense, believing that political action for social change is futile.[86] These isolated demonstrators tended to resort to extremes. This would suggest that their lack of connections with established institutions loosens the restraints on violence.

But, the role of outsiders should not be exaggerated. Political activity is still typically spearheaded by people who are well integrated into the society—that is, middle-class students from well-educated families situated in national, public institutions of the highest prestige.

Reservations. While the university's relationship to the political system is an obviously crucial part of the explanation, as was true of the previous explanations, it is incomplete when taken by itself. It does not entirely account for why some universities are more politically active than others. To answer this more precise question we must consider a final ingredient—the contextual and internal conditions within the universities and high schools themselves.

How Do Educational Organizations Contribute to Activism?

The discussion up to this point has concentrated on conditions that predispose people to become activists and then nourish and sustain their efforts. We have not yet identified the mechanisms located within the structure of educational institutions that actually *trigger* activism. Many of the factors already identified often converge in educational institutions where they are activated. Thus, perhaps it is no coincidence that surveys and studies of American, Asian, and Latin American students have indicated that the more years a student spends in the university the more likely he is to move to the left.[87] Students have often directed their aggression directly at school-related conditions: the nature of classroom instruction; lack of respect toward students; school disregard of serious societal ills; lack of response to legitimate grievances; irrelevant curriculum; interracial tension in schools populated by large numbers of black and white and brown students; the extent of administrative and teacher control over student behavior; and the division of status and privilege that separates teachers from students. We now consider a few of the conditions that are frequently cited as immediate sources of protest.

ECOLOGICAL FACTORS

Several ecological factors have been cited as catalysts of discontent. For example, students are likely to be more aware of political issues when attending universities located near a political capital, and it appears that student movements are often headquartered in the national universities, which selectively attract students from around the nation and the world. In addition, social control is difficult to maintain in universities having concentrations of students who are living away from home and living off campus where they are less subject to supervisory controls.

Also, the fact that many universities are large and are concentrated in urban centers facilitates communication among the students. Indeed, congested living conditions found around most major universities of the world resemble those of ghetto slums in many respects: they are densely populated by a mobile, homogeneous age group who are uniformly without property or family ties but who are affiliated by membership in a common institution and confronting common problems. The dense concentration of this homogeneous group fosters rapid communication, the development of social organization, and the emergence of a distinct youth culture with its own language, value system, and ideologies. In view of the fact that student organizations are hampered by rapid turnover, they probably would not be able to survive without the benefit of these favorable ecological conditions.

SIZE AND ALIENATION

It is perhaps not a coincidence that student activism gained momentum during an era when the number and size of universities was mushrooming at an accelerated pace and when the size of high schools was doubling. As noted in Chapter 1, although there is little evidence, many observers believe that this growth in the scale of educational organizations has contributed to impersonality, sense of alienation, and educational routine that is meaningless for the individual student. Social scientists in the United States, France, and Italy have attributed the rise of student protests to the growth of university student bodies.[88]

The evidence does overwhelmingly indicate that larger institutions are more protest prone than smaller ones. The Syracuse study of 27 high schools found that larger schools had more problems, and that the size of the student body was more important than the size of the city in which the school was located.[89] Hodgkinson's survey of several hundred universities revealed that, regardless of the highest degree awarded, as the size of the student body rose, the percentage of institutions reporting student protests also rose.[90] Peterson's Educational Testing Service survey also verified that organized protest was related to college size.[91] While there was not a perfect one-to-one relationship, the very large campuses were far more subject to organized protest than the medium and small ones, especially with regard to certain types of issues, such as racial discrimination by the university administration, censorship, and off-campus issues (civil rights and the Vietnam War, for example). Almost half of the 50 largest universities (compared to only 18 percent of the total sample) indicated that outbreaks were prompted by racial circumstances; one contributing factor was that the largest campuses were more likely to have black organizations and student leftist groups, but they also contained numerically more morally sensitive students and nonstudents who rejected traditional middle-class standards.

Still another study found that large complex, high-quality "multiversities" located in large communities had a much higher rate of demonstrations per school than small, structurally simple, low-quality schools.[92] However, further analysis revealed that large schools did not produce more demonstrations *per thousand students* than the small schools. In other words, demonstrations were not a result of numbers alone. They were produced by a combination of size, administrative complexity, and social heterogeneity. Nevertheless, since many of these characteristics were associated with size, the size of the student body was the best *single* predictor of incidents of student demonstration.

The authors of that study argued that the more bureaucratic an educational institution, the greater the status and power differences between students, faculty and administrators, and the more socially isolated the students are from the administrators, faculty, and other students. This isolation and powerlessness, they conjectured, make students feel neglected, manipulated, and dehumanized. Paradoxically, as a larger percentage of university students marry, become mobile, financially independent and more insistent on personal freedoms, many schools seem to have become more bureaucratic and regimented. Lacking channels for personal contact with higher administration, students seek to redress their grievances in illegal or extralegal protest actions that cannot be easily ignored by lower-level bureaucrats and that attract even more of the highly radicalized and politicized students.

However, there is not much support for this "alienation" theme. Only one-third of the deans surveyed in 1968 reported organized complaints about classes being too large or institutions too impersonal.[93] Moreover, the students continue to enroll voluntarily in the large institutions that they must suspect are impersonal and bureaucraic. Advocates of the alienation theme, of course, might argue that the focus of the protest need not be on the conditions that produced it. This kind of collective behavior is not necessarily so rational. However, if there is no connection it also would be extremely difficult to demonstrate that factors such as size and impersonality have anything to do with protests. Perhaps too much weight has been given to size in comparison to other, more fundamental characteristics associated with size.

QUALITY OF THE UNIVERSITY

Many of the prestigious, high-quality academic institutions are large, suggesting that there may be something about the *quality* of institutions that provokes activism. In Peterson's study, activism was clearly related to the quality of institutions (measured by percentage of Ph.D.s on the faculty).[94] Hodgkinson also concluded that as institutional quality (measured by the number of Ph.D.s on the faculty, satisfaction ratings by freshmen, and selectivity of students, for example) increased, so did the incidence of student protest.[95] He attributed this finding almost entirely to the competence of the students, but Kahn and Bower's research indicated that there was clearly something apart from the student's social background, academic commitment or field of study that promoted activists' involvement in the higher quality colleges and universities.[96] They conjectured that in addition to promoting intellectualism and critical social thought, the better institutions also serve as symbolic and strategic *targets* of protest. Since these schools often set the standards and styles for the entire system of higher education, students realize that widespread educational reform cannot take place until these institutions are changed. Moreover, the fact that these institutions generally play an important role in community and national affairs makes them desirable targets for other reasons already suggested; that is, by attacking the institutions, the students can attack the basic problems in the society itself.

STUDENT BODY COMPOSITION

It already has been seen that the type of student subculture that dominates a college or high school has a bearing on the extent of activism. Large institutions are especially receptive to the evolution of activist subcultures, for even if the *proportion* of radicals on campuses is constant from campus to campus a larger *number* of activists will be concentrated on the larger campuses. Also, the heterogeneity of large campuses, aside from sheer size, can lead to polarization and politicalization. The racial composition of the student body is an important aspect of heterogeneity. The Syracuse study of high school disruptions reported a positive correlation between disruptions and the amount of racial integration in the school; schools that were almost all black or white were less likely to be disrupted than racially mixed schools. Undoubtedly, integration not only increases the tension among the students themselves, but also is likely to increase tensions between students and teachers. Evidence of this tension was found in the Syracuse study. Integrated schools with higher proportions of black students were more likely to be disrupted if they had predominantly white staffs than if they had black staffs.

Also, teachers have not been adequately prepared to deal with the growing number of students who are indifferent to schooling and who only a decade ago would have dropped out of high school. Nor is there reason to believe that professors are prepared to cope with the growing numbers of low-ability students now going to college.

THE REWARD SYSTEM: TEACHING VERSUS RESEARCH

It is often contended that neglect of teaching in favor of research has been a major source of provocation for activist students. Some critics have observed that students who are attracted to major universities by famous teachers often find that they are met only in large lecture courses along with several hundred undergraduates; that many of the famous names are too socially distant and too busy with research and writing commitments to have much time for personal contacts with undergraduates; and that much of the teaching is done by teaching assistants whose major preoccupation is meeting their own degree requirements.[97] Critics have observed that the less a person teaches, the higher is his status, and that the proximity of an undergraduate menaces the managerial purity of the modern professor.[98] Kerr sees a cruel paradox in the fact that a superior faculty means inferior teaching, that as the university gets better and better, teaching gets worse and worse. In Marx's system, say the critics, there was an increasing misery of the proletariat as the capitalist system made technological advances and moved toward a zero rate of profit, whereas in the modern university, there is a comparable increase in the misery of students as the university system moves toward intellectual advance with a zero rate of teaching, which encourages students to think of themselves as a new "class," a "lumpenproletariat."

In support of these accusations, Hodgkinson reported that, in comparison to a national sample, the faculty in the high-protest universities devoted more time to research and less to teaching and service to the university in recent years.[99] However, as a more direct test of this explanation, one considers the nature of the issues. The 1968 survey of deans reported that issues involving poor instruction, "publish or perish" issues, as well as censorship and related freedom of expression issues were relatively unimportant as targets of student protest.[100] Less than 15 percent of the deans reported protests over curriculum inflexibility, testing, grading, and poor quality of instruction. Indeed, some of the small liberal arts colleges that are noted for the high caliber of instruction and individual attention have been the scene of protest. "Poor teaching" appears to be a superficial symptom of the more basic fact that, as indicated in Chapter 2, modern mass universities are not effectively or economically organized to meet both the demands of today's undergraduate student bodies and the demands of the society for research and service.

NARROW SPECIALIZATION AND FORMALIZATION

The debate over teaching and research does touch upon a more fundamental problem that probably is involved when students complain about the curriculum and teaching, that is, the effects of excessively narrow specialization and unbending professionalism. Bendix has observed that among student radicals there is a strong distrust of "reason" and antagonism toward science.[101] This observation could provide an important clue to a basis for their unrest. What accounts for the "distrust of reason"? Is it simply another form of the intellectual's historical mistrust of official authority and his quest for a return to the sacred qualities of life?[102] Or, is it a reaction to what MacLeish[103] referred to as the separation of "knowledge" from "feeling"? Bendix argues that man attempts to overcome his feelings of excessive alienation and relativism through a highly subjective radical commitment to action and impatience with neutral science.

But "distrust of reason" merely describes a personal reaction; it is not the structural source of the issue. People distrust reason because of its narrow intellectual basis, not because it is opposed to feeling. This narrowness stems from the tendency of scientific disciplines to become separated from other *intellectual* currents. Snow called attention to the increasing polarization between science and the humanities in the western world, and Ortega y Gasset before him lamented the increasing narrowness of fields of science that were producing progressive isolation among its separate branches.[104] Accordingly, Holton considers the need to restore reciprocal contact between science and intellectual traditions to be the most critical challenge today before scientists and other scholars.[105]

Referring to a related tension between *scholarship* (which draws upon and is constrained by an established body of knowledge) and *creativity* (which requires the risk of breaking away from established fact and paradigms), Barzuns notes that the curiosity of students is sometimes curbed by rigid professional expectations that professors impose on their students and by administrative rules.[106] When narrow specialization, exacting standards of inquiry, unyielding rules and requirements, and professionalism converge on the student, he has little latitude to follow his own imagination and curiosity. Some students who go to college in search of philosophical answers to complex issues soon learn that the answers cannot be found within any one discipline, and yet they are expected to master the technical knowledge associated with a discipline while the broad issues and underlying assumptions may be entirely ignored.

At least some of the activism, then, must be seen as a response to the threat of ethical perversion that occurs when the traditions of humane intellectual scholarship no longer serve as guidelines for the uses to which scientific knowledge is put. Student activists have called attention to these problems and have demanded a new synthesis between research and significant intellectual and moral issues.

CONTROL STRUCTURE

Many student activists and observers believe that the authority structure of educational institutions has been a major target of student unrest. Although there are differences in degree between the authority structures of high schools and colleges, both are shaped by the mandatory nature of attendance and the necessity of controlling the students. Spady argues that as long as students accept the power of their teachers and professors to give poor grades and withhold other rewards as a legitimate right, they will not rebel. The source of legitimacy is the students' respect for the teacher's technical competence (in both subject matter and pedagogy) *and* his empathy for students.[107] In reality, he argues, many teachers cannot meet these competency tests and are forced to rely on their bureaucratic positions to provide the power they need in order to maintain control. In effect, students are rebelling against the teachers' *bureaucratic* authority that they use to compensate for the fact that they have not met *professional* standards of authority.

This explanation cannot be easily applied to the universities. It seems unlikely that students have a low regard for their professors' technical competence. And while perhaps they do not admire professors for their teaching ability, as just noted, there is little evidence of widespread hostility to professors on this basis. The problem can be more adequately explained by the fact that professors are overspecialized and, perhaps, have low empathy for students. Nevertheless, there may be a kernel of truth in Spady's argument, even at the university level. *Administrators* cannot readily point to a body of specialized knowledge that justifies their authority. Administrative actions, therefore, rely on bureaucratic authority that can appear arbitrary to students. Students have often expressed resentment about the attempts of administrators to set dress codes and dormitory regulations, to control political activities, to establish the curriculum and required courses, and to govern grading and placement policies. Moreover, student careers are subject to irrevocable career sorting processes controlled by school authorities, through which they are assigned to a curriculum, or a "track," on the basis of precarious assumptions and limited knowledge about their innate ability, interests, and motives. This unites entire groups of students with a common fate against their professors.

FACULTY HIERARCHY

Neither high school "teachers" nor college "professors" should be categorically portrayed as the primary target of student hostility. For, there are wide differences among high school and among college teachers (as well as some important differences between them). Some faculty members, especially in universities, not only have encouraged activism but have exercised leadership in student movements. Many young faculty members and graduate assistants, in particular, have essentially become "marginal" men and women in recent years. They have turned their sympathies and loyalties from research and other narrow professional concerns to the problems of undergraduate students.

The magnitude of the gap between younger and older faculty members was revealed in a large national survey of academic men in 300 colleges across the country sponsored by the Carnegie Commission on Higher Education in the spring of 1969. By a ratio of 2 to 1 the younger men were less likely to oppose violence to achieve political goals and more likely to approve radical student activism and the right of undergraduates to be formally consulted on decisions about the provision or content of courses.[108]

Young professors are in close contact with undergraduate students by virtue of their teaching roles and their age; on the other hand, they occupy university positions that allow them to exert leadership with respect to undergraduates. Keniston believes that the presence of large numbers of underpaid, frustrated teaching assistants (and instructors) is an essential ingredient for organized protest.[109] They tend to be politically liberal, partly because education has a liberalizing effect and partly because the students who persist in graduate school tend to be more liberal than those who drop out. Furthermore, the frustrations of graduate students and young faculty members, especially at large public universities, make them particularly sensitive to general problems of injustice, exploitation, and oppression.

EXTRACURRICULAR ACTIVITIES

Schools and colleges traditionally have tried to channel student energies into extracurricular activity programs partly to divert their attention from more serious matters. In Japan during the 1920s, there was a self-conscious effort to reduce radicalism by relaxing restrictions on high school love affairs. Sports in colleges in the United States were organized partly to divert energy from the town-gown brawls. High schools customarily use extracurricular activities as incentives for students to conform to the school's academic and personal standards of conduct; in probably a majority of high schools, grades are required for eligibility in athletics, student government, cheerleading, and other activities. It is speculated that where extracurricular activities do not exist, students are more likely to satisfy their leadership ambitions by focusing on issues that are more central to the school.

However, this hypothesis presumes that activities are accessible to the students who might be inclined toward activism. Insofar as they are not accessible, the extracurricular program can become the source of further discontent. As institutions have grown larger, it has become more difficult for large numbers of highly qualified students to gain recognition through extracurricular activities. At each stage of his career, the student enters a larger institution affording fewer opportunities to achieve recognition than the one from which he has graduated. For example, a boy who was elected president of the ninth-grade class finds overwhelming competition for the post of student body president in a large, urban high school, and once in college will find almost overwhelming odds against obtaining a similar position of leadership. Girls have even fewer chances to attain leadership positions through legitimate channels. The situation is aggravated in many universities that selectively recruit students from the top of their high school graduating classes, since these are the very students who are most likely to have held leadership positions in their high schools. Student activism can help to compensate for this form of status deprivation. It provides *alternative channels of recognition* for students who otherwise find their status in college to be entirely inconsistent with the positions of leadership they were accustomed to in high school.

A related factor is that there is no longer much distinction in attending college. Whereas only 20 percent of the high school graduates went to college only a generation ago, today the figure is over 60 percent, and for upper-middle-class students in states like California it is closer to 80 percent. This fact, coupled with the fact that many of these youths feel compelled to be in college because there are few alternatives, helps to explain much of the alienation.

WHAT CAN BE DONE ABOUT STUDENT ACTIVISM?

STUDENT POWER

One of the important findings from the Equality of Educational Opportunity survey was that blacks who believed that they could control their own fate achieved higher scores on tests than students who did not believe this. This suggests that achievement might be improved by giving students more opportunities to participate in the governance of educational institutions. However, there is no evidence that giving students more voice in university government does in fact curb activism. On the contrary, one form of political activity seems only to stimulate other forms of political activity. For example, 80 percent of the campuses in Hodgkinson's study reporting an increase of student control over institutional policies also reported an increase in protest. Whereas 64 percent of the national sample of institutions reported increased student control, 80 percent of the high protest sample reported an increase in student control in institution-wide policy making.[110]

Changing the internal authority structure of universities alters only one dimension of the equation. If the political structure remains in turmoil, students may simply use their internal power leverage for waging attacks on the larger society. This seems to be the case in revolution-prone South American universities, where students sometimes comprise up to one-third of the governing bodies of the universities.

SELECTIVE RECRUITMENT

Where activism is instigated by a handful of "troublemakers," it might be controlled by recruiting fewer of the potential troublemakers. This might become absurd, however. As a practical matter, this would mean recruiting fewer bright students from affluent, liberal, middle-class homes and, instead, giving preference to (1) the vocationally oriented, upwardly mobile Protestant and Catholic students of average ability or below from lower-middle-class homes, and to (2) the vocational curriculum over the social sciences and humanities. Both policies would distort the historical, intellectual mission of universities. The first policy, in effect, would screen out the most academically able students, which would have serious repercussions for both the intellectual mission of the university and the society. The people who are committed to maintaining the very policies that produced activism in the first place would be channeled into leadership positions. The second policy would produce a generation of narrowly trained leaders and citizens deprived of a broader perspective on the values and type of society in which they live.

RECRUITING MORE MATURE STUDENTS

The notion that activists are immature suggests that colleges might require students to gain some kind of job experience, travel, serve in the military, or work in the Peace Corps or similar programs before entering college. This approach awaits the development of better alternatives to college for those students who do not want to be there, and it would require more appropriate university policies for dealing with mature students.

LIMITED ENROLLMENTS

The thesis that activism is the response of college students whose status aspirations have been frustrated suggests that activism could be reduced by limiting enrollments to a number that would assure appropriate jobs for all students who complete college. This policy would represent such a major reversal of the society's apparently unquenchable thirst for universal formal schooling, however, that it probably could not be implemented at the present time; although it might become more feasible as some of the previously mentioned alternatives to formal schooling are made available.

The main question here, however, is not whether it would be feasible to limit college enrollments but whether it would curb activism. Indeed, another explanation is that the status security of affluent activists is responsible for their willingness to take the risks involved in activism. Conversely, therefore, activism might *decline* during periods of intense competition among college graduates. Competition might promote insecurity that would force students to conform.

LOWER ACADEMIC STANDARDS

To the extent that student activists are simply concerned with advancing their own self-interests, as some critics have argued, activism might be minimized by lowering academic standards and providing more electives within the system. Such a policy would perhaps relieve some of the pressure on the less-able students and thus deprive student movements of some essential support from the rank-and-file students. However, it is not likely to have much effect on the idealistic leadership, who might become even more disillusioned with the university by such policies.

SUPPRESSION

Writers who advocate that generational conflict, with its psychological propensity toward self-destruction, violence, and destruction of the university and the society, is at the bottom of the problem advocate more stringent controls, retaliation, and repression. Six percent of the high schools in Bailey's study reported resident policemen, and two-thirds of the schools said that the police are "on call."[111] Many university administrators have relied on the force of police and the militia as well. Reliance on force, however, sometimes has provoked even more sympathy for the militants and more aggression and tends to undermine the rapport between teachers and students to the point where administrators, professors, and students confront one another on opposing sides of a "militarized zone."

SOCIAL REFORM

The other version of the generational conflict thesis, which stresses that value conflicts lie at the heart of the problem suggests very different policies. If activism is produced by the value system and structural inconsistencies, then activism can be reduced only by eliminating the social conditions that activists are reacting to—racial and social inequalities, war, repressive moralities, and adult oppression, for example. This approach suggests that legislation is required to strike down privileges based on class, race, and adult status, to liberalize school policies, and to enlarge the sphere of student involvement. Recent legislation revising the draft system, giving 18-year-olds the right to vote, and withdrawing from the Asian war are part of this approach and may have been partially responsible for cooling off the students.

DISENGAGEMENT

One logical (although probably not very feasible) alternative at this point in history would be for universities to disengage from socially relevant programs. Although universities have always been subject to outside pressures, as long as they maintained their "ivory tower" role they were less subject to politicalization and provided a better atmosphere in which to engage in long-range research than is presently true as universities attempt to increase their practical relevance.

DECENTRALIZATION AND STRUCTURAL DIFFERENTIATION

Finally, the organizational and ecological dimensions of the problem lead to a variety of other suggestions: breaking down universities into smaller institutions and dispersing colleges more widely throughout each state; encouraging students to live at home; insulating undergraduate teaching from research and graduate training and providing more rewards for undergraduate teaching careers; and opening up more opportunities for students to gain recognition within the university's social system.

The reader will have to judge for himself whether activism *ought* to be controlled and, if so, which of its many forms should be suppressed and which encouraged. Since no one knows for sure what causes activism, it is not possible to say definitively which proposal will provide the most effective form of control, although we have seen the obvious weaknesses in some of them. Militancy is probably a product of many causes, and therefore no one policy in itself will be entirely effective in controlling it. It should be noted, however, that some proposals are intended only to suppress the activists, while other proposals would lead to wide-scale social and educational reforms, at least some of which could represent an improvement in education for many individuals. Student protest, then, has been a positive as well as a negative force. For this reason, activism has had, and will continue to have, an important part to play in public education.

CONCLUSIONS

It is clear that the speculations about student activism are far more plentiful than the available factual information, but the range of speculation does at least demonstrate how extremely complex the problem is. We have tried to build a cumulative explanation by weaving together many isolated themes. But, as John F. Kennedy once said, "Just because there is a problem, doesn't mean there is a solution." Any explanation, or set of explanations, is still largely conjectural, warranting only some limited conclusions.

To briefly recapitulate, although there is a long history of student activism in this country, during the 1960s protests became more militant, more extensive, more focused on the educational and social structure, and more hostile to established authority and to institutions not only within universities but in the larger society as well. Certain types of students and institutions have been involved more frequently than others. We noted the curious anomaly that the best students tend to be actively involved and that their target often is precisely the best academic institutions. During the discussion, we touched on some of the reasons. The fact that the better students come from high-status, economically secure homes protects them from some of the risks involved in exercising militant leadership; they have been exposed to liberal values; they have already experienced positions of authority within their own homes and in high school; they have the leisure time to think about social issues; and they are cognizant of national and worldwide problems. The best institutions are the targets of attack not only because these institutions attract militant students but also because they encourage critical thinking, support academic freedom and, most important, are the leaders of academe and are closely linked to the political and economic affairs of the nation. They are excellent symbolic targets. Whether one is speaking about universities or individuals, then, there seems to be a general principle at work: activism is associated with the intellectual, academic culture. It arises where the academy develops influence over political and economic policies. Conversely, the more integrated an individual or university is into the vocational world, the less likely activism is to flourish. Student activism may be a natural by-product of intellectual life. If so, the only way to curb it is to radically change the mission of universities, in effect, to destroy their intellectual core.

Activism is produced by a coalition of elites and the rank-and-file, but these two groups are probably motivated by very different concerns. Elites are idealistic and politically oriented. They have encountered status inconsistencies, are disillusioned with the society, and are distrustful of the adult generation's competence to solve the problems. Many of the rank-and-file, by contrast, are less-intensively idealistic, although liberally inclined and sympathetic, and they are perhaps more motivated by self-interest—often the economic and social worth of the college degree.

Several explanations of activism were reviewed. The *predispositions* of individuals are important but do not provide a sufficient answer because there is evidence that whether or not a person acts in accordance with his personal predispositions depends on his social context, including characteristics of the institution. The idea that activists are immature adolescents overlooks the recent emergence of an independent youth subculture, a "counterculture" of values and norms at variance with the traditional culture. The generational conflict hypothesis does take this conflict of values into account, but too often it has been interpreted psychologically, which misses the fundamental *institutional* sources of the problem. These are found in the youth culture that supports a value climate conducive to militancy and in social change, which has outmoded the future orientation and stress on achievement that are endorsed by the adult generation. This change in values is responsible for contradictions that are intensely experienced by the activists.

In addition to the personal predispositions, a conducive value climate, and selective experience with the cultural contradictions, activism requires *structural support* in the form of linkages between the university and the political system. The university must be sufficiently well incorporated into the political system to provide political support but yet maintain enough autonomy to resist being co-opted by the dominant political group.

Finally, there must be *triggering* mechanisms within educational structures themselves to activate this coalition of forces in particular places and times. They include ecological factors (such as location of the institution and the physical concentration of students), organizational size and complexity, quality of the institution, the reward system, specialization, student body composition, official policies, faculty structure and support for activism, and lack of opportunities for students to be heard and recognized through legitimate channels.

It can be seen, then, that activism is caused by a combination of ingredients, and that organizational characteristics of educational institutions are among the most essential of these ingredients. Since many of the necessary forces converge in universities, the university holds the final key as to whether or not activism materializes. Although activism perhaps has become a fundamental condition of the structure of higher education, it can be moderated by changing the structure of educational institutions. In view of the fact that changes in student participation, voting rights, and other policies already have been taken as steps toward reducing some forms of activism, perhaps the most significant effect of activism will be to produce lasting structural change in the educational, social, and political systems of this country. To that extent, activism will ultimately affect not just the few who participate but large numbers of Americans for generations to come.

REFERENCES

1. Lewis Feuer, *Conflict of Generations.* New York: Basic Books, 1969, p. 329.

2. The generic term, "student activism," is used to refer to a range of social and political activities including rebellions, disruptions, civil disobedience, open protest, peaceful demonstrations, and verbal confrontations. This term also encompasses the more peaceful demands of students to participate in making educational policy and in officially recognized political and social organizations on campus. However, since these latter activities, which fall within the legitimate system, are less problematic they are less applicable to this discussion. The term "student movement" refers to a specific form of activism—that is, organized and sustained action on the part of students

unified by a radical political ideology. The discussion will, at various points, allude to some parallels between activism in colleges and high schools. However, since more is known about the colleges, primary attention will be given to them in this abbreviated discussion.

3. Feuer, *op. cit.*, p. 436.

4. Cited in U.S. President's Commission on Campus Unrest, *The Report of the President's Commission on Campus Unrest.* New York: Arno Press, 1970, Chapter 1.

5. *Ibid.*

6. Philip Jacob, *Changing Values in College.* New York: Harper, 1957.

7. Feuer, *op. cit.*

8. Jerome H. Skolnick, *The Politics of Protest: The Skolnick Report to the National Commission on the Causes and Prevention of Violence.* New York: Ballantine Books, 1969.

9. U.S. President's Commission on Campus Unrest, *op. cit.*

10. Kenneth Keniston, "The Sources of Student Dissent," *Journal of Social Issues, 23,* July 1967, 201.

11. Skolnick, *op. cit.*

12. Richard E. Peterson, *The Scope of Organized Student Protest, 1964–65.* Princeton: Educational Testing Service, 1966 and Richard E. Peterson, "The Student Left in American Higher Education," *Daedalus,* Winter 1968, 293–317.

13. Harold Hodgkinson, "Student Protest—An Institutional and National Profile," *Teachers College Record, 71,* May 1970, 537–555.

14. Cited in Stephen Bailey, *Disruption in Urban Secondary Schools.* Washington, D.C.: National Association of Secondary School Principals, 1970, p. 7.

15. *Ibid.*

16. *Ibid.*

17. National Association of Secondary School Principals, "Report on High School Disruption," unpublished manuscript, Washington, D.C., 1969.

18. Bailey, *op. cit.*, Tables 1 and 2, pp. 7 and 8.

19. John W. Meyer, Chris Chase-Dunn and James Inverarity, "The Expansion of the Autonomy of Youth: Responses of the Secondary School to Problems of Order in the 1960's." Stanford University: Laboratory for Social Research, 1971 (mimeo).

20. Feuer, *op. cit.*

21. Peterson, *op. cit.*, 1966.

22. Seymour Martin Lipset and Sheldon S. Wolin, editors, *The Berkeley Student Revolt: Facts and Interpretations.* Garden City, N.Y.: Anchor Books and Doubleday, 1965.

23. Dean R. Hoge, "College Students' Value Patterns in the 1950's and 1960's," *Sociology of Education, 44,* Spring 1971, 170–197.

24. Daniel Seligman, "A Special Kind of Rebellion," *Fortune*, January 1969, 68.

25. Harris Poll, May 1970 (Student Activism) cited in "College Generations and Their Politics," Seymour M. Lipset and Everett C. Ladd, Jr., *New Society*, October 7, 1971, 654.

26. "Campus, 65: The College Generation Looks at Itself and the World Around It," *Newsweek*, March 22, 1965, 43–63.

27. Louis Harris, "Crisis in the High Schools: The Life Poll," *Life*, May 16, 1969, 24–25.

28. *Ibid.*

29. Robert H. Sommers, "The Mainsprings of Rebellion: A Survey of Berkeley Students in November 1964," in *The Berkeley Student Revolt: Facts and Interpretations, op. cit.*

30. Brewster M. Smith, Norman Haan, and Jeanne Black, "Psychological Aspects of Student Activism on Two Bay Area Campuses," Berkeley: Institute of Human Development, University of California (mimeo).

31. Marshall W. Meyer, "Harvard Students in the Midst of Crisis," *Sociology of Education, 44*, Summer 1971, 245–269.

32. U.S. President's Commission on Campus Unrest, *op. cit.*, Chapter 2.

33. Peterson, *op. cit.*, 1968.

34. Michiya Shimbori, "Zengakuren: A Japanese Case Study of a Student Movement," *Sociology of Education, 37*, Spring 1964, 229–253.

35. James Coleman, et al., *Equality of Educational Opportunity*, Washington, D.C.: U.S. Government Printing Office, 1966.

36. Bailey, *op. cit.*

37. These four types of conditions can be applied to each of several different levels of analysis: personal characteristics of individuals, cultural values, institutional structure, and characteristics of schools and colleges and of their social environments. For example, certain factors within schools might be considered to be predisposing conditions (i.e., student body composition), others to be facilitating conditions (i.e., quality of the institution), others to be structural supports (i.e., faculty structure), or still others to be triggering mechanisms (i.e., size and complexity of the system). Moreover, a more refined analysis would show that the same conditions can, at different times, act as supporting or activating mechanisms. However, in order to simplify the presentation, these more refined distinctions will not be discussed here. For our purposes, in most cases it will be sufficient to combine the two dimensions of the typology.

38. Keniston, *op. cit.*

39. Richard Flacks, "The Liberated Generation: An Exploration of the Roots of Student Protest" in *Black Power and Student Rebellion*, James McEvoy and Abraham Miller, eds. Belmont, Cal.: Wadsworth Publishers, 1969, pp. 354–378.

40. Clement H. Moore and Arlie R. Hochschild, "Student Unions in North

African Politics," in *Students in Revolt*, S.M. Lipset and P. Altbach, eds. Boston: Houghton-Mifflin, 1969; Michiya Shimbori, "Zengakuren: A Japanese Case Study of a Student Movement," *op. cit.*; and C. J. Lammers, "Student Unionism in the Netherlands," Leyden: Institute of Sociology, University of Leyden, 1970 (mimeo).

41. Sommers, *op. cit.*

42. Richard G. Braungart, "Family Status, Socialization, and Student Politics: A Multi-Variate Analysis," *American Journal of Sociology*, 77, July 1971, 108–130.

43. Roger M. Kahn and William J. Bowers, "The Social Context of the Rank-and-File Student Activists: A Test of Four Hypotheses," *Sociology of Education*, 43, Winter 1970, 38–55.

44. Hanan C. Selvin and Warren O. Hagstrom, "Determinants of Support for Civil Liberties," *British Journal of Sociology*, 11, March 1960, 51–73: Also William J. Crotty, "Democratic Consensual Norms and the College Student," *Sociology of Education*, 40, Summer 1967, 207.

45. Donald K. Emmerson, *Students and Politics in Developing Nations*, Donald K. Emmerson, ed. New York: Praeger, 1968, pp. 390–426.

46. Selvin and Hagstrom, *op. cit.*

47. Lionel S. Lewis, "Intellectualism on Campus," *College and University*, 44, Winter 1969, 173–181.

48. Feuer, *op. cit.*, p. 3.

49. Skolnick, *op. cit.*, p. 80.

50. *Ibid.*

51. Kahn and Bowers, *op. cit.*

52. David Nasatir, "A Note on Contextual Effects and the Political Orientation of University Students," *American Sociological Review*, 33, April 1968, 210–218.

53. Stephen Cole and Hannelore Adamsons, "Determinants of Faculty Support for Student Demonstrations," *Sociology of Education, 42*, Fall 1969, 315–329.

54. Erick H. Erickson, editor. *Youth: Change and Challenge*, New York: Basic Books, 1963.

55. Ivan Turgenev, *Fathers and Sons*. New York: Modern Library, 1961.

56. Feuer, *op. cit.*

57. *Ibid.*

58. Philip E. Slater, *The Pursuit of Loneliness: American Culture at the Breaking Point*. Boston: Beacon Press, 1970, p. 100.

59. Flacks, *op. cit.*

60. *Standard Education Almanac*. Los Angeles: Academic Media, 1970.

61. Norman Birnbaum, *The Crisis of Industrial Society*. New York: Oxford University Press, 1969; S. N. Eisenstadt, *From Generation to Generation*. New York: Free Press, 1962; Kingsley Davis, "The Sociology of Parent-Youth Conflict," *American Sociological Review*, 5, August 1940, 523–535;

and Margaret Mead, *Culture and Commitment: A Study of the Generation Gap.* Garden City: Doubleday, Natural History Press, 1970.

62. The role of cultural change in producing conflict between the generations can be readily seen in many underdeveloped countries in the process of modernization where there is an especially marked contrast between the old and new institutions. Universities play a uniquely strategic role in such countries. As products of the Western culture, universities are cosmopolitanizing forces. Where illiteracy is high, the educated and the elite rival the military for control of the society. University students in such societies become identified with the Western countries and become alienated from their own traditions. They develop feelings of superiority to their families, especially because they are faced with a changing job structure and can no longer rely on their family status for their own futures but, instead, must demonstrate technological competence that comes with formal training. Since the ability of their nation to adapt to a changing world will determine their own future, these students become future oriented, progressive, and internationally minded.

63. Keniston, *op. cit.*

64. Skolnick, *op. cit.*

65. Keniston, *op. cit.*

66. Richard Flacks, "The Liberated Generation: An Exploration of the Roots of Student Protest," *Journal of Social Issues, 23,* 1967, 52–75; and Keniston, *op. cit.*; also *Youth in Two Worlds.* San Francisco: Jossey-Bass, 1972.

67. Denise Kandel and Gerald Lesser, "Parental and Peer Influence on the Educational Plans of Adolescents," *American Sociological Review, 34,* April 1969, 213–222; also, *Youth in Two Worlds.* San Francisco: Jossey-Bass, 1972.

68. Samuel Lubell, "How Much Radicalism is There on Campuses?" *Columbus Citizen Journal,* 7, No. 144, Monday, April 25, 1966.

69. Flacks, *op. cit.*

70. More precisely, activism can be seen as a product of the *relationship* between the economic importance of the degree and access to it. Either side of this equation may produce dissatisfaction. First of all, for a given level of access, the lower the value of the degree, the more reason the students have to be dissatisfied with the educational system. However, the less accessible the degree is, the more discontented the students will be. This can be expressed as a series of ratios: (1) the proportion of graduates who are employed in positions requiring their level of training; (2) the proportion of students enrolled in a college who graduate; and (3) the proportion of applicants to a college who are admitted.

71. Arthur L. Stinchcombe, *Rebellion in the High School.* Chicago: Quadrangle Books, 1964.

72. George Z. Bereday, "Student Unrest on Four Continents: Montreal, Ibadon, Wassau, and Rangoon," in *Student Politics,* S. M. Lipset, ed. New York: Basic Books, 1967.

73. Keniston, *op. cit.*

74. Max Weber, *From Max Weber: Essays in Sociology.* Hans H. Gerth and C. Wright Mills, eds. New York: Oxford University Press, 1946.

75. Slater, *op. cit.*

76. Skolnick, *op. cit.*

77. Bailey, *op. cit.*

78. "Most Protests Not Violent Survey Shows," *Chronicle of Higher Education, 4,* January 26, 1970, 1, Urban Research Corp.

79. Rodney T. Hartnett, "Differences in Selected Attitudes and College Orientation between Black Students Attending Traditionally Negro and Traditionally White Institutions," *Sociology of Education, 43,* Fall 1970, 419–436.

80. Donald P. Dore, "Education: Japan," in *Political Modernization in Japan and Turkey,* R.E. Ward and D. Rustow, eds. Princeton University Press, 1964, pp. 180–187.

81. Ian Weinberg and Kenneth N. Walker, "Student Politics and Political Systems: Toward a Typology," *American Journal of Sociology, 74,* July 1969, 77–97.

82. Seymour Martin Lipset, ed., *Student Politics.* New York: Basic Books, 1967.

83. Clarence E. Tygart and Norman Holt, "Examining the Weinberg and Walker Typology of Student Activists," *American Journal of Sociology, 77,* March 1972, 957–966.

84. Cited in George F. Rothbart, "The Legitimation of Inequality: Objective Scholarship versus Black Militance," *Sociology of Education, 43,* Spring 1970, 159–174.

85. Skolnick, *op. cit.,* and Bailey, *op. cit.*

86. William A. Watts and David Whittaker, "Profile of a Nonconformist Youth Culture: A Study of the Berkeley Non-Students," *Sociology of Education, 41,* Spring 1968, 178–200.

87. S.M. Lipset and Gerald Schaflander, *Passion and Politics: Student Activism in America.* Boston: Little, Brown, 1971.

88. Alan E. Bayer and Alexander W. Astin, "Violence and Disruption on the U.S. Campus, 1968–69," *Educational Record, 50,* Fall 1969, 337–350.

89. Bailey, *op. cit.*

90. Hodginkson, *op. cit.*

91. Peterson, *op. cit.,* 1966, 1968.

92. Joseph W. Scott and Mohammed El-Assal, "Multiversity, University Size, University Quality and Student Protest: An Empirical Study," *American Sociological Review, 34,* October 1969, 702–723.

93. Peterson, *op. cit.,* 1968.

94. *Ibid.*

95. Hodgkinson, *op. cit.*

96. Kahn and Bowers, *op. cit.*

97. Clark Kerr, "For the Record," *The New Leader,* January 18, 1965, 8–9.

98. Clark Kerr, *The Uses of the University*. Cambridge: Harvard University Press, 1963; Feuer, *op. cit.*

99. Hodgkinson, *op. cit.*

100. Peterson, *op. cit.*, 1968.

101. Reinhard Bendix, "Sociology and the Distrust of Reason," *American Sociological Review, 35*, October 1970, 831–943.

102. Edward A. Shils, "The Traditions of Intellectuals," in *The Intellectuals*, George de Huszer, ed. New York: The Free Press, 1960, pp. 55–61.

103. Archibald MacLeish, *Poetry and Experience*. Cambridge, Mass.: Houghton–Mifflin, 1961.

104. C.P. Snow, *The Two Cultures and a Second Look*. New York: New American Library, 1964 and Jose Ortega y Gasset, "The Barbarism of 'Specialization,'" reprinted in George B. de Huszer, *op. cit.*, pp. 176–179.

105. Gerald Holton, "Modern Science and the Intellectual Tradition," reprinted in George B. de Huszer, *op. cit.*, pp. 180–191.

106. Jacques Barzuns, *The House of Intellect*. New York: Harper & Row, 1959.

107. William G. Spady, "The Authority System of the School and Student Unrest: A Theoretical Exploration," National Society for the Study of Education, *1974 Yearbook in Education*, C. Wayne Gordon, ed., forthcoming.

108. Martin Trow, *The Expansion and Transformation of Higher Education*. Morristown, N.J.: The General Learning Press, 1972.

109. Keniston, *op. cit.*

110. Hodgkinson, *op. cit.*

111. Stephen Bailey, *Disruption in Urban Public Secondary Schools*, Washington, D.C.: National Association of Secondary School Principals, 1970.

CHAPTER 5
TEACHER MILITANCY

"We have been on the verge of a revolution in teacher-administrator-school board relations."[1]

Over a decade ago, on April 11, 1962, 40,000 teachers affiliated with the powerful labor movement paralyzed the largest system in the nation and in so doing dramatized the determination of teachers throughout the nation to strike out against the great educational system.[2] After that strike, others were to occur with accelerating frequency until eventually nearly every major city would be affected. But it was not until six years later, in February, 1968, when half of Florida's public school teachers resigned and walked out of the schools in the nation's first statewide teacher strike, that the nation became fully aware that a new era of teacher militancy had arrived.[3] Sam Lambert, NEA executive secretary, described the mass resignation of 30,000 teachers throughout Florida as "one of the biggest show-and-tell demonstrations in the history of education." The fact that the Florida strike was eventually defeated is now less important than the fact that it served notice that teachers, once aroused, would use their dormant power. Suddenly, the specter of a nationwide strike was a distinct possibility, and the public faced up to a new force in American life.

WHAT IS THE NATURE OF TEACHER MILITANCY?

The most visible and dramatic evidence of teacher militancy is, of course, the strike. But contrary to popular impressions perhaps, teacher strikes are not an entirely recent development in this country. Between 1918 and 1962 there were more than 130 work stoppages involving teachers.[4] In the years 1946–1948 some 12,000 teachers in 48 communities struck for an average of nearly 10 days in each instance. Many other threatened strikes were averted during the same period.[5]

How Widespread Is Teacher Militancy?

What is new is the prevalence, scope, strength, and defiance implied in teacher strikes. According to the NEA and the U.S. Bureau of Labor Statistics, during the two decades of the 1940s and 1950s there were 86 work stoppages involving 23,000 people, whereas in the brief seven-year span between 1960 and 1967, 75 work stoppages occurred involving 100,000 people.[6] The number of work stoppages has accelerated exponentially since that time. In 1967–68 there were 114 work stoppages, several times as many as during the entire preceding decade. September and October, 1967, were marked by nearly as many strikes of public school teachers as once occurred in all government employment throughout the country for an entire year. School teachers struck in such diverse communities as Paducah, Kentucky; Groton, Connecticut; East St. Louis, Illinois; Fort Lauderdale, Florida; and Janesville, Wisconsin. By the fall of 1968, 10 percent of the nation's teaching force was on picket lines. There were 131 work stoppages in that year. There were 12 strikes that fall in the state of Michigan alone and in New York City some 50,000 teachers and a million pupils were out of classes for 36 of the first 48 days of the term. The number and length of work stoppages reached an all-time high of 181 in 1969–1970, exceeding comparable statistics for all other groups of public employees. The work stoppages in that year alone accounted for 25 percent of the 720 work stoppages that occurred between 1960–1972. The figures have declined only slightly in recent years. There were 130 stoppages in 1970–1971, 89 in 1971–1972, and over 120 in 1972–1973.

There can be little doubt, then, that teacher militancy has become a permanent part of the mainstream of education. The previously timid National Education Association and its local affiliates, representing 80 percent of the nation's two million teachers, had not been involved in a single work stoppage between 1952 and 1963 but participated in one-third of the 1966 work stoppages; 80 percent of the striking teachers that year were NEA members. The NEA and its affiliates have initiated 70 percent of the 720 work stoppages, strikes, and interruptions of service since 1960, while teacher unions have accounted for 70 percent of the six million man-days lost by teachers. The percentage of teachers who believe it is *right* for teachers to strike also has risen sharply in the last few years. Whereas only 1 out of 2 teachers surveyed by the NEA in 1965 supported the right to strike, by 1970 9 out of 10 teachers supported some type of group action, and 3 out of 4 believed that at least in some circumstances teachers should strike.[7] In 1972, 7 out of 10 teachers who approved of strikes said that striking is justified to remedy unsafe conditions for pupils, obtain higher salaries, achieve satisfactory teaching conditions, improve the instructional program, or obtain a negotiation agreement.

In 1965, the majority of teachers considered none of these reasons justifications to strike with the exception of the remedy of unsafe conditions.

These trends signify growing tension between teacher groups and members of the public who oppose the potential increase in school costs implied by teacher demands. Traditionally, the general public has not approved strikes and other forms of public protest, and according to a 1969 Gallup poll the majority of Americans (59 percent) still oppose the teacher's right to strike.[8] The 1962 New York City strike was prohibited by law and challenged the authority of not only a major city but an entire state. The strain between teachers and parents was dramatized in the teachers' strike in New York City in the fall of 1967 when, during a mass public meeting, the president of the teachers' union declared, "Many of our schools are becoming unsafe because parents and community groups are hostile. They're hostile because their kids are not learning. It will not mean anything to go back with a good salary increase—but then be driven out of the schools."[9]

What Forms Does Militancy Take?

The tension rises to this level, of course, only under extraordinary circumstances. But even in less-troubled moments there seems to be a prevailing undercurrent of hostility, which takes forms that are more subtle than the strike. One of the serious mistakes that many observers have made is to concentrate on only the most visible militant activities to the neglect of equally effective low-profile tactics, including political lobbying, campaigns in school board municipal elections, public criticism of boards of education, day-to-day disputes with administrators, resignations, work slowdowns, professional holidays, mass resignations, withholding signed contracts, and blacklisting of uncooperative school districts.

ORGANIZED STRENGTH

The National Education Association (NEA), with over one million members, is one of the world's largest labor organizations. Over half of the nation's teachers belong to the NEA, and over 80 percent belong to local NEA affiliates. In recent moves, the NEA has attempted to strengthen the position of teachers by limiting the authority of school administrators within the organization who, in the past, had exercised power greatly in excess of their numbers.[10]

Also, 1 out of 5 teachers now belong to the American Federation of Teachers (AFT). Although a considerably smaller organization, it is nevertheless very powerful, partly because it has the backing of organized labor and partly because it represents teachers in many of the largest, most bureaucratized trend-setting cities where there is the greatest concentration of teachers. Within the space of a few years, AFT competition revolutionized the NEA leaders' attitude toward bargaining and the use of sanctions. It is ironic that perhaps the most significant achievement of the AFT has been to transform the NEA from a sleeping giant into a major political force, and it is even more ironic that, in the process, the AFT necessarily has become less effective. The NEA's broad membership base equips it far better to deal with the state and national levels where, more and more, the major issues are being decided.[11]

The two organizations have become so similar that it seems likely that they will merge in the near future. Nevertheless, there are still some major differences between the two organizations. One study surveyed 185 teacher leaders in nine organizations in five large cities and found sharp contrasts in the orientations of the NEA and AFT leadership. Leaders heading AFT locals were considerably more likely than their NEA counterparts to advocate a decisive participatory voice, attribute greater power to their own group than to other participants, and express combativeness and a willingness to take forceful action.[12] A merger could have the effect of toning down the teacher movement.

Higher Education. Comparable developments have been emerging almost unnoticed in higher education. The younger faculty members, in particular, are turning to collective action. The Carnegie Commission-sponsored Survey of Higher Education in 1969 reported that "when asked, 'Do you feel that there are circumstances in which a strike would be a legitimate means of collective action for faculty members?' fewer than a third of the older men gave even a qualified yes, while over 60 percent of the young teachers did so. When presented with the statement that 'Collective bargaining by faculty members has no place in a college or university,' about half of all the academic men over thirty-five agreed, at least with reservations. Under thirty-five the proportion dropped to under a third."[13]

Lieberman predicts that the unionization of college faculties will be one of the most important developments in higher education in the next decade.[14] Even though only about 6 percent of the country's more than 800,000 faculty members are presently employed under the terms of a union contract, involving only 180 campuses (out of a total of 2700), the NEA and the AFT are enrolling professors at a much faster rate than the traditional American Association of University Professors. The NEA has succeeded in winning statewide bargaining contracts in several states, and about 15 states have enacted legislation authorizing collective bargaining in higher education. More than two-thirds of private higher education institutions are now under the National Labor Relations Board jurisdiction. A majority of voting faculty members at four of the six largest state college systems have expressed approval of joining the AFT.[15] College teachers have gone on strike in state and city colleges in San Francisco and

New York City. These trends are likely to accelerate in view of the fact that everywhere higher education is under unprecedented budgetary pressure that is threatening basic salary structures and tenure provisions and creating financial squeezes. Future support for higher education is uncertain in view of the increased number of students and the rapid creation of new institutions, particularly junior colleges. Periods of student militancy add another element of uneasiness as students increase their decision-making power within the university.

This intensification of organized militancy among university professors could produce significant shifts in the balance of power between professors, administrators, and boards of control. The union has opposed all loyalty and disclaimer oaths for faculty and students, holds that tenure status should be conferred on all full-time staff members within three years after the initial appointment, advocates that faculty salaries should start at $10,000 per year and be increased by annual increments to $30,000, and supports sabbaticals every eighth year with full pay. Unionization also will give professors more political leverage with state legislatures, and it might stimulate the organization of student unions in self defense against organized faculty members.

COLLECTIVE BARGAINING

The burgeoning teacher organizations provide the basis for *institutionalizing* conflict, especially in the forms of collective bargaining and binding arbitration. An increasing number of local school districts are providing for some form of collective negotiation. Twenty-five states have passed laws mandating teacher organizations. By 1972 nearly half of the nation's nearly two million public elementary and secondary school teachers in 1800 school districts were working under some form of written agreement between a board of education and a teacher organization. Over 700,000 teachers are now covered by contracts that contain salary schedules, clauses covering working conditions, and professional matters.[16] In cities such as New York, the bargaining between teachers and school boards has become an almost continuous, year-long process. The scope of bargaining also has been considerably broadened to encompass practically every problem that teachers might encounter, including not only wages, hours and conditions of work, and class size but also making educational policy as well. In this latter respect, teachers have gone beyond most other labor groups. For instance, some contracts provide for teachers' representation in groups that set curricular policy, select textbooks, and recommend educational programs.[17]

Ultimately, statewide and nationwide negotiations are likely to bypass local school boards, and eventually more of the control of education will be in the hands of centralized teacher organizations that are as remote from classrooms and as bent on standardization as the local and state agencies they oppose. More will be said about this development in Chapter 6.

POLITICAL ACTIVITIES

While public controversy has centered around the right of teachers to strike and to bargain collectively, teachers themselves have become increasingly aware that these instruments have very limited effectiveness. These tactics can be directed at only one school district at a time and, even when successful, they do not guarantee teachers the right to control or influence decisions that vitally affect the status of the profession, such as control over licensure; in most states teachers are not well represented on the state licensing boards that certify teachers and accredit teacher training programs. Consequently, teacher organizations are beginning to flex their political muscle, aiming for sweeping legislative changes that would enhance their legal authority over the profession and perhaps transform the system of control over education.

The New York City AFT spent a quarter of a million dollars to defeat the community control legislation before the New York legislature.[18] Over half of the NEA state affiliates have political arms, and more are in the process of political organization. In some cases teachers have been asked to donate substantial sums for the purpose of lobbying. Some observers claim that teacher support was an important factor in several congressional, state legislative, and gubernatorial races in 1970.[19] In many states, teachers themselves won seats in state legislatures, and in California grass-roots teacher support was considered to be the big difference in the election of a black state superintendent of schools.

This flirtation with politics represents a sharp about-face. Historically, teachers have been reluctant to use collective action for political purposes, either within or outside schools. The traditional ideology dictated that schools should not be involved in "politics," that teachers should not align themselves with political parties, and that the stature of the profession would suffer if teachers were to become involved in politics.[20] A 1957 national survey reported that the majority of teachers at that time thought it inappropriate to attempt to persuade others to vote for the political candidate of the teacher's choice, serve as party precinct workers, conduct partisan elections, or give political speeches.[21] But, whereas in 1956 only 23 percent of the nation's teachers thought they should work actively as members of political parties in elections, by 1968, 81 percent of the men and 71 percent of the women favored campaign work.[22]

What Issues Lie Behind Teacher Militancy?

Three intertwined types of issues have prompted teachers to resort to increasingly militant actions: salaries, working conditions, and policy issues.

SALARIES

Generally speaking, money has been the primary overt issue in negotiations with teachers, and salary disputes have been the major cause of strikes and other overt manifestations of power. In districts that are engaged in formal bargaining, and where teachers have either threatened to use excessive collective power or have gone on strike, teachers have received more money and fringe bnefits than they would have without formal negotiations.[23]

WORKING CONDITIONS

Among the nonmonetary issues frequently negotiated have been reducing the school year to legal minimum, shortening of the school day, reducing the class load, providing duty-free lunch periods and extra compensation for overtime, and "due process" protections through grievance procedures and arbitration for discipline, dismissal, and demotion.[24]

POLICY ISSUES

But, in addition to and often underlying these issues, there have been numerous struggles over the control of educational policy. It is still true, as Rosenthal concluded, that teachers' organizations play a negligible part in determining school policies in most instances.[25] Nevertheless, numerous examples indicate that teachers' influence over policy is becoming more important. For instance, in the fall of 1967, New York City teachers went on strike to enforce their demand to extend the expensive "More Effective Schools" program to all inner-city schools. In the following year they struck three times in a struggle over decentralization and community control during an escalation of a basic conflict that far transcended the normal negotiating process.[26] A number of contracts have resulted in committees that provide joint decision-making about the curriculum, methodology, textbook selection, promotion to the principalship, screening and recommendation of candidates for openings in any level of the system, methods of achieving pupil and teacher integration in the system, and pupil discipline. Some contracts provide teachers the right to challenge administrative judgment on teaching methods and to propose guidelines for promotion policies, placement and transfer of teachers, grading practices, and criteria to be used to evaluate teachers. In some cities teachers have bargained for integrated textbooks, changes in discipline practices, the introduction of minority group history into the curriculum, and the establishment of compensatory education programs.[27]

In his study of 28 high schools in Southern California, Dull found that teachers expressed more support for militancy where they had less influence over school policy and disagreed more with material inducements.[28] My survey of over 1500 teachers in 28 high schools in the Middle West also revealed that, although there was a considerable amount of self-interest and petty, selfish infighting in the high schools, most of the conflicts in one way or another reflected critical policy issues.[29] The vast majority of teachers at least wanted to share with the administration decisions about selecting required textbooks; establishing the essential minimum knowledge that students taking a particular course should derive from it; determining what concepts and values are to be taught in a particular course; identifying the appropriate method for teaching particular courses; and specifying the appropriate number of hours of homework and the appropriate grading curve.

Nearly half of the conflicts reported by teachers were classified as authority problems. One in four involved authority disputes with the administration. The majority of teachers believed that they should exercise the ultimate authority over major educational decisions. Many of these issues revolved around the students. They argued over student discipline and competed for their share of the best students. Teachers were possessive of the good students and went to some lengths to assure that their colleagues did not violate the territorial claims they staked out over them. Competition for students often spilled over into the extracurricular activities. Coaches and music teachers often competed for the same students.

A survey of Philadelphia school teachers also revealed that teachers were dissatisfied with the central-level decision-making.[30] Many seemed to feel that the educational bureaucracy in large cities is incapable of adequately dealing with a number of important policy and administrative decisions. Thus, two thirds of the sample wanted the procedures for disciplining students to be made at the local school level rather than at either the central level or the local district level. Nearly half of them wanted control over teacher evaluation, decisions about the content of the curriculum and courses taught, and setting educational objectives for each grade level to reside at the local school level. They also wanted the local schools to participate with the districts in decisions to establish the qualifications for teaching in culturally deprived areas and selecting paraprofessionals.

The survey of Philadelphia teachers also concluded, incidentally, that the status of teachers might be affected by decentralization of big city systems. The teachers' organization would at first bargain with the district that it thinks will be most vulnerable and most likely to agree to the best settlement terms. Eventually, the authors of that study predict, school district boards will join together in self-defense, thus reducing teachers' bargaining power in the long run.

Reservations. However, although many teachers are growing more discontented with their authority, probably just as many are relatively content with their present level of authority. For example, in the writer's survey referred to above, two-thirds of the teachers thought that they should be prepared to adjust their teaching to the administration's views of good educational practice, and half of them believed that teachers who are openly critical of the administration should be encouraged to leave.[31] This acceptance of the status quo among the rank-and-file teachers has often restrained even the militant leadership from being more assertive about policy issues.

For example, despite the seriousness of the controversy over racial integration and busing in recent years, teachers have not as yet taken a forceful stand on this issue. As Swanson has pointed out, teachers are seldom consulted on integration matters. Moreover, although the most powerful teachers' organization in New York City, the United Federation of Teachers, has taken a stand in support of integration, the Federation has been quick to protect the teachers from forced transfers to different schools.[32] The paralysis of teacher organizations on racial issues was revealed in a survey of approximately 400 teachers in one city school system.[33] Less than 10 percent of the teachers could be classified as militant enough on racial issues to be willing to stage a teacher demonstration at a board meeting, demand the ouster of conservative board members, or demand adoption of a plan for desegregation pending a teacher strike. Three-fourths of the teachers did believe that teacher groups should influence decisions on school racial balancing through more passive means (such as a pro-integration position in the local newspaper or a pro-integration article in the organization's journal), but members of the local Classroom Teachers Association (an NEA affiliate) were split on the issues of busing white students to predominantly black schools to achieve racial integration (53 percent in favor) and busing blacks to white schools (60 percent in favor). In addition to this internal dissent, teachers were impeded from acting positively on this issue by threat of reprisals from community leaders, greater priority given to wage negotiation and to policy issues not involving racial issues, and possible loss of membership. But what is perhaps most important were the internal pressures from conservative members within their own group.

WHAT ARE THE SOURCES OF TEACHER MILITANCY?

Teacher militancy, like student unrest, arises from a complicated chain of circumstances. The events that have prompted both developments are comparable in certain respects, although they also have some very different historical and social roots. I will try to build a cumulative explanation based upon the types of conditions identified in the preceding chapter: (1) predisposing conditions, (2) conducive, or facilitating, conditions, (3) structural supports, and (4) triggering mechanisms.

What Characteristics of Teachers Predispose Them to Be Militant?

Surveys suggest that certain types of teachers are more prone to take militant actions than others.

GENDER

A steady increase in the proportion of men teaching in secondary schools may help to explain rising teacher militancy; between 1955 and 1970 this ratio increased from 69 to 76 percent. Sex and militancy have been found to be highly correlated. Males are more likely than females to join teachers' unions and to engage in militant actions. Dull found that males were significantly more predisposed to militancy, as measured by his scales, than were women.[34] Lowe's investigation of one school district revealed that men were more inclined to join the more militant AFT locals and women more inclined to join the NEA.[35] Rosenthal also found that in Boston and New York City, men were more likely than women to join a teachers' union.[36] My study as well confirmed that, in general, men teaching in high school were more belligerent than the women teachers. Older women, in particular, were among the most compliant, least militant teachers.[37] However, that study also revealed wide variations. Being a woman did not rule out being militant. Many of the militants were women. The aggressiveness of men can be explained partly by the way men have been socialized and partly by the fact that more men than women regard teaching as a lifetime career and have greater need of the financial and ego benefits that militancy brings. Committed career women, then, can be as militant as men.

My study also suggested that in addition to being more militant, men are slightly more professionally oriented than women. Yet the correlation between the militancy and professional orientation (to be discussed later) was higher for the women. Even slight increases in their professionalism produced marked increases in militancy. Perhaps because there are fewer incentives from the general culture to encourage women to be aggressive, the professional role conception is more important to them as a source of motivation and justification.

AGE AND EXPERIENCE

Age and teaching experience are also related to militancy. Generally speaking, younger teachers are more militant than older and more experienced teachers. Cole found that teachers over 50 years of age were less militant than younger teachers.[38] Also Dull reported that the militantly oriented teachers in his sample had been teaching less than 10 years.[39] In addition, my study showed that the oldest group of teachers (over 45) were not inclined to become involved in disputes.[40] Younger teachers have been more exposed to the currents of change and militancy within the general society and have received fewer rewards from the status quo. By contrast the older teachers who often began teaching at a time when jobs were scarce experienced rising incomes and, as they near retirement, risk more from militant actions. Therefore, it is significant that the average age of teachers has declined from 43 to 35 between 1955 and 1970; in the former period less than one-fourth of the teachers were under 30 years of age, whereas 37 percent were younger than 30 in 1970.

However, when the teachers in my study were divided into three groups, the youngest teachers were found to be less militant than the *middle-aged* teachers who have been in teaching for a few years. Dull also found that teachers who have taught 5–10 years were more militant than *either* new teachers (with 0–5 years experience) or those who have taught over 10 years. In my study, the younger men did express more defiant *attitudes* than older ones, but the ones who had been in the occupation for a while were the ones who became involved in overt disputes and confrontations. This pattern suggests that more than age is involved. Perhaps, a teacher must be in the occupation a sufficient length of time to establish the social support needed to make his opinions felt in overt disputes. The middle-aged men have been in the profession long enough to have established themselves as leaders but not so long that they have been co-opted by the administration, and they are still mobile. Personal predispositions, then, are not sufficient to produce militancy. There must be structural support for the predisposition; in this case the respect of peers among other things apparently provided the necessary support for middle-aged men.

FAMILY BACKGROUND

Cole examined teachers' support for the United Federation of Teachers, the New York City affiliate of the AFT, and found that in addition to sex and age, their religion, political affiliation, and class of origin influenced their inclinations about being militant.[41] Finding that Jewish religious affiliation, Democratic party allegiance and lower-class origins created militant predispositions, he conjectured that people in these statuses had undergone prior socialization experiences that predisposed them to respond positively when UFT called its strikes to improve salaries and working conditions. It appears that a major cause of the union's success in the late 1950s and early 1960s was the result of a change in the composition of the city's teaching staff. Most of the people entering the system in the first three decades of the twentieth century were Christians, whereas the majority entering since then have been Jewish. Also, the percentage of male teachers rose from 11 percent in 1920 to 20 percent in 1960 and the number of young teachers in the system also increased significantly.

RESERVATIONS

However, the personal motivations of the individuals who enter teaching cannot, in themselves, explain the rise of militancy within teaching because militancy is a collective action. It is necessary to explain why the inclinations of disparate individuals converge and explode in certain times and places but not in others. The explanation must identify the opportunities and values that *facilitate* or impede militant actions.

We have already seen that, despite their more belligerent attitudes, the youngest teachers are not as likely as middle-aged teachers to become involved in conflict because, I maintained, they are not sufficiently integrated into the status system. This factor indicates that characteristics in the situation play an important role. In addition, Rosenthal's data showed that in both cities he studied, men and women teachers were more likely to join unions when they were in predominantly male schools than when in schools with a high proportion of women, which also demonstrates that school climate can independently affect teachers' behavior over and above the personal characteristics of the individuals involved.[42] Moreover, Cole was able to demonstrate that some teachers did not always act according to their personal predispositions.[43] During the 1960 New York City teacher strike, for example, those teachers who were without social support, even when personally predisposed to be militant, found it difficult to support the strike. Only 38 percent of the personally militant teachers who had little social support backed the strike (by refusing to punch a time clock, by walking the picket line, by calling in sick, or by staying home). How much they were influenced by their colleagues depended on: (1) the amount of cross pressure they were under—for example, they had some friends who favored the strike and others who opposed it; and (2) the importance they attached to their colleagues' favorable opinions of them.

In short, the social background factors in themselves are not all that is involved. The social *context* can modify the extent of teachers' support for a strike even when they are personally predisposed in a different direction. Thus, we turn to consider institutional and related factor that induce individuals who have militant attitudes to act out their aggression.

What Institutional Developments Facilitate Teacher Militancy?

Teacher militancy is not a reaction to despair. Instead, it stems from teachers' optimism that their situation can be changed. This optimism is fed by a number of changes throughout the society.

NATIONAL RELEVANCE OF EDUCATION

One of the major changes is the previously noted "revolution" in technology, which has thrust institutions of formal education into unpre cedented positions of economic importance. However, the price has been high and the limited resources available to schools and colleges have been strained by their new responsibilities. Teachers therefore might feel that they are being asked to assume major responsibilities for prepar ing children for college and a changing job market without adequate authority, support, and rewards.

SOCIAL CHANGE AND DEAUTHORIZATION

In addition, inadequate financing, student discipline, dropout rates student unrest, and other problems have often given schools the stigma of failure. Changes have undermined the authority of administrators School organization is better adapted for the unified, small-town America that used to prevail than for modern conditions. The authority system is premised on teacher compliance and justified by the legal fiction that administrators can be responsible for literally every facet of the system Insofar as administrators have tried to live up to these responsibilities they are blamed for problems that are essentially beyond their control Teachers are expected to display unquestioning loyalty to a system of authority that has not successfully come to grips with pressing problems The result is a power vacuum: administrators can no longer possibly make the critical decisions by themselves, while teachers do not have the authority to do so. Administrators have often reacted by attempting to reassert their power with more and stricter rules, stiffer sanctions and the like, only aggravating the tensions.

These tensions are also aggravated by generational differences. Most administrators were trained in an era when the problems of classroom teaching could be reduced (so it was thought) to the psychology of indivi dual learners and when the central administrative problems seemed to revolve around efficient internal management. The current generation of teachers, by contrast, has been reared in a sociological era characterized by rapid social change and group conflict. Administration has become largely a matter of managing an increasingly complex balance of forces from outside as well as from within the schools. Many school administrators still in positions of authority today are not trained to cope with these problems.

THE CLIMATE OF INNOVATION

The sustained attacks on the schools by the public and teachers have produced a climate receptive to innovations intended to reorient schools from systems of routine to problem-solving devices. Innovation is not new to schools, but innovation has been elevated to the level of a principle. Not only has the pace been stepped up but, as will be noted in the next chapter, the scope of some of the changes proposed promises to be more sweeping than usual, encompassing entire systems and regions rather than individual classrooms.

Since administrators normally have the upper hand at the local level, many of the proposed changes have been aimed at improving classroom *teachers* through in-service programs for teachers and modified teaching procedures and curricula, rather than at fundamental alterations in the system itself. Many proposals seem to imply that poor teaching has produced the existing problems. Consequently, innovations often make teachers defensive, because imminent changes can threaten their status. As far as teachers are to be held responsible for the problems, they naturally want the right to exercise more of a voice in solving them.

AFFLUENCE

The expensive demands of teachers make sense only within the context of a revolution in expectations that has fed on our national wealth and the mass media. The ability of local communities to compete for these national resources, however, varies widely, and the war in Asia and inflation drastically altered expected resource allocations. Moreover, teachers must compete for limited resources with even better-organized local employees, such as nurses, policemen and transit workers, which has inevitably thrust educators squarely into the political arena.

RESERVATIONS

Thus, a value climate and related institutional conditions have developed in recent years that encourage and nourish militancy. There are many conditions to fuel and support the ambitions of militant individuals. However, in addition, the occupation itself must provide the conditions necessary to support the visions of a few leaders and to translate their aspirations into concrete action. We now consider some of the conditions within teaching itself that promote teacher militancy.

Which Characteristics of the Occupation Facilitate Militancy?

Several recent developments are providing an unprecedented level of support for the militant teachers.

INCREASED STATUS AND POWER OF THE OCCUPATION

Traditionally in this country the teacher has been thought of as an obedient servant of the public, principal, and the school board. In his remarkable account of the recent history of public education in the United States, Curti documented the submissiveness of teachers to the various groups that dominated each era and the vocation's willing complicity in its low stature. Regardless of the personal attitudes of educational leaders on social issues, in their actions they have readily complied with the demands of the dominant groups of the day. Of a leader whose personal philosophy was as liberal as that of Horace Mann, Curti could say, "Yet Horace Mann, as an educator, was bound in all he did, or permitted others to do, by the framework of the system in which he worked."[44]

Other evidence supports these impressions. Male and female students studying education in a major state university have been identified as one of the most conservative and "other directed" groups of students in American colleges.[45] Observers like Friedenberg charge that the typical school faculty is "composed chiefly of individuals who have achieved their own basis of security by cautious attention to external norms and these not the most generous."[46] Kaufman and others portray teachers as puny employees huddled before the time clock waiting to leave, raising their hands in faculty meetings for the right to speak, being told what supplies to place in center drawers of their desks, and willingly subjecting themselves to administrative caprice and indifference.[47]

However, these images do not correspond with the increased incidence and intensity of collective militant action on the part of many teachers that we have been describing. Ironically, the same New York City teachers whom Kaufman satirizes have been the leading force behind teacher militancy in this country. Clearly, the substantial alterations in the traditional status and role of teachers brought about by recent events have produced curious contradictions in the popular images of teaching. Even though perhaps the majority of individual teachers remain obedient servants, the *occupation* as a whole has amassed a substantial reservoir of power.

SOURCES OF THE OCCUPATION'S POWER

Several sources of this power base can be identified: legislation, characteristics of the community, patterns of recruitment, specialization, and professionalization.

Legal Support. By 1970, 21 states had enacted legislation mandating negotiations between local teacher groups and boards of education.[48] In one sense this legislation granting organizing and bargaining rights to public employees is an effect of militancy, but the legislation provides legal support for subsequent militant actions.

At the same time, there are also still legal restrictions on the activities of teachers in many areas. The legal right to strike, in particular, is still in dispute or clearly outlawed in most areas of the country; few states require binding arbitration; and perhaps most important, teachers do not have the kind of legal control over their occupation that is enjoyed by physicians, lawyers and even barbers, who dominate their respective state licensing bodies. Their lack of legal control over the occupation is probably a major reason that teachers have been more ready than physicians and lawyers to resort to collective action as a means of making their influence felt. The net effect is legislation that denies teachers the legal authority to control their work and, at the same time, that encourages direct *collective actions*.

The Community Context. Teacher organizations also are influenced by the amount of integration or cleavage within the local community and region. According to one study, a community characterized by a high degree of disintegration facilitates teacher action. Cultural heterogeneity, conflicting local attachments, and competing interests (which might be suppressed in a more harmonious setting) are more likely to be exposed and magnified in less harmonious situations.[49]

Recruiting Patterns. As already pointed out, in recent years more of the types of people who are predisposed to want and to exercise power are being attracted into teaching, especially individuals attracted to the profession as a way of improving their social status. In occupations like teaching, where there is little opportunity for individual mobility, each individual must rely on the collective mobility of the occupation as a whole to improve his status.

The status of teaching has improved considerably over the past 60 years. Since 1930, the average length of teaching careers has doubled (from 7 to 14 years). The number of men in teaching increased in the past decade at twice the rate of increase in the women; most of the high school teachers are now men. Moreover, teachers of both sexes are better trained than ever before. Between 1940 and 1960 the proportion of male teachers without college degrees was cut in half; for women teachers it was reduced by 40 percent. Also, the fact that, in dollars of constant purchasing power, the salaries of teachers have increased more than threefold since 1910, almost doubling since 1940, perhaps has attracted more competitive people.[50]

In sheer numbers alone teachers have amassed an important political base. The proportion of teachers in the work force expanded four times faster than the general population explosion during the 1950s and 1960s. In addition, if the *proportion* of militants does not grow, their absolute power is bound to grow because of the numbers and concentration.

Specialization. Another important basis of teacher power is the growing specialization within the occupation as knowledge increases, as pedagogical techniques are developed for distinct populations, and as separate career lines for teaching various classes and types of students become more distinct. Although not in widespread use, there are specialized technologies for teaching subjects like modern math and the initial teaching alphabet, for working with handicapped and advanced children, and for coping with problems of low-income schools. The number of specialized journals and magazines in teaching, for example, doubled between 1955 and 1972 (from 46 to 91). There are approximately 150 separate publications for teachers. As a result of this growing information base, the traditional role that line administrators have played as "curriculum leaders" became unfeasible years ago. Although administrators are still responsible for evaluating the competence of teachers in different pedagogical techniques and subject matter areas, the time may be rapidly approaching when it will be difficult, if not impossible, for administrators to even attempt to assume the exclusive responsibility for evaluating teachers.

Professionalization. Finally, and perhaps most important, teachers are attempting to advance their professional status. Although by many criteria teaching is not yet a mature profession, many of the militant leaders *aspire* to make teaching more professional.[51] Basically, professionalization represents a quest for status and power. Professional associations were originally formed in order to free vocations from lay control. They invariably challenge the traditional ideologies of control by laymen and administrators. Unless leaders in control are willing to relinquish their power, teachers must become militant if they want to professionalize. Shanker has observed, "Power is never given to anyone. Power is taken and it is taken from someone. Teachers, as one of society's powerless groups, are now starting to take power from supervisors and school boards. This is causing and will continue to cause a realignment of power relationships."[52]

Thus, the chances are that as an occupation increases its aspirations for professional status, it will become more aggressive in its quest to wrest power from those in control. Without denying the economic interest and material gain that is undoubtedly involved behind some forms of teacher militancy, the distinctive significance of militant professionalism in teaching is that it is part of the politics of status.[53] Indeed, it is precisely the fact that material rewards cannot compensate for the low professional stature of the occupation that underlies much of the discontent in teaching.

Professionalism As a Structural Support

Because professionalism plays such an important role in teacher militancy, we shall now turn attention to it before considering how professionalism is transformed into militancy by characteristics of schools. There are at least three questions about the nature of professionalism that should be answered. The answers will help to illuminate how professionalism supports militancy.

Is Militancy "Professional"?

The answer to this question, of course, depends on which characteristics of a profession one chooses to emphasize. The question may not even be productive. Commenting on the problems of identifying professions, Hughes said in an earlier study of real estate agents that it is misleading to ask whether or not "these men are professionals." For the concept of "professional" in all societies is not so much a descriptive term as one of value and prestige.[54] But, ignoring that fact for a moment, there is nothing in the sociological definition of the term that would preclude organized militant action on the part of an occupation in the name of professionalism. Kornhauser identifies four criteria of a profession: specialized competence having an intellectual component; extensive autonomy in exercising this special competence; strong commitment to a career; and responsible use of this special competence.[55] Goode reduces professionalism to only two dimensions: (1) prolonged training in a body of abstract knowledge over which the occupation maintains a monopoly and (2) a collectivity with a service orientation.[56]

However, many citizens and educators have another image of a profession. They tend to confuse being "professional" with being an obedient employee. In effect, they emphasize the teachers' *obligations* to their students and to their colleagues—for example, to stay late to work with students, to cooperate with the administration, to come to work on time, or to obey school rules.

Suppose that members of an occupation attempt to act in accord with these professional tenets; that is, they receive training in a well-developed technology and attempt to exercise their autonomy on behalf of what they consider to be the best interests of their clients. Then suppose that these members are blocked by administrative fiat, by parents, or by legislation. They must decide either to abandon their claim to professional stature, or they must fight for the prerogative to make decisions over matters within their sphere of competence.

Being a professional person, then, involves more than living up to a list of obligations and conducting oneself with propriety. A professional person has some control over his work. If physicians seldom strike, it is not because striking is "unprofessional." It is because physicans have not *needed* to strike since they already have relatively effective forms of political control over major facets of their work. Control in some form is the essential basis of a profession.

In my study of conflicts among the teaching staffs of 28 high schools, the most professionally oriented teachers also tended to be militant (within bounds).[57] The incidence of most types of conflicts in schools increased with the average level of professionalism of the faculty. The *faculties* that were the most professionally oriented to their work (as measured by the average of the teachers' responses to a series of specially designed statements) also had the highest incidence of conflict episodes. In almost every test, as a faculty's average professionalism rose, its conflict rates rose accordingly. In fact, in the half dozen most professionally-oriented schools, at least twice as many disagreements and disputes were reported (based on the average number reported per interview) as in the least professionally-oriented schools.

Also, on the average, the most professionally oriented *teachers* in the sample had higher rates of conflict than the typical teacher. Teachers with the strongest professional orientations, for example, were involved in twice as many authority issues with the administration as their counterparts with the weaker orientation. The opposite also occurred, that is, the most-loyal employees were involved in fewer conflicts than the less-loyal employees.

WHO ASPIRES TO PROFESSIONAL STATUS?

We are concentrating on how an occupation's *aspirations* for professional status can influence its behavior. There is no claim being made that teaching *is* a profession in any rigorous sense of the term. The ambitions of an occupation are not shaped by the majority rank-and-file members but by a small minority of leaders who spearhead the movement.[58] The presence of a few determined leaders who are not reluctant to confront administrators and laymen has changed the complexion of entire vocations.[59] The critical question, then, is whether the leadership in teaching aspires for professional status for the occupation.

Who Are the Most Professionally Oriented Militant Leaders? Are the militant professionals marginal, "deviant" types of people, then, or are they the respected leaders in the occupation? I found that the most militant professionals in my sample of 1500 teachers (1) had more support from colleagues, (2) were mentioned more frequently as highly respected teachers, and (3) had more formal training then *either* the rank-and-file members in the sample or the teachers of equally high professional conviction who had not been engaged in a conflict incident.[60] In short, the professionally oriented militants in the sample were informal leaders who were supported and respected by their colleagues.

RESERVATIONS

The growing professionalism of teachers and the power of teacher organizations provide *support* for militancy, then. However, we have not yet identified the conditions that provoke and *trigger* militancy in particular situations. We shall now consider the thesis that much militancy in teaching has been a response to conflicts between professionalism and the organizational principles that underlie many school systems.

Which Organizational Characteristics Trigger Militancy?

School systems are bureaucratic in varying degrees, along several dimensions of bureaucracy, as discussed in Chapter 1. Some of these bureaucratic characteristics block professionally-oriented teachers from carrying out their professional roles, causing them to rebel. In the discussion that follows, it is assumed that the fundamental tension is *not* between the individual and the system. It arises between parts of the system—between the professional and the bureaucratic principles of organization.[61]

BUREAUCRATIZATION

Some observers believe that the trend toward bigger school systems and larger schools results in centralization of decision making and widens the gap between alienated classroom teachers and school executives.[62] Ironically, some of the attempted solutions such as attempts of administrators to encourage the rank-and-file teachers to participate in certain decisions, perhaps have aggravated the problem by raising their expectations for power.[63]

PROFESSIONAL-EMPLOYEE ROLE CONFLICTS

Bureaucratization poses special problems for *professional* employees. Professions and bureaucracies represent alternative and, in some ways, competing modes of organization.[64] For instance, if teachers had more professional status, they would have more decision-making authority over the classroom, especially over curriculum content, than they have been permitted to take within most school systems. To take another example, the rules and procedures of a school might interfere with the teacher's judgment about what the students' own best interests would dictate in a situation. A professionally-oriented teacher might find himself in direct opposition to the school's procedures. Thus, militant professionals might actively support busing, integration, or school consolidation if they think it is in the best interests of the students, even if the administration and school board oppose it; they might fight the administration's attempts to ban important American authors such as Steinbeck or Faulkner if they think students could benefit by reading their books; or they might choose to violate the curriculum guide by spending more time than they are supposed to on reading and less on science, if they think that reading will be of more benefit to their particular students. As bureaucratic employees, however, teachers are expected to subscribe to the expectations of the administration and the community. Hence, a teacher can be successful as an employee while failing to fulfill professional obligations, or vice versa.

There is evidence from a variety of settings that inconsistencies of this type between professional and employee principles create tension. For example, the professional roles of physicians in the military have been found incompatible with the bureaucracy in which they operate.[65] The professional person's self-conception as an individual capable of critical ability and capacity for original thought could be only superficially followed in the structure of the military organization, according to McEwan, who maintains that the bureaucratic principles on which the military is organized—such as standardization of positions and superordination-subordination by rank—are, in practice, incongruent with the need for creative thinking and peer relations that prevail among professionals.[66] The principle of delegating authority seems to be especially inconsistent with the idea that professional authority is independent of the sanctions applied by a particular organization.[67]

THE POINTS OF CONFLICT

There are three points of potential conflict between bureaucratic and professional principles: (1) the form of specialization, (2) the way work is regulated, and (3) the decision-making process. Each of these dimensions can be visualized as a separate continuum, ranging from more to less bureaucratic (see Table 5-1). The configuration of these variables determines whether or not members of an organization can act professionally in their relations with clients, colleagues, the administration, and the public, and the amount of pressure that is exerted on them to behave as bureaucratic employees in these relationships.[68]

Specialization. Bureaucratic employees specialize on the basis of particular tasks or techniques (as illustrated, in the extreme, in the factory assembly line); this was referred to as structural specialization in Chapters 1 and 2. Their skill is based on practice and repetition. By contrast, professionals specialize on a functional basis, that is, in terms of broad objectives, such as maintaining the general health of particular patients or curing all diseases involving a particular part of the body. Their claim to competence is based upon their grasp of abstract knowledge about the problem and, although this knowledge can sometimes be enhanced by

Table 5-1 Contrasts in the Bureaucratic and Professional-Employee Principles of Organization

Organizational Characteristics	Bureaucratic-Employee Expectations	Professional-Employee Expectations
Specialization		
Basis of division of labor	Stress on efficiency of techniques; task orientation.	Stress on achievement of goals; client orientation.
Basis of skill	Skill based primarily on practice.	Skill based primarily on monopoly of knowledge.
Standardization		
Routine of work	Stress on uniformity of clients' problems.	Stress on uniqueness of clients' problems.
Continuity of procedure	Stress on records and files.	Stress on research and change.
Specificity of rules	Rules stated as universals; and specific.	Rules stated as alternatives; and diffuse.
Authority		
Responsibility for decision-making	Decisions concerning application of rules to routine problems.	Decisions concerning policy in professional matters and unique problems.
Basis of authority	Rules sanctioned by the public.	Rules supported by legally sanctioned professions.
	Loyalty to the organization and to superiors.	Loyalty to professional associations and clients.
	Authority from office (position).	Authority from personal competence.

practice, practice itself is no substitute for the abstract principles that must guide decisions in particular cases.

As Gouldner has observed, much organizational tension can be attributed to the fact that administrators frequently supervise and evaluate professional subordinates who are more specialized and, hence, technically more competent in their work than they.[69] It is difficult for nonspecialized administrators to assess professional skill and competence. As a solution, seniority and loyalty to the organization are used to reward workers in lieu of evaluation. The expert is expected to remain loyal to the organization even though he identifies more closely with other experts in his field who are employed elsewhere. Blau and Scott report that the social welfare workers they studied, who were most closely oriented to their profession, were also less attached to the welfare agency, more critical of its operation, and less confined by its administrative procedures.[70]

Their specialized competence also produces tensions with clients. Since the latter are not considered to have enough training and experience to accurately assess professional performance, their opinions tend to be ignored or discounted by professionals who tend to become indifferent to them. This indifference creates severe problems in public organizations like schools where (as discussed in Chapter 1) neither the professional nor the client has much choice in entering the relationship.[71]

Standardization. Standardization can limit the discretion of professionals. This is a problem not so much because it interferes with individualism but because it can discourage creative and original thought and initiative, which are necessary if organizations are to adapt to individual needs of clients and to changing environments. From the short-run perspective in which administrators and workers see their daily problems, predictability and consistency often appear more convenient than the risks of flexibility. It is interesting, for example, that usually it is not sufficient to demonstrate that a proposed change will be no *worse* than the existing situation, and typically it must have potential for a *marked* improvement; change is avoided when possible.

However, it should also be recognized that standardized procedures can support professionals in some ways, too. Moeller concluded that, contrary to his expectations, standardized school systems sometimes provided teachers with a sense of power that cannot exist where there are no clear guidelines; a clear policy reduces particularism and increases predictability.[72] Thus, teachers often demand rules, for example, with respect to student discipline. The question is not so much whether there are rules but who makes and interprets them.

Centralization. Bureaucratic and professional principles also provide different ways of legitimizing authority.[73] In bureaucratic organizations, one derives his authority primarily from the position that he holds. He might also have professional expertise in a specific area, but his right to give orders stems more directly from his rank in the organization. That is, he has the right to the last word because he is *officially* the superior.

This notion of hierarchical authority is also found in professional organizations, but it is not supposed to be the overriding factor. Instead, the last word presumably goes to the person with the greater knowledge or the more convincing logic. In other words, the professional employee's obligations to do a job do not mean that he must always obey his official superiors; indeed, he is sometimes obliged to disobey by ethics and law. Whereas the bureaucratic employee is hired to "do what he is told," the professional already knows what he is to do and how to do it. He always has split loyalties between the organization that employs him and his profession.

It is important to note, then, that when Peabody compared school employees, police officers, and welfare workers on the degree that each group stressed these two bases of authority, the elementary school teachers attached far more importance to the professional basis of their authority, even though their typical reaction to conflict was acquiescence to the authority of position, particularly among the less experienced members of the sample.[74]

STRUCTURAL VARIATIONS IN ROLE CONFLICT

The way bureaucratic-employee role conflicts impinge on teachers to produce more or less tension depends on where they are located within the educational system, as well as their own professionalism. For example, in addition to the fact that there are more male teachers at the secondary than at the elementary level, the former are more specialized, which (as I argued above) places them in a better position to engage in militant actions. Also, a teacher's militancy is likely to vary by type of specialty he has or department he is in. Administrators, counselors, and teachers in the more professionally oriented social science departments were among the most militant people in my high school sample.[75] Teachers of athletics and those working in extracurricular areas also often got into disputes. On the other hand, teachers in vocational programs and in home economics had relatively low rates of conflict. In other words, it seems that certain positions are conflict-prone regardless of who staffs them.

Also, these professional-bureaucratic role conflicts will tend to be highly pronounced in the more complex school systems. On the one hand, because of the greater need for coordination in complex organizations, administrators (whose function is to coordinate the system) tend to have more power in such systems. On the other hand, complex organizations tend to employ more specialized personnel who can use their expertise as a basis of power. A high level of tension can be expected where there are these two strong groups.

Some Evidence. Several findings from my study of militant professionalism reflect the kind of tension between professional and bureaucratic principles discussed here:

1. The single most frequent type of conflict (one in every four identified) concerned authority problems between teachers and administrators. These authority issues were of greater concern to the professionally-oriented militants than to the rank-and-file teachers. In fact, authority issues were the prevailing concerns among the most professionally-oriented, belligerent leaders.

2. Many of the disputes occurred where teachers had the most authority over routine decisions in the classroom, probably because those teachers with some authority had more to fight about and found more occasions on which it was necessary to fight.

3. The authority structure seemed to be especially unstable in precisely the largest, centralized, specialized, and complex schools that relied most heavily on administrative authority.

4. The previously noted positive relationship between professionalism and conflict was particularly true in the more professional schools. There was evidence to suggest that when a conservative, loyal person found himself in a liberal professional environment, he was less inclined to withdraw from conflict than when he was in an environment where all employees were relatively loyal to the administration.

5. The positive correlation between professionalism and conflict was also stronger in the more bureaucratic schools compared to the less bureaucratic ones. In other words, a strong commitment to the profession was the most likely to lead to conflict in the most bureaucratic schools. On the other hand, conflict seemed to diminish when *less* professionally oriented faculties were staffing bureaucratized schools.

ALTERNATIVE THEORETICAL PERSPECTIVES

Up to this point we have been considering several types of conditions that can produce teacher militancy if they happen to converge in a particular way. Now we shall try to amplify the explanation further by considering the theoretical foundations that underlie each type of variable considered.

Personal Deviance

Probably most people would be inclined to start with the assumption that conflict simply represents another phase of the Hobbesian war of "all against all," which is sustained by certain types of deviant, belligerent people who have abnormal degrees of vanity, drive for recognition, inability to adjust to others, and emotional instability, for example. I have argued that, without denying the relevance of such factors, these characteristics are more likely to manifest themselves in certain situations than in others and, indeed, in many situations conflicts seem to be kindled almost independently of the people involved. For example, teachers of academic subjects typically have some complaint against teachers in the extracurricular programs because of the class disruptions created by activity practices and special events. Similarly, vocational teachers often express antagonism toward academic teachers and counselors who monopolize the "good" students and send them the "castoffs." And schools with high rates of faculty turnover seem to be more conflict prone than more stable schools. Moreover, the most belligerent, professionally oriented teachers, far from being marginal or "deviant" characters, were clearly better educated and more respected, and received more group support from their colleagues than the typical teacher. Although the number of teachers who were both professional and militant was proportionately small, they were backed by a broad base of teachers.

In short, while many teachers might have personality problems that became manifest under pressure, the sources of the pressure itself are the important factors, and they are sociological in nature. Yet, school personnel policies continue to be premised on individual psychology.

The Frustration-Aggression Hypothesis

It is a short step from explanations based on deviant personalities to some versions of the *frustration-aggression* hypothesis that portrays conflict as a generic human response to social constraints (rather than as the product of unique personality traits). From this perspective, it appears that teachers have become belligerent because they have been prevented from obtaining their group objectives.

While in a sense this may be true, the interpretation is vague, rather mechanistic, and does not explain very much since the hypothesis itself does not account for either the origins of the objectives frustrated or the sources of frustration.

The Alienation Hypothesis

The popular alienation thesis elaborates on the frustration-aggression hypothesis.[76] The roots of frustration are presumed to be social, that is, disenfranchisement, marginality, and powerlessness. The person's objective presumably is to find his identity, to control his destiny, or to participate more meaningfully in life. Engaging in conflict itself can provide some people with a sense of meaningful participation in their society. This last possibility received some support in my study, where it was found that both the personal job satisfaction of teachers and their overall morale increased with the conflict rates of the faculty members, considered both individually and as a group.

The alienation thesis would also help to explain why the militant teachers tend to be relatively young members of the occupation, since they are closest to the current generation of alienated youth. And yet, to focus on alienation is to focus on only the negative side of a larger equation. It is not accurate to picture militant teachers only in rebellion against something, because at least some of them also seem to be working for something: a positive alternative to bureaucracy embodied in professional standards. Teachers who are integrated into a professional organization cannot be described as alienated or as simply opposed to "the system." It is more accurate to say that, caught between competing parts of the system, they have been forced to choose between divergent but legitimate versions of the organization.

THE RELATIVE-DEPRIVATION HYPOTHESIS

Introducing the dynamic element of competing alternatives begins to tap the complexity of the situation. To bring the problem into better focus, we shall draw on two concepts that can help to illuminate how competing standards can produce conflict, *relative deprivation*, and *reference group theory*.[77]

The former concept refers to the difference between a person's present situation and some outside standard, either a former state of his own being or the achievements of his contemporaries. The latter concept calls attention to the fact that the standards that people set for themselves are usually advocated by, or exemplified in, some social group to which they may or may not belong. For example, teachers compare their station in life with members of other occupations who have equivalent education or income, expecting rewards that are at least equivalent to those obtained by people with similar levels of education. Moreover, even when they are making progress, they might become discontented if they are not progressing as rapidly as their reference groups. Thus, although in recent years teachers' average income has increased faster than that of industrial workers (20 percent increases during some recent five-year periods), they remain discontented because they still lag behind other professional groups.

Structural Explanations

THE STATUS-CONSISTENCY HYPOTHESIS

A still more sophisticated way to treat comparative statuses is provided in the notion of *status congruency*, which explicitly focuses on convergences and divergences among a person's different statuses.[78] Incongruence among statuses has become a critical feature of modern changing societies. There is no longer a close connection between various dimensions of status, such as salary, authority, and level of education; winning salary increments, for example, does not in itself provide access to power. The status-consistency hypothesis holds that a group tends to compare its achievements in a particular area with its achievements in other areas as well as with the achievements of other people and will strive to bring its achievements in various areas up to a level commensurate with its highest area. For example, teachers will expect their salary, occupational prestige, and authority to keep pace with their rising level of formal education. The consistency of expectations that other people have about them, and the demands that they can make of others, depends on how consistently they rank on the various status dimensions. The assumption is that a group's position will be reinforced as long as his statuses are congruent, whereas incongruence leads to confusion because the lower statuses detract from the more notable achievements. Therefore, people with incongruent statuses will try to improve themselves in those areas in which they are lagging.

Ironically, a significant advance in one form of status can merely illuminate the disparities in the overall status pattern; progress in one respect, far from satiating the status quest, can stimulate one's efforts to improve in other respects as well. It is relevant in this connection that Goffman found that, for people occupying middle- and upper-middle-class positions, there was an inverse relationship between the consistency of their statuses and their preference for extensive change in distribution of power in the society.[79]

One gets the impression that any increases that teachers may have made in their authority have not kept pace with their advances in salary and education in recent years; they have almost closed the education gap that once existed between them and administrators. The authority discrepancy could be an important incentive behind their recent efforts to achieve new levels of authority. However, whatever modest gains they *have* been able to make in their level of authority have created serious imbalances in the *equilibration* of the *total system*. That is, their gains in authority are upsetting their traditional relationships with administrators and challenging parents and other citizen groups. At the same time, middle-class parents now appear to be more anxious than ever before about their children's educational achievement, while the civil-rights movement has mobilized previously lethargic lower-class parents who, along with teachers, are demanding a greater voice in the schooling of their children. Experiments with community control over inner-city schools will bypass teachers and increase the authority of laymen at precisely a time when teachers want more authority for themselves. Then, too, the teacher's authority is being threatened by young people as they advance their status in the wake of student activism and the adolescent revolt; in school after school teachers complain about discipline problems, slowdowns, and outright violence against teachers. These imbalances in the system promote power struggles that stimulate teacher militancy.

THE EXCHANGE HYPOTHESIS

The quest of teachers for power has transformed the teacher-administrator relationship from one of clear-cut subordination into naked bargaining. *Exchange theory* is a way of systematically analyzing bargaining relationships.[80] A more extended period of training for teachers and the current affluence of this country has increased the teachers' career alternatives and reduced the risks involved in losing. As teachers have achieved their own leverage, they do not need to rely on administrators to do their bargaining for them—especially since the latter operate under different constraints.

In the past few years, the dramatic increase in the supply of teachers has reduced their individual bargaining power in the short run but, ironically, in the long run their bargaining power is likely to increase because today's oversupply of teachers will make it possible to raise the standards of entry to the occupation in the future. The teachers who enter in the future are likely to be even better educated and more committed to their careers than those now in teaching.

Some Implications

It is important to note that the exchange and consistency models give different answers to a crucial question. From a strictly bargaining point of view, for example, one might have expected that teachers would feel that they have been adequately compensated for their low authority and prestige by recent gains they have made in salaries. But, within the consistency framework, a salary increase might simply whet the ambitions of employees to achieve other forms of advancement. The bargaining model in itself does not indicate what a group will and will not be willing to bargain away, which depends on their present status. Less well-educated groups seem to be more willing to settle for salary as a compensation for their lack of authority, while better-educated groups appear to be less willing to tolerate extreme disprepancies between income and authority. The bargaining model, then, must be interpreted against the background of status congruency.

SOME QUALIFICATIONS

Each source of teacher militancy identified here contributes in small part to the total explanation. But now that we have sketched in the outlines, it is still necessary to add some detail by way of elaboration and qualification to what has been said to avoid any misunderstanding.

First, despite all the discussion about teacher militancy in recent years, it should be remembered that only a minority of teachers are militant, and an even fewer—probably no more than 15 percent—are professionally-oriented militants. Although some surveys show that almost 9 out of 10 classroom teachers support some type of group action, and that most believe strikes are justified under some circumstances, most teachers remain essentially conservative in their behavior. What I have stressed is that as teachers have become more densely concentrated in large cities, even small proportions can be *numerically* large enough to be decisive. Moreover, militant professionals constitute a mature, experienced, core leadership group backed by the majority of teachers. Professionalization is being advanced by the most respected, influential segment of teachers.

Second, discussions of militant professionalism should not be permitted to become clouded by nebulous speculations about whether or not teaching is, in fact, a "profession." How it is defined by social scientists is less important than the fact that a large portion of teachers *believe* that they are entitled to more recognition and authority than they now have, and use professional ideology to justify their claims.[81]

As a third qualification, it would be a mistake to assume that militancy is simply a reaction to a presumed *loss* of control on the part of teachers because of the fact that schools have become less personal and more bureaucratized. Perhaps there are elements of this, but the data show that in the larger, more hierarchical schools where there is the most conflict, teachers actually have more decision-making authority over the classrooms than teachers in less bureaucratic schools. Their aspirations seem to be fanned by modest advances.

The fourth and related point is that increases in the decision-making authority of teachers seem to lead to more, rather than to less, conflict in the school. It is unlikely that teachers can be pacified by minor concessions. Their expectations seem to be increasing faster than their achievements. Success feeds aspiration; and participation in the decision-making process, even in a minor way, can plunge teachers into a wider range of issues than they would otherwise have become involved in. But there is an important exception: there were fewer *severe* conflicts where teachers had more opportunity to participate in decisions. In other words, participating in decision-making seems to promote *numerous*, but not *severe*, disputes. Apparently, engaging in minor disputes permits employees to "let off steam," thus preventing grievances from accumulating to erupt eventually in major outbreaks.

Fifth, professionalization obviously does not *necessarily* lead to conflict, especially to the extent that schools are beginning to adapt and to accommodate the professional aspirations of teachers. For example, faculties in the sample that were most committed to professionalism also reported more decision-making authority over classroom matters. Moreover, professionalism entails less conflict in the least bureaucratized schools since there are fewer bureaucratic principles to oppose it. Conversely, even in the bureaucratized schools, if a critical mass of professionally-oriented teachers is not present, conflict is less likely to occur. Probably even more militancy could be found if the professionally-oriented teachers were concentrated in only the most bureaucratized schools, instead of being randomly distributed throughout all types of compatible as well as incompatible situations.

Sixth, the corollary to the previous point, of course, is that bureaucratization in itself does not necessarily lead to conflict either. The problems occur primarily when attempts were made to apply close supervision, standardization, tight rules, and centralized decision-making in faculties that are attempting to increase their professional status. But where faculties are not professionally oriented, the use of such bureaucratic devices does seem to be effective in controlling conflict. The effectiveness of administrative practices is, therefore, obviously not inherent in the practices themselves but depends largely on the setting in which they are applied. Administrators often do not systematically tailor their practices to fit the changing conceptions of their faculties.

Seventh, professionalization fragments teachers and produces conflict among them as well as with the administration.

Eighth, there are many sources of militancy other than professionalism, including organizational complexity and the authority structure, general conditions within the society such as the adolescent revolt, and the civil right's movement in the big cities.

Ninth, militancy can take a variety of forms and degrees of intensity in addition to work stoppages. Strikes are only the most visible sign of challenge to authority. The most professionally-oriented militants often shy away from "major incidents" that involve sustained, heated conflicts among many persons. The major exception occurs in the *most bureaucratic* schools, where professionalization seems to be associated with even the frequency of major incidents. Whether or not professional leaders are the ones actively leading the teacher strikes remains a matter of conjecture.

Tenth, the fact that teacher militancy is more likely to arise in bureaucratized schools than in less-bureaucratic ones suggests that bureaucratic controls sometimes *provoke* conflict, and that the same administrative principles that prove to be effective in one situation can backfire in another. Administrators might have to put up with some friction if they want to maintain professionally-oriented faculties. But, on the other hand, supporting professionally-oriented teachers could prove to be a more effective way to control major incidents than attempting to suppress them through bureaucratic control. Yet precisely where militant professionalism is strongest administrators will be the most tempted to impose additional control. If, instead, administrators were to support teachers, teacher militancy could provide them with an effective leverage against community pressures.

Finally, it is clear that the behavior of teachers can be explained better in terms of principles of social power than exclusively in terms of either mundane economic considerations or their idealism. Although teachers are motivated by self-interest, they want more than money. They are in a struggle for power and cannot afford to confine themselves to only legitimate tactics. Self-interest seems to be characteristic of all professions, but professions eventually rationalize and legitimate their private gains in terms of public benefits. For example, medical schools set selective admissions presumably to maintain high medical standards even though selectivity also conveniently restricts the supply of physicians, enabling them to command high fees. There are parallels in teaching. Teachers maintain that they cannot do their best for students under poor working conditions, without sufficient authority, and on low salaries that repel qualified people. It is no accident that these conditions also benefit teachers and that the claims are difficult to prove or disprove. There can be no clear-cut answer to the question of the "real" motives of teachers.

Administrators also subscribe to contentions that are equally difficult to disprove, such as the notion that "employees must be supervised," that there is a special class of "decision makers" in schools, and that school boards' sovereignty must remain inviolable in a democracy. Each group uses these ideologies to define the public interest to suit its own purposes.

CONCLUSIONS

Teacher militancy has been bred within a larger context of discontent that has swept this country in recent years. Existentialism, with its doctrine of personal commitment and decisive action, finally has come of age during this generation. It is a generation that blames most of its problems on a self-conscious sense of alienation rooted in the failure of existing social arrangements. Large segments of the population have lost any sense of meaningful control over their destiny. Group militancy represents an alternative for people not content with this fate. With the assistance of the mass media, and the voices of blacks and alienated adolescents, many partially disenfranchised groups are beginning to be heard. Militancy has become a matter of course, a common response to pervasive sociological tensions, and a generic symptom of the failure of existing social institutions. The militancy of teachers, as well as of their students, must be understood in this context.

But though the environment is receptive, in itself it does not explain the aggressiveness of teachers. Other forces facilitate and trigger their militancy. Teaching has been confronted by two major issues in recent years: (1) the proper role of experts in a democratic society—where the growth of knowledge has almost forced laymen to forego their right to make many technical decisions, notwithstanding a widespread belief that ultimately only public control will safeguard public interests, and (2) the appropriate role of professional employees in complex organizations. In large part, teacher militancy is a product of the simultaneous professionalization and bureaucratization of American society.

These developments have produced a curiously contradictory image of teachers, first as obedient, loyal employees and second, as militant professionals. The aspirations of a small but important segment of teachers have led them to a quest for more power, which cannot be achieved within the traditional hierarchical authority structure and system-wide uniformity. Teacher militancy aims to make basic changes in the underlying structure of public education.

The problems of education and the interests of the American people are so varied and intricate that no one group will be permitted to dominate the system for long without being subject to attack. The situation is now well beyond the point where school policy can be made by proclamations from administrators; and yet, that is the myth that has been inherited and that we continue to live with. The only basis for stability is to recognize the growing power of teachers by including them more centrally in the decision-making process. Historically in this country we have had to learn either to include the excluded or live with strife. Until teachers create a more central place within the system for themselves they will continue to go around it.

It is not necessary to romanticize the motives of teachers to recognize that teacher militancy, at the very least, provides an important countervailing force in education. Like student activism, it must be seen as part of a larger system of "checks and balances" comprised of conflicting but equally legitimate, valued principles. Teacher militancy provides a defense for professional principles in an otherwise alien, often hostile, bureaucratic environment. At the same time, professionalism can be detrimental if there are no internal checks on it. Recognizing that many problems might be a product of professionalism itself, some observers have advocated deprofessionalizing professional roles by relying more on persons from outside established career routes and on paraprofessionals and untrained laymen from social backgrounds comparable to those of their clients and by better training to reduce the social distance between professionals and their lower-class clients.

REFERENCES

1. Charles Cogen, "The American Federation of Teachers—Force for Change," in *The Collective Dilemma: Negotiations in Education*, Patrick W. Carlton and Harold L. Goodwin, eds. Worthington, Ohio: Charles A. Jones Publishing Co., 1969, p. 59.
2. Leonard Buder, "The Teachers Revolt," *Phi Delta Kappan, 43*, June 1962, 370–376.

3. James Cass, "Politics and Education in the Sunshine State—The Florida Story," *Saturday Review, 51,* April 20, 1968, 63–65, 76–79.

4. Ronald W. Glass, "Work Stoppages and Teachers: History and Prospect," *Monthly Labor Review,* August 1967, pp. 43–46: Also Wesley A. Wildman, "Teacher Employment, Financial Aspects," in *Encyclopedia of Education, 9,* New York: Macmillan, 1971, 1–7.

5. *Ibid.*

6. See *American Teacher,* published 10 times a year by the American Federation of Teachers and *Negotiation Research Digest,* published 10 times a year by the National Education Association, Research Division. Also NEA Research Memo 1972–18, "Teacher Strikes, Work Stoppages, and Interruption of Service, 1971–72," October 1972.

7. "Teacher Strikes" (Opinion Poll), *Today's Education, 58,* November 1969, 10, National Education Association, Research Division.

8. George Gallup, "How the Nation Views the Public Schools," Princeton, N.J.: Gallup International, 1969: Also Charles Winick, "When Teachers Strike," *Teachers College Record, 64,* April 1963, 593–604.

9. "A Talk with Albert Shanker," *Phi Delta Kappan, 49,* 1968, 255–256.

10. "Nation's Teachers Flex Political Muscles," *Columbus Dispatch,* Sept. 29, 1971, p. 19A.

11. Myron Lieberman, "Implications of the Coming NEA-AFT Merger," in *The Collective Dilemma, op. cit.,* pp. 44–56.

12. Alan Rosenthal, "Teacher Militancy," *Encyclopedia of Education, 9, op. cit.* 36–42.

13. Martin Trow, *The Expansion and Transformation of Higher Education.* Morristown, N.J.: The General Learning Press, 1972, p. 6.

14. Myron Lieberman, "Professors, Unite!" *Harpers Magazine,* October 1971, 61–71.

15. Harry A. Marmion, "Unions and Higher Education," *The Collective Dilemma, op. cit.,* pp. 44–56.

16. *Negotiation Research Digest, op. cit.*

17. Charles R. Perry and Wesley Wildman, *The Impact of Negotiations in Public Education: The Evidence from Schools.* Worthington, Ohio: Charles A. Jones Publishing Co., 1970: Also Cogen, *op. cit.*

18. H. Kaufman, "Administrative Decentralization and Political Power," Paper presented to APSA meeting in Washington, D.C., September 1969.

19. NEA News, "Political Participation Gets the Nod for More Teachers." Press release, October 18, 1968.

20. Cf. L. Iannacone, *Politics in Education.* New York: Center for Applied Research in Education, 1967; M. W. Kirst and E. K. Mosher, "The Politics of Public Education," *Review of Education Research, 39,* December 1969, 623–637; D. Tyack, "Needed: The Reform of a Reform" in *New Dimensions in School Board Leadership.* Evanston: National School Boards Association, 1969; and H. Ziegler, *The Political World of the High School*

Teacher. Eugene: Center for Advanced Study in Educational Administration, University of Oregon, 1966.

21. "Voting and Politics," *NEA Research Bulletin,* vol. 35, February 1957, Washington, D.C.: National Education Association, pp. 33–35.

22. Robert D. Hess and Michael W. Kirst, "Political Orientations and Behavior Patterns: Linkages Between Teachers and Children," *Education and Urban Society, 3,* August 1971, 453–476: Also, "Teacher Opinion Poll," *NEA Journal, 57,* November 1968, 8.

23. Charles R. Perry and Wesley A. Wildman, *The Impact of Negotiations in Public Education, op. cit.,* 1970.

24. Wesley Wildman, "Teacher Employment, Financial Aspects" in *The Encyclopedia of Education, 9, op. cit.,* 1–7.

25. Alan Rosenthal, *Pedagogues and Power: Teacher Groups in School Politics.* Syracuse, N.Y.: Syracuse University Press, 1969.

26. Perry and Wildman, *op. cit.,* 1970.

27. *Ibid.*

28. Roy Dull, "Teacher Militancy in the Secondary Schools," unpublished Ph.D. dissertation, Claremont Graduate School, 1970.

29. Ronald G. Corwin, *Militant Professionalism: A Study of Organizational Conflict in High Schools.* New York: Appleton-Century-Crofts, 1970.

30. Michael H. Moskow and Kenneth McLennan, "Teacher Negotiations and School Decentralization" in *Community Control of Schools,* Henry M. Levin, ed. Washington, D.C.: The Brookings Institution, 1970.

31. Corwin, *Militant Professionalism, op. cit.*

32. Bert E. Swanson, *School Integration Controversies in New York City,* New York: Institute for Community Studies, Sarah Lawrence College, 1965, p. 53.

33. Shirli M. Vioni, "An Exploratory Study of Teacher Opinions on a Human Rights Issue," unpublished paper, Ohio State University, Department of Sociology, March 1972.

34. Dull, *op. cit.*

35. William T. Lowe, "Who Joins Which Teachers' Groups?" *Teachers College Record, 66,* April 1965, 614–619.

36. Alan Rosenthal, *Pedagogues and Power: Teacher Groups in School Politics, op. cit.* Also Alan Rosenthal, "The Strength of Teacher Organizations: Factors Influencing Membership in Two Large Cities," *Sociology of Education, 39,* Fall 1966, 359–380.

37. Corwin, *Militant Professionalism, op. cit.*

38. Stephen Cole, "The Unionization of Teachers: Determinants of Rank-and-File Support," *Sociology of Education, 41,* Winter 1968, 66–87.

39. Dull, *op. cit.*

40. Corwin, *Militant Professionalism, op. cit.*

41. Cole, *op. cit.*

42. Rosenthal, *op. cit.*, 1969.

43. Stephen Cole, "Teachers' Strike: A Study of the Conversion of Predisposition into Action," *American Journal of Sociology*, 74, March 1969, 506–520.

44. Merle Curti, *The Social Ideas of American Educators*. Paterson, N.J.: Littlefield, Adams and Co., 1959, p. 138.

45. Carl Bereiter and Marvin B. Freedman, "Fields of Study and the People in Them," in *The American College*, Nevitt Sanford, ed. New York: Wiley, 1962, pp. 563–596.

46. Edgar Z. Friedenberg, *The Vanishing Adolescent*. New York: Dell Publishing Company, Inc., 1962, p. 125.

47. Bel Kaufman, *Up the Down Staircase*. Englewood Cliffs, N.J.: Prentice-Hall, 1964.

48. Perry and Wildman, *op. cit.*, 1970.

49. Rosenthal, *op. cit.*, 1969.

50. John K. Folger and Charles Nam, *Education of the American Population*. Washington, D.C.: Bureau of the Census, 1967.

51. The term "profession" is conventionally applied to a set of *structural* characteristics (i.e., an organized occupational group with a legal monopoly over recruitment and knowledge); but most of what might be called professional behavior is, in fact, the striving of a group to achieve the right to claim the title of a profession. In other words, to study professions is to study process. See also Howard S. Becker, "The Nature of a Profession" in *Education for the Professions*, Sixty-first Yearbook of the National Society for the Study of Education, Part II. Chicago: University of Chicago Press, 1962.

52. Albert Shanker, "Teacher-Supervisory Relationships: A Symposium," *Changing Education*, *1*, Spring 1966, 23: Also, "A Talk with Albert Shanker," *Phi Delta Kappan*, *49*, 1968, 255–256.

53. Cf. Richard Hofstadter, "The Pseudo-Conservative Revolt," in *The Radical Right*, Daniel Bell, ed. New York: Doubleday, 1963, pp. 57–96.

54. Everett Cherrington Hughes, *Men and Their Work*. New York: The Free Press, 1958, p. 44.

55. William Kornhauser, *Scientists in Industry: Conflict and Accommodation*. Berkeley: University of California Press, 1962, p. 8.

56. William Goode, "The Librarian: From Occupation to Profession?" *Library Quarterly*, *31*, October 1961, 306–320.

57. Corwin, *Militant Professionalism*, *op. cit.*

58. Rue Bucher and Anselm Strauss, "Professions in Process," *The American Journal of Sociology*, *66*, January 1961, 326–334.

59. Hughes, *op. cit.*

60. Corwin, *Militant Professionalism*, *op. cit.*

61. Parsons has warned of the dangers in analyzing occupational behavior on

the basis of individual motives. See Talcott Parsons, "The Professions and the Social Structure," *Social Forces, 17,* May 1939, 457–467.

62. Edwin M. Bridges, "Teacher Participation in Decision Making," *Administrators' Notebook, 12,* 1964.

63. Wesley Wildman, "Implications of Teacher Bargaining for School Administration," *Phi Delta Kappan, 46,* December 1964, 152–158: Also, Wesley Wildman and Charles R. Perry, "Group Conflict and School Organization," *Phi Delta Kappan, 47,* January 1966, 244–251.

64. Cf. Ronald G. Corwin, "The Professional Employee: A Study of Conflict or Nursing Roles," *American Journal of Sociology, 66,* May 1961, 604–615.

65. William J. McEwan, "Position Conflict and Professional Orientation in a Research Organization," *Administrative Science Quarterly, 1,* September 1956, 208–224.

66. There is also a hierarchy among professionals, but it has a different basis of authority; and communications between ranks of professionals are more nearly reciprocal.

67. Walter I. Wordwell, "Social Integration, Bureaucratization and Professions," *Social Forces, 33,* May 1955, 356–359.

68. Adapted from Ronald G. Corwin, "Professional Persons in Public Organizations," *Education Administration Quarterly, 1,* Autumn 1965, 1–22.

69. Alvin W. Gouldner, "Organizational Analysis" in *Sociology Today,* Robert Merton, et al., eds. New York: Basic Books, 1959, pp. 400–428.

70. Peter Blau and W. Richard Scott, *Formal Organization.* San Francisco: Chandler Publishing Company, 1962, p. 244.

71. The factor of choice is an important control mechanism for both clients (who can boycott professionals from whom they receive little benefits) and for professionals (who probably can be more effective with clients who have faith in them). Private practice, however, overcompensates for the first problem because of the professional's dependence on private fees; and bureaucratic employment accentuates the second problem. The fact that teachers are arbitrarily assigned students who are compelled to accept the service is a serious strain on the teacher-student relationship.

72. Gerald H. Moeller, "Relationship Between Bureaucracy in School Systems and Teachers' Sense of Power," unpublished Ph.D. Dissertation, Washington University, 1962. Centralized authority systems support professional autonomy by resisting outsiders (as when principals defend teachers against interfering parents) and by refusing the use of essential facilities to competing groups.

73. Gouldner, *op. cit.*

74. Robert L. Peabody, "Perceptions of Organizational Authority," *Administrative Science Quarterly, 6,* March 1962, pp. 463–482.

75. Corwin, *Militant Professionalism, op. cit.*

76. Robert Blauner, *Alienation and Freedom: The Factory Worker and His Industry.* Chicago: University of Chicago Press, 1964.

77. Robert K. Merton, "Contributions to the Theory of Reference Group Behavior," in *Social Theory and Social Structure*, R. K. Merton, editor. Glencoe, Ill.: The Free Press, 1957, pp. 225–280.

78. Gerhard Lenski, "Social Participation and Status Crystallization," *American Sociological Review, 21*, August 1956, pp. 458–464.

79. Irwin W. Goffman, "Status Consistency and Preference for Change in *Power Distribution,*" *American Sociological Review, 22*, June 1957, pp. 275–281.

80. Peter Blau, *Exchange and Power in Social Life*. New York: Wiley, 1964.

81. Corwin, *Militant Professionalism, op. cit.*

CHAPTER 6

THE FUTURE OF PUBLIC EDUCATION

"The pieces of an educational revolution are lying around unassembled."[1]

Most observers seem to agree on the need for some type of educational reform, even though they might have different reasons for this conclusion. Some, perhaps most, of the critics believe that educational reform will improve the academic achievement and life chances of the children and young adults who are socialized in schools and colleges. Other writers doubt that improving the quality of schooling will materially affect what students learn or improve their life chances but nevertheless agree that reform is desirable if only to make schools more satisfying places for the teachers and children.

But the preceding chapters repeatedly pointed to the sluggishness with which the educational system is responding to the changing demands being made on it. This resilience has blunted the force of repeated demands for reform. The evidence and theory reviewed provide some convincing reasons why educational structures might be at the root of the current unresponsiveness and responsible for many of the problems. Clearly, the solutions will have to be targeted toward the structure of education itself. This chapter reviews some of the changes being contemplated and speculates about what might take place in the future as the system responds to the problems.

Looking into the future can be a precarious occupation. As a product of both crescive, evolutionary forces and deliberate innovations, the future of education will hinge on thousands of slippery contingencies. In this clockwork of events every deliberate action can reverberate in unforeseen ways, which virtually precludes any kind of precise forecasting. As Bell pointed out, public authorities each year face more problems than they have in previous times in history because social issues are more intricately related to one another and because the impact of any major change is itself quickly felt throughout the national and international system.[2] Moreover, the solutions to one set of problems will themselves create still others. Computer technology, which helps us deal with increasingly complex social problems, is a prime example of this point. Computers require esoteric and detailed information, techniques, and concepts that most people do not understand and that could give the people who understand computers a disproportionate influence over the direction and style of the decisions in local and federal government.[3]

The complexity of the task has not prevented writers from attempting to predict the future, however. Some authorities have little confidence in the ability of the society to cope with the problems and expect the educational enterprise to remain substantially unchanged. Such a note is sounded by Anthony Oettinger, author of *Run, Computer, Run,* who observes that the American school system seems almost ideally designed to resist change. He predicts that 10 years or so from now, the schools will be pretty much as they are today.[4] Such predictions have become almost cliches, but in support of his gloomy forecast he notes how school economics, national organization, internal school hierarchies, inadequately trained staff, and simple human inertia all militate against substantial change. He also has the support of E. M. Cornford who wryly observed that "nothing should ever be done for the first time."[5] Observing Cambridge University as it began to stir to the modern world at the beginning of this century, Cornford added, "Nothing is ever done until everyone is convinced that it ought to be done, and has been convinced for so long that it is now time to do something else."[6]

Other writers, however, are just as convinced that drastic reform is in the offing. While noting that the purposes, forms, and functions of schools in 1970 look much as they did in 1960, Fischer predicts that "what has happened during these ten years is that pressures of the sort that produce and usually must precede institutional change have accumulated to the point where significant reforms are not only possible but inevitable."[7] It seems inconceivable to him and to many other observers that schools can continue to resist the pervasive forces for change that are now at work in this country: the greater use of complex and changing technologies, the diffusion of existing goods and privileges throughout the society, centralization of the American political system, and a closer relationship of the United States with the rest of the world.

In this chapter we will assume that some kind of reform is highly probable, given the right conditions. The final chapter is devoted to an analysis of some of those conditions that must prevail before the proposed reforms to be reviewed here can materialize. This chapter will provide a brief overview of the range of experiments, models, and innovations that are being tried or proposed. The innovations selected for this discussion are merely intended to illustrate some possible directions for the future. I have not tried to be inclusive, nor does space permit a thorough analysis of any one type of innovation; the reader is referred to the educational literature for more detailed discussions. The chapter will serve its purpose if it conveys a sense of the ferment in the field today.

The chapter is organized around the five problems considered in each of the preceding chapters: changes in the organization of public schools, changes in the structure of higher education, the implications of racism and poverty for the future of education, the prospects for student unrest, and the prospects for teacher militancy.

HOW WILL THE PUBLIC SCHOOL SYSTEM BE REORGANIZED?

Before reviewing some of the innovations being advocated for public education, it will be useful to identify several trends in the society that, it seems likely, will sustain the momentum of innovation and influence the direction of future experiments.

Trends

First, as more people come to recognize that formal schooling has become a serious economic necessity that accounts for a large portion of this nation's economic growth over the last few decades, there will be more pressure to improve the effectiveness of schools. Second, declining public confidence in many social institutions, including educational organizations, will support the demand for reform. Third, there is a shifting balance of power within the society that is breaking down old monopolies over education, most notably the shift from rural-to-urban dominance and the increased power of ethnic and racial minorities in the central cities. These new sources of pressure will generate more momentum for change. Fourth, the fact that public enrollments and the demand for teachers have leveled off, for the first time in many years puts the public in a position to think about something other than the problems of growth in the public schools, perhaps including ways to improve their quality. Finally, the federal government has become a major source of leadership because it is one of the few sources of leadership capable of coping with national problems posed by rapid social change.[8] It serves as a source of outside leverage on local educational institutions.

There is, however, a wide range in the scope of changes likely to be produced by these forces—from relatively simple modifications of classroom activities to revolutionary proposals to dispense with formal schooling. By far the majority of the innovations being contemplated fall near the former extreme, but the future ultimately hinges more directly upon what happens to the more sweeping proposals for wholesale reform.

What Reforms Are Occurring Within the Classroom?

CURRICULUM CHANGES

The curriculum appears to be one area of public schools that can be changed quite rapidly, perhaps because changes in the content or procedures of instruction do not create serious disturbances throughout the remainder of the school. Thus, 20 percent of the schools had adopted the "modern physics" curriculum in four years, and modern math swept the country so rapidly that it was taught in nearly every high school only six years after it was introduced. Sex education courses also have spread in recent years. Some observers now believe that in the coming years there will be a comparable transformation in the social sciences and humanities with more stress on social problems and on preparing students to cope with the future.[9]

There were two dominating approaches to curriculum during the 1960s. One was programmed instruction designed to individualize instruction. Learning was organized into "small step" learning sequences. However, as a Ford Foundation report notes, interest in the approach soon waned because early materials were poorly constructed and available in a limited number of subject matter areas, and because the mechanical approaches created problems of student motivation.[10] However, elements of the approach have survived, including the principles of behavioral objectives, carefully constructed learning sequences, and criteria tests used at each stage to help plan the learner's experiences.

The second approach was the curriculum-reform movement generated by professors at Harvard and MIT. Building on central concepts of a discipline, some of these materals were sophisticated, but they also tended to be expensive and demanded extensive teacher preparation. The Ford Foundation report concludes that where the packaged curricula are accompanied by teacher training, they tend to continue, and where the curricula are locally produced, expensive, or require substantial changes in faculty behavior, they tend to be discontinued. But in either case, the efforts at least resulted in less reliance in a single textbook and use of a wider variety of materials.

EARLY CHILDHOOD EDUCATION

A growing number of school systems have converted to the concept of early childhood education based on the idea that some form of schooling should be provided almost from birth if the child is to successfully survive in the first grade. Some psychologists believe that at least half of all human intelligence is developed by the age of four, a belief that has gained wide acceptance and is rapidly being translated into educational practice.[11]

About 40 percent of all three-to-five year olds in the United States are enrolled in some kind of preprimary program. There are now more than 100 infant programs in the United States.[12] The effect is to extend the influence of the formal school over the child and his family for longer periods of his life. However, studies of Head Start-trained children indicate that children who are trained early often lose most of whatever preschool gains they had made because the elementary schools do not build on this early foundation. In the future, it seems likely that more attention will be given to planning a curriculum at the elementary school level that anticipates the needs of children who have already experienced two, three, or four years of formal schooling.

THE INFORMAL CLASSROOM

This concept, designed to break down the status differences between teachers and students, includes relaxed multimedia learning centers, cooperative student-teacher ventures, growing opportunities for pupils to plan and assume independent responsibility for their education, and relaxation of the personal controls that teachers have traditionally exercised over students. Such programs in this country are modeled around experimental schools in England where a variety of alternative settings, materials, and projects are provided for children who work at their own rate. Indirect, "psychological" techniques of discipline are used, such as reasoning, appeals through guilt, and withdrawal of love (versus direct methods such as physical punishment, scolding, or threats). In the classroom there is an aversion to the single test, drilling on organized curriculum, and teacher-questioning-pupils approaches.[13]

Underlying the specific proposals is a renewed emphasis on humanism, rejection of the strictly "scientific" concept of teaching, and a shift in the focus away from "teaching" to "learning." For example, some schools are experimenting with "cross-age" teaching, where older children assume the responsibility for teaching certain subject matter skills to younger children. The assumption is that students learn more from one another than they can learn directly from the teacher.

There is some reason to believe that children who are reared with the more permissive techniques tend to excel over other children in self-control, achievement, responsibility, leadership, popularity, and general adjustment. But the critics consider this approach to be little more than warmed-over progressivism that was advocated by Dewey. Moreover, often the children have not been taught how to live with the increased responsibility. As Herndon says of his experiment with nondirected learning,

"What we were doing was offering the kids an intolerable burden. We offered to make them decide what they would do. But they couldn't decide, because they had been in school for seven years and besides that they knew from their lives—long all about the expectations of their parents and of the country of America. They were not free, no matter how often we said they were. No more than we were."[14]

Whether the approach is merely a fad, or whether it is the vanguard of a sustained drive to debureaucratize the schools, it does highlight the significance of the *setting* in which learning is to take place. It has become apparent that to improve education, it will be necessary to do more than improve teaching in a limited sense.

CROSS-AGE TEACHING

At hundreds of schools, high school and junior high students are tutoring elementary pupils and even their own classmates in such basic subjects as reading and math. Some of the tutoring sessions are informal, free-periods; at other schools student-teachers work on a formal schedule. According to one limited study in Dallas, more than 40 percent of the tutored youngsters raised their grades by one letter or more; only about 10 percent received lower grades, and of students whose grades were unchanged, most would probably have slipped without tutoring.[15]

CONTRACT LEARNING

Noting all of the problems with informal schooling, some authorities advocate another extreme, that is, to *formalize* the teacher-learning relationship by means of individual "contracts" geared to the student's present achievements and his own rate of progress. But in making students formally accountable for their accomplishments, contracts also allow teachers to relax their day-to-day supervision and permit a greater variety of behavior to be carried on in the classroom simultaneously. The school must be on a flexible, modular schedule that divides up the day into short periods (e.g., of 30 minutes each) and that can be combined into longer periods as desired. As the student accomplishes each task, he is "programmed" at his own rate step-by-step through an orderly sequence leading towards specific, measurable objectives. Motivation is based on "operant conditioning," or "contingency management" principles, through which desirable behavior is positively reinforced with tangible rewards such as tokens that the students "cash" to purchase jump ropes, puzzles, soft drinks, and other goods and activities they enjoy.

A number of problems have been reported with this procedure. One is that existing technology is not sufficiently advanced to measure many of the significant educational objectives other than academic achievement. Also, many critics still are not satisfied because "individualized" does not mean "humanized" learning; all that is individualized is the *rate* of instruction.[16] Opponents charge, in fact, that programmed instruction often dehumanizes the learning process. And finally, as Mecklenburger observes, performance contracts exemplify what Illich characterized as the "school mentality"—that knowledge can be defined as a commodity whose value can be determined by its contribution to *institutional* objectives rather than to the objectives of the child."[17]

DIFFERENTIATED STAFFING AND MULTIUNIT SCHOOLS

Another widely acclaimed innovation—differentiated staffing—would produce more coordination problems but would also alleviate the burdens of teaching as new responsibilities are heaped upon the schools. Three kinds of new specialists are being introduced to cope with specific tasks—clerks, general aids (to sell tickets, supervise nonstudy areas, and police traffic), and instruction assistants (with some college training) to supervise independent study areas or grade papers.

Several developments have made a new division of labor almost mandatory, including the following:

1. The first (and, in a sense, foremost) development is the knowledge explosion. The structure of knowledge has become so complex that there is no way for it to be either comprehended or treated as a whole. Indeed, in view of the full range of forces that are now known to influence education, it is fair to say that no one occupation can handle the responsibility for schooling in the future; closer collaboration will be required between teachers, social workers, nurses, psychologists, businessmen, and other groups.

2. The current efforts to professionalize teaching have encouraged greater specialization of work roles—and in particular a functionally based form of specialization that carries broad authority for specialists to find the means necessary to fulfill given responsibilities.

3. Increasing bureaucratization has imposed many duties on teachers that have deflected their attention from their primary functions. Specialization allows teachers to delegate work to other positions and, hence, provides a means of separating out bureaucratic duties.

4. Finally, technology is revolutionizing the self-contained classroom, not only by creating additional roles, but by providing the means by which teachers can specialize.[18]

Implementing differentiated staffing on a broad scale could shake up established lines of authority, and it could help to increase the sense of commitment on the part of teachers who enter and remain in the field. Teachers have been adamant about minimizing status distinctions among themselves, perhaps partly in order to protect themselves from the capriciousness of administrators. Differentiated work roles could change that and provide career ladders for teachers. Career ladders might increase the internal competition among teachers within a particular school, but they could circumvent the "dead end" quality of teaching as it is presently constituted, which seems to have prompted many teachers to leave the classroom. In addition to increasing commitment to teaching in general, career ladders could be used to increase commitment to specific fields within teaching. Teachers who have been effective in working with certain types of problems—for example, working with disadvantaged children—could be promoted *without* requiring them to forsake their area of specialization.

The Ford Foundation report on its Comprehensive School Improvement Program concluded that innovations in staff utilization clearly emerge as the most successful and most permanent of the innovations it funded, "since changes in teacher behavior and attitude could be effected within a school or inside a few classrooms with a minimum of disruption, and often without the community's full awareness."[19] There is some evidence that team teaching and other forms of differentiated staffing are at least more satisfactory for teachers than the traditional self-contained classroom. Using a combination of survey and behavioral observation techniques, sociologists at Stanford's Center for the Study of Teaching compared nine open-space schools with eight self-contained schools and found that teachers in the first situation were decidedly more likely than teachers in the second situation to discuss their work with their colleagues, to exert more influence over each other's teaching practices and over school policy, to maintain more autonomy over their own work, and to be more committed to teaching.[20]

Nevertheless, there is still strong resistance to the forces pushing for reorganization of the teacher's role. After surveying the situation, Roy A. Edelfelt concluded:

"Differentiated staffing got off to a great start in the talking stages. Two years ago it was one of the hottest innovations in education. Reorganizing school faculties to differentiate roles had appeal because it satisfied so many good causes. . . . All these good ideas ran smack into a series of stone walls. . . . School board members soon realized that differentiated staffing wouldn't save money. . . ."[21]

He observes that teacher organizations resisted differentiated staffing because of their suspicions about merit pay, and superintendents did not support it because it implied decentralized power. All these second thoughts emerged as the nation moved into the economic recession. Only

24 of these projects were funded. In most cases, the funding was so minimal that not much could happen that is really experimental.

In addition to the projects to which Edelfelt refers, however, team teaching and other forms of differentiated staffing are being incorporated into larger instructional systems called "multiunit" schools. These experimental schools consist of nongraded instructional units and individually guided instruction. Teachers work together in groups, assisted by various kinds of specialists. Such schools typically include several teaching units consisting of approximately five professionals each and 150 students. Each unit has a lead teacher, and the unit teachers and principal form a faculty council responsible for coordinating school-wide affairs.[22] There are at least 500 of these schools in existence in 15 states.

Since each unit sets its own objectives and must move at a separate pace, multiunit schools require different forms of decision making and communication. The units must devise ways to plan, instruct, and evaluate cooperatively. Some decisions that traditionally have been made in the central office must be decentralized, while some decisions that were formerly made by individual teachers must be centralized. Similarly, this organizational mode is likely to encourage more horizontal communication among teachers as well as more communication among the different levels of the hierarchy. It is possible that the principle of group decision making leads to a wider range of alternatives, more informal decisions and more effective implementation.

The Center for the Advanced Study of Educational Administration at the University of Oregon has been studying how differentiated staffing in multiunit schools is affecting the authority of teachers. There is some evidence that, once staff reorganization has been achieved, teachers are more satisfied with their jobs and exercise more authority.[23] It is very likely that changed patterns of work and activity might produce more horizontal communication among teachers and more informal communication among them and the administration, which in turn would enhance their authority.

However, case studies reported by the Oregon researchers also reveal a number of chronic problems in these attempts to reorganize, including the resistance of teachers to directed change, unclarity surrounding the roles and objectives of differentiated staffing, work overloads and time pressures, lack of resources, inadequate training for new responsibilities, and undue reliance on structural change (via job descriptions, new titles, or altered organizational units) as a way of changing behavior.[24] (Some of these underlying barriers to change will be discussed more systematically in the final chapter.) Even if they do succeed, it can be expected that differentiated staffing and multiunit schools will aggravate still other problems, such as the problems of overlapping authority lines, competition among teachers, and coordinating and evaluating independent teachers and other professionals who will have to cooperate closely. New administrative hierarchies are likely to evolve in response to these problems, but most specialized personnel could find themselves assuming more of the administrative duties that will remove them further from their clientele.

CHANGES IN TEACHER TRAINING

Finally, many of the proposals for change within the classroom will require better and more thoroughly trained teachers. During the 1960s many "fifth-year" teacher programs were introduced. These programs typically admit students with good undergraduate records, place only moderate stress on education courses, and involve prospective teachers with practical experience as interns in local schools.

Several teacher training institutions are experimenting with individual-paced "competency-based" training programs. A program is tailored to suit each student on the basis of his present skills and needs. The student makes a contract with the university, agreeing to complete certain tasks that have been designed to achieve a specified set of explicitly defined outcomes. It is possible to measure the extent that the intended outcome has been achieved on the basis of skills, attitudes, and behavior that the materials have produced. The program is organized around a flexible scheduling system and "modules" consisting of pretested materials and experiences that take varying amounts of time to complete. Continuous evaluation determines when a student is ready to undertake his next assignment.

The largest of these programs is the Teacher Corps, a federally sponsored program that grew out of the "war on poverty" along with the Peace Corps and Vista. This program is designed to train teachers for poverty schools and to introduce teaching innovations into such schools. Unlike many master teacher programs, the Teacher Corps places less priority on the undergraduate records of the recruit than upon recruiting idealistic young people into teaching. My study of 10 of these programs indicated that, in comparison to conventionally recruited new teachers, the Teacher Corps interns were more socially and politically liberal, more change oriented, and more closely identified with minority group children. The interns subscribed to a very humane philosophy of education, preferred to work with minority children, endorsed racial integration, emphasized the creative potential of these children over maintaining discipline in the classroom, expressed confidence in the ability of their pupils to learn, and were concerned for the children's welfare.[25]

They were rated as good teachers by their supervisors, but many of the older teachers considered the interns to be too "radical" and too "naive" to make good teachers. A substantial minority of them, having become frustrated by their attempts to introduce change into public schools and universities, became alienated and radicalized during the program and did not enter teaching. But others seemed to adapt their attitudes to the realities of the situation. They will perhaps become a new "hybrid" type of teacher, one who is humanistic and innovative but also realistic and patient enough to develop feasible strategies for changing the profession.

SOME RESERVATIONS

Although these and other experiments are being tried in a few places, they are widely resisted and remain rather isolated in a few classrooms or a particular school. Most teaching still comes down to ordinary conventional teaching and discipline.[26] Most teachers appear to be comfortable in their routines; most "innovations" are used only infrequently. Despite all of the rhetoric about "innovation," it seems unlikely that significant new departures can be made in the classroom until modifications are made in the larger structural context that entraps the classroom in its traditional routines.

Is Power Being Redistributed?

The important changes of the future will be those designed to directly modify the system itself. Several efforts are now being made to revise the decision-making structure.

DECENTRALIZATION

Decentralization of education can mean one of two things: (1) decentralization of decisions within the administrative hierarchy, principally when central office administrators delegate more authority to local school principals and teachers and (2) sharing more control with citizen's groups in the local community or neighborhoods.

Administrative Decentralization. Perhaps principals could relate to the local citizens more effectively if they had more discretionary powers in dealing with the local groups. But decentralization would also deprive them of the backing of strong central administrators, leaving them vulnerable to local pressure groups.

Some proponents also advocate a form of decentralization within schools, that is, breaking up large high schools consisting of thousands of students into smaller "houses." Each house would be further subdivided into "resource units" that include a few hundred students and a dozen or so teachers and other staff members. Architecturally, the research unit ("pod") would be the basic learning block of the school. The various houses would provide a variety of atmospheres and learning climates, thus affording the student a choice of the type of environment most compatible for him.

Community Decentralization. Administrative decentralization leaves control in the hands of school officials, which fails to satisfy the critics who charge that schools have been too insulated from criticism. Many observers believe that schools must be forced to become more responsive and accountable to the public. That the average lower-class child from the Northern city can graduate from high school reading at less than the tenth-grade level is seen by many citizens, correctly or not, as evidence that the professional bureaucracy has not taken its responsibilities seriously. Although social scientists have customarily accepted, at face value, the claims of professionals that outside interference undermines their ability to administer treatment with fairness and technical competence, an equally valid argument can be made that hostile self-interest groups, including parental organizations and student organizations aid in maintaining an effective professional relationship.[27]

One answer is to decentralize monolithic school systems by breaking them down into smaller, independent districts run by communities or neighborhoods within the large city. Decentralization could provide an important step toward debureaucratizing the schools. It is widely assumed that decentralization will energize the system by redistributing power to parents so that those with fresh ideas will be able to exert more influence; promote wider participation in the schools; permit communities to supplement the work of professional teachers; reduce the size of the bureaucracy, thus increasing the overall efficiency and reducing the alienation of students and parents; and prompt professionals to improve the academic achievement of children by making them accountable to the parents.[28]

However, the decentralization movement is not an entirely new phenomenon in American education. It has failed before because it encourages excessive parochialism. During the early part of the nineteenth century, parent groups, or "democratic localists" as Katz refers to them, combated the trend toward incipient bureaucratization. Their stress was on variety, local adaptability, and rapport between the school and community. They maintained an antiprofessional attitude, being hostile and suspicious of educators.[29] At its best, democratic localism embraced a broad and humanistic conception of education that combated narrow utilitarian education. But, Katz observes, the failure of democratic localism was predictable from the start, because it permitted tyrannical local groups to impose their narrow sectarianism and political biases into the schoolroom.[30] Decentralization also fosters resegregation and further isolates neighborhoods from the larger community, thus depriving low-income ethnic groups of the advantages of integrated classrooms that were reported in Chapter 3. Moreover, since local neighborhoods cannot raise their own revenues, they must rely upon the central board to allocate funds. Yet, lower-class neighborhoods are seldom able to muster the political power necessary to compete for resources with middle-class neighborhoods; they are not likely to be able to pull themselves up "by their own bootstraps" without the close and sustained cooperation of middle-class students and parents.

There are also serious practical obstacles to be overcome. Many low-income communities are split among themselves and lack the political organization necessary to maintain representative government. Thus, community schools might either increase ethnic clashes or result in low voter turnout; in either case, a few influentials could gain control for their own purposes. Also, there has been strong resistance from the teacher unions that, while preferring decisions to be made at the local level, want professionals to make them. Still other costs include the added time and effort required to run the program and loss of efficiency and flexibility that is likely to result when citizens participate in decision making. Some critics also fear that citizens may demand actions that are inconsistent with other public programs and objectives or that are impractical, unethical, or contrary to law.

DEPROFESSIONALIZATION

There have been parallel attempts to break up teaching monopolies in the wake of growing discontent with the professional educators' hold over formal education, especially in view of widespread alienation between professionals and their lower-class clientele. The teacher aide and student careers movements represent two efforts to deprofessionalize teaching. The number of indigenous laymen working as teacher aides in American schools increased over 800 percent between 1960 and 1968.[31] In 1971 it was estimated that between 200,000 and 300,000 aides were employed in the schools.[32]

Teacher aides are noncertified persons who directly assist a teacher with his instructional responsibilities. They usually assume a wide variety of educational tasks, ranging from housekeeping functions to teaching dance and supervising field trips. No matter what their role, however, they can provide a link to the community by acting as mediators and interpreters between the bureaucracy and the community. Since this is an emergent role, there has been a great deal of conflict surrounding it, especially over the kind of training that the aide should have and his proper relationship to the teacher. The aide concept challenges the assumption held by most professionals that one's authority in education should stem from his technical skills. Instead, the aide's authority in large part rests on his firsthand knowledge of the situation and rapport between him and the client. Teacher organizations have proposed that aides should be certified, fearing that the aide program can become a back door to teaching and will weaken professional standards. Certification is also advocated as a way of providing job security for aides and providing a career ladder within the educational profession.

There is no conclusive evidence as yet concerning the effects of aides on the learner, but in at least one school in New York City, children's reading scores improved measurably during the four years that paraprofessionals worked there, and another study in Minneapolis concluded that there was a clear-cut improvement in the achievement of children in a kindergarten class when an aide was used. But the latter study showed that when two or more aides were used, ironically, it created problems of supervision that interfered with effective teaching.[33] This latter possibility, together with the skepticism and resistance from teachers, points to the types of problems that the aide movement is likely to produce as it becomes institutionalized.

What Alternatives Are There to the Public Schools?

Community control and deprofessionalization are long-range proposals to break up the monopolies that various groups exercise over the system of education as it now exists. Other reforms are being proposed that would break up the system itself and establish other types of educational institutions within and alongside the present system.

PERFORMANCE CONTRACTING

Performance contracting represents a modest step toward creating alternative forms of schooling. The school system delegates responsibility for conducting classes to an external agency but retains final control. Several schools around the country have contracted with private firms to teach reading to a specific group of underachieving pupils, with the understanding that the firm will be paid a specific sum for every pupil whose reading level improves by an agreed-on amount. Dozens of performance contracts in education have been awarded in recent years.

One of the most ambitious programs to date was a six-and-a-half million dollar contract with one private firm to take over responsibility for teaching in schools in 18 cities involving more than 27,000 children. Another contract was signed by the school system of Gary, Indiana, with Behavioral Research Laboratories to run an entire elementary school on a money-back guarantee basis if the firm failed to bring 840 black inner-city students up to or above the national average in reading and mathematics in three years. Several learning systems employ only a few certified teachers, replacing them with paraprofessionals or assistant learning directors, who are usually local parents. A few systems have replaced teachers entirely.

Performance contract firms are unencumbered by the school administration and rules of the school system that have constrained other teachers. Supporters claim that performance contracting ties teacher performance to *results,* rather than schedules, seniority, and protected mediocrity. But the practice is still controversial with an uncertain future. Although most members of the National School Board Association are sympathetic to it, the American Federation of Teachers decries it as a form of hucksterism and resents the use of noncertified teachers by the independent firms. A Rand Corporation study for the U.S. Office of Education found that public school programs run by private business firms have produced very little overall gains. The five school districts studied showed gains averaging about seven months' growth for nine months' instruction—the usual rate for children in poverty-area schools. Only one program, in Gary, Indiana, showed gains above the usual rate.[34] The Office of Economic Opportunity, after analyzing 19 separate programs conducted by six different companies across the country, also concluded that there were no significant gains in the reading and mathematics performances of students who were exposed to these programs and "control groups" that had not been exposed to performance contracting.

THE VOUCHER SYSTEM

In performance contracting, the decisions regarding contracts remain in the hands of school boards and administrators. Other proposals have been advanced aimed at breaking up this monopoly by giving the individual citizen the right to choose where he will send his children. A committee of the NEA has recommended abolishing compulsory attendance laws now on the books in all states except Mississippi (although they are widely violated under school policies of suspension and expulsion). This would give citizens more choice in where and how their children are educated. However, the available options are still limited by both the absence of alternatives and the lack of a sound basis of financing. The voucher plan is designed to meet these problems.[35]

Under this system, state governments could require children to receive a minimum level of schooling at a variety of institutions of their choice financed by giving parents vouchers redeemable for a specified maximum sum per child per year if spent on a variety of approved educational activities. Parents would then be free to spend this sum and any additional sum they themselves could provide on purchasing educational services from an approved institution of their own choice. This would include private enterprises operated for a profit, non-profit institutions, or a specific public school within their metropolitan area. The GI Bill is a similar plan on the college level that has been in operation for many years.

One idea behind the plan is that the teachers and administrators who devise the most interesting or effective curriculum should attract the most students and therefore the most money. Those programs that students dislike or that parents feel are not effective are expected to lose students and money until, in theory, they either improve or go out of business. However, they also might be tempted to "water down" the curriculum as a basis of popular appeal.

DIRECT COMPENSATION FOR LEARNING

The voucher system foreshadows what could turn out to be an even more revolutionary incentive system, namely, making direct payments to the teacher, parent and student for what the student has learned. One evaluation study concludes that providing financial incentives for the teachers alone does not seem to improve the reading and math levels of the children.[36] Teachers must be helped to find substantive ideas about how teaching can be improved; they need more than incentive. However, the study notes that there is some hope of improvement if the *parents* are eligible for payments based on their child's progress.

Making direct payments to the children might be even more effective. Direct compensation would focus the incentive system on the learner himself instead of on the teacher or administrator, and even the parent, and thus eventually cut out the "middle man." It would elevate learning geography or English literature to a plane at least comparable to pumping gas or delivering papers and other jobs for which young people are paid in after-school employment, and that compete directly with certain school requirements.

ALTERNATIVE SCHOOLS

Another sweeping reform is called the "alternative schools" movement. It is estimated that there are now between 400 and 500 private school systems in operation throughout the country initiated and run by groups of citizens. They range from "storefront schools" in Harlem and preschools operated by the YWCA to the traditional parochial schools. The growth of these private schools reflects a new commitment to pluralism, with its concomitant value of free choice. Additional proposals have been made for regional, state, and federal schools; open schools run by colleges; industrial demonstration schools financed by commercial firms; labor-union sponsored schools; and army schools.[37]

The survival rate of these schools is low. Only one third of the private schools founded since 1969 have survived; their average life span is about two years. They face many obstacles, especially financing problems and extreme disagreement among those within the movement over the goals. Some want the schools to function as therapeutic communities. Others want them to develop alternative "life styles," and still others want to create "counterculture schools" with a radical orientation. Grubard believes that they will become increasingly political, a development which will reduce the odds of survival even further.[38] On the other hand, Teuber reports evidence that the survivors tend to become increasingly like the public schools they are designed to replace, as a condition of survival.[39] Whether they become more radical or more conservative, or develop in different ways will strongly depend upon (1) whether a more stable base of support evolves, through vouchers or a similar system and (2) the ability of public school systems to provide alternatives *within* the system. This latter development would rob the alternative school movement of its middle-of-the-road supporters, leaving the private schools with the most alienated, radicalized parents, as Grubard predicts.

The federal government has been promoting some new alternatives through the U.S. Office of Education's $25 million Experimental Schools Program to establish a nationwide system of experimental schools. For example, a project in Berkeley, California, is designed to build on an integration plan that uses large-scale busing to mix up a racially divided student body. The students spend part of their time with students of different backgrounds, the other part in programs of their choice geared to their own racial or ethnic groups. Options include traditional schools, open classrooms, a Spanish language school, a black-awareness section of a high school, and a new school comprising 100 students and their families who will determine the program themselves. In Pierce County, Washington, the schools operate on highly flexible scheduling. A child might go to school four days a week, or five mornings or afternoons. Depending on a computer assisted diagnosis of the instruction he needs, the student will be in school as little as 180 days or as much as 240 days a year.

To some degree, all of these schools are in competition with the traditional public schools for students and other resources. The movement probably will not replace public schools, and the quality of education in alternative schools is undoubtedly quite varied and may be no more effective on the average than what is provided through traditional public education. However, by challenging the monopoly of professional educators and by creating an element of competition and free choice, the *existence* of such alternatives could force other schools to become more responsive and accountable to a wider range of publics.

Schools Without Walls

Several proposals have been made to broaden educational settings in order to break down the artificial boundaries to learning that are imposed when it is confined to schools.

Experience-based Curricula. Some schools have experimented with giving course credit for extra-school experience, such as working in apprenticeships and participating in organized activities like VISTA or summer-long tutoring programs. These experiences would supersede required courses and diplomas and substitute in their place competitive examinations when the student feels prepared.

Educational TV. One of the most promising developments capitalizes on the creative use of TV for educational purposes in the home, as reflected in the widely acclaimed success of "Sesame Street," for example. The show has consistently demonstrated the effectiveness of television as a medium for teaching preschool children, according to studies completed by Educational Testing Service.[40] Findings show that youngsters who watch more tend to learn more and, among frequent viewers, disadvantaged youngsters gain as much as those from advantaged homes. Three-year-old frequent viewers gain more and have higher post-test results than older children who watch less frequently. Gains in vocabulary, mental age, and IQ have never been objectives of "Sesame Street," but research indicates that the program may have positive impact within these areas as well. One significant conclusion reached by evaluators was that there is no basis for fears expressed by some observers that children accustomed to the fast paced, rapid-fire television format would be "turned off" by the conventional classroom when they started school.

Satellite television is now available to capitalize on these educational values of television. It can be exploited to provide dramatic learning opportunities, whether it is a riot in Chicago, a Congressional hearing, or a 10-week series of programs on the recent developments in Asia. Because students can observe what is taking place at the time it takes place, satellite television might encourage students to become more cognizant of the world society.

But it should be noted that any reform that has the effect of relocating education in the home can have some serious consequences for disadvantaged groups who, many critics believe, are already held back by their home environments, and for women who will be tied to the home at a time when they are trying to break out from it.

Community Schools. "Community schools" are designed to serve not only children but all members of the community on a 14-hour-a-day, six-days-a-week, year-round basis. In Boston, for example, urban renewal plans for residential and commercial building are closely tied to plans for community schools. A Secondary Education Complex for 5000 students, to be located in the black neighborhood of Roxbury, includes commercial services such as movie theaters and restaurants and some housing for faculty. The new Quincy Elementary School building also includes commercial and community services as well as private apartments. However, in many cases there seems to be no clear idea whether what is wanted is a school with deep ties to its local neighborhood or a school that will draw both its pupils and participating adults from throughout the city and beyond.[41]

Media Networks. Perhaps the most extreme possible future has been painted by Illich, who proposes to abandon schools altogether. He points out that the Title I federal-aid program has distributed approximately

$1 billion a year with very little sign that the learning of "disadvantaged" children has improved.[42] Alluding to two centuries ago when the United States led the world in a movement to disestablish the monopoly of a single church, Illich calls for the disestablishment of the monopoly of the school, which he says legally combines prejudice and discrimination. He calls for a law forbidding discrimination in hiring, voting, or admission to centers of learning based on previous attendance at some curriculum. The advantage of abandoning schools, he says, would be to remove discrimination that now favors the person who has learned with the largest expenditure of funds, usually with the advantage of a favorable family environment conducive to learning. Maintaining that most learning habits begin casually, Illich calls for new educational institutions that would break apart the pyramid of preschools, grade schools, high schools, junior colleges, and colleges—which have created a lockstep system of education.

Starting from the premise that people learn more outside of the school than in school, the alternative that Illich sees is to rely on self-motivated learning. Instead of employing teachers "to compel or bribe" the student to learn an arbitrary curriculum, he would substitute networks of media and reference services—including libraries, laboratories, museums, theaters, airports or farms available to students as apprentices or on off-hours, skill exchanges that permit persons to list their skills and the conditions under which they are willing to serve as models for others who want to learn these skills, and a communication network that permits persons to describe the learning activity in which they are interested. These educational networks would be operated by professional educators who would need skills and aptitudes similar to those expected of a museum staff, a library, or an employment agency. An extensive educational establishment would not be required because there would be no need for staffs to maintain student discipline, public relations, hiring, supervising of teachers, curriculum making, textbook purchasing, and the maintenance of grounds and facilities.

Youth Communities. Finally, Goodman, among others, regards widespread rebellion in high schools and colleges as evidence that the majority of students do not want to be there. He maintains that an academic environment is an inappropriate means of educating most young people, including most of the bright ones.[43] As a substitute for the coercive nature of most modern school systems, he advocates a system of "incidental education" in which students take part in the ongoing activities of society as the chief means of learning. Youth communities would be substituted for high schools, and college training would follow rather than precede entry into the professions. The main use of academic teaching, Goodman believes, should be for those already in the sciences and the professions who need academic courses along the way.

However, critics of these plans to disestablish the schools point out that the school does perform important functions that should be preserved and strengthened: (1) it can counteract the crass and corrupt values conveyed through the mass media and sanctioned in some homes and by the unsupervised peer group; (2) it can provide a resource for disadvantaged groups to promote group solidarity if they can gain control over it; (3) it provides job training for a large sector of society who are the most vulnerable to unemployment; and (4) it is a source of firm direction for the vast numbers of children who are not self-motivated.[44] The critics contend that these functions are of special benefit to the disadvantaged youths who would be the first to suffer if the society were deschooled.

In final analysis, then, the fact that there are strong sources of resistance to most of these experiments makes it hazardous to guess precisely what schools will be like one generation from now. But it is clear that serious thought and effort are being devoted to ways of reforming education in this country. It does seem plausible that something different might evolve from all of this movement. It also seems likely, however, that whatever the nature of the new form that evolves, it will represent a modification of what now exists, not a radically different system. It is more likely to be the product of compromise than of revolution.

WHAT CHANGES ARE IN STORE FOR HIGHER EDUCATION?

While there are some differences between the trends in elementary-secondary education and trends that appear to be developing in higher education, there are also many parallels. The future will depend on how three types of dilemmas are resolved: (1) whether to make the changes necessary to accommodate an increasing variety of students or to attempt to restore the traditional academic authority of the universities by enforcing standards of intellectual achievement; (2) whether to give students a greater voice in policy and control over their own education or to try to maintain the present course and credit machinery; and (3) whether to try to maintain a detached and neutral setting for scholarship or to become more "relevant" and join the struggle against social ills.[45]

Trends

Orlans notes that the universities are under multiple pressures for change caused by the side effects of federal support, the demands of regional and community developments, the creation of cross-disciplinary centers, the fading boundaries between training and work, and the demands from the new society of the young.[46] As a result, it is expected that a variety of new organizational forms linked more closely to community needs, to work, and to the industrial, political, and educational life of the traditional community will evolve.

The Carnegie Commission on Higher Education has identified several sources of strain produced by social change—doubtful financial support from both states and the federal government, changing job requirements, a new life-style among youth, a fluctuating birth rate, and innovative educational technology. Many of the problems stem from the growing scale and complexity of colleges and universities, which has taken place within the past decade. Despite a recent slowdown in the growth rate, enrollments are expected to double again in the next 30 years.[47] As pointed out in Chapter 2, this growth has radically transformed traditionally aristocratic institutions into mass institutions. Higher education's time-honored answer to a burgeoning student population—simply building more and bigger institutions—will not solve these problems.[48]

This growth rate will bring to college students who have a wide range of academic abilities and interests. On the one hand, today's *best* young people are far superior intellectually to those of the recent past. The average American 16-year-old has had five years more schooling than his counterpart in 1920 and scores approximately one standard deviation above the student of a generation ago on standardized performance tests. A student who places in the middle of his graduating class today would probably have placed in the top 15 percent 30 years ago.[49] Some of these changes perhaps can be attributed to commercial television, which entered the homes almost 15 to 20 years ago. Many young people in college today have watched television about 20 hours a week during their childhood for an annual total greater than the number of hours they spend in school.

On the other hand, as pointed out in Chapter 3, the bulk of the increase in college enrollments will be made up of low-income, low-socioeconomic status students who only a decade ago would not have entered college. By 1967, as many as a third of the lower-socioeconomic males in the lowest ability groups were attending college, and the majority of low-ability males in the upper socioeconomic group were in college.[50] As many as five percent of the students who entered college in 1960 scored in the bottom fifth of the aptitude distribution, and as many as 21 percent scored in the bottom half. Thus, the total range of ability found among high school graduates in this country is represented in the population now in college. The range in the student population will be further compounded by a considerable increase in the number of adults enrolled in higher education institutions.

Another force that has to be taken into account is the drift toward nationalization. There has been an explosion of federal funds for education, not only in the U.S. Office of Education but in many federal agencies; the Department of Defense and Veterans' Administration combined spend more money on education than does the U.S. Office of Education. Because most problems today are national in scope, and because of geographical mobility and the existence of national labor markets, colleges and universities will be forced, more and more, to respond to outside national forces. With greater frequency than ever before they will be influenced by outside groups who are not subject to the control of professionals and administrators. As Sussman notes,

"The truly major changes in university life have been initiated from the outside, by such forces as Napoleon in France, ministers of education in Germany, royal commissions and the University Grants Committee in Great Britain, the Communist Party in Russia, the emperor at the time of the Restoration in Japan, the lay university governing boards and the federal Congress in the Unted States— and also, in the United States, by the foundations. The foundations, quickly responsive to needs and possibilities, have been the main instruments, for example, in the reform of medical education, the introduction of interdisciplinary studies, the involvement of universities in world affairs."[51]

The universities can be expected to evolve new procedures and standards as they accommodate themselves to these trends.

The continuing explosion of knowledge is still another source of problems. Campuses cannot handle the new knowledge within their traditional framework. Campus faculties have multiplied and splintered and now must regroup. The idea that there is a fixed "body of knowledge" to be delivered has become archaic, and with it the use of faculty-student ratios, years of residence, and credit hours for courses and grading have become useless as measures of performance.

Finally, as these problems have begun to directly affect more people, there has been growing pressure to integrate the various levels of education. However, as yet there is no truly effective way to permit or compel institutions at the various levels to combine their talents and resources on attacks of central problems that affect all levels.

How are institutions of higher education responding to these developments? As in the case of the public schools, the scope of proposed reforms extends from modest technological and procedural changes confined to the classroom to more fundamental structural reforms.

What Reforms Are Taking Place Within the College Classroom?

Several types of changes are being discussed that could change the typical college classroom.

GRADING PROCEDURES

One academic reform that gained widespread acceptance in recent years was the substitution of the pass-fail approach for alphabetical or numerical rating systems. The idea was to make college work less competitive in the hope that it would encourage students to explore ideas of interest to them. Some colleges reported that the pass-fail system significantly reduced academic pressures without adversely affecting students' prospects for graduate study.[52] However, some students in pass-fail courses have had trouble getting into graduate school. Thus, many colleges have had second thoughts. For example, whereas in 1969 over half of Brown's undergraduates chose pass-fail in a majority of their courses, by 1972 the figure had dropped to only 29 percent. This reversal illustrates that even relatively minor changes in classroom practices often do not take root. In this case, the barrier comes from other levels in the system. The innovation is likely to be more effective in colleges not typically sending many of their graduates to graduate school.

PROBLEM-ORIENTED CURRICULA

As indicated in Chapter 2, there seems to be growing disenchantment with the specialized curricula organized around specific subject matter. Orlans predicts that by the year 2000 the major problem confronting universities will be how to impart a common culture to counteract excessive specialization. Liberal arts colleges will continue to fulfill this vital function in collaboration with specialized universities.[53] Traditional curricula are slowly being supplemented by more interdisciplinary, problem-oriented work. Some authors believe that colleges and universities soon will have worked out procedures so that a group of students interested in a common problem can locate a professor who will work with them in a course-like setting.[54]

General education—organized so that all students will do intensive work in literature, philosophy, history, science, mathematics, and the social sciences—could easily comprise the bulk of undergraduate training. Vocational training might gradually cease being a major preoccupation of the undergraduate schools. While a few courses might extend over a semester, there is pressure to make most into year-long efforts, thus allowing enough time for students to become more deeply involved. Comprehensive examinations in the student's major field, which now supplement examinations in separate courses, might eventually replace them.

INFORMAL CLASSROOMS

Flexible programs have been envisioned that are designed to impart a more individualized faculty-student relationship. The plan is to transform the professor from a purveyor of information into the senior scholar in a joint intellectual adventure and the advisor who helps direct the student's learning experiences.[55] One writer predicts that the middle-size classes of 25 to 50 will be supplanted by instruction in quite large groups of 500 or more and in quite small groups of 5 to 10.[56]

EDUCATIONAL TECHNOLOGIES

At the same time, colleges will be pressed to use audio-visual and related machines to improve the quality of mass education. Some authorities hope that closed-circuit television and films may help to offset the differences in university quality that stem directly from the variable quality of faculty members teaching at private and public, and at four- and two-year colleges.

Perhaps the paperback book will become an even more valuable teaching device than television. One author believes that mass textbooks and other printed materials of smaller, more specialized scope probably have done more than educational television to contribute to individualization and the use of problem-solving formats.[57]

TEACHER TRAINING

These developments could force colleges to pay more attention to the challenge of preparing professors to teach students with different backgrounds and ability levels. Students, college administrators, and professors themselves have become more concerned about finding ways to systematically evaluate the teaching performance of college teachers in order to hold professors more responsible for the effects of their teaching on their students. Some universities now grant a special advanced teaching degree distinct from the traditional research-oriented degree as a step toward specialized training programs for college teachers.

What New Forms of Organization Are Emerging?

Notwithstanding the limited number of innovations noted above, the fact remains that, as yet, American higher education is structurally much the same today as it was 50 years ago. This is all the more remarkable in view of the range of functions that have been thrust upon universities, their enormous growth in size, and the increasing heterogeneity of their student bodies. However, a number of changes seem to be underway.

REVISED CALENDARS

At the simplest level, many university schedules are being rearranged, particularly in state-supported institutions, in order to permit more nearly year-round use of physical facilities.

ADMINISTRATIVE DECENTRALIZATION

But more fundamentally, many colleges are experimenting with ways to divide student bodies into smaller units and to decentralize their administration. Student activism on the large campuses provided one stimulus for this thrust. Some universities have been experimenting with units of 50 to 100 students and a few faculty advisors. The "Harvard Houses" represent a long-established prototype of this kind. Each house provides board and room for approximately 400 students, but is also the center for social and cultural activities, academic tutorials, extra credit seminars, lectures, and discussion groups. A number of younger faculty members reside in the house as tutors, and other faculty members are affiliated with it. Each house is administered under the guidance of a senior professor who has a wide latitude in the performance of his role.

One study of the Harvard Houses demonstrated how living arrangements can affect students. The authors concluded that the direction of change in student values and attitudes during the course of their college education was primarily determined by the content of the goals of the house where they lived. The extent of change was also linked strongly to the student's involvement in the house and to the amount of consensus between the staff and the students on the central goals.[58]

STRUCTURAL DIFFERENTIATION

With the growth of universities, the problems of undergraduate teaching are likely to crowd out much of the large-scale applied research now being conducted in universities. The majority of researchers in chemistry and other physical science disciplines have already left the campus, and some social scientists have taken jobs outside of universities. As non-university research settings proliferate and grow, in effect, higher education will become even more variegated than it already is. Ways will have to be found to link research institutes and centers to universities if the former are to keep abreast of the broader intellectual currents.

Although efforts to separate the undergraduate and graduate research programs have failed,[59] the fact is that sustained, large-scale research is not central to universities, either with respect to their current mission or historically.[60] Indeed, the founders of early universities in this country had difficulty getting research adopted. It has been an essentially part-time activity subsidized by the undergraduate program, attached to other enterprises within the university, supported from outside funds, and subordinate to teaching in some respects. Some recent developments make universities even less attractive for research. In addition to the obstacles to research posed by teaching responsibilities, divisive disciplinary ideologies and protective departments have served as barriers to interdisciplinary cooperation and have insulated academic researchers from the stimulation of applied fields. Now there is an oversupply of Ph.Ds in many fields, in comparison to the demand for them in universities. This is likely to open new markets for Ph.D. graduates and force social scientists into other settings outside universities.

Shifts in government research budgets anticipate these developments. One agency, the U.S. Office of Education, is illustrative. In 1964, colleges and universities received the lion's share of available funds (75 percent). By 1968 contributions to universities and colleges accounted for less than one half of a nearly $100 million budget (41 percent). Regional educational laboratories and profit and nonprofit research corporations and state agencies received 21 percent. The remainder went to university-based research centers (19 percent).[61]

Community Colleges. In addition to the changes in the university's internal structure and the differentiation between teaching and research settings, a variety of other settings are evolving to serve the wide-ranging interests of students.[62] One of these is the community college. The safest prediction is that more two-year, community colleges will be established, especially for low-income and ethnic groups in urban areas where such institutions are now in strikingly short supply. These tax-supported institutions are likely to have completely open enrollment policies, in effect, extending universal education to the college level for many individuals who, a few years ago, probably would not have graduated from high school.

New Settings for Vocational Training. A few universities will become highly specialized settings in which scholarship is the primary activity; but in view of the diversity of students now entering universities, many others will be forced to drop the pretense of being the major centers of intellectual life. But it is not yet clear what their role will be. With the upgrading of jobs, employer demands for more technically trained workers, and surpluses of college graduates in recent years, some colleges might begin to examine forms of vocational training other than professional training. Yet, in view of the phenomenal rate of change in the job structure, it is doubtful whether colleges will be able to gear themselves to provide highly technical training for thousands of jobs that are rapidly coming into existence and just as rapidly becoming obsolete each month. Thus, the responsibility for job training perhaps will be assumed by institutions other than colleges. For example, much of the technical training needed in such complex fields as electronics might be provided by the prospective employers, who are in a better position to provide the newest procedures and the equipment with which to conduct training. This would signal a return to an apprenticeship system not only in the skilled trades but in the service and managerial industries as well.[63]

Consortia. As higher education becomes more diversified, it will become necessary to find ways to share resources and to reintegrate the system at a higher level. New consortia of institutions concerned with education will provide some of this integration. These consortia will include elementary and secondary schools as a means of coordinating their curricula with college offerings.⁶⁴ Some universities and public schools are now trying joint ventures. For example, the City University of New York has suggested that its College of Education should run an elementary school in Harlem both as a training ground for teachers and an exemplary school. Such a plan was carried out, with some poor results, by the Adams–Morgan elementary schools in the District of Columbia in conjunction with the Antioch College–Putney Graduate School of Education.⁶⁵ In addition, Orlans expects many private companies to become more closely linked to higher education by supporting more long-range fundamental research pertinent to the general problems in their field.

Patterns of Stratification. These new divisions of labor will inadvertently accentuate patterns of stratification among institutions of higher education. At least a few universities are likely to remain intellectual centers; still others will retain their positions as means to the attainment of desirable social positions; and junior colleges are likely to get the less-talented faculties and students. It is indeed ironic and unfortunate that the life chances for the students who attend the junior colleges, who come predominantly from poverty and minority backgrounds, will remain relatively poor. The minorities who just now are entering institutions of higher education are being channeled into precisely these institutions, which occupy the lowest rung of the higher education ladder.

What Alternatives to College Are Evolving?

A growing number of college students are not really convinced of the value of a traditional college education. The society is searching for new, alternative forms of post-secondary education. The Peace Corps, VISTA, Nader's Raiders, military service, travel, temporary employment before college, social action programs, and political work sponsored by universities represent (often feeble) attempts to provide other alternatives.

THE OPEN UNIVERSITY

Probably the most widely accepted alternative to the traditional college is represented in several plans to enable students to earn academic credit and college degrees without having to live on a campus or even attend classes. For many years a *few* colleges have been sponsoring a work year or a year abroad as an interlude in the college student's career. But recent plans go far beyond these programs. One prototype is Britain's "open university," which permits adults to earn academic degrees in three to six years at a total cost to the student of less than $1000. Students listen to radio lectures, go through correspondence course packets, watch television courses, and read in local libraries to prepare for examinations taken in one of 250 local study centers, which are staffed with tutors and counselors who act as study assistants and advisors. Students also attend a week of summer school at one of 12 regional centers or at one of the established colleges.

A similar program in this country, called "university without walls," is sponsored by 19 cooperating institutions ranging from major universities to small community colleges. Part of the time students take traditional courses at their home colleges, but they may also move about to co-operating colleges, serve supervised internships in businesses, hospitals or museums, or study independently with the aid of reading lists, televised lectures, records, and tapes.

The "national university" is still another version of these programs in this country. This refers to a proposed national board that would sponsor college level examinations and thereby permit students to earn degree credits for materials they have learned on their own.

UNIVERSITY CITIES

The open university will inevitably reach into the theaters, museums, industrial laboratories, libraries, and centers of financial, social, and political research housed in other urban institutions. "Higher education" is thus being transformed into a series of experiences of different types, interspersed through much of one's lifetime after the adolescent years.[66] This transformation will drastically alter the environment surrounding the university. Graubard anticipates that entire cities will evolve around universities.[67] The faculties of these university cities are not likely to be corporate groups set apart, but will be intimately related with other professional groups. Scholars and teachers may divide their time between several cities teaching and studying regularly both in this country and abroad. Great numbers of postdoctoral and professional adults of all ages will congregate in these intellectual and cultural centers for longer or shorter periods of time, seeking something quite different from what is today quaintly called "continuing education." Businessmen might spend a sabbatical year in these places. University cities will make it possible for men and women from all walks of life to pursue two or three different careers in succession by returning to these cities for retraining. These cities also will attract a great variety of industries, particularly those that depend heavily upon technical competence.

In short, the university is becoming fused with other organizations and with urban institutions. The boundaries between the university and the rest of society will become less distinct, and new forms of collaboration with other educational institutions, businesses, homes, and offices will develop as it takes its place in the center of the economic and social mainstream. These changes will be far more important than the less problematic changes within classrooms.

WHAT IS RACISM AND POVERTY DOING TO PUBLIC EDUCATION?

One cannot assume that the stubborn problems of poverty and racism will disappear in the foreseeable future. At the same time, the magnitude of these problems and the forms they take are changing.

Trends

The national struggle to incorporate American blacks and other racial groups into the urban industrial system is part of an irreversible trend toward cultural integration. However, there is still a long way to go. The segregation of minority students in the large cities in the North and West has continued. The persisting gap between the rising academic demands and results in central city public schools will continue to be a major source of discontent and conflict. Organized groups of parents in the central cities have been the prime force behind recent experiments in community control, and racial issues have been prominent sources of campus unrest. Subtle, but perhaps no less militant political activities have replaced the violence of the late 1960s.

Any effective solution will cost more money and accentuate the competition between the social classes for scarce funds. Every additional dollar spent per child per year requires an addition of $46.5 million to the national educational budget. An increase of even $1 billion per year for education would hardly put a movie projector in each classroom. It would not begin to pay for improvements that are needed to help low-income children catch up. The local property tax structure cannot support more substantial innovations, even in the middle-class communities. Middle-class schools are likely to continue to draw off the limited funds available for innovation unless provisions are made to insure that low-income schools receive a greater share of the tax dollar.

In response to these pressures, several types of changes that are designed to close the gap between white and black children are now being tried or advocated: compensatory education; busing; new methods of districting, changed housing patterns, and educational parks; and extreme modifications in the base for financing education.

How Effective Is Compensatory Education?

Compensatory education for educationally disadvantaged learners has been tried in New York City, Syracuse, St. Louis, and many other major cities. Usually, these programs involve more counselors and special teachers assigned to selected schools, efforts to increase the range of educational experiences available for children, including the use of extensive field trips, and efforts to improve the cooperation between the school and the home and neighborhood agencies.

Does it Work?

Most of these programs have a similar history. In the early stages they have shown great promise; the St. Louis project, for example, raised eighth-grade reading scores during the first year. But, generally, these gains have not been sustained; in St. Louis after seven years in the program, students were still one year or more below the national average. The "Higher Horizons" program in New York City was another promising program in the late 1950s and early 1960s. At the outset of the program, after per-pupil expenditures had been increased by $80 a year for 700 selected junior high school pupils, 147 of the 250 pupils who had begun the program in the seventh grade gained four years in reading achievement in two-and-one-half years. But as the program spread throughout the city, it was watered down, and after five years there were no significant differences in either the achievement or the attitudes of children who had participated in the program and those in schools without the program.[68]

Probably the most highly regarded compensatory program is the government-sponsored "Head Start," which is premised on (1) the fact that early childhood is the time when learning occurs most rapidly and on (2) growing recognition that their family environment has handicapped many lower-class children. Thus, the objective of many compensatory programs is not only to counteract the family influence, but to isolate disadvantaged children from their families at an earlier age and for longer periods of time throughout the day and throughout the year. While originally established with grants from the federally supported antipoverty program, these programs are now accepted features of most large school systems. Many of them have had at least limited success. Nevertheless, the evidence compiled from hundreds of these programs to date gives little reason to suppose that they are uniformly effective.

What Are the Sources of Problems?

Critics charge that compensatory programs simply attempt to prepare children to accept presently inadequate educational programs. The emphasis in such programs is not on changing the educational institutions but on changing the youngsters to fit into existing programs. Compensatory education has been called a form of "psychological radicalism," by which the world is changed by changing children. This notion clashes with "sociological radicalism," which assumes instead that institutions must be changed first.

Instead of trying to bring children up to arbitrary standards set by industry, universities, and high schools, say the critics of the compensatory approach, it would be better to do away with formal requirements and, indeed, the whole system of credentials that relies on formal education. The intent of credentials is to minimize the risk of accepting an unacceptable job applicant. But they also increase the risk of rejecting applicants who are acceptable and exclude people from the economic mainstream, rather than bringing more people into productive employment. The stress on degrees and diplomas makes it extraordinarily difficult for those from families whose parents have low education, whatever their own ability, to move into productive positions. Preliminary findings of Berg's study, which was cited in Chapter 3, show that at every occupational level, persons with less education do better than those with more education. The less educated have lower absenteeism and higher job satisfaction. As employers become more aware of these facts, they may begin to question their preference for more education than the job demands.

In sum, besides the contradictory results of compensatory programs, they have been severely criticized for their emphasis on rehabilitation, for giving the child concentrated doses of the same thing—more teachers, more trips, and more assignments—in a misplaced attempt to transport middle-class schools into the slums. Moreover, insofar as compensatory education is premised on the assumption that the inadequacies reside within the learner, some critics are concerned lest it deflect attention from the critical problems caused by the system itself.

How Effective Is Busing?

Busing, on the other hand, is intended to alter a vital underlying characteristic of the system: residential segregation patterns. A reanalysis of the Equality of Educational Opportunity survey by the Civil Rights Commission strongly suggested that children do not learn as well in homogeneous schools as they do when they attend schools with students from mixed social backgrounds. Busing children to schools outside of local neighborhoods has been seen as a remedy.

As in the case of compensatory education programs, preliminary studies of busing did indicate favorable results.[69] For example, when black students who were participating in a compensatory program in predominantly black elementary schools in Syracuse were matched with comparable black children bused to majority white schools without compensatory programs, the bused children achieved at more than double the rate of students in compensatory programs. Preliminary results in Boston also indicated that bused children had higher test-achievement scores than comparable children who were not bused. Similar results were reported in Berkeley, California, and Philadelphia. Katz reported that *in an atmosphere of social acceptance*, Negro pupils were likely to want to meet high academic standards of white classmates; favorable evaluation by white adults and peers provided an added incentive.[70] He believes that although low-ability Negroes tend to be highly anxious about their school work when in desegregated situations, the opportunity that the situation provides them to compare themselves and identify with white peers may tend to raise their self-evaluations.

SOME RESERVATIONS

However, in view of the history of compensatory education, one wonders whether the academic gains from busing will be sustained over time or whether, like compensatory education, busing is only a temporary remedy that will have to be supplemented with more basic changes in the system. The Boston survey, for example, found that the longer the children were in the program, the more deterioration that occurred in the rate of improvement. Also, as pointed out in Chapter 3, there is some evidence that when racial integration is accompanied by racial tension, students do not do as well in school. Research summarized by Katz on black children in biracial educational settings indicates, on the negative side, that sudden integration by busing or other means can be socially threatening for some lower-class black children.[71] When black students are rejected by the white majority group, the ensuing fear, anger, and humiliation could be detrimental to learning. There is evidence that where feelings of inferiority are acquired by black children, they are likely to have a lower expectancy of academic success and low-achievement motivation in integrated classrooms. It seems plausible that lower-class black children who score several years behind white children might be thrown off-balance when they find themselves competing with academically advanced middle-class peers.

The most pessimistic picture to date was drawn by Armor, who used data gathered from tests of black children bused in Boston; Hartford; New Haven; White Plains, New York; Ann Arbor, Michigan; and Riverside, California.[72] In some cases, the black children were bused to suburban schools. In other cases, the children were mixed into majority-white schools in the same school district. All busing was voluntary. In all cases, comparable groups of black, nonbused children were studied over periods ranging from one to five years. The effects of integration on learning, aspirations, and racial attitudes were compared by testing bused and nonbused black children. Among the findings:

• None of the studies has been able to conclusively demonstrate that integration has had an effect on academic achievement as measured by standardized tests.

- Bused students do not improve their aspirations for college. The same is true for occupational aspirations.
- Minority children tend to have lower self-esteem before integration and integration does not seem to affect the self-esteem measures in any clearly consistent or significant way.
- Integration heightens racial identity and consciousness, enhances ideologies that promote racial segregation, and reduces opportunities for actual contact between the races.
- Black students actually have higher aspirations than white students at similar levels of achievement, but blacks may be overaspiring for college education.
- Bused students are much more likely to start college than nonbused students, but they drop out at a much higher rate so that by the end of the second college year almost the same proportion of bused and nonbused blacks remain in college.
- However, bused students attend what are generally considered high-quality colleges compared to colleges attended by nonbused blacks, an indication that busing has an important "channeling" effect not found in black schools.
- The busing programs seem to have considerable support from both the black and white communities, but none of the programs studied involved mandatory busing of whites into black communities.
- Younger-bused black pupils supported busing and held more positive racial views than older-bused blacks, and black girls had a more difficult time adjusting to busing and to integrated schooling than black boys.
- Academic grades of bused blacks dropped considerably because these children experienced stiffer competition in white, middle-class schools.
- Bused black students who had college aspirations but also had grade averages of "C" or lower stood out as clearly more "pro-Black Panther" than black youngsters with higher grades. Armor said this "increased militancy . . . may arise partly from the fact that aspirations remain at a very high level even though performance declines to the point where the pupils question their ability to compete with whites."

The Boston-area study reviewed by Armor covered 1500 black pupils bused to 28 suburbs. Its tests showed no significant gains in reading or mathematics among bused black grade- and high- school pupils, compared with nonbused black children or with middle-class whites. Instead, the bused blacks slipped slightly as they grew older. The same was true in White Plains, Ann Arbor, and Riverside. Three years later (in Riverside) the integrated black students were even further behind the white students than before the integration project began. Hartford and New Haven results were "mixed" but not promising.

Armor's verdict should not be regarded as conclusive. Other social scientists have been quick to attack Armor's study. Thomas Pettigrew, together with Harvard colleagues, contends, among other things, that Armor's report is based on a "biased and incomplete selection of studies." Seven other studies in other cities, Pettigrew observes, show evidence that the academic achievement of blacks improves when they are bused to white schools. He also points to serious methodological problems in Armor's own research. In any event, Pettigrew contends, the contact theory—which maintains that the performance and attitudes of blacks improve upon contact with whites—is not damaged by Armor's findings about student attitudes since all the required conditions such as "equal status" contact may not have been fulfilled.[73]

At times, desegregation has been actively promoted by white moderates for reasons other than egalitarian considerations. Specifically, integration plans have been conceived as mechanisms for reducing the threat of black in-migration to specific white and integrated communities by anchoring whites that still reside in these areas. Integration plans set racial quotas and thereby stabilize changing areas to the advantage of the conservative whites. Very little is known about how to bring about integration in order to maximize its benefits. One question has not yet been answered: In what *situations* does integration by race or class improve achievement? In addition to considering the composition of the student body, one must take into consideration the way integration is achieved, the organizational and contextual properties of these situations, and the characteristics of the professional staff.

What Are the Prospects for Metropolitan School Districts?

Ultimately, school segregation cannot be eradicated unless traditional school district boundaries are erased. Metropolitan-wide school districts, supplemented by educational "parks" or campuses, might serve that purpose. There are overwhelming pressures in favor of such parks. A U.S. Office of Education study, the National Finance Project, recommended consolidation of 80 percent of the 18,000 school districts nationwide on the grounds that existing districts do not have sufficient enrollment to support even minimally adequate programs and to warrant the excessive costs of maintaining these districts. This could involve the abandonment of many suburban school districts. Moreover, a national survey found that there was support for metropolitan school district consolidation in all but the very largest suburbs.[74] A very high proportion of residents in all areas, including the largest suburbs, would favor metropolitan consolidation if it would guarantee a reduction in taxes. Given the economies of scale and with the stimulus of federal financing, metropolitan-wide school districts are distinct possibilities.

Two other related developments should be mentioned. One is the "new towns" being built with federal assistance that feature open occupancy. A major purpose in building them would be to provide places so attractive that families without hardened prejudices could be lured out of the city suburbs into a variety of small satellite racially and socially balanced communities that could assimilate low-income families. Still another possibility is suggested in a plan being considered to apply fair housing legislation guidelines more stringently in order to achieve racial balance in the sale and rental of all federally-assisted housing projects, which represent a large proportion of the housing being built today. Also, there has been some discussion of ways to encourage municipalities to build lower-class housing in middle-class suburbs and to provide middle-class housing in ghetto neighborhoods.

WHAT CHANGES ARE BEING MADE IN METHODS OF FINANCING EDUCATION?

Some corollary changes in the basis of financing public education also are being considered. Projections show that the cost of public education will reach $48 billion by 1980, up $1.5 billion from 1970, and that the per-pupil cost will soar from $593 (in 1968) to $989. These increased costs come on the heels of a property taxpayer's revolt, signified by a high rate of school-bond defeats at the polls in recent years; the majority of the public school requests for public funds were turned down by the voters in 1971. This revolt partly stems from the fact that local property constitutes only eight percent of the national wealth in today's industrial society; yet over half of school costs are financed by local property taxes. Clearly in the future only the federal government, which alone has authority to tax the wealthy corporations that control the lion's share of the economy, will have the capacity to collect the necessary monies and distribute them equitably to communities not fortunate enough to have direct access to an industrial tax base.

In addition to the fact that the present system of financing seems to have reached the saturation point, there are gross inequities in the way the available monies have been distributed. According to the four-year National Finance Project, America's richer school districts spend up to $5.50 per child for every $1.00 spent by the poorest districts.[75] The authors of the finance study concluded that the American idea of equal educational opportunity is a myth.

WHAT IS LIKELY TO HAPPEN?

Among the changes being contemplated, then, are consolidation of the wealthier and the poorer school districts, less reliance on the property tax, and more reliance on federal taxing powers. The finance study called for drastic reform. It advocated that the federal share of school financing should increase from the present 7 percent to between 22 and 30 percent and that states should boost their share from 40 percent to 55 percent. Localities that now carry 52 percent of the burden, the study advocated, should pay no more than 15 percent of the cost.

These recommendations came in the wake of recent far-reaching court decisions in California and Minnesota, holding that traditional property tax-based school financing systems are unconstitutional. The California court concluded that California's dependence on local property taxes discriminates against the poor by tying the quality of the child's education to the wealth of his parents and neighbors while wealthy districts can provide a high-quality education for their children by paying lower taxes. These decisions have been modified by subsequent Supreme Court rulings, but the proposal is still viable.

WHAT IS HAPPENING TO STUDENT ACTIVISM?

It is still too early to tell whether the militancy of students during the late 1960s was a fleeting fashion of the times or an integral part of educational institutions, but there is no doubt that it has left an indelible mark on educational institutions, and it could flare up again at any time.

Trends
SOME SOBERING FACTS

The students have lost much of their taste for militant activism. There have been changes in a number of conditions that, according to the explanations reviewed in Chapter 4, can help to explain the changed mood of students.

The change in draft laws and withdrawal of troops from Southeast Asia reduced the threat to the students' own self-interests. At the same time, the prospect of political repression and growing violence (climaxed in the death of students at Kent State University in the spring of 1970) discouraged many of the students. Also, students were confronted with a new practical reality—the shrinking job market. As a result of the economic squeeze on the teenagers and college youth who enter the job market during the decade of the 1970s, this is rapidly becoming a nation of underemployed, well-educated citizens. Although higher education will continue to be a nearly necessary condition for social mobility, it will no longer guarantee entry into the prestigious positions (however, the ability of a college degree to provide a passport to riches has always been overestimated—see Chapter 4). During each year of the 1970s it will be necessary to find jobs for 40 percent more people than in each of the past 10 years. Many more college-trained people will be out looking for jobs; and teaching jobs, the largest single source of jobs available in the 1960s, will almost completely dry up. It is estimated by the end of the decade there might be as many as a million-and-a-half unemployed schoolteachers alone in this country. There will be an increasing overabundance of college graduates, which will continue to the end of the decade, even if the economy starts to expand at a fast rate. Contrary to one interpretation, which suggests that an oversupply of highly educated people is a cause of rebellion, the new economic realities seem to be forcing youths to once again turn their attention to the immediate problems of career and status. Just as expectations and demands for improvement appear to rise in an expanding economy, they appear to decline in a contracting one, providing some diversion from activism. At the same time, a growing number of college students coming from lower-middle-class families are vocationally oriented and must work their way through college, leaving them with less time or interest to pursue political action.

These conditions—the new draft laws, political repression and violence, the changing job market, and a growing number of vocationally oriented students—support the "status threat" explanations that presume that student activism is motivated by self interest. However, there is also some support for other explanations. One important factor was the changing political situation. On the one hand, the sheer power of young adults that comes from numbers was curbed by a drastic alteration in the population structure. Peter Drucker observed that 1970 was the last year in the foreseeable future in which teenagers—that is, 17- and 18-year-olds—would form the center of gravity of our population.[76] During the 1970s, 17-year-olds will no longer grow in numbers at the previous rate, and they will lose their place as the largest single group in the nation. From now on, the center of population gravity will shift steadily upward, and Drucker predicts that soon the dominant age year will be 21 or 22. The total number of 17-year-olds in the population will drop sharply by 1985.

At the same time, political channels have opened to students that make direct confrontation less necessary. Legislation granting 18-year-olds the right to vote and corresponding changes within universities have opened new channels of influence that a few young people are trying to use at least temporarily. The status inconsistency problem has been minimized by the greater voice of students on university councils and a relaxation of paternalistic dormitory and related regulations over their personal lives. In addition, universities have made some adaptations to student demands, such as new black studies programs, deemphasis on ROTC, and initiation of environmental-studies programs. In effect, the government and university administrators made just enough of an accommodation to drain off the broad base of support that radical student leaders depend upon. Moreover, because the universities seem to have backed off from their traditional *in loco parentis* role of providing protection to students who get into trouble with legal authorities, they are no longer a safe base of operation for militant forays into the society.

PERSISTING SOURCES OF DISCONTENT

Despite the decline in activism, there is reason to believe that the underlying discontent has not subsided and, in fact, might be intensifying in some ways.[77] The proportion of students describing themselves as "radicals," which rose to a high point of 11 percent in May of 1970, declined again to between 4 and 7 percent during the "ebbing wave" of 1971. Yet, even in late 1970, 44 percent of the college students said that violence is justified to bring about social change in the United States (compared to 14 percent of the public at large); and nearly half of them maintained that personal freedom and the right of dissent are being curbed in the United States. More than a third of them (37 percent) described themselves as "far left" or "left" politically, compared with 17 percent who called themselves "right" and "far right."[78]

After analyzing the political orientations of succeeding generations of college students, Lipset and Ladd have arrived at the basic conclusion that the liberalism of the college-educated voter is largely a function of his age. The younger the voter, the greater the preference for the more liberal nominee.[79] They concluded that if past American experience is any guide, it is likely that the students who experienced the radical and activist politics of the late 1960s will become more moderate and less committed to current proposals for major changes as they grow older. However, they also point out that there has been a historical drift of political attitudes toward a more liberal position over time. Thus, although today's generation will become *relatively* more moderate over time, they may remain more liberal than preceding generations.

This tendency of the succeeding generations to become more liberal than preceding ones (despite the tendency of *individuals* to grow relatively more moderate within each generation) is particularly important in view of the growth of the college population, which in the late 1960s was approximately seven times as great as that of the late 1930s. Even if the percentage of committed radicals does not increase, the absolute number of radicals seems bound to grow. The left-inclined students are now large enough to sustain a wide variety of countercultural institutions on and off campus. The leftist students of today may find a broader support for their radical views than the environment of the 1930s provided after the radicals had graduated from college.

Many factors can be readily identified that could revive the radicals' discontent. In the first place, certainly the big issues that emerged over the past 20 years—notably race and civil rights, the urban crisis, and the environment—will not go away. Moreover, the large reservoir of frustrated, underemployed college graduates that is expected to accumulate is a potential source of leadership to spearhead new activist movements in the future. In the coming generation, also, more students will come from the social backgrounds that produce activists—that is, the affluent, better-educated, liberal, upper-middle-class families. In particular, levels of affluence and education, which are known to nourish activism, will continue to rise; and the segment of the middle-class that produces the most activists—the service-oriented occupations—will continue to grow rapidly in the foreseeable future.[80] In addition, the trend toward universalism that fuels much activism shows no sign of abating.

Consequently, in the future, there should be a higher proportion of families who hold universalistic, humanitarian, equalitarian, and individualistic and related values subscribed to by the protesters. Keniston predicts that in the next decades, barring a major world conflagration, criticisms of American society will probably intensify on two grounds: first, that it has excluded a significant minority from its growing prosperity and second, that affluence alone is empty without humanitarian, aesthetic, or expressive fulfillment.

The spreading estrangement of millions of Americans from the two traditional political parties also increases the possibility that a significant new national political base will develop. At the present time about one out of four voters claims to be an independent, and the volatile young people are slowly becoming more actively involved in politics. Another factor that could nourish activism is the growing influence and continued growth of American universities, with an increased amount of stratification among and within these institutions. In view of recent efforts on the part of integrated institutions to attract high-ability black students, for example, it seems likely that racial issues will be even more important on campuses in the future. At the same time, the young demonstrators of today will take positions of responsibility within institutions of higher learning. Many of them will become the assistant and associate professors of tomorrow. Their positions of responsibility are likely to tone down their zeal, but they might continue to arouse and give moral support to activist students.

In short, while activism seems to have reached a crescendo in the late 1960s, and probably will not be repeated as frequently or as vigorously in the next few years, a smoldering discontent lingers on college campuses that could easily flare up again in widespread disruption if the proper spark were provided. Activism in some form seems to have become an integral part of the fabric of education. It is not likely to entirely disappear but will remain as a force to be dealt with in one form or another.

Administrators, parents, students, and politicians will still be wondering what to do in years to come. What these groups are able or willing to do about activism depends on how they interpret its causes and its probable long-range consequences. The explanations reviewed in Chapter 4 suggest radically different reactions to the problem.

WILL TEACHERS BECOME MORE MILITANT?

A decade of militant teacher action has already made indelible alterations in the authority structure of schools and, more recently, in universities; and it seems clear that teacher militancy is not likely to abate in the near future. But as militancy has gained momentum, it has also changed form. Each year there are still many local strikes, but they are being supplemented by regional actions, and perhaps ultimately they will be entirely superseded by new forms of institutional conflict.

Trends

Two developments are likely to dampen the aggressiveness of teachers, at least temporarily. One is a sudden reversal in the teacher supply-demand ratio that occurred in the late 1960s and early 1970s. Since 1968, as the population growth has leveled off, the acute teacher shortage that dominated the 1950s and 1960s has reversed itself; an oversupply of teachers has accumulated. This situation will temporarily reduce their bargaining power. Second, some of the innovations being introduced to meet the teachers' problems could slow down the momentum of teacher organizations, if these changes help eradicate the more serious sources of teacher discontent.

However, the effects of the oversupply of teachers are likely to be only temporary. In the long run, the effect might be to fuel teacher militancy because teacher-training institutions will begin to recruit more selectively from better applicants and will require more years of schooling for certification. In other words they will recruit and train precisely the types of teachers who are most inclined to be militant. Similarly, the second factor might be illusory. There may be an element of naiveté or wishful thinking on the part of individuals who believe that improving the conditions of teaching will in itself pacify teachers. On the contrary, improvement often seems to fan expectations. It seems likely that teachers will become even more demanding if their present demands are met. Moreover, teachers oppose some of the proposed innovations, such as contract teaching, vouchers, community control, and proposals to deprofessionalize teaching. The talk of change might only convince teachers that they must fight harder for more control. And finally, it now appears that teacher organizations have become sufficiently large and powerful, and so fully integrated into the body politic, that they will never revert to their passive, reticent posture of only a few decades ago. Officials of the individually powerful

NEA and AFT are seriously considering a controversial merger that could substantially strengthen all teachers' bargaining power. The New York State NEA affiliate has already merged with the New York United Federation of Teachers to form one of the most powerful labor organizations in the nation.

What Will Be the Consequences of Teacher Militancy?

There is reason to believe that militant behavior by teacher groups has had an impact on (1) organizational growth, (2) the distribution of power within school systems and teacher participation in the resolution of educational policy issues, (3) administrative structures and grievance machinery, (4) styles of administration, (5) the capacity of the educational system to innovate, and ironically (6) a movement to deprofessionalize teaching.

ORGANIZATIONAL GROWTH AND POWER

The drive by the teachers' union in Boston to win sick-leave benefits and duty-free lunch periods and the 1962 strike by the UFT in New York City both resulted in large gains in group membership.[81] The 1962 strike, in particular, noticeably enhanced the appeal of the UFT. The way the strike was run, rather than the benefits that accompanied its settlement, had a major impact on the organization's growth. The rise of teacher organizations has increased the power of teachers, enabling them to act in concert with their colleagues and to establish procedures for collective negotiation. The main question is no longer *whether* school authorities will negotiate with their personnel but, instead, *how* the authorities will negotiate and on what kinds of issues.

REDISTRIBUTION OF POWER

Militant behavior has also begun to change the distribution of power. The American Association of School Administrators has pledged to resist any effort to displace the superintendent and his authority in matters affecting the interest and welfare of school personnel.[82] But in large cities where teachers have been most militant, the authority of superintendents, school boards, and especially principals has noticeably diminished.[83] Teacher organizations are likely to become an even more important force to be dealt with by local, state, and national political groups whenever educational issues arise. A rising number of political contests will probably focus on educational issues. With this development, statewide negotiations will probably become a standard procedure.

Ironically, however, the power of groups *outside* the school system also seems to have grown, which neutralizes some of the teachers' gains.[84] City mayors and state governors are being forced to intervene in school negotiations with greater frequency and forcefulness. Teacher groups have tried to bargain directly with the governors of Florida and New York, for example. Also, in the larger cities, neighborhood groups of community parents have been provoked to demand more control in response to teacher militancy. In New York City the prolonged teacher strike of 1967 aroused discontent in the ghetto communities and incited the development of Negroparent power.

Administrative Authority Structures

If, as I have argued, the sources of organizational tension are structural, teacher militancy is likely to produce structural reforms. One author has predicted that a dual authority structure will evolve modeled after university faculty committees and senates.[85] A possible model is provided in the dual lines of authority that sometimes have developed between physicians and hospital administrators. One study reports that this dual system of authority helped to minimize professional-employee conflicts.[86] The hospital administration maintained the right to make certain administrative decisions, such as scheduling and chart review, and the right to give advice. However, physicians reserved the right to accept or reject administrative suggestions about patient care. It was up to the physician actually attending the patient to make the final decision. Physicians interpreted the official right of the administrator to supervise as the right to "advise" rather than to make the decisions. This consulting relationship was even more acceptable because respected physicians held the administrative positions. Whether or not physicians accepted advice with which they disagreed depended on whether they considered the decision to lie within the administrative or professional sphere. Although physicians did not closely follow administrative regulations when they conflicted with their professional tasks of taking care of patients, they did otherwise comply with them; since by complying in strictly administrative spheres, physicians gained freedom from administrative responsibility, which they considered to be onerous.

Goss, the author of the study, concluded that although the hierarchical organization of the hospital might appear to conflict with the essence of professional autonomy, in fact the hospital avoided this conflict by using this kind of separation of spheres of authority.

In thinking of organizations, many people often seem to have had in mind a stereotype of military bureaucracy based on the assumption that the central office must have authority over every decision throughout the organization. However, this is only one blueprint for organizations, and it is one that denies authority to the very employees who have firsthand acquaintance of their client's problems and who have received specialized training for dealing with them.

As teachers assume at least some of the traditional responsibilities of administration, administrators will have to find new roles. Perhaps teachers will take over more of the internal matters and administrators will devote more of their attention to managing the schools' external relationships, which administrators have often had to neglect because of the press of internal problems.

GRIEVANCE MACHINERY

It is expected that more effective grievance machinery will also be established. This will include an "appeal system" providing for hearings by impartial parties outside of a particular school. Special committees composed of administrators, teachers and, in some cases, parents and students might be convened to hear special problems. And possibly, collective bargaining will become a nearly continuous, institutionalized process among full-time representatives of teacher groups, administrators, school boards, and citizen groups. A "defender role" might evolve consisting of someone who functions as a "defense lawyer" representing teachers, students, or other groups whose salary would be paid from a nonlocal source, such as a state or federal agency. Such machinery might provide the additional protection and incentive that teachers need if they are to raise questions about the underlying principles of the system that might threaten their colleagues and the people in authority.

STYLES OF ADMINISTRATION

The prospect of growing conflict among professionals within school systems and of new administrative structures probably will alter the patterns of school administration. More and more, the job of the administrator will be to mediate between groups in conflict, not to "direct" the organization. "Benevolent" styles of administration interfere with this mediating role. The issue is not whether school boards and administrators will "allow" teachers to participate more in the decision process, but whether teachers will have the *authority* to do so. So-called "democratic" administration permits subordinates to participate only at the discretion of the administration and can be withdrawn at any time. One study found, in this connection, that when wards in a hospital were operated according to so-called "democratic" principles of administration, the actual result was far from democratic.[87] On the wards where only an illusion of democracy was perpetuated, the professionals were more frustrated and negative than those working on wards that were admittedly less democratic.

Administrators will also have to develop a more coherent philosophy for evaluating their professional employees and for guiding their own conduct with respect to professional-employee conflicts. The teachers who are the most loyal employees, and the ones who make the administrator's job easier, are not always the most professional teachers. Conversely, professionally-oriented teachers who bend school rules to protect their students bear the brunt of criticism for problems created by the system. What is to be the fate of a teacher who is guilty of "insubordination" while attempting to protect his students from a textbook or a curriculum guide that he believes would be ineffective or detrimental to students? How should an otherwise effective and respected teacher who leaves the building early be treated? The same issues, of course, apply to adminstrators. Will a superintendent who has been requested by a school board to violate a professional ethic (e.g., fire a competent teacher for prejudicial reasons) dare to be insubordinate?

CAPACITY TO INNOVATE

Teacher's demands (for reduced loads and equalization of assignment, for example) have forced a tightening of schedules in some districts, which has reduced the discretion and flexibility that can be exercised by the local school principal.[88] Wildman predicts that teacher militancy and collective bargaining, far from revolutionizing education may, in fact, result in further centralization and standardization of education in this country, which will reduce the flexibility of school systems and freeze them into the present mold.[89] If teacher organizations continue to grow and to increase their capacity to strike, the states may find it necessary to centralize decision making on salaries and other personnel matters. Centralization would help to achieve parity among districts of all states and among teachers and other public employees, but statewide (and perhaps ultimately nationwide) salary schedules would diminish the significance of local teacher groups and school boards and make it difficult for local schools to depart from standard practices and conditions on which uniform salaries are based.

DEPROFESSIONALIZATION

It is ironic that the advances that teachers have mde toward professionalization have produced a backlash that could ultimately tarnish the professional image they want to create and reverse the gains they have made. Teaching sets achievement standards applicable to all students regardless of their individual circumstances. These same standards release the professional from responsibility for the pupil's failure. Professional ideology places blame for the pupil's failure on the pupil himself. As we saw in other chapters, many critics of education accuse teachers of being too concerned with pleasing their colleagues or superiors and neglecting the best interests of their students.

The question of whether the teachers who subscribe to professional standards are more competent classroom teachers than less professionally-oriented teachers cannot be answered with any degree of confidence at this time. The answer depends partly on the criteria used to assess effectiveness. Are professionally-oriented teachers better liked by students and parents? Do they have a better grasp of subject matter, and do they communicate more effectively? Perhaps the professionally-motivated teachers will work to protect students from the worst features of educational bureaucracies. Or professional standards might help to protect the children from pressure groups in the community intent on violating professional norms and from community pressures to maintain an outmoded curriculum or to censor the literary works of major American authors. And, finally, to the extent that professionals are not strongly committed to a particular system of administration, they at least have the potential to act as a force for change in the system.

But many citizens and critics alike are beginning to question these presumed advantages. Indeed, teacher militancy seems to be on a collision course with the civil-rights movement in the big cities as lower-class parents assert their authority. The clash between the teachers' professional status and community demands to control public education was highlighted in the 1965 school boycott that affected 17 racially segregated schools in New York City when 6000 children stayed away from school for several weeks. The boycott had been organized by a group of parents and community leaders to protest *de facto* segregation. The protesters made some demands that challenged the status of teachers, most notably their call for appointing 200 Negro and Puerto Rican teachers to supervisory positions.[90]

One of the protesters' motives in attempting to gain control was to force teachers to accept more responsibility for how their students learn. One of the major complaints of the parents and students was that teachers expected and accepted substandard performance of Harlem pupils and, more basically, that teachers had lost faith in the ability of their pupils to learn. Correspondingly, the community lost faith in the schools' ability to teach. The boys and girls blamed many teachers for being incompetent to teach them, and many other teachers were charged with deliberate efforts to downgrade and humiliate the students, including invasion of privacy and insults to personal dignity.[91] One girl said,

"I don't like my French teacher at all. I like French but I don't like the teacher because she figures because she knows French that we should know it too. And if you make a little mistake she's quick to call you stupid and especially me. We don't get along together at all and she's always calling me stupid. And so I don't like her."[92]

A boy noted,

". . . I left school last week because . . . they bore me . . . not really bore me but they make me doubt myself, you know, they show me so much to doubt. The teachers and the deans and all; and they tell me—'You're not going to pass any-thing anyway even if you come so I don't know why you're telling me about boycotting.' "[93]

If community control materializes, any autonomy that teachers may accumulate will have to be accommodated to citizen groups. They may be forced to become more accountable for the failure of their pupils. These pressures may result in more radical modification in the status of teachers than those ever contemplated by middle-class parents.

Implications

Throughout history, education has been dominated by other groups, such as religion, business, or elite families in control of the political struc-ture. If teacher militancy maintains momentum, this could become the first time in modern history when teachers have a good chance of control-ling education. Trends toward better teacher training and increased spe-cialization are on their side. It should be remembered, of course, that there are powerful forces working against them as well. The press by citizens' groups to debureaucratize and deprofessionalize education and student militancy in high schools will probably cut the teachers' gains, even as they make inroads in the prerogatives of administrators. But even with these compromises, teachers are likely to have more authority over education in the future than ever before. For the first time they will be in a position to ward off the pressures exerted by special interest groups to use schools for their distorted private purposes. The challenge will then be to find ways of assuring that teachers will use their power in the pub-lic's interest instead of their own.

CONCLUSIONS

Some common threads run through the disparate changes anticipated here. First, with respect to all of the problems, several proposals have been made that would have the effect of *redistributing power by debureau-cratizing education and breaking up traditional monopolies.* Within class-rooms, informal techniques would give the children more opportunity to influence the learning process by reducing the social distance between them and teachers. Educational technologies would open up the tradi-tional self-contained classroom to outside influences, and interdisciplinary work will have the effect of breaking down the monopoly of disciplines that now retards curriculum revision. Within the school, there have been several proposals to give students more decision-making power and to establish more equitable balances of power between teachers and adminis-trators. Within the school system, community control, the use of vouchers, and performance contracting would put policy-making machinery within reach of the typical citizen and weaken the monopoly that all along has been exercised by professional teachers. Finally, within the larger society, the monopoly that schools and universities hold over schooling would be broken by alternative forms of education being developed to replace formal schooling.

However, whether education *can* be debureaucratized in line with these proposals is another matter. Decentralization threatens to produce other forms of stratification by isolating powerless groups from the social mainstream. Deprofessionalization could dilute academic standards and promote debilitating conflict that ultimately victimizes the students. And the alternative-schools movement is plagued by erratic results and financial instabilities. These problems are the very ones that professional bureaucracies were invented to combat in the first place. The fact that these problems are emerging once again calls attention to the often forgotten functions that bureaucracy does serve. In the long run, therefore, existing organizational forms probably will not be replaced by completely new forms. Instead, it seems more likely that the existing forms will be modified and adapted without being destroyed. This also means that the *innovations* will have to be adjusted to fit the modified structures; the proposals will not be adopted in their pure form. The future will be a compromise between the existing and proposed forms of education.

As part of this compromise the growing influence of students over school policy, teachers' increased militancy and political activities, and the demands of parents for more direct control over educational policy will generate new alliances. The traditional generational and hierarchical divisions of authority between these groups are likely to give way to divisions between militants, loyalists, and passives erupting within each group, while new alliances will cut across these traditional lines.

Second, in nearly every case, proposals have been made that would *increase the degree of specialization and structural differentiation* within and among formal educational institutions. Experiments to better prepare teachers to teach minority group children in low-income schools, proposals for differentiated staffing (with the variety of roles and new specialties it entails), and new divisions of labor that appear to be emerging between teachers and administrators all point to further specialization within teaching. Beyond the boundaries of the individual institutions, an increasing amount of specialization is developing among the institutions. Separate settings are available for teaching and research, and selective recruiting produces distinctive missions for different institutions. As a result of these trends the institutions will become highly stratified among themselves.

Third, step by step, *educational institutions are developing into total institutions,* extending further and further into the society and into the life space of the child as the length of schooling lengthens in both directions—from early childhood education through adult education. Informal classrooms, preschools, diminished social distances, and efforts to break up large systems are intended to create an atmosphere where teachers can more effectively exert personal influence over the student in the hope that educational institutions can command a wider range of the child's personal behavior. "Motivation" is being seen more and more as something that is produced by situations that are subject to control.

Fourth, *educational institutions are becoming more fully assimilated into the society.* New practices and institutions, such as the community school, educational TV, apprenticeships, problem-oriented curricula, and systematic efforts to capitalize on the educational value that can be gleaned from the political and social service activities of students are breaking down the walls of schools and universities. The political activities of classroom teachers and professors and federal funding could plunge learning institutions more deeply than ever before into the controversial social issues.

Finally, several proposals are designed to promote *new cultural accommodations and new forms of assimilation.* Controversies over busing and compensatory education, efforts to develop educational parks, metropolitan school districts and proposals to lower academic standards and open up universities to all applicants reflect a renewed national commitment to incorporate disenfranchised groups into the fabric of society through education.

In this chapter, we have anticipated the trajectory that educational reform could take over the next generation, on the basis of some current developments. Probably some, and perhaps many, of these experiments will turn out to be dead ends or mere fads; and no one can be sure of what the piecemeal effects will be despite the impressive rhetoric and flurry of activity. As yet, there has been no widescale reform, except for some curriculum revisions. There is little evidence about the effects of most of these developments, and most of the evidence that is available is indecisive. Possible disadvantages as well as advantages of many reforms were noted. Thus, it is still a matter of speculation whether education will indeed be much different in the near future than it is today and, if different, whether the differences will lead to improvement in some sense. All that can be said now is that in the turmoil of today there is the *potential* for profound reform leading to possible improvements. There is room for only cautious optimism.

One contingency is whether the country is sufficiently prepared to capitalize on the experimental climate. The innovations cannot be introduced on a wide scale without deliberate and sustained effort guided by effective change strategies. Therefore, in the next chapter, we will consider what little is known about how to implement innovations.

REFERENCES

1. John W. Gardner, "Agenda for the Colleges and Universities," in *High School: 1980*, Alvin C. Eurich, ed. New York: Pitman Publishing Co., 1970, p. 3.
2. Daniel Bell, "The Year 2000—The Trajectory of an Idea," *Daedalus, 1,* Summer 1967.
3. Donald Michael, *The Next Generation.* New York: Random House, 1965.
4. Anthony Oettinger, *Run, Computer, Run.* Cambridge: Harvard University Press, 1969.
5. F. M. Cornford, *Microcosmographia Academica: Being a Guide for the Young Academic Politician.* Cambridge, England: Dunster House, 1923, p. 32.
6. Cornford, *Ibid.*, p. 600.
7. John H. Fischer, "Who Needs Schools?" *Saturday Review*, September 19, 1970, 78.
8. Bell, *op. cit.*
9. Alvin Toffler, *Future Shock.* New York: Bantam Books, 1970, p. 422.
10. The Ford Foundation, *A Foundation Goes to School: The Ford Foundation Comprehensive School Improvement Program, 1960–1970.* New York: The Ford Foundation, 1972.
11. "Never Too Young to Learn," *Newsweek,* May 22, 1972, 93–98A.
12. *Ibid.*
13. Charles Silberman, *Crisis in the Classroom.* New York: Random House, 1970.
14. James Herndon, *How to Survive in Your Native Land.* Glenview, Ill.: Simon and Schuster, 1971, pp. 125, 126.
15. *Newsweek,* Feb. 5, 1973, 57. Also Frank Riessman, et al. *Children Teach Children.* New York: Harper and Row, 1972.
16. James A. Mecklenburger and John A. Wilson, "Learning COD—Can the Schools Buy Success?" *Saturday Review, 54,* September 18, 1971, 62, forward.
17. *Ibid.*
18. Ronald G. Corwin, "Enhancing Teaching as a Career," *NEA Journal, 58,* March 1969, 55.
19. Ford Foundation, *op. cit.*
20. John Meyer and Elizabeth Cohen, "The Impact of the Open-Space School upon Teacher Influence and Autonomy," Technical Report No. 21. Stanford: Center for Research and Development in Teaching, 1971 and R. F.

Molna, "Teachers in Teams: Interaction, Influence and Autonomy," Stanford: Center for Research and Development in Teaching, 1972 .

21. Roy A. Edelfelt, "Differentiated Staffing," *National Elementary Principal, 51,* January 1972, 46–48.

22. Herbert J. Klausmeier, "The Multi-Unit Elementary School and Individually Guided Education," *Phi Delta Kappan, 53,* November 1971 and *Multi-Unit Newsletter, 4,* October 1972. Also Roland J. Pellegrin, "Some Organizational Characteristics of Multiunit Schools," Eugene, Oregon: Center for the Advanced Study of Educational Administration, Occasional Paper Series, November 1969. See also Maurie Hillson and Ronald T. Hyman, eds., *Change and Innovation in Elementary and Secondary Organizations.* New York: Holt, Rinehart and Winston, 1971.

23. Roland J. Pellegrin, "Professional Satisfaction and Decision Making in the Multiunit School," Eugene, Oregon: Center for the Advanced Study of Educational Administration, Occasional Paper Series, November 1969.

24. W. W. Charters, Jr. and Roland J. Pellegrin, "Barriers to the Innovation Process: Four Case Studies of Differentiated Staffing," *Educational Administration Quarterly, 9,* January 1973, 3–14.

25. Ronald G. Corwin, *Reform and Organizational Survival: The Teacher Corps as an Instrument of Educational Change.* New York: Wiley, 1973.

26. John I. Goodlad and M. Frances Klein, and Associates, *Behind the Classroom Door,* Worthington, Ohio: Charles A. Jones Publishing Co., 1970.

27. Fred Katz, *Autonomy and Organization,* New York: Random House, 1968.

28. Simon Marcson, "Decentralization and Community Control in Urban Areas," New Brunswick, N.J.: Rutgers University, 1971, (mimeo).

29. Michael Katz, "From Voluntarism to Bureaucracy in American Education," *Sociology of Education, 44,* Summer 1971, 297–332.

30. *Ibid.*

31. William S. Bennett and R. Frank Folk, *New Careers and Urban Schools: A Sociological Study of Teacher and Teacher Aide Roles,* New York: Holt, Rinehart and Winston, 1970.

32. *Ibid.*

33. "The Paraprofessionals," *Newsweek, 78,* July 26, 1972, 47.

34. *Science News, 100,* December 18, 1971, 409.

35. Christopher Jencks, "Is the Public School Obsolete?" *Public Interest,* Winter 1966, 18–27.

36. *Columbus Dispatch,* Tuesday, January 30, 1973, 8A.

37. Kenneth B. Clark, "Alternative Schools" in *High School: 1980, op. cit.,* pp. 89–102 and Bonnie B. Stretch, "The Rise of the 'Free School' ", *Saturday Review, 53,* June 20, 1970, 76–79.

38. Allen Grubard, *Free the Children: Radical Reform and the Free School Movement.* New York: Pantheon Books, 1973. See also "Schools with a Difference," *Newsweek,* April 23, 1973, 113, 116.

39. Margareth Teuber, "The Dynamics of Free School Survival: A Sociological Analysis of Organizational Attributes and Member Perceptions." Unpublished Ph.D. dissertation, Department of Sociology, Ohio State University, 1973.

40. *Columbus Citizen Journal*, Monday, December 6, 1971.

41. Leila Sussman, *Innovation in Education—United States*, Paris: Technical Report, Organization for Economic Cooperation and Development, June, 1971, p. 19.

42. Ivan Illich, "Education Without School: How It Can Be Done," *The New York Review of Books*, January 7, 1971.

43. Paul Goodman, "High School is Too Much," *Psychology Today*, October 1970, 25 and forward.

44. Gertrude S. Goldberg, "Deschooling and the Disadvantaged: Implications of the Illich Proposals," *IRCD Bulletin*, Vol. VII, December 1971, 2–10.

45. Robert Nisbet, *The Degradation of the Academic Dogma: The University in America 1945–70*, New York: Basic Books, 1971; Harold Taylor, *How to Challenge Colleges: Notes on Radical Reform*, New York: Holt, Rinehart and Winston, 1971; Judson Jerome, *Culture out of Anarchy: The Reconstruction of American Higher Learning*, New York: Herder and Herder, 1971.

46. Harold Orlans, "Educational and Scientific Institutions," *Daedalus*, Summer 1967, 823–831.

47. "Stop and Go," *Newsweek*, November 18, 1971.

48. *New Students and New Places*, Carnegie Commission on Higher Education, New York: McGraw-Hill, 1971.

49. Ernest L. Boyer and George C. Keller, "The Big Move to Non-Campus Colleges," *Saturday Review*, July 17, 1971, 46 and forward.

50. K. Patricia Cross, *New Students and New Needs in Higher Education*, Berkeley: Center for the Study of Higher Education, 1972.

51. Sussman, *op. cit.*, p. 306.

52. "Pass-Fail Pitfalls," *Newsweek* 79, January 3, 1972, 34.

53. Orlans, *op. cit.*

54. Lewis B. Meyhew, "The Future Undergraduate Curriculum," in *Campus: 1980*, Alvin C. Eurich, ed. New York: Delacorte Press, 1968, p. 213.

55. Elizabeth Paschal, "Organizing For Better Instruction," in *Campus: 1980*, *Ibid.*, 227.

56. Meyhew, *op. cit.*, p. 215.

57. C. R. Carpenter, "Toward a Developed Technology of Instruction—1980," in *Campus: 1980*, *op. cit.*, pp. 236–53.

58. Rebecca Vreeland and Charles Bidwell, "Organization Effects on Student Attitudes: A Study of the Harvard Houses," *Sociology of Education, 38*, Spring 1965, 233–50.

59. Christopher Jencks and David Riesman, *The Academic Revolution*, Garden City, N.Y.: Doubleday, 1968, p. 199.

60. Joseph Ben-David, "Scientific Productivity and Academic Organization in Nineteenth Century Medicine," *American Sociological Review, 25,* December 1960, 838–43 and Joseph Ben-David and Abraham Zloczower, "Universities and Academic Systems in Modern Societies," *European Journal of Sociology, III,* 1962, 45–84.

61. U.S. Office of Education, *Educational Research and Development in the United States*, Washington, D.C.: Government Printing Office, 1969.

62. John Folger, Helen S. Astin, and Alan Beyer, *Human Resources and Higher Education*. New York: Russell Sage Foundation, 1970.

63. Meyhew, *op. cit.,* p. 210.

64. Orlans, *op. cit.*

65. Sussman, *op. cit.,* p. 19.

66. *Ibid.,* p. 73.

67. Stephen R. Graubard, "University Cities in the Year 2000," *Daedalus,* Summer 1967, 817–22.

68. James Cass, "How Much Progress is Enough," *Saturday Review,* July 17, 1971, 41.

69. U.S. Commission on Civil Rights, *Racial Isolation in the Public Schools.* Washington, D.C.: U.S. Government Printing Office, 1967.

70. Irwin Katz, "Desegregation or Integration in Public Schools? The Policy Implications of Research," *Integrated Education, 5,* December 1967, January 1968, 15–27.

71. *Ibid.* One case study of a high school in Cincinnati, Ohio, indicated that as the school shifted from predominantly white to black within a period of a few years, the hostility between black and white students increased. White students took on the characteristics of a minority group, withdrawing from school activities and complaining that they were being discriminated against by the teachers. See Michael Sanow, "A Case Study of Race Relations Among Students in a Transitional High School." Ph.D. dissertation, Ohio State University, 1972.

72. David J. Armor, "The Evidence on Busing," *The Public Interest, 28,* Summer 1972, 90–126.

73. Cf. Tom Alexander, "The Social Engineers Retreat Under Fire," *Fortune, 86,* October 1972, 136.

74. Basil G. Zimmer and Amos H. Hawley, "Resistance to Reorganization of School Districts and Government in Metropolitan Areas," USOE Cooperative Research Project, Brown University, 1966 (mimeo).

75. Roe L. Johns, *Future Directions for School Financing*, Gainesville, Fla.: National Educational Finance Project, 1971.

76. Peter F. Drucker, "The Surprising Seventies," *Harpers Magazine,* July 1971, 35–39.

77. Dean R. Hoge, "College Students' Value Patterns in the 1950's and 1960's," *Sociology of Education, 44,* Spring 1971, 170–197.

78. Seymour M. Lipset and Everett C. Ladd, Jr., "College Generations and Their Politics," *New Society,* October 7, 1971, 654–657.

79. *Ibid.*

80. Kenneth Keniston, "Social Change and Youth in America," *Daedalus,* Winter 1962, 145–171 and "The Sources of Student Dissent," *The Journal of Social Issues, 23,* July 1967, 108–137.

81. Alan Rosenthal, "The Strength of Teacher Organizations: Factors Influencing Membership in Two Large Cities," *Sociology of Education,* 39, Fall 1966, 359–380.

82. T. M. Stinnet, et al., *Professional Negotiation in Public Education.* New York: Macmillan, 1966.

83. Joseph H. Cronin, "School Boards and Principals—Before and After Negotiations," *Phi Delta Kappan, 49,* November 1967, 123–127 and *The Control of Urban Schools: Perspective on the Power of Educational Reformers.* New York: The Free Press, 1973.

84. Alan Rosenthal, "Teacher Militancy," *The Encyclopedia of Education, 9,* New York: Macmillan, 1971, pp. 36–43.

85. Daniel E. Griffiths, "Board-Superintendent-Teacher Relations: Viable Alternatives to the Status Quo" in *Struggle for Power in Education,* Frank W. Lutz and Joseph J. Azzarelli, eds. New York: Center for Applied Research in Education, 1966, pp. 96–110.

86. Mary E. W. Goss ,"Influence and Authority Among Physicians," *American Sociological Review,* 26, February 1961, 39–50.

87. Mark Lefton, Simon Dinitz, and Benjamin Pasamanick, "Decision-Making in a Mental Hospital, Real, Perceived, and Ideal," *American Sociological Review, 24,* December 1959, 822–829.

88. Wesley Wildman, "Teacher Employment, Financial Aspects," *The Encyclopedia of Education, op. cit.,* pp. 1–7.

89. *Ibid.*

90. Estelle Fuchs, *Pickets at the Gates.* New York: The Free Press, 1966.

91. *Ibid.*

92. *Ibid.,* p. 145.

93. *Ibid.,* p. 147.

CHAPTER 7
STRATEGIES FOR EDUCATIONAL REFORM

"For a generation our school masters have gone on developing the system, the public supporting it with abundant money and influence; and now, when the work is called perfect, and we are being called on to fall down and worship at the sound of music. It is seen by the discerning that . . . the new system has become inflexible and tyrannous . . ."[1]

"A more receptive attitude toward new ideas must be cultivated in school administrators—at the state as well as the local levels—in the schools of education, and among parents. Methods of determining what is useful and accelerating the adoption of proven ideas may well be the greatest need of all in our educational system."[2]

The previous chapters identified several sources of pressure for sweeping educational reforms and reviewed a number of innovations being proposed to breathe new life into education. But it is far from certain that these glowing promises will be realized in the near future. We learned from the binge of innovations attempted during the 1960s that the task of reform is far more difficult than anyone expected. As noted in the preceding chapter, on the basis of past history, some critics believe that the prospects of revamping educational institutions are bleak. Certainly, the intractability of school systems, colleges, and universities has been a persistent problem in this country. The first opening quotation above, lamenting the inflexibility of school systems, was written nearly a century ago. The second, written in 1968 by the Committee for Economic Development, continues to echo the same concern. These are but two of the nearly continuous frustrated calls for educational reform sounded during the past century. Even when schools change—as they often do intermittently when school board incumbents are defeated and superintendents are fired and replaced by outsiders—there is often widespread dissatisfaction with the pace of the change. Typically there is a lag of at least five years before school districts respond to the shifting demands of the citizens. This determined resilience of educational institutions is cause to wonder whether anything will produce more changes during the next century.

The amount of change that takes place will be a product of both (1) unplanned, crescive *social changes* that cannot be easily controlled by policy makers and (2) deliberate, planned *organizational innovations*. Unfortunately, sociologists have not given much thought to the latter type of change, perhaps because they tend to assume that social systems have an independent life of their own beyond man's control. This fatalistic assumption could be disastrous in this rapidly changing organizational society where lives are controlled by the complex organizations in which people live, work, and play. The outcome of the educational reforms being proposed today hinges on the prospect that we can learn how to *implement* planned organizational change. Therefore, this chapter will review what is known about planned change.

For our purposes here, an innovation will be defined as (1) a planned intervention, (2) which involves a change in the technology or structural relationships within particular organizations, and (3) which could lead to secondary unplanned change. The definition highlights several important features. First, although an innovation is a deliberate intervention, it can have unanticipated effects. Second, the targets of major innovations are either the technological procedures in use, or the relationships among the people involved, or both. It can be assumed that changes requiring altered or new social relationships, and changes affecting the basic curriculum, are of greater importance than mere additions to what is present or changes in extracurricular activities or other peripheral activities. Thus, team teaching, the introduction of black history, mixed-age grouping, and the use of indigenous laymen are more innovative than the addition of another section of an existing course, the use of films, or the establishment of a new photography club, for example. Hostility between teachers and administrators or lowered academic performance would be examples of unplanned, secondary changes. Third, in contrast to an *invention*, which refers to the first time a practice is used in a profession as a whole, an *innovation* refers to the first time an invention is used in a particular organization. Thus, the significance of an innovation must always be judged within the context of the particular schools, colleges, or organizations involved. For example, although motion picture equipment is standard equipment in most wealthy suburban schools, it could represent an innovation when introduced into poverty-stricken rural Indian reservations. Moreover, even if it had always been available, it could be used in innovative ways: for example, elementary school children might film a documentary on racial relations in schools for a local TV station.

WHAT IS THE RATE OF INNOVATION IN EDUCATION TODAY?

The many types of innovations cited in the previous chapter leave the impression that education is in ferment and undergoing rapid transformation. As Miller points out, school systems have been inundated from the shock waves of Supreme Court rulings on desegregation, programs for the gifted and for the culturally deprived, an unprecedented federal aid bill in 1965, substantial assistance to vocational education, new preschool programs, team teaching, ungraded schools, foreign language in the elementary schools, and major curriculum revisions—in physics, mathematics, and biological sciences and, more recently, social sciences—educational television, programmed learning and teaching machines.[3] In a national survey of instructional practices, over 10 years ago, over half of the elementary principals responding reported that some change had taken place in their schools, and one-third indicated that much change had taken place; only 17 percent reported little or no change at all.[4] Within five years after the introduction of language laboratories, 17 percent of the school systems had adopted them; in eight years 18 percent adopted teachers' aids in the high schools; 12 percent adopted team teaching in five years, and 20 percent adopted the "modern physics" course in four. By the earlier formula, less than 2 percent of the systems would have adopted these innovations within five years.[5] Perhaps the most striking instance of change has been the rapid diffusion of modern math, which was 88 percent complete in six years.[6]

Moreover, the findings from a 1967 Gallup survey of a cross-section of parents, school board members, and teachers and administrators revealed that all three groups sampled were prepared to accept innovation and change.[7] Each group looked upon changes in curriculum and teaching methods as imperatives. Prestige for these groups appeared to lie on the side of accepting change. At least two-thirds of the teachers, administrators, and school board members approved of the use of schools as community centers and supported classes in how to think and study, team teaching, movable partitions for classrooms, guidebooks for parents, programmed instruction, classes assigned by level of achievement, vocational training in school, and independent study time. With the exception of movable partitions for classrooms and programmed instruction, where slightly less than two-thirds of the parents agreed, the parents also overwhelmingly approved these innovations. (However, less than half of each group approved reducing summer vacation to four weeks, increasing the school day by one hour, standard high school tests for all seniors, and marks for "pass" and "fail.") Educators probably have not appreciated how far the public *is* ready to accept change. The authors of the study concluded that "it could well be that the public, in respect to education, is as far ahead of educators as it is of its legislative leaders in the field of government."[8]

Nevertheless, many observers still have the uncomfortable feeling that little basic change has occurred in the school system. "The observer of social organizations," notes Griffiths, "is forced to the conclusion that organizations are not characterized by change."[9] There is some weighty evidence on his side. On the basis of a systematic review of over 200 studies, Mort reached the gloomy conclusion that it takes 15 years before 50 percent of the nation's school systems have adopted an innovation like the kindergarten, and it could take up to 50 years for complete diffusion.[10]

Mort's conclusions were reached on the basis of evidence reported many years ago, but a comparable judgment was made less than 15 years ago on the basis of a survey of the diffusion of innovations in 161 teacher-education institutions and associated laboratory schools.[11] Recently, Gideonse reported that less than 15 percent of elementary and secondary schools in the nation make team teaching, nongraded classes, or programmed instruction available to all eligible students.[12] He adds:

"(In a special 1968–69 study) more than half of the 33,731,000 students included in our projection get no exposure to 13 of the 17 specified innovations . . . it seems clear that in most subjects the great majority of the students in our projection of 33,731,000 are studying curriculums that are unchanged since 1965; and that in the important field of science, mathematics, and reading roughly half are using relatively old materials. In general, a lower percentage of students in the smaller districts have access to new curriculums than in the larger districts."[13]

Moreover, on the basis of the observations of 158 classrooms of 67 urban schools in 13 states, one group of observers concluded, ". . . many of the changes we have believed to be taking place in schooling have not been getting into classrooms; changes widely recommended for the schools over the past 15 years were blunted on school and classroom door."[14] They noted that although many teachers thought they were being innovative, actually the innovations were being only partially applied at best. The experiments were so dimly conceived and so twisted to fit familiar patterns of schooling that very little of importance was taking place. For example, team teaching, more often than not, was a pattern of departmentalization and nongrading that looked like a form of homogeneous grouping. Similarly, the new content of curriculum projects tended to be conveyed with the "baggage of traditional methodology."[15] These observers concluded that in most schools there is no way to implement countervailing ideas and models; the system is geared to self-preservation, not self-renewal. Evans reached similar conclusions about the resistance to change from professors of higher education.[16] After reviewing the outcomes of its $30 million investment in innovative education projects during the 1960s, the Ford Foundation report cited in Chapter 6 concluded that the outcomes were limited changes that could be effected within the existing classroom structure.

In sum, while there are many new forces for change, and while numerous efforts are being made to adapt the educational system to those forces, there is still widespread recalcitrance to change. The question, then, is what is it about educational institutions, and perhaps about innovations themselves, that accounts for the renowned inflexibility of educational organization in this country?

Why Aren't Innovations Being Fully Utilized?

There is no way to fully answer this question at this time. However, there are several clues worth considering. The way an innovation is received seems to depend on at least five characteristics that are always involved in the innovation process: (1) characteristics of the innovation itself; (2) the scope of the change; (3) the way it is introduced; (4) characteristics of the system into which the innovation is introduced; and (5) characteristics of the members of the social system.[17]

Aspects of the Innovation Itself

Rogers lists five factors viewed from the standpoint of individual or group perceptions that past research has found to effect the rate of adoption:[18]

1. *Relative advantage.* The individuals involved will attempt to assess the relative advantage of an innovation on the basis of whether they think it is superior to the ideas that it supersedes. Typically, individuals weighing the costs of change against the advantages will not be satisfied with only slight improvements, and often they will expect the innovation to remedy not one but many different problems at the same time.
2. *Compatibility.* The more compatible an innovation is seen to be to existing values and practices, the more receptive members of the system will be. However, almost by definition, the more compatible the innovation, the less difference it will make to the system. Radical changes that require extensive revision will have

little support, except in complex systems where compatibility will vary from division to division.

3. *Complexity*. The more complex an innovation, the more it will cost to implement. Costs must be calculated not only in the cash outlay but also in the time and loss of status and prestige to the people involved. For example, an innovation that requires long special training on the part of all members of the system not only would be relatively expensive to introduce but would probably upset the existing status system. Miles concludes that "other things being equal, innovations which are perceived as threats to existing practice rather than as mere additions to it are less likely of acceptance; more generally innovations which can be added to an existing program without seriously disturbing other parts of it are likely to be adopted."[19]

4. *Divisibility*. Innovations that can be divided into separate parts or stages do not require full acceptance or complete rejection. Certain segments of the innovation can be adopted on a limited basis, or they can be adopted experimentally, which makes later abandonment easy and almost inevitable. One of the reasons that many schools appear to have adopted innovations without visible results, undoubtedly, goes back to their tendency to adopt things piecemeal, rejecting the parts that are incompatible with the existing system.

5. *Communicability*. The degree that the effects of an innovation can be known and communicated to others will affect its acceptance. Sometimes the negative and sometimes the positive effects can be more easily communicated.

SCOPE OF CHANGE

These characteristics of the innovation point to the importance of the scope of change that is taking place. Chin identified five types of changes based on their scope: (1) *substitution*, where one element is substituted for another element already present; (2) *alteration*, or an apparently minor addition to what has already been adopted; (3) *perturbations* and *variations*, involving temporary experiments or fads that create variations in a system rather than any lasting change in a structure; (4) *restructuring*, which is a basic social change requiring reorganization; and (5) *value orientation change*, involving change in deep-seated cultural value clusters.[20] These types can be looked upon as points in a continuum ranging from a smaller scope to a broader scope of change. The more complex the innovation, the greater the scope of change that will be required, and the greater resistance that it will encounter.

The scope of change also can be described in terms of a distinction between cultural goals and alternative means to reach those goals. Generally speaking, "innovators" subscribe to the cultural *goals* but reject the *means* being used to achieve them and seek alternative means.[21] Dubin further distinguished between (1) innovation in values versus behavioral innovation and (2) innovations at the institutional, normative, and operative levels.[22] Equal educational opportunity would be an example of a largely unquestioned cultural *value* (normative goal) in this country, which prompts many educational innovations. But continued patterns of segregation, for example, testify to the disparity between this goal and behavior.

The more radical forms of behavioral innovation require substitution of new *institutions*, as exemplified in the alternative schools movement, for example. Most of the proposed innovations fall short of that extreme, although they often do require modifications in the *normative rules*, for example, proposals to use indigenous, untrained lay teachers or college graduates without professional training, as classroom teachers.

Finally, recent curriculum innovations and changes in teaching practices illustrate change at the *operating level*; new math and team teaching, for example, are confined to the operating level. In general, it can be expected that innovations designed to modify behavior will encounter less resistance than innovations designed to modify values, and that innovations confined to the operating level will encounter less resistance than those aimed at the normative or institutional levels.

How Innovations Are Introduced

The way a system receives an innovation will depend on who introduces it and under what conditions it is introduced. Innovative programs can be classified along two dimensions: the level in the system at which the innovation is introduced (i.e., from the top down or broad-based participation); and whether or not the innovation is initiated within the operational setting or in an insulated context (see Table 7-1).[23] Although the introduction of change from the top down has the advantage of providing full administrative support for the change, it also can be easily sabotaged by subordinates if they are not consulted, since they must implement it on a day-to-day basis. However, if subordinates are consulted, they are

Table 7-1

Setting of the Innovation	Level at which Innovation Is Introduced[a]	
	Administration	Subordinates
Operational setting	1	2
Insulated setting	3	4

[a]Adapted from Bessent and Moore.

likely to modify the innovation to suit their self-interests and professional goals and, if they propose the change, there is no guarantee that they will receive the necessary administrative support. Turning to the second dimension of the typology, there is another dilemma. When experimental programs are implemented within the ongoing operational setting, they are confronted from the outset with stifling red tape and customary procedures, without having the leverage of the established programs that they are designed to replace. Yet, if they are developed solely within an insulated setting, they will not be in a position to gain broad support, and they cannot be easily transported into more practical complex situations.

System Characteristics

Some observers contend that certain social systems are less responsive to change than others. Rogers characterizes the inflexible system as "traditional," which by comparison to the more innovative "modern" system, has less well-developed technologies and less communication between the members and persons outside of it.[24] Most members of traditional systems are provincials rather than cosmopolites and are slow to recognize new roles or easily learn new social relationships involving themselves. Such systems tend to support conservative "fundamentalistic" attitudes.[25]

Street attributes the inflexibility of school systems to a number of built-in structural constraints, which include: (1) a heavily institutionalized set of universalistic standards, "the inheritance of an earlier age of fighting off corruption and political influence"; (2) a great "in-growness" in the selection of administrative staff; (3) weak methods of socialization and control seen, for example, in the token quality of most in-service training; (4) the overcentralization of curriculum construction and managerial decision making; (5) rigidities in the division of labor, which mitigate against the full use of subprofessionals—paid and volunteer—to solve the great problem of insufficient financial and human resources to staff the schools; (6) defensiveness toward outsiders, which minimizes the opportunities for fruitful collaboration with external agencies and preserves marked social distance between the schools and lower-class parents; (7) rigid practices of grouping and dividing students into grade levels, which formally assume that all children learn at the same rate; and (8) "internal structural inertia" and external cross-pressures, which make effective, entrepreneurial top leadership difficult.[26]

A Ford Foundation study of its Comprehensive School Improvement Program, for which the Foundation granted $30 million in the 1960s for innovative projects, concludes that projects were more effective when, among other things, (1) the individual leader who directed day-to-day operations was committed to the project, (2) the innovation was confined to a few classrooms in a single school, (3) the school was relatively small,

(4) parent school districts made financial commitments, and (5) the schools were located in middle-size suburbs—homogeneous enough to avoid heated debate but large enough to provide broad-based support.[27]

MEMBERSHIP CHARACTERISTICS

Finally, it helps if the members of the organization are personally committed to the desirability of change. A composite picture of such individuals, the "innovators," is presented by Rogers.

"Observers have noted that venturesomeness is almost an obsession with innovators. They are eager to try new ideas. This interest leads them out of a local circle of peers and into more cosmopolite social relationships. Communication patterns and friendships among a clique of innovators are common even though the geographical distance between the innovators may be great. They travel in a circle of venturesomeness, like circuit riders who spread new ideas as their gospel."[28]

Barnett developed a typology based on the characteristics of innovators as follows:

1. *The dissident*, who consistently refuses to identify with some of the conventions of his group.
2. *The indifferent*, who is prepared to accept new ideas because he has not dedicated himself irretrievably to a custom or ideal of his society.
3. *The disaffected*, who is at odds with his society as a result of such possible variables as marginal status, disillusionment, frustration, circumvention by specified enemies, generalized social anxiety, and guilt depression.
4. *The resentful*, who is susceptible to a suggestion of change because he has less to lose by accepting it, often nothing to lose.[29]

It is reasonable to assume that the more members in an organization who are innovators, the more receptive it will be to a proposed change. However, it should be clear from the other factors identified above that it takes far more than well-intentioned individuals to institute change. All four of the characteristics discussed above act in concert in any situation to determine whether the innovation is accepted or rejected.

Nature of the Innovation Process

There seem to be some general patterns or stages that most innovations seem to go through, which can be described as follows:[30]

1. *Structural lag*. During the first stage there is a change in the functional needs of a society. Structures designed to serve particular functions become inadequate for new demands placed

upon them. Public expectations tend to accelerate during periods of change and even during periods of improvement, but the more structured the component, the more difficult it is to change or substitute it in order to accommodate these rising expectations.

2. *Crisis.* Eventually the strain between the structure and function becomes sufficiently intense to provoke public pressure for change. The pressure reaches its peak when the lag becomes part of a general social crisis effecting a large number of institutions. During these crisis periods leaders, who in normal times are under conservative pressures, are expected to innovate; rules are suspended and new opportunities arise for exercising ingenuity.

3. *Outside intervention and polarization.* New structures are proposed by concerned outsiders who are in a position to exercise personal leadership and have less investment in a given structure. This outside leadership is resisted by the established leaders of a profession, but it is supported by members of the new generation in the profession for whom the innovation is a source of status; they can use their mastery of new content areas and procedures to challenge the authority of the established leaders.

4. *Dialectic process.* Sorokin viewed the pattern of change in the Western world as a series of alterations between the "sensate" and the "idealistic" value systems.[31] Blau and Scott notice a parallel process in organizations; that is, the solutions to one set of organizational problems will create new ones; the existing organization represents a synthetic compromise of its past solutions and present problems as it evolves through some distinctive cycle.[32] Usually, the ramifications of a change in one part of an organization will modify other parts, often in unforeseen ways. Conversely, sometimes organizations act defensively with only token changes to forestall more fundamental changes. As an ironic consequence, some innovations have enabled organizations to maintain their traditional procedures despite the pressures for more fundamental change.

5. *Variations and adaptations.* The experimental nature of most innovations and the widely varying circumstances and pressures under which they must be implemented, produce many variant forms of a given innovation, the original conception being only one of the alternative forms. No one innovation will be suitable in its original form for the variety of circumstances under which it must be implemented. In the course of a short period of time these variant forms may come to have very few features in common, even though they are associated together ideologically and coordinated through a common administration and funding source.

6. *Natural selection.* In the majority of cases, these variant forms become so well adapted to their local circumstances and so thoroughly overwhelmed by existing forces that they reach extinction. However, in some cases, through a process akin to natural biological selection, an optimal match occurs between the innovation and local conditions. In these cases, the innovation will survive and eventually become institutionalized. It is these circumstances, under which a particular form of an innovation survives and does not survive, that must be identified in order to explain the process of innovation and, indeed, in order to understand the innovation itself. The effectiveness of an innovation cannot be meaningfully assessed without recognizing the widely varying circumstances under which it is introduced and its many forms.

7. *Routinization.* Finally, once an innovation has been established, it is subject to the same institutionalizing forces that originally created the need for it. The innovation's routinization and increased size and complexity, its capture by special interest groups, and the pressures of traditionalism force the innovation into a stabilized mold.

HOW CAN INNOVATIONS BE IMPLEMENTED?[33]

Drawing upon some of the characteristics of the innovation process just outlined, and also upon sociological theories of social change, we can begin to identify some promising alternative strategies for implementing innovations. In the sociological literature there are several distinct, although overlapping, streams of thought about social change that can serve as guidelines for different approaches to organizational innovation.

The Socialization Approach

Many of the classical writers, from Plato, Montaigne, and Rousseau to Freud, were preoccupied with the assumption that a society is largely a product of the way it socializes its children. Many people, including leading sociologists share this assumption.[34] For that reason one of the most popular—and perhaps the prevailing—strategy for change that is implicit in many of the current reform programs is based upon the simple assumptions that (1) institutions are the reflections of the people who operate them and consequently (2) institutions can be best changed by changing the people responsible for managing them. This simple formula immediately suggests that it is advisable to reach people early and systematically in the socialization process.

Is It Possible to Train Innovative Professionals?

But the evidence regarding the feasibility of reshaping the attitudes and values of prospective teachers and other professionals with training programs is equivocal. While there is evidence that from the freshman to senior years of undergraduate college, some changes in attitudes and values occur[35]—in particular, students tend to adopt more liberal social and political attitudes—the degree and extent of change depends upon the nature of their experience, the setting, and the group's approval of new attitudes. Moreover, it has not yet been conclusively demonstrated that changes occurring during these periods are a result of college rather than other experiences associated with growing older.

Even less is known about the extent of change that occurs specifically as a result of *professional* education. Even if new recruits to a profession are persuaded to modify their attitudes and behavior during the training period, the changes are not always permanent. They will be under sustained pressure to adapt to their work situation after graduating. The ability of new recruits to withstand these pressures from their colleagues on the job depend upon (1) the creativity of the training program, (2) the initial amount of similarity and dissimilarity between prospective and experienced teachers, and (3) characteristics of their place of employment. But, in general, there seems to be a tendency for young professionals to become disillusioned with the professional role beginning during their training program and extending at least into their first jobs. Studies of student nurses, medical students, and law students indicate that, during training, students become progressively disillusioned with the professional school itself and later, after graduation, with their idealistic conceptions of the profession.[36] At the very least, the exotic and dramatized professional image that students often bring with them to professional school is gradually replaced by routine and pedestrian elements as they learn to cope with the problems in their work situation.[37]

Human-Relations Techniques. Human-relations techniques have been widely used as one means of counteracting this disillusionment process and to enhance or maintain the individual's receptivity to change. Human relations is based on the assumption that a social system consists of opposing forces. The reduction of tension is the chief mechanism of change. The primary reason that systems do not change, it is supposed, is because the *individuals* in them resist change. Participation in decisions becomes one means of reducing tension.[38] Another approach is to use interpersonal influence, especially through sensitivity training and group therapy (T-groups), to influence the individual directly. For example, employees or newcomers to a profession might be isolated in retreats and other "temporary systems" in order to analyze themselves and their interpersonal relationships. The main initial objective of the T-group is personal change or self-insight. Presumably, giving therapy leads to self-understanding and provides the ego-strength necessary to undergo change.[39]

Reservations. The gradually accumulating evidence on the effectiveness of the socialization approach is not very promising, however. Attitude changes in people who are participating in therapy sessions do not necessarily lead to altered behavior; for example, one study reports that although the *attitudes* of physicians towards medicare changed after the introduction of legislation supporting medicare, their *behavior* did not change in a corresponding way.[40] Moreover, the changes that do occur tend to be temporary, with individuals reverting to their usual attitudes once they have returned to the normal pressures of their jobs.[41]

But, more important, in view of the prevailing pressures in social situations, even if it were possible to train people to be personally receptive to change, their presence in itself would not necessarily be enough to reform an occupation. The assumption that organizational change will occur if only the organization has enough members who are favorably oriented to change is, to say the least, open to question. One study found that the attitudes of an organization's members towards change were virtually unrelated to the amount of program change that actually occurred, although one of the authors reported later that the leaders' attitudes were more important than those of the rank-and-file members.[42]

The Diffusion Approach

In line with the assumptions behind the socialization strategy, change is often "explained" by describing the characteristics of a specific type of person, that is, the innovators or, in other words, the first members of a system to adopt new ideas. Tarde was one of the first social scientists to stress the importance of the first adopter.[43] He contended that change consists of (1) an invention and (2) imitation of that invention by others. This process, he said, occurs in three stages: repetition, opposition to it, and adaptation of the invention by individuals who imitate it. For Tarde, then, all change was the product of one person exerting "mental influence" on another.

What Are the Characteristics of First Adopters?

Berelson and Steiner have summarized the findings to date in a number of different fields. Innovators are more likely to be younger than persons who resist change, of higher social status, and more oriented to the outside world; they take less time to adopt the new idea in practice, and they discontinue using the idea less often.[44] Rogers characterizes innovators as being young, of relatively high social status (i.e., educated, prestigeful, and of high income), cosmopolitan, with access to impersonal sources of communication, with ability to excite opinion leadership but viewed as deviants by their peers and themselves.[45] In short, members of a profession who are younger, politically and socially liberal in orientation, cosmopolitan, and higher in status generally will tend to be more receptive to an innovation than members who are older, socially and politically conservative, locally oriented, and lower in status.

THE INTERPERSONAL STRUCTURE

Much of the early literature in this dissemination tradition was based on an image of the practitioner as a rational decision maker. It was taken for granted that if information about successful practices were disseminated to innovators through impersonal channels, it would have the power to change their behavior. However, subsequent research has shown that it depends on how the information is communicated. Some individuals act as "gate keepers." Depending on whether they learn of the information and their attitudes toward it, it may or may not get through to, or be accepted by, the innovative members of the organization. These "gate keepers" are either people who have high group status, or who are marginal to the group but in positions where they have an opportunity to both receive new ideas from outside of the group and then filter them out and pass some of them on to members of their own group.[46] This communication system is sometimes referred to as the "two-step" flow of information. According to the model, if one is to modify an organization, he must first persuade the opinion leader who disseminates the information to other members of the group.

An example of the two-step flow was found in Carlson's study of the adoption of modern math in two states (Pennsylvania and West Virginia).[47] After plotting the friendship cliques of superintendents in each state, he found that the rate of adoption related to the way the superintendent fit into the friendship groups. The *first* superintendent to adopt tended to be an *isolate* and a cosmopolitan. He was younger, knew fewer peers, received higher professional ratings, had shorter tenure on his job, and sought out administrators *outside* of the region. Once he adopted modern math, it was quickly adopted by the central friendship group, and then it spread more slowly to others who were on the periphery of the friendship group. Thus, the number of friendship choices received by a superintendent was directly related to the speed with which he adopted modern math. Also, the status of the superintendent (measured by combination of level of education, professionalism as judged by the superintendents, salary, and opinion leadership) was directly related to adoption rates.

The Replacement Approach

If it is assumed that the type of individual in the organization makes a difference, then it follows that organizations can be changed by replacing the more conservative members with members who are more receptive to new ideas. The larger the turnover rate in the organization, the more change that should occur.

WHEN WILL RECRUITING OUTSIDERS PRODUCE CHANGE?

However, several other considerations also enter the picture. First, the number of sources from which recruits are drawn would make a difference. The fewer restrictions to recruit only within a specific territory and the wider the basis for selecting recruits, the more likely that new recruits will hold conceptions different from those prevailing in the organization.

Second, the level at which new recruits are brought in will influence their impact on the organization. Turnover at the leadership levels probably has different implications than at the subordinate levels.

Leadership. Pareto argued that the receptiveness of a social system to change depends on the outcome of perennial struggles between governing and "nongoverning elites,"—capable persons not in positions of power.[48] The elites in turn are divided into the liberals ("speculators") and the conservatives ("rentiers"). The system moves through cycles of change, depending on the fluctuating power of these elite groups.

Michel's widely accepted "iron law of oligarchy" is closely related to Pareto's theory about change.[49] Michel maintained that there is a universal tendency for a small group to gain control of organizations. Whereas Pareto emphasized the *circulation* of elites, Michel emphasized the capacity of the group in power to maintain its control. The elite is able to minimize the opposition by co-opting potential challengers into the leadership ranks. As a result, divergent opinions are seldom encountered, and the organizational goals become subordinated to the interests of the group in power.

Accumulating evidence indicates that cosmopolitan, career-oriented administrators, recruited from outside an organization, tend to be more supportive of change than the locals promoted from within an organization itself.[50] For example, Carlson found that superintendents were more likely to be hired from outside the system where the school board was unsatisfied with the present system.[51] Outsiders were looked to for creativity, while insiders were hired to maintain stability. The insider adapted or modified himself to fit the office. It would be difficult for an insider to effect change even if he wanted to. He would not be as likely to have the school board's support for change, and he would risk being identified by the teachers, on the basis of his past and by virtue of his promotion, as the "school board's man." On the other hand, superintendents from the outside were in a better position to bargain than were the insiders. The outsiders were less likely to make rules to maintain the status quo whereas they were more likely to make rules that altered internal commitments or external ties of the system. For example, while insiders made rules about the technical-managerial facets of the school, such as "all principals are responsible for making classroom observations and follow-up conferences," rules made by outsiders affected the institutional level of the organization and changed its character; for example, the outsider might wish to establish a kindergarten or employ social workers to serve the school.

However, the appointment of outsiders to top positions also can provoke opposition, especially if they alienate the rank-and-file members or if they divide the organization to the extent that its energies are dissipated by infighting.[52] Moreover, the impact of the outsider depends on the history of the organization. For example, on the basis of case histories of three innovative colleges—Antioch, Reed, and Swarthmore—Clark concluded that change efforts are usually successful when initiated by a strong, charismatic leader, but only provided that one of three social conditions was present: (1) a new organization not hampered by tradition; (2) a period of financial or other crisis that forces the organization to make some kind of accommodation; or (3) ambitious members who desire improvement.[53] Only if a leader who seeks change finds one of these conditions can his mission be transformed into a success. Any change he introduces cannot be maintained without the efforts of tenured faculty, who are able to replace themselves with men of similar beliefs, and of a strong group of believers among the student body and the alumni. These supporting conditions and groups are as important as the objectives of the leader for instituting and maintaining the thrust of change.

The Membership. In contrast to the priority that the above writers give to the top positions of the power structure, others have called attention to the fact that turnover at subordinate levels also can lead to change if it brings people into the organization from subcultures distinctly different from the prevailing one, especially if a large enough number of subordinates are recruited.[54] The research (reported in Chapters 1 and 2) on the influence that student subcultures can have on student performance and aspirations and on college value climates is indicative of the impact that student subcultures can have.[55] Clark's description of the changes that took place when the students who were recruited into a junior college held objectives and values different from those of the officials is illustrative (see Chapter 2). The college's original mission as a terminal vocational school was transformed to that of a transfer liberal arts college because it unintentionally recruited college-bound high school graduates.[56]

Third, the number of *echelons* in an organization that are invaded by new recruits will influence the rate of change. If all of the newcomers are brought in at the bottom of both the professional and the organizational hierarchies, the chances of change occurring are less than if they are complemented by a new supportive administration.

Another important condition is the *density* of the new membership, that is, the number of new members assigned to a given organization or, more precisely, the ratio of newcomers to experienced members in the organization. The greater the "critical mass" of creative individuals in an organization, the more social support they can give to one another in their efforts to effect change.

Structural Approaches

The foregoing approaches provide valuable but very restricted views of the change process. Whether learning, interpersonal influence, or recruitment are effective depends on the larger situations where they occur. None of these approaches takes into account the many situational and external pressures that can undergird or block change, especially the organizational *context* that sets limits on what individuals can do. The structural approach, by contrast, presumes that change in the content or in technologies of education cannot occur, or at least will not persist, unless adjustments are made in the organizational structure. There is a tendency for organizations with similar technologies to also have similar structures (despite the variety of products involved). This suggests that new technologies require that corresponding changes be made in the structure.[57]

At least one study provides evidence that the structure plays an important role in organizational innovation.[58] Structural properties of 16 welfare organizations were closely associated with the rate of program change, and they were more closely related than the staff's attitudes towards change. Program change was correlated with organizational complexity, professional activities, decentralization, and job codification.

Gracey's case study of classrooms provides an agonizing account of how the school structure can frustrate the efforts of even the best-intentioned teachers.[59] His study is testimony to the fact that, although most teachers go along with the traditional approaches, teachers are not entirely to blame for the heavy hand of traditional education. A group of teachers who were committed to a nontraditional, child-centered educational approach were straitjacketed by parents' and administrators' expectations of what skills ought to be imparted through the curriculum, students' desires for grades, the school's requirements for order and quiet in the classroom, and the large size of classes. Some teachers tried to work out an unsatisfactory compromise: most children worked at their individual desks under a highly structured system of control, which enabled the teacher to spend much of her day working with individuals or small groups of children.

The public has recognized this need to revise the educational structure as a means to lasting reform in proposals for desegregation, decentralization, increased participation of laymen in the decision making process, team teaching, new grouping procedures, and other proposals that will lead to the abandonment of self-contained classrooms. It will be useful, then, to consider some of the key structural characteristics in greater detail.

THE DECISION-MAKING PROCESS

The question of *who* sponsors the change is an important one. Approaches have variously focused on the role of administrators and subordinates, or some combination of the two.

How Important Are Administrators? Certainly, in large organizations, it is helpful, if not mandatory, for official leaders to be strongly in support of the new proposal.[60] Officials play important gate-keeping roles by mediating between local and national forces, and by determining which innovations are acceptable and how much backing is to be given to them. The Ford Foundation study previously cited concluded that individual leadership was a critical factor in the success of experiments. The most effective projects were those whose directors were present at the planning and retained their leadership through the implementation, evaluation, and adoption phases. The individual leader who directed day-to-day operations was more important than the size of the project and the amount of money it received, and even more important than the type of policy or governing body.[61]

As Griffiths has pointed out, it seems to be easier for changes to be made from the top down than from the bottom up.[62] Moreover, administrators are sometimes more aware than teachers of the system-wide problems that demand change and the adjustments that have been made in other places to meet the demands.[63] Conversely, if administrators do not support an innovation, its chances for success will be minimized. A study of an innovative program in the public schools revealed that one of the major reasons for its failure was that, even though everyone initially was in favor of the proposed changes, adjustments that would have been necessary to accommodate the program to the system were not made because of the lack of administrative support.[64]

One question, then, is how supportive of change are most administrators? Perhaps as some writers believe, the emphasis on stability and boundary maintenance in schools and colleges, which is underscored by their hierarchical nature and the segregation between roles, cause official leaders to be conservative.[65] Many sociologists have concluded that it is unlikely that basic changes will come from the group traditionally in control of the organization.[66] However, this is not always the case. As Marris and Rein have pointed out, the administrators who negotiate for new programs often have the least reason to be threatened by them, and they have the most to gain financially and in terms of public relations.[67] What seems to be critical is not the official position but the amount of status security and vision that the position provides.

The Role of Subordinates. Whatever part that administrators play in the change process, it should not be allowed to obscure the equally important role of subordinates. Cillie found in this regard that in schools that had adopted more new programs—for example, continuous revisions of courses of study, more experimentation with new methods, and adoption of more recent instructional materials—the decision-making process was not as highly centralized as one would expect were administrators the critical factor.[68] The fact that these schools were decentralized indicates that subordinates played an important role in adoption. Indeed, sometimes the major impetus for change comes primarily from professional subordinates. For example, it has been found that the adoption of language laboratories in high schools was initiated by teachers who were familiar with the innovation and who had been trained in language laboratories during their college training.[69]

However, subordinates do not always want change, and they are sometimes in a position to block it. Because they are not completely powerless participants, at the very least they can influence the capacity of administrators to promote change. The outcome depends on (1) the relative influence and power of administrators *in comparison to* their subordinates' power and (2) the extent that subordinates accept the intent of the new program and are willing to cooperate in it.

Power Equalization. The "power equalization" principle represents a middle ground between complete control by administrators and control by professional subordinates. On the premise that planned change is most likely to be successful when decision-making power is shared by all levels, the approach gives subordinates an opportunity to participate in, and influence alternatives proposed by, the administration. An effort is made to reduce status differentials between supervisors and subordinates as a means of soliciting subordinates' support for the innovation. The more that members of all levels of the organization participate in the decision to implement the change in other words, the more successful it should be. The underlying assumptions are (1) that people who are alienated from an organization, like those who are blindly committed to it, will be reluctant to undertake the commitment necessary to change it;[70] (2) that participation will minimize alienation and reduce the threat involved when innovations are unilaterally induced by administrators; and (3) that consequently, subordinates will be more willing to cooperate in the changes that are agreed on. The popularity of this approach is reflected in Greiner's finding that all nine published accounts of large-scale change efforts reviewed by him involved power-equalization models.[71]

Some of the studies support the thesis. In one study, for example, organizations that had undertaken many joint programs with other organizations had slightly more representative decision-making structures (and were more highly professionalized) than those with fewer joint programs.[72] The greater the participation in agency-wide decisions, the greater was the rate of program change in the organization. Participation in decision making was found to be the one variable most closely associated with program changes when other variables were controlled. Nevertheless, the approach can easily backfire since, when participation is widespread, subordinates are in a position to co-opt the new program. Moreover, the strategy places an undue amount of reliance on the cooperative attitudes of individuals; despite its concern with power, the approach is blind to many other important factors in the situation.

Structural Heterogeneity and Complexity

Marx, Veblen, and Weber were among the major theorists who stressed the central role that organizational structure plays in *social change*.[73] For Marx, social change was produced by prior changes in the structure and technologies associated with different modes of production; Weber believed that the rationalization of the Western world was a manifestation of bureaucratization and related structural changes; for Veblen, the structural isolation of the leisure classes from the rest of the society produced a lag that retarded the ability of the society to adapt to social change.

Recently, writers have made comparable observations about *organizational change*. Thompson, for example, has pointed out that in the less-bureaucratized organizations there tends to be more conflict and uncertainty, which seems to lead to more innovation.[74] He proposes that innovation is encouraged when there is a wide diffusion of uncertainty, stimulating the whole organization to "search" activity. It appears, too, that certain types of organizational structures generate uncertainty. Several authors have observed that the innovative organization is characterized by structural looseness, free communication, and relatively flexible stratification systems and diversity of inputs.[75] In short, the rate of innovation should increase with the heterogeneity of the organizational context into which the innovations are introduced.

Planned Change. However, this general proposition needs to be qualified, depending on whether one is talking about planned or unplanned change. Concentrating on deliberate, planned change, Wilson proposed that *the greater the diversity of an organization, the greater the probability that major innovations will be PROPOSED.*[76] A proposal from one part of the system will stimulate counterproposals from other parts seeking to protect their positions and to forestall changes that would threaten them. A study cited previously provides some support. A direct relationship was found between complexity and the rate of change in *programs*.[77] It was also found that the number of occupational specialties in an agency and the agency size were correlated with the rate of program change.

But at the same time, Wilson also noted that the diverse groups typically found in complex organizations will be affected differently by a proposed change. Many of them will resist the change in order to protect themselves. A special part of the system, such as inner-city schools facing unique problems, for example, will develop special interests that are not compatible with the existing system. For that reason it will resist proposals that other parts of the system might favor. Moreover, the more complex the organization, the less control that administrators will have over it, compounding the difficulty of trying to impose change from the top. Any effort to introduce an innovation into this situation is likely to result in a series of bargains that compromise the original proposal. For these reasons Wilson proposed that *the greater the diversity of an organization, the smaller the proportion of proposed innovations that will be ADOPTED in their original form.*[78]

Unplanned Change. Nevertheless, note that the last proposition refers to the *rate* of adoptions. Since, in sheer *numbers*, more new proposals are likely to be made in the more complex organizations, it is possible that more proposals will also be accepted in them than in less-complex organizations, despite the high failure *rate*. Moreover, even though *deliberate* changes might be frustrated or compromised in complex organizations, the rate of *unplanned* change is likely to be higher in heterogeneous social systems than in homogeneous ones.[79] The likelihood of an innovation being compromised increases even though the probability of a visible innovation being adopted in its entirety diminishes with the complexity of the organization. The compromises tend to promote unplanned change.

One reason that the rate of unplanned change is likely to be higher in more complex organizations is that there are more points of contact, or "linkages," that must be established.[80] Every time there is another point of contact in the organization, bargains must be made with the people responsible for it and resources must be exchanged (e.g., money, prestige, assistance, and political support, for example). Another reason is that many innovations themselves tend to be highly complex, requiring more extensive modifications in the system and more intricate coordinating procedures than are required by simpler innovations.

Consensus on Goals and Roles

Because of their novelty, innovations seldom have the advantage of being considered to be fully legitimate (with some exceptions, perhaps, such as fads). Disagreements about the legitimate goals of an innovation are therefore numerous. In the wake of disagreement, a large number of goals frequently are imposed on innovations. Supporters of a new program seldom have enough resources or influence to be able to stick to one objective over others when various groups expect it to accomplish different things.

In addition to variations in the number and priority of goals, some of the goals will be more specific than others. At the most abstract level, an innovative program might have as a very general objective simply to "un-freeze" the existing system so that its members will be free to break out of traditional patterns and entertain unspecified alternatives. At the other extreme, an innovation might be expected to achieve very specific measurable objectives. One of the dilemmas is that when goals are not pre-determined, the unanticipated directions in which an innovative program might go cannot be controlled; whereas when the goals are specific, the participants will tend to resent the amount of control and manipulation required to implement the objective.[81]

Multiple goals have both disadvantages and advantages. On the one hand, the more goals to be achieved, the more widely dissipated the efforts will be, the more vulnerable the innovation will be to outside pressures, and the greater the likelihood that disagreement will arise among various people concerned about their respective roles with respect to the innovation. On the other hand, the more goals claimed for an innovation, the wider will be its base of support and the more readily it can adapt to changing outside circumstances.

Disagreement among the people involved can defeat a particular plan for innovation, but it can stimulate unplanned change by freeing the people involved from uniform standards and providing them with a wider latitude for interpreting their respective roles. Lack of agreement, and competition within the organization for scarce resources, can force the parties involved to accommodate their goal orientations to one another. Again it can be seen that even if an innovation does not completely suc-ceed in terms of the original plans, it can nevertheless force unplanned changes on an organization.[82] For these reasons, Moore singles out the conflict in goal priorities as one of the three primary sources of institu-tional change.[83] In short, the rate of natural change within a system can be expected to increase with (1) the number of goals, and (2) conflict over goal priorities.[84]

ROLE CONSENSUS .

Lack of consensus on roles would tend to have similar effects. When members do not understand their roles within an organization, a par-ticular innovation will be less successful than when everyone does under-stand his role (but again dissent can stimulate unplanned change). Gross and his colleagues found that one of the major organizational barriers to a planned change in the school they studied was the lack of clarity about the innovation that members of the host system were being requested to implement.[85]

RESOURCES: THE OPERATING GOALS

No matter how many goals there are, the real priorities are reflected in the way the available resources are allocated throughout the organization.

The total costs of innovation include the costs of inducing people to accept it, and the costs of reassignments, retraining, and taking temporary jobs or other risks. These costs are frequently underestimated because they are borne by the rank-and-file members. But they are real costs to the people displaced by change. Seldom are enough resources available to pay these costs directly.

But while innovations are expensive, it does not follow that the wealthier school systems will be more innovative. Contradicting an earlier study,[86] Carlson's study showed that expenditures in themselves were not related in a consistent manner to the number of innovations adopted by a school system.[87] The important economic factor, it seems, is not the total level of wealth available to an organization, but the amount of "organizational slack," that is, uncommitted funds available to absorb the "start-up" costs that are connected with an innovation over and above normal operating costs.[88]

The need for extra resources to pay for the costs of an innovation helps to explain why even relatively wealthy organizations are willing to enter into agreements with each other and with outside agencies, such as the federal government, despite the fact that these arrangements jeopardize their highly valued autonomy.[89] Considering the fact that acceptance of outside money is likely to cost an organization some autonomy, for a specific level of funding, its receptivity to outside sources of support should depend upon (1) the bargaining power of the organization (e.g., as determined by its prestige) and (2) the stringency of conditions for participating in the innovation. To be more specific:

- For organizations of comparable bargaining power, receptivity to an innovation sponsored by an outside group will increase with the amount of funds involved and decline with the stringency of conditions for being accepted into the program.
- For a specific level of funding and stringency of conditions, the willingness of an organization to participate in an innovation sponsored by an outside group will decline with its level of prestige.

Thus, one consequence of the strings usually attached to outside funds is to attract the vulnerable but less-prestigious organizations that are in most need of outside funds and to repel the most prestigious, pace-setting organizations.

STRUCTURAL COMPATIBILITY

As mentioned, there are social as well as economic costs attached to an innovation. The social costs increase with the incompatibility between (1) the innovation and (2) the values and practices of the organization. According to the theory of "cognitive dissonance," individuals feel compelled to adopt interpretations of events that are consistent with one another.[90] There is dissonance any time a person has information or an opinion that, when considered by itself, would lead him not to engage in some action which he engages in anyway. The person will try to reduce dissonance either by changing his actions or by changing his beliefs and opinions. If he cannot change the action, opinion change will ensue. Applied to innovation in organizations, the theory would mean that the more incompatibility between new and existing programs, the more disruptive the innovation will be and the more resistance there will be to it, at least until it has been successfully introduced for a period of time.[91]

THE STATUS AND INCENTIVE SYSTEMS

The degree of resistance to a proposed change then, will depend on how it might affect the status of people in different parts of the system. Teachers belong to a formal hierarchy in a school, to a primary group of other teachers in the school, to teachers' organizations, to organizations in the community, and to primary groups of family and friends. Any educational innovation affecting any of these statuses of the teacher could shake the whole structure.[92] Thompson proposes that the social cost of an innovation can be computed as the extent that status rewards must be redistributed.[93] To be more precise, the amount of resistance can be calculated as the ratio of (1) the number and level of positions whose status will increase in comparison to (2) the number and level of positions that are threatened by status loss.

A fundamental characteristic of the school's status system is that teachers are rewarded for emulating higher levels of education and, consequently, a teacher's status is directly related to the difficulty of the subject he is teaching.[94] Teachers who handle the academic responsibilities—such as teaching in advanced placement programs—usually have higher status than those who teach in industrial arts or vocational training. Persons who teach vocational subjects or students who are less-academically inclined and the lower-class students tend to have less prestige than persons who teach English and other academic subjects and the middle-class students. Any change that threatens to reverse this status pattern is likely to encounter resistance.

Even proposals for change that seem to be reasonable in the abstract can create unperceived status threats. Thus, even minor departures from typical classroom practices might be resisted if staff members feel that the changes might create invidious comparisons among them. The status of "good employees" depends on the continued legitimacy of the present system in which they have achieved. They can be the biggest losers in any proposed change. For this reason, an insured, even if inadequate result is often more highly valued by employees than uncertainty about potentially better results.[95] This explains why even though teachers might wish to have additional help, they are sometimes threatened by the presence of aides in the same classroom who might be "getting too close to the children."[96] Working with children tends to be a major source of personal satisfaction, especially for elementary school teachers, and particularly in the inner-city schools where many other sources of satisfaction are not present.[97] In general, they will resist any innovation that puts them in competition for the emotional attachment of the children and removes them as the central figure for each child.

Carlson has reported how the objectives of programmed learning were defeated by teachers in one school system because of the status problems that this particular innovation posed.[98] It removed teachers from the focus of attention; they had to constantly repeat instructions to pupils moving at their own pace; there was no provision for students who finished a course before the end of the semester, except to shift them into an art class; and the principals did not know how to evaluate teachers who were not standing in the front of the room lecturing, except to praise the teachers who "walked around" the room while the students studied.

Status problems also resulted from the way "modern math" was introduced into many schools in this country. Many experienced math teachers resisted the change, despite the fact that this would become one of the most rapidly disseminated innovations in educational history. Because the innovation was introduced through the universities, in effect, the newly trained teachers assumed the burden of introducing it. This meant bypassing the experienced teachers, who resented the usurpation of their professional leadership by newcomers. Once the problem was recognized, summer institutes were rapidly established to give experienced teachers the opportunity to keep sufficiently abreast to maintain their leadership positions.

Social-Contextual Approaches

The way an organization is related to its social environment is still another factor that has a crucial bearing on its ability to adapt to changing circumstances. Insofar as it is integrated into the broader social fabric, an organization will be hampered from making changes that would be incompatible with the environment, and it will be compelled to change when the environment changes. As schools and colleges have become more central institutions, they have encountered more pressures to change from outside pressure groups.

MODERNIZATION OF REGIONS

Whole societies and different regions within a society vary in the degree that they are subject to change. Schools and colleges located in *modernized* regions, which are characterized by sharp social divisions and rapid social change, will tend to be swept up in rapid changes and the pervasive conflicts that typically arise in these areas over racial and social desegregation, pressures from groups in ghetto communities for community control, decentralization of school districts, and militant teacher and student demands for redistributions of power between administrators and professional associations. On the other hand, educational institutions located in more remote areas can preserve their traditional forms by finding special "niches," or by making a contribution to higher systems (through symbiotic relationships). Such areas are characterized by what Parsons calls "fundamentalism"—traditional value systems that resist change.[99] Organizations located in these areas typically resent any effort on the part of outsiders to control them and attempt to limit changes to purely technical matters that can be easily adapted within the existing framework. The personal beliefs and close personal relationships of people located in these regions predispose them to remain loyal to local traditions and to resist both the intrusions of impersonal nationalizing influences and remote government pressures.[100]

The Historical Situation. The history of innovation in the region is especially critical. Working in a cross-cultural setting, investigators have found that in cultures under transformation, radical innovators gain prestige compared with innovators in more stable or disintegrating cultures.[101] More generally, it seems likely that if an innovation is introduced into organizations located in an area that has a history of innovation, it will be more successful than if introduced into an area that has not been innovative.

Community Cleavage. However, the pressures for change that characterize modernized environments also are often offset by cleavages between groups that usually are found in these areas. For example, Rogers noted the inability of the civil rights groups in New York City to establish an effective coalition because of competition among themselves, which was a major reason for the failure of desegregation efforts in that city.[102] The Ford Foundation study of its Comprehensive School Improvement Program concluded that innovations had a poor chance of success while there was a crisis in the community. Financial commitment from the community was an important ingredient of success.[103]

INTERORGANIZATIONAL RELATIONSHIPS

Other organizations make up an important part of the social environment. When one changes, it can affect the other organizations that are closely linked to it.[104] An organization will provide an incentive for another to change primarily where either (1) the organizations are symbiotically related or (2) they are competitively related.

Symbiotic Relations. Two types of symbiotic relationships can be distinguished—confederation and role hybridization:

1. *Organizational confederation.* Coalitions of organizations are necessary to counteract the narrow divisions of labor that arise among organizations and that serve as one of the major barriers to change in modern society. Wayland has noted how the division of labor among local governments, textbook publishers, and teacher training institutions has often blocked educational change.[105] Each organization is compelled to limit its attention and responsibilities to certain aspects of a complex problem, yet it monopolizes resources (skills, money, and manpower, for example), thus depriving other organizations of these resources. Once such jurisdictions have been established, it is difficult to coordinate the work of the separate organizations dealing with interrelated problems.

   The only way to cope with highly intricate and complex social problems is through a broad-front attack waged by a coalition of organizations. Where they exist, coalitions can cut across jurisdictional boundaries and bring to bear a range of influence, skills, and other resources that no one organization would have available by itself. Modern math and the physical science high school curriculum were products of precisely this kind of confederation of loosely linked public agencies at the federal and local levels and private groups acting in concert.[106]

2. *Role hybridization.* Innovation also seems to be stimulated by the cross-fertilization of ideas and compromises that must be made when people in two or more disparate roles are forced to cooperate. New ideas and, ultimately, new hybrid roles seem to evolve from the merger and resynthesis of old ideas and established roles. For example, entire new sciences—such as bacteriology, experimental psychology, and psychiatry—were the products of the cross-fertilization of intellectual fields by individuals occupying dual and incompatible roles.[107] All of this suggests that the rate of innovation will be highest where there is a high rate of interaction between incompatible systems and lowest where the rate of interaction is low and compatibility is high.

Competition. Competition is another type of interorganizational relationship that can induce change. A notable example is the remarkable transformation of the NEA into a militant organization, which many observers believe was in response to fierce competition for membership with the AFT in the major cities.

Conversely, the traditionalism of the educational institutions is probably due, partly at least, to the lack of competition; they have a guaranteed enrollment and public funds. As noted in the previous chapter, as a means of breaking the educational monopoly, a number of writers have proposed establishing a large variety of private as well as public schools based on open, competitive enrollment policies; a series of alternative public school systems ranging from regional, state, and federal schools to industrial- and labor union-sponsored schools might break the protected public monopoly of local school systems; so could a system of vouchers redeemable for a specified sum if spent on any one of a wide range of educational services that extend well beyond traditional schooling, including travel. Noting that neighborhood-based schools no longer perform the socializing functions they were intended to perform, the present writer has advocated separate schools for specialized clientele within metropolitan-wide school systems as a way of promoting change.[108] For such a system to function effectively and avoid the "track" characteristics of present specialized programs within schools, each school would be forced to compete for students with whom it intends to specialize, and personnel would have to be evaluated and rewarded primarily on the success of the school in accomplishing its announced specialized objective.

In sum, a very promising approach to deliberate change is to introduce a competitive structure into an organization or to introduce competitors into the environment. The organization must adapt in order to compete.

A COMPARISON OF STRATEGIES[109]

Because many government programs are attempting to manipulate precisely the structural variables that theory suggests are important, they can sometimes be illuminating. Therefore I studied the Teacher Corps over a period of five years as a way to compare the relative effectiveness of some of the change strategies discussed above. The Teacher Corps is a nation-wide, multimillion dollar government program intending to promote educational reforms in low-income schools through innovative teacher training programs. In particular, it provides a route into teaching for liberal arts graduates and members of minority groups who otherwise might not have entered the profession. Because it was designed to attack complex social problems on a national scale, the program has attempted to mobilize a coalition of organizations, each of which contributes special resources and skills needed to improve teaching in low-income schools.

Structure of the Teacher Corps

A special two-year internship gives interns experience working in several cooperating public schools that employ them while attending college part-time. Colleges of education are expected to experiment with curriculum and personnel policies and to establish cooperative relationships with schools and communities and with other departments in the university. In the words of one Teacher Corps brochure, the program seeks to utilize the team approach for training purposes, to provide for special and continuous supervision of interns, to incorporate the spirit of the Peace Corps, to establish a closer relationship between theory and practice, to set up a route into teaching for some who might have otherwise been excluded, and to involve the community as a training ground by extending the walls of the classroom into the community. The program is divisible into two main parts and several components: a preservice program for interns, which includes graduate courses in education as well as some observation of schools and/or the community; and a tripartite, in-service period consisting of university study, a practical internship in poverty schools, and experience with poverty children and their families in the community.

Typically, a group of 30 to 50 liberal arts graduates (interns) and several experienced teachers who serve as team leaders receive about eight weeks of special preservice training at a college or university. Following preservice the group is broken into four to six teams composed of three to eight interns and one team leader. Each team is assigned to a school serving a poverty area, usually an elementary school, where they spend 60 percent or more of their time on a weekly basis. In the beginning they may work with small groups of students on specific lesson plans and, as they gain experience, their tasks become more complex. They have experimented with cross-age tutoring, sociodrama, multiethnic centers, black history courses, and multilingual programs, for example. They are expected to spend about 20 percent of their time with academic coursework at the university, which includes interdisciplinary work in the social sciences as well as in colleges of education and leads to teacher certification and a masters degree in two years. Finally, the interns also are supposed to devote about 20 percent of their time on community activities, conducting surveys, working with social agencies, visiting parents, and participating in civic and (sometimes) political activities as a way of familiarizing themselves with the environment in which their students have grown up and to try to bridge the gap that exists between the school and the low-income community that it serves.

There has been a pervasive goal conflict between the national office, which stresses the objective of educational reform and the local schools that often attempt to use the resources provided by the Teacher Corps to supplement their existing programs. The assumptions of this program are at variance with the traditional training model, which holds veteran professionals responsible for socializing the novices. Interns have been led to view themselves as autonomous colleagues of the experienced teachers and as agents of change, a view that is not shared by most teachers and many professors, who insist on placing the interns in traditional teacher-trainee roles. More fundamentally, the entire program attempts to act as a unique type of change agent, consisting of a complex network of organizations acting in concert and designed to promote innovation within member organizations and in organizations outside the immediate network. Generally, the literature has overlooked organizations in the role of "agents of change" intent on changing other organizations. But the literature on interorganizational relationships provides a starting point, and the Teacher Corps can be used as one strategic case.

Methods

Indicators of the different strategies were derived from questionnaires and interviews with new teacher-interns, experienced teachers, and college professors who were part of this national experiment to train teachers for low-income schools. The analysis was based on 42 public schools and 10 universities located throughout the United States. The dependent variable is the number (and innovativeness) of new technologies introduced into schools through the program (derived from a content analysis of interviews).

The many indicators that were used formed seven major factors that seemed to be involved in the different explanations. In general, the number of technological innovations adopted by a school appeared to be produced by a combination of (1) a dominant outside organization (university) staffed by competent and liberal members; (2) competent, receptive boundary personnel (team leaders) in the host organization; and (3) functional interdependence between the school and university and channels for cooperation to take place. These conditions underscored the importance of characteristics of the general organizational context in which innovation is taking place.

Relationship to the University

The most salient factor was the quality and interdependence of the boundary personnel, which included four variables: competence of the university faculty members (as rated by the interns); faculty members' political liberalism (based on their own self-identity); the extent of cooperation between the school and the university (assessed from a content analysis of the interviews); and the competence of the experienced teacher-supervisors—the team leaders (based on the combined ratings of teachers and interns). Interns' ratings of the faculty members' competence and the faculty's political liberalism were probably more important than either the university's prestige or its resources. Perhaps the better universities were too socially remote and too well-integrated into the academic system to have developed the interest or competence for this kind of problem.

The Ford Foundation review of its school improvement program concluded that universities seldom functioned as a force for improvement in the quality of elementary and secondary schools. The findings summarized here do not contradict this indictment, but they do suggest the reason: colleges seldom have established effective linkages with schools. However, where these linkages do exist, the university can be a very potent force for change. The overriding importance of the university faculty supports the contention of some writers that organizations change primarily in response to an outside stimulus. But, more specifically, it reinforces the generally acknowledged significance of interorganizational relationships, and underscores the crucial role played by boundary personnel in particular, in this case represented by the team leaders from the school and the university faculty members. In this sense, the findings support the diffusion approach with its emphasis on the importance of the openness of boundary personnel to change. While the technical competence of the occupants of both boundary roles appeared to be important, the attitude climate set by the university faculty seemed to be even more important.

The dominating role of the university can be attributed to several sources. First, in comparison to schools, universities are more cosmopolitan, relying on regional or national financial and recruiting bases and exporting their products throughout the nation and the world. In addition to this institutional base, faculty members probably tend to be more professionalized than teachers and less tied into the local political structure. Moreover, they have less investment in the existing technology of the schools (as opposed to their investment in their own institutions). Finally, the fact that universities are the prime contractors for this program, the program director being a faculty member, enhances the university's influence. However, this leverage for change, no matter how great, cannot be applied unless there is a channel through which the university can exert its influence, that is, a working relationship between the universities and schools. Competent and receptive team leaders are a necessary component of such a channel.

Comparison with Other Environmental Conditions

To put it another way, the major dimension of the environment contributing to innovation was the amount of cooperation between the school and the university. With that factor controlled, modernization of the state made only a small contribution. There was some support for the contention that innovation can be promoted by adding outside resources, and there was slightly more change in schools associated with larger universities, but these variables were relatively unimportant in comparison to other factors examined. The number of training programs at the university was inversely associated with program change, which suggested that change does not always occur more readily in otherwise changing environments as speculated above. Perhaps some allowance should be made for a ceiling effect, that is, the fact that it is also more difficult for a program to make additional changes when there is already a high rate of change.

Organizational Control

The second critical factor was the extent of internal control exercised by schools. This factor included four variables: centralization of the school system's decision-making structure; stress that classroom teachers and administrators place on rules and procedures; emphasis that teachers place on pupil control (i.e., strict discipline); and the proportion of program funds controlled by the schools.

This factor reflects the other side of the coin—the capacity of the cooperating, host organization to filter and shape the changes proposed by the cooperating outside organization. The first two variables form a "containment dimension," through which an organization develops the capacity to control its members and which determines how effectively it can regulate its members' reactions to proposed changes. However, these two variables operated in opposite directions. The positive correlation between the centralization of the decision-making structure and technological change was at variance with the widely held assumption that decentralized systems are more adaptable. The higher administration was usually responsible for introducing this program to the schools. Under these conditions, the more that power is concentrated at the top, the more effective the program will be. In other words, a centralized organization does not for that reason necessarily resist change; instead, centralization gives it the capacity to select and enforce innovations as well as to resist them. At the same time, where teachers emphasize classroom discipline. it probably both reflects and reinforces strong administrative control.

There was a tendency for innovations to decline as the proportion of funds controlled by the local schools increased. This reflected the conflict in goals between these two institutions. Control over the funds provides a leverage for co-opting the program. Schools attempted to use funds to supplement their existing programs rather than for innovations. There may have been a slight tendency for the more competent principals to gain more control over program funds. While it is probably true that educational decisions are moving up and out, placing initiative outside of the local system, local school boards often maintain final veto power over changes that they do not want.

The Role of Dissonant-Change Agents

The third factor reflects the amount of dissonance between the change agents and the members of the host organization. But, contrary to the theory, the correlation was negative. Independent field observations and interviews also confirmed that interns were often a source of friction and tension in the local schools, and that schools tended to react defensively when even a few of these critical, liberal, change-oriented newcomers were introduced. Perhaps the resulting conflict was not entirely counterproductive, however. There were small positive correlations between innovation and (1) the amount of conflict between interns and other members of the program and (2) the number of teachers reporting that the program had created problems for them. These correlations supported the notion that conflict often accompanies change. But the fact that the correlations were not higher also suggested that conflict does not necessarily produce extensive change under certain circumstances.

An attempt to influence the change process by introducing change agents as an independent force can be effective under only limited conditions, which were not present in this case. Even with the two most influential factors controlled, the more liberal the interns in a school, the less innovation that occurred. This fact indicates that their ineffectiveness was not simply a product of the institutional balance of power, but that it was inherent to the strategy itself as employed in this program. The tactics used in this program, of course, provide an extreme test of the replacement approach. The attempt to marry the change-agent roles to the apprenticeship system placed the interns in a precarious position between two powerful organizations. They were representatives of the outside organization in the schools, but could count on little direct support from remote university professors, while they were directly supervised by defensive teachers. Sensing this resistance to them, and often finding the schools conservative toward change, in most programs a vocal minority of interns resorted to confrontation tactics. However, the conflict theory of change presumes a balance of power that did not exist in this case. As inexperienced newcomers to the profession, still in training and temporarily assigned to schools under direct supervision of experienced teachers, the interns could not gain leverage within the schools—even though, ironically, these very characteristics enabled them to maintain the autonomy that encouraged them to take risks involved in promoting change. Nor did the interns constitute a sufficiently critical mass in any of the schools to provide power from numbers or to promote the development of a strong peer group. They were so outnumbered and over-whelmed by the structural defenses available to school administrators and teachers that the schools were able to neutralize their efforts. Indeed, the interns' militancy gave the teachers little latitude to compromise without jeopardizing their authority, which created a win-lose situation. Teachers retaliated by completely withdrawing their support for interns' proposals. Thus, while some change accompanied conflict, the fact that interns had little leverage from which to wage a successful conflict helps to explain the negative correlation between technological change and the proportion of liberal arts interns in the program.

This suggests that two additional conditions must be present that were not present in this case: (1) the change agents must be introduced in sufficiently large numbers, and (2) the agents must be introduced at more than one echelon in the hierarchy. The impact might have been modified either by assigning a higher ratio of interns to each school or by recruiting interns into the administrative ranks. But, in any event, the experience in this program suggests that caution should be exercised in employing the replacement strategy for purposes of innovation without further examination of the conditions under which it can be successful.

Professional Competence

Finally, despite the theoretical importance that could be attributed to variables relating to professionalism and competence of the administrators and teachers, these variables were less important than the characteristics of other boundary personnel who were more directly associated with the program. Teachers' participation in the proposal is the other side of administrative centralization discussed above. Their participation had only a minor effect and, contrary to expectations and findings from other studies, the small effect that appeared was negative.

The power-equalization model presumes that changes are produced from the consent of the parties involved. However, some innovations are forced into a system, which arouses suspicion or opposition of the incumbents. This was frequently the case in this program. When subordinates fail to agree on the objectives or strategies of these proposed changes, but are relatively professionalized, their participation in the decisions places them in a better position to sabotage the innovation; and when their participation is only nominal, the strategy can backfire by producing unrealistic expectations. Thus, the strategy can inhibit as well as promote innovation, depending on the initial balance of power, the degree of consensus, and the status threat involved.

The competence of the teaching staff was negatively correlated with change, and there was a low correlation with their professionalism and liberalism. Both of these findings question the assumption that status security and professionalism necessarily promote change.

Some of these latter findings may have implications for the current decentralization issue concerning demands for community control that are being made by residents of ghettos in the large cities. First, the data support the contention of many critics that the professionalism and technical competence of teachers in itself provides no assurance that efforts will be made to improve the schools. Second, administrative decentralization could reduce the capacity of central administrators to impose change from the top down and, more important, perhaps the whole controversy over the schools' relationship with their communities has eclipsed an equally important relationship: the relationship of the schools with innovative universities.

IMPLICATIONS

The antecedents of the preceding approaches can be traced to several macrotheories of change, albeit the linkages are imperfect and often overlap.[110] For example, socialization and diffusion are the peaceful mechanisms of natural adaptation underlying various forms of "equilibrium" theory"; "evolutionary" and "neoevolutionary" theories give priority to structural differentiation and the sociohistorical and environmental context; and replacement and status maintenance, insofar as they imply an unstable balance of power and pressure for redistributions of power, are ingredients of "conflict" theory.

Any model that purports to guide deliberate efforts to introduce change should be linked to (derived from) a general theory of social change. What is needed is a model that systematically incorporates these various theoretical traditions. Therefore, in these closing pages, it is only fitting that we begin to consider such a model in a more systematic way than we have done to this point. What is proposed below, however, is only a tentative, first approximation.

Underlying Assumptions of the Model

The model rests on the assumptions already outlined earlier in the chapter. By way of summary, these assumptions are as follows:

1. The way an innovation is conceived and implemented results from a combination of forces inside and outside of the organization; its success or failure will vary with the conditions under which it is introduced, as well as the internal characteristics of the organization or of the innovation itself.
2. Characteristics of both occupation and organization must be taken into account in order to explain innovation; attempts to change an occupation will be influenced by its organizational context, and organizational innovations will be influenced by

the occupational structure that dominates the organization.

3. Innovation occurs in response to an environmental crisis created when an organization fails to adapt rapidly enough to a changing environment; consumers consequently pressure the organization to improve its performance.

4. During crisis periods leaders, who at normal times are under conservative pressures, are expected to be innovative; these leaders come predominantly from among influentials outside of the organization who have less investment in its present structure.

5. An internal split develops between the established leaders and a new generation identified with the outside leaders who stand to gain from new roles that promise to open new channels of success and circumvent the status monopoly controlled by traditionalists.

6. A coalition develops between influential outsiders and the competitive internal leadership; they develop new techniques, identify new specialties that they can monopolize, make provisions for transmitting the new knowledge, and assign the new roles as specialized functions to new or established units.

7. New specialties and units will be created by redistributing existing tasks that formerly were the responsibility of other units; for that reason, the new units will be resisted; a dialectic develops in which the traditional, conservative procedures are reasserted or slightly adapted in order to compete with new procedures.

8. Variant forms of the innovation evolve as it is adapted to different circumstances, the variant forms being only loosely associated through ideology and a common administrative and funding source.

9. Most variants become extinct or so well adapted as to be indistinguishable from the existing forms but, through a process of natural selection and cross-fertilization of values and technique, new hybrids do arise in some cases from an optimal match between the innovation and local conditions.

10. Finally, once established, the innovation becomes subject to the same institutionalizing forces that originally brought it into existence.

Some General Principles

With these assumptions in mind, we consider some general principles that should influence attempts to institute deliberate change:

1. Change in an organization occurs because of one of the following overlapping conditions: (a) passive adaptation on the part of

members of the organization to changes going on outside the organization—for example, the rising demand for formal education brought about by technological change; (b) deliberate initiatives on the part of a group in control of the organization; (c) complete displacement of existing practices and values by entirely new ones that have been interjected into the system; and (d) a shift in priorities among competing practices and values already present in the system.

2. The first and last conditions are more typical than the other two; complete displacement occurs only rarely—during revolutionary times—and only seldom does a group in power have either the authority or leverage to allow it to impose change without meeting resistance.

3. Shifts in priority result from conflict among status groups that subscribe to different practices and values; more specifically, priorities change when the dominant group is successfully challenged by a previously subordinate group, which then seeks to institutionalize its ideas.

4. The probability of the subordinate group's being successful in asserting its power will be greater when it aligns itself with outside groups than when it acts in isolation; groups contending for control over education historically have sought to align themselves with the political, economic, religious groups, and elite families (status groups).

5. A challenge is fully successful when the subgroup completely *displaces* the dominant group; it is partially succcessful when it asserts its right to coexist or otherwise is able to increase its *share* of control.

6. To wage a successful challenge, the subgroup must accomplish one of the following:
   a. Break the dominant group's monopoly over necessary resources by either finding other sources of supply or establishing an alternative system.
   b. Gain authority through legal channels using the pressure of group organization and numbers, or by force.
   c. Replace the prevailing ideology with a competing ideology.

An Application

These principles were implicit in the cases of both student activism and teacher militancy considered in previous chapters. Student activism is a response to the strains created as universities become transformed into mass institutions. As students have become more closely aligned with powerful economic, political, and social strata they have gained leverage and are now in a better position to press both recent and age-old grievances. They have challenged the faculty's and administration's exclusive monopoly over the curriculum, control over their time, and the right to speak for the university and to engage in political activity. They have used rhetoric, pressure, and force to bargain for more legitimate decision-making roles. And they have questioned the time-honored ideologies that have traditionally governed the university—the supremacy of scholarship over political action and the supreme right of administration and faculty to govern the institution—advocating instead an alternative value system that they firmly believe is morally superior. Educational institutions, under pressure from a variety of sources, are making efforts to passively adapt to these demands.

Teacher militancy follows a similar pattern. Individual teachers traditionally have registered personal grievances against their administrators, but their organized protest occurred only sporadically until teachers forged mammoth national professional associations that were aligned with powerful labor unions. More important, momentum was not fully sustained until teachers entered the political arena, seeking to gain the backing of political groups for their demands. Teachers have sought to break the administrator's monopoly over critical political decisions using both force and legal channels. They have challenged traditional ideologies about lay control and the supremacy of the bureaucratic hierarchy and substituted competing ideologies justifying the dual authority system on the basis of student welfare.

CONCLUSIONS

During the 1960s politicians formed unprecedented alliances with social scientists to convert academic theories into ambitious social reform programs that were intended to alleviate the problems of poverty, crime, and unequal social opportunity. The results of these efforts have been disappointing. For example, this writer concluded his study of the Teacher Corps with this comment.

"In one sense, this has been another study documenting the disappointing failures and modest successes of another government program. The federal program attempted to cooperate with relatively autonomous local organizations to bring about reform from within the established system by adding resources to the present system and making minor adjustments in it. But strong opposition, nationally and locally, prevented the program from receiving the full share of authorized funding; structural concessions were made to local organizations, giving them greater freedom to run the program, and in many instances to go against the policy and purposes of the legislation. On the local level, the program had to face the reality of strong opposition by organizations and professions whose established positions might be threatened by visible accomplishment of the program's goals; the resources available to the federal program were too little and too thinly dispersed to make a striking impact on the organizations they were designed to change. In order to survive, the federal organization had to keep subtly redefining its goals behind a smoke screen of ideologies used to disguise and compensate for the fact that extensive change was not occurring. The federal program sought acceptance, legitimacy, and institutionalization within the federal bureaucracy. Some of its power was given to other agencies, and, internally, a succession of leaders and personnel resulted in less emphasis on "reform" and more emphasis on technical specialists. In short, this program demonstrated the tendency of such organizations to remain prisoners of the coalition of conflicting forces that created them. In final analysis, the Washington office was bargaining the possibility of creating a dramatic and visible effect for a more modest impact and ultimately for its very survival.

"I suspect that many of these same observations—the frustrating obstacles the Teacher Corps encountered at each turn, and the subsequent goal displacements, co-optation, and disillusionment of its participants—could be made with equal validity about a host of other government programs, ranging from the New Deal's Tennessee Valley Authority to more recent Office of Economic Opportunity Community Action and Model Cities antipoverty programs, the Head Start program, the Ford Foundation's Gray Area programs, and the Peace Corps."[111]

At least four quite-different explanations of these failures have been advanced. At one extreme, several psychologists and sociologists have begun to explain human behavior in ways that challenge the key assumption underlying reform programs, that is, that human behavior is entirely malleable and can be altered by deliberately changing the social environment.[112] Arthur Jensen, Richard Herrnstein, Lionel Tiger, Robin Fox, and Bruce Eckland, to name a few, challenge this assumption on grounds that many personal, traits including personality, intelligence, tastes, and temperament are inherited. They postulate that, through selective mating and inbreeding, entire subgroups (i.e., social classes or races) are preprogrammed from birth with propensities that go back millions of years to ancestry. Insofar as this is true, the failures of the reform programs can be attributed to the basic intractability of human nature and inherent resistance of people to being modified by schemes for improving society.

But most social scientists and many policy makers doubt that genetic factors explain the failure of reform programs. Instead, some writers have taken a second extreme, arguing that the failures only reflect the *igno-rance* of social scientists about how to alter human behavior, not the inherent intractability of human nature itself. Despite years of research, many social scientists will admit that not enough is known about what needs to be changed or how to change it. Perhaps the willingness of social scientists to tackle the problems and the eagerness with which policy makers have tried their solutions is more of a tribute to their desperation than to any evidence that social scientists are prepared for these awesome responsibilities.

Although there is no denying that social scientists know too little, there is still a third way to explain the failures of reform programs—policy makers have not made use of what little that *is* known. Failure is virtually inevitable as long as the nation's leadership continues to concoct programs without any effort to provide some of the conditions known to be necessary to the survival and the effectivenesss of new programs. The government itself often has been responsible for erecting many of the barriers that compromise these programs, including insufficient funding and constant changes in policy. The programs might be more successful if the persons who conceive and administer them devoted as much attention to the problem of cultivating and propagating them, once instituted, as they devoted to their original design. We know that innovations cannot be installed simply by announcing that they are available; and as suggested in this chapter, we are beginning to learn more about how to implement them.

Finally, the political constraints on reform programs constitute a fourth explanation for why they fail. Politics enters into every facet of reform. Reform programs are not entirely rational systems. The leaders in charge of these programs seldom have enough control to implement them as planned. The political process does not stop when Congress has enacted legislation authorizing a new program. The political process is reenacted at each stage of implementing the program. The reason is that citizens in changing democratic societies seldom fully concur on the seriousness of social problems or how to go about solving them. Controversy and opposition continues even after a program has been implemented. Leaders of the program cannot concentrate solely on implementing the ideal plan if they are faced with opposition. They must also search for underlying points of consensus and strike feasible compromises if the program is to survive. Thus, the reform programs cannot achieve their full potential because of the necessity of making these compromises.

But, although reform programs seem doomed to "fail" in one sense, they can achieve still another purpose. They provide concrete settings in which fundamental value conflicts—between those in the society who want the reforms and those who do not—can be mediated, and the details of this compromise can be worked out in an operational way. What is lost by way of specific reform is sometimes compensated for by the opportunity for people to resolve their differences. In the final analysis, then, educational reform is as much a part of the democratic political process as it is a part of the educational process. The future of education will be determined by politics as well as by rational planning and deliberate reform efforts.

In this chapter, we have considered several ways that policy makers might approach reform efforts with more effective results than have been achieved. The discussion suggests that organizational innovation requires a *combination* of several conceptual approaches. By proposing a general model we have tried to move beyond the individual strategies identified in the earlier discussions in this chapter. Apparently, there is a great deal of both truth and fiction in the various streams of thought that were identified above. Various types of variables seem to supplement one another, but even in combination, they explain only a part of the problem. Some strategies might be more effective than others, but the crucial element seems to be the way they *interact*. The situation into which an innovation is introduced seems to be as critical as the strategy used. Perhaps the fundamental dimension underlying the variables that were considered here is the way local organizations are insulated from, or integrated into, the larger context. Thus, decentralization gives local interests leverage over unwanted changes, while centralization more closely links the system to the broader system, as do institutional cooperation and liberal and competent boundary personnel. In the future, more thought will have to be given to the conditions that enable organizations to maintain functional autonomy within an interdependent, changing society.

We have intentionally skirted some fundamental moral issues about whether change is always desirable or whether some changes are better than others. Our strategy has been to discuss some alternative futures (in the preceding chapter) and then to consider in this chapter how at least some aspects of these futures might be implemented. This is not meant to imply that change is always better than stability, or that all changes are equally desirable. We have assumed, instead, that the answers to these questions depend on different conceptions of the "good" and "bad," and the difference in these conceptions must be resolved politically. The answers cannot be prescribed by the findings of social scientists although individual social scientists can and perhaps should try to guide the conclusions.

REFERENCES

1. *Our Common School Education, with Special Reference to the Reply of Supt. A.J. Rickoff, to R.A. Hinsdale* (Cleveland, 1878). Reprinted in *School Reform: Past and Present*, Michael B. Katz, ed. Boston: Little, Brown and Co., 1971, p. 268.

2. Committee for Economic Development, *Innovation in Education: New Directions for the American School*. New York: Committee for Economic Development, 1968, p. 7.

3. Richard I. Miller, *Perspectives on Educational Change.* New York: Appleton-Century-Crofts, 1967, pp. 1–2.

4. *The Principals Look at the Schools.* Washington, D.C.: National Education Association, Project on Instruction, 1962, pp. 8–9.

5. Paul R. Mort, "Studies in Educational Innovation from the Institute of Administrative Research: An Overview" in *Innovation in Education,* Matthew Miles, ed. New York: Teachers College, Columbia University, 1964, pp. 317–328.

6. Richard O. Carlson, "School Superintendents and Adoption of Modern Math: A Social Structure Profile" in *Innovation in Education, ibid.,* pp. 329–342 and *Adoption of Educational Innovations.* Eugene: Center for the Advanced Study of Educational Administration, 1965.

7. *Administrators' and Teachers' Reactions to Educational Innovations.* Princeton, N.J.: Gallup International, May 1967.

8. *Parents' Reactions to Educational Innovations.* Princeton, N.J.: Gallup International, May 1966, p. 8.

9. Daniel E. Griffiths, "Administrative Theory and Change in Organizations" in *Innovation in Education, op. cit.,* pp. 425–436, p. 425.

10. Paul R. Mort, *op. cit.* Also Paul R. Mort and Francis G. Cornell, *American Schools in Transition,* New York: Bureau of Publications, Teachers College, Columbia University, 1953.

11. Margaret Bushnell, "Now We're Lagging Only 20 Years," *The School Executive, LXXXVII,* October 1957, 61–63. Also Thomas W. Barrington, *The Introduction of Selected Educational Practices into Teachers' Colleges and Their Laboratory Schools.* New York: Bureau of Publications, Teachers College, Columbia University, 1953.

12. Hendrick Gideonse, *Educational Research and Development in the United States.* U.S. Office of Education, Washington, D.C.: Government Printing Office, 1970.

13. *Ibid.,* p. 147.

14. John I. Goodlad, M. Frances Klein, and associates, *Behind the Classroom Door.* Worthington, Ohio: Charles A. Jones Publishing Co., 1970, p. 97.

15. *Ibid.,* p. 72.

16. Richard I. Evans, *Resistance to Innovation in Higher Education.* San Francisco: Jossey-Bass, Inc., 1968, pp. 14–32.

17. *Ibid.*

18. Everett M. Rogers, *Diffusion of Innovations.* New York: The Free Press of Glencoe, 1962. Also, "What are Innovators Like?" *Change Processes in the Public Schools.* Eugene, Oregon: Center for the Advanced Study of Educational Administration, University of Oregon, 1965.

19. Matthew Miles, ed., *Innovation in Education, op. cit.,* p. 638.

20. Robert Chin, "Models and Ideas About Changing," paper presented at the Symposium on Identifying Techniques and Principles for Gaining Accept-

ance of Research Results of Use of New Media in Education, November 24–27, 1963, Lincoln, Neb.

21. Robert K. Merton, *Social Theory and Social Structure*. Glencoe, Ill.: The Free Press, 1957, pp. 176–181.

22. Robert Dubin, "Deviant Behavior and Social Structure: Continuum in Social Theory," *American Sociological Review*, 24, April 1959, 147–164.

23. Adapted from Warland Bessent and Hollis A. Moore, "The Effects of Outside Funds on School Pursuits" in *Perspectives on Educational Change*, Richard I. Miller, ed. New York: Appleton-Century-Crofts, 1967, pp. 101–117.

24. Everett Rogers, 1962, *op. cit.*, p. 169.

25. Talcott Parsons, "Evolutionary Universals in Society," *American Sociological Review*, 29, June 1964, 339–357.

26. David Street, ed., *Innovation in Mass Education*. New York: Wiley-Interscience, 1969, pp. 6–7.

27. "What Makes Innovation Work?" *Ohio Schools*, December 22, 1972. Also, *A Foundation Goes to School*. New York: The Ford Foundation, 1972.

28. Everett Rogers, *op. cit.*, p. 169.

29. Homer G. Barnett, *Innovation: The Basis of Cultural Change*. New York: McGraw-Hill, 1953, p. 381.

30. R.W. Gerard, "Problems in the Institutionalization of Higher Education: An Analysis Based on Historical Materials," *Behavioral Science, 2*, April 1957, 134.

31. Pitirim Sorokin, *Social and Cultural Dynamics*. Totawa, New Jersey: Bedminster Press, 1939–1941.

32. Peter M. Blau and W. Richard Scott, *Formal Organizations*. San Francisco: Chandler Press, 1962.

33. Parts of this section are adopted from Ronald G. Corwin, *Reform and Organizational Survival: The Teacher Corps as an Instrument of Educational Change*. New York: Wiley-Interscience, 1973.

34. J.M. Baldwin, *The Individual and Society*. Boston: The Gorham Press, 1911; J. Dewey, *Human Nature and Conduct*. New York: Holt, 1922; F.P. Giddings, *The Theory of Socialization*. New York: The McMillan Co., 1897; G.H. Mead, *Mind, Self and Society*. Chicago: University of Chicago Press, 1934; W.I. Thomas and F. Znaniecki, *The Polish Peasant in Europe and America*, 4 volumes. Boston: Richard C. Badger, 1918–20; and C.H. Cooley, *Human Nature and the Social Order*. New York: Scribner's, 1920. Rev. ed., 1922.

35. John A. Clausen, "A Historical and Comparative View of Socialization Theory and Research" in *Socialization and Society*, John A. Clausen, ed. Boston: Little, Brown and Co., 1968, pp. 18–72. Also, Allen H. Barton, "Studying the Effects of College Education" in *The College Student and His Culture: An Analysis*, Kaoru Yamamoto, ed. Boston: Houghton Mifflin, 1968, pp. 326–330.

36. Howard Becker and Blanche Geer, "The Fate of Idealism in Medical School," *Harvard Educational Review, 28,* Winter 1958, 70–80; Ronald G. Corwin, M.J. Taves, and J.E. Haas, "Professional Disillusionment," *Nursing Research, 10,* Summer 1961, 141–144; and Dan Lortie, "Laymen to Lawmen: Law School, Careers, and Professional Socialization," *Harvard Educational Review, 29,* Fall 1959, 352–369.

37. Lortie, *Ibid.*

38. Harold J. Leavitt, "Applied Organizational Change in Industry: Structural, Technological and Humanistic Approaches," *Handbook of Organizations,* James March, ed. Chicago: Rand McNally, 1965, pp. 1144–1170; Ronald Lippett, "The Youth Culture, The School System, and the Socialization Community" in *Schools in a Changing Society,* Albert J. Reiss, ed. New York: The Free Press, 1966, pp. 99–120; and Ronald G. Havelock and Kenneth D. Benne, "An Exploratory Study of Knowledge Utilization," *Concepts for Social Change,* Goodwin Watson, ed., Washington, D.C.: Cooperative Project for Educational Development, 1967, pp. 47–70.

39. Matthew Miles, *Learning to Work in Groups.* New York: Teachers College, Columbia University Press, 1959. Also, W.G. Bennis, "A new Role for the Behavioral Sciences: Effecting Organizational Change," *Administrative Science Quarterly, 8,* September 1963, 125–165.

40. John Colombotos, "Physicians and Medicare: A Before-After Study of the Effects of Legislation on Attitudes," *American Sociological Review, 34,* June 1969, 318–334.

41. Sam D. Sieber, "Images of the Practitioner and Strategies of Educational Change," *Sociology of Education, 45,* Fall 1972, 362–385.

42. Jerald Hage and Michael Aiken, "Program Change and Organizational Properties: A Comparative Analysis," *American Journal of Sociology, 72,* March 1967, 503–519.

43. Gabriel de Tarde, *Laws of Imitation,* rev. ed. Gloucester, Mass.: Peter Smith, 1962.

44. Bernard Berelson and Gary Steiner, *Human Behavior: An Inventory of Scientific Findings.* New York: Harcourt, Brace and World, 1964.

45. E. Rogers, *op. cit.,* 1962.

46. Herbert Menzel, "Innovation, Integration and Marginality: A Survey of Physicians," *American Sociological Review, 25,* October 1960, 704–713.

47. R. Carlson, *Adoption of Educational Innovations, op. cit.*

48. Vilfredo Pareto, *The Rise and Fall of the Elites.* Totawa, N.J.: The Bedminster Press, 1968.

49. Robert Michels, *Political Parties.* Glencoe, Ill.: The Free Press, 1949.

50. Alvin Gouldner, *Patterns of Industrial Bureaucracy.* Glencoe, Ill.: The Free Press, 1954.

51. Richard O. Carlson, *Executive Succession and Organizational Change: Place-Bound and Career-Bound Superintendents of Schools.* Chicago: Midwest Administrative Center, University of Chicago, 1962.

52. Robert Guest, "Managerial Succession in Complex Organizations," *American Journal of Sociology, 68,* July 1962, 47–54.

53. Burton R. Clark, *The Distinctive College: Antioch, Reed, and Swarthmore.* Chicago: Aldine Press, 1970, Chapter 10.

54. Howard S. Becker and Blanche Geer, "Latent Culture: A Note on the Theory of Latent Social Roles," *Administrative Science Quarterly, 5,* September 1960, 304–313.

55. David Gottlieb and Benjamin Hodgkins, "College Student Subcultures: Their Structure and Characteristics in Relation to Student Attitude Change," *Social Review, 71,* Fall 1963, 266–289 and Edward McDill, Leo C. Rigsby, and Edmund D. Meyers, "Institutional Effects on the Academic Behavior of High School Students," *Sociology of Education, XL,* Summer 1967, 181–182.

56. Burton R. Clark, *The Open Door College: A Case Study.* New York: McGraw-Hill, 1960.

57. Joan Woodward, ed., *Industrial Organization: Behavior and Control.* Oxford, England: Oxford University Press, 1970.

58. Hage and Aiken, *op. cit.,* 1967. Also see, by the same authors, *Social Change in Complex Organizations.* New York: Random House, 1970.

59. Harry L. Gracey, *Curriculum or Craftsmanship: Elementary School Teachers in a Bureaucratic System.* Chicago: University of Chicago Press, 1972.

60. Eli Ginzberg and Ewing W. Reilley, assisted by Douglas W. Bray and John L. Herma, *Effecting Change in Large Organizations.* New York: Columbia University Press, 1957.

61. "What Makes Innovations Work?" *op. cit.; A Foundation Goes to School, op. cit.*

62. Griffiths, *op. cit.*

63. Mort and Cornell, *op. cit.,* 1941.

64. Neal Gross, Joseph B. Giacquinta, and Marilyn Bernstein, "Complex Organizations: The Implementation of Major Organizational Innovations," presented at the 1968 Annual Meeting of the A.S.A., Boston, Massachusetts, August 1968 and *Implementing Organizational Innovations: A Sociological Analysis of Planned Educational Change.* New York: Basic Books, Inc., 1971, Chapter 7.

65. Barnett, *op. cit.*

66. Berelson and Steiner, *op. cit.,* 1964; Carlson, *op. cit.,* 1967.

67. P. Marris and M. Rein, *Dilemmas of Social Reform.* New York: Atherton Press, 1967.

68. Francois Cillie, *Centralization or Decentralization: A Study in Educational Adaptation.* New York: Teachers College, Columbia University Press, 1940.

69. Ralph N. Haber, "The Spread of an Innovation: High School Language Laboratories," *The Journal of Experimental Education, 31,* Summer 1963, 359–369.

70. Victor A. Thompson, "Bureaucracy and Innovation," *Administrative Science Quarterly, 10,* June, 1965, 1–20.

71. L.E. Greiner, "Organization Change and Development," unpublished Ph.D. dissertation, Harvard University, 1965.

72. Michael Aiken and Jerald Hage, "Organizational Interdependence and Intra-Organizational Structure," *American Sociological Review, 33,* December 1968, 912–930.

73. Max Weber, *The Theory of Social and Economic Organization,* New York: Oxford University Press, 1947; Thorstein Veblen, *The Theory of the Leisure Class,* New York: New American Library, 1957; and Karl Marx, *Das Kapital,* Frederick Engels, ed., New York: The Modern Library, 1936.

74. James D. Thompson, *Organizations in Action.* New York: McGraw-Hill, 1967.

75. Thompson, *ibid.* Also, Tom Burns and G.M. Stalker, *The Management of Innovation.* Chicago: Quadrangle Books, 1961.

76. James Q. Wilson, "Innovation in Organization: Notes Toward a Theory" in *Approaches to Organizational Design,* J.D. Thompson, ed. Pittsburgh: University of Pittsburgh Press, 1966.

77. Aiken and Hage, *op. cit.,* 1968.

78. Wilson, *op. cit.*

79. Berelson and Steiner, *op. cit.,* 1964.

80. Charles P. Loomis, "Tentative Types of Directed Social Change Involving Systemic Linkage," *Rural Sociology, 24,* December 1959, 383–390.

81. Marris and Rein, *op. cit.*

82. Terry Clark, "Institutionalization of Innovations in Higher Education: Four Conceptual Models," *Administrative Science Quarterly, 13,* June 1968, 1–25.

83. Wilbert E. Moore, *Social Change.* Englewood Cliffs, N.J.: Prentice-Hall, Inc., 1963.

84. In addition to the distinction between natural and deliberate change, it is necessary to distinguish between the goals of the innovation and the goals of the host system. The optimal condition for innovation is when there is a high consensus on the goals of the innovation among those responsible for its implementation, together with low consensus among members of the host system on the goals of that system. The least optimal condition for implementing change is when there is low consensus on the goals of the innovation and high consensus on the goals of the host system.

85. Gross, et al., *op. cit.,* 1968.

86. D.H. Ross, ed., *Administration for Adaptability.* New York: Metropolitan School Study Council, 1958.

87. Carlson, *Adoption of Educational Innovations, op. cit.*

88. Harold Guetzkow, "The Creative Person in Organizations" in *The Creative Organization,* Gary A. Steiner, ed. Chicago: University of Chicago Press, 1965.

89. Aiken and Hage, *op. cit.*, 1968.

90. Leon Festinger, "The Theory of Cognitive Dissonance" in *The Science of Human Communication*, Wilbur Schramm, ed. New York: Basic Books, 1963.

91. Berelson and Steiner, *op. cit.*

92. John W. Riley, Jr., and Matilda White Riley, "Sociological Perspectives on the Use of New Educational Media," in *New Teaching Aids for the American Classroom*, Wilbur Schramm editor. Washington, D.C.: U.S. Office of Education, 1962.

93. J.D. Thompson, *op. cit.*, 1967.

94. Ronald G. Corwin, *Militant Professionalism: A Study of Organizational Conflict in High Schools*. New York: Appleton-Century-Crofts, 1970.

95. Willis Sibley, "Social Structures and Planned Change: A Case Study from the Phillipines," *Human Organization, 19*, Winter 1960-61, 209-211.

96. Ronald Lippett, *op. cit.*

97. William W. Wayson, "Securing Teachers for Slum Schools," adapted from the address to the Annual Meeting of American Association of School Administrators, Syracuse University, February 19, 1964.

98. Richard Carlson, "Unanticipated Consequences in the Use of Programmed Instruction," in *Adoption of Educational Innovations*. Eugene, Ore.: Center for the Advanced Study of Educational Administration, 1965, p. 63.

99. Talcott Parsons, "Evolutionary Universals in Society," *op. cit.*, 1964.

100. Victor A. Thompson, "Administrative Objectives for Development Administration," *Administrative Science Quarterly, 9*, June 1964, 91-108.

101. Snell Putney and Gladys I. Putney, "Radical Innovation and Prestige," *American Sociological Review, 27*, August 1962, 548-551.

102. David Rogers, et al., *New York City and the Politics of School Desegregation*. New York: Center for Urban Education, 1968.

103. "What Makes Innovations Work?" *op. cit.; A Foundation Goes to School, op. cit.*

104. Shirley Terreberry, "The Evolution of Organizational Environments," *Administrative Science Quarterly, 12*, March 1968, 590-613.

105. Sloan Wayland, "Structural Features of American Education as Basic Factors in Innovation," in *Innovation in Education, op. cit.*, pp. 587-613.

106. Burton R. Clark, "Interorganizational Patterns in Education," *Administrative Science Quarterly, 10*, September 1965, 224-237.

107. Joseph Ben-David, "Roles and Innovations in Medicine," *American Journal of Sociology, 65*, May 1960, 557-568 and Joseph Ben-David and Randall Collins, "Social Factors in the Origins of a New Science: The Case of Psychology," *American Sociological Review, 31*, August 1966, 451-465.

108. Ronald G. Corwin, *A Sociology of Education: Emerging Patterns of Class, Status and Power in the Public Schools*. New York: Appleton-Century-Crofts, 1965.

109. This section adapted from Ronald G. Corwin, "Strategies For Organizational Innovation: An Emperical Comparison," *American Sociological Review*, *37*, August 1972, 441–454.

110. Richard P. Applebaum, *Theories of Social Change*. Chicago: Markham Co., 1970.

111. Ronald G. Corwin, *op. cit.*, 1973, pp. 393–394.

112. Tom Alexander, "The Social Engineers Retreat Under Fire," *Fortune*, October, 1972, 132–150.

AUTHOR INDEX

Numbers in parentheses indicate the pages on which the full references appear.

SUBJECT INDEX